THE ALLIES

ALSO BY WINSTON GROOM

NONFICTION

Conversations with the Enemy (1982, with Duncan Spencer)

Shrouds of Glory (1995)

The Crimson Tide (2002)

A Storm in Flanders (2002)

1942 (2004)

Patriotic Fire (2006)

Vicksburg, 1863 (2009)

Kearny's March (2011)

Shiloh, 1862 (2012)

The Aviators (2013)

The Generals (2015)

FICTION

Better Times Than These (1978)

As Summers Die (1980)

Only (1984)

Forrest Gump (1986)

Gone the Sun (1988)

Gump and Co. (1995)

Such a Pretty, Pretty Girl (1998)

El Paso (2016)

THE ALLIES

Roosevelt, Churchill, Stalin, *and the* Unlikely Alliance That Won World War II

WINSTON GROOM

NATIONAL
GEOGRAPHIC

WASHINGTON, D.C.

Published by National Geographic Partners, LLC
1145 17th Street NW Washington, DC 20036

Library of Congress Cataloging-in-Publication Data

Names: Groom, Winston, 1944- author.
Title: The allies : Roosevelt, Churchill, Stalin, and the unlikely alliance
  that won World War II / Winston Groom.
Description: Washington, D.C. : National Geographic, [2018] | Includes
  bibliographical references and index.
Identifiers: LCCN 2018027574 | ISBN 9781426219665 (hardback)
Subjects: LCSH: World War, 1939-1945--Biography. | Roosevelt, Franklin D.
  (Franklin Delano), 1882-1945. | Churchill, Winston, 1874-1965. | Stalin,
  Joseph, 1878-1953. | Heads of state--Biography. | BISAC: HISTORY /
  Military / World War II. | HISTORY / Modern / 20th Century. | BIOGRAPHY &
  AUTOBIOGRAPHY / Presidents & Heads of State.
Classification: LCC D736 .G735 2018 | DDC 940.53092/2--dc23
LC record available at https://lccn.loc.gov_2018027574

Since 1888, the National Geographic Society has funded more than 13,000 research, exploration, and preservation projects around the world. National Geographic Partners distributes a portion of the funds it receives from your purchase to National Geographic Society to support programs including the conservation of animals and their habitats.

National Geographic Partners
1145 17th Street NW
Washington, DC 20036-4688 USA

Get closer to National Geographic explorers and photographers, and connect with our global community. Join us today at nationalgeographic.com/join

For information about special discounts for bulk purchases, please contact National Geographic Books Special Sales: specialsales@natgeo.com

For rights or permissions inquiries, please contact National Geographic Books Subsidiary Rights: bookrights@natgeo.com

Interior design: Nicole Miller

Printed in the United States of America

18/QGF-PCML/1

To Susan Helmsing Groom,
whose mere presence is
a brilliant inspiration.

WORLD WAR II EUROPEAN THEATER

ATLANTIC

OCEAN

Legend:
- Allied controlled areas
- Axis controlled areas
- Neutral nations
- Greatest area under Axis military occupation Nov. 1942
- □ Conference
- ✷ Major battle
- → Allied advance
- U.K. Nation in control of territory

Modern names are in parentheses.

0 — 400 mi
0 — 600 km

North Sea

IRELAND

UNITED KINGDOM

DENMARK

NORWAY

NETH.

London
Battle of Britain July 1940–May 1941 ✷ ★

Dunkirk
Arnhem

English Channel

BELGIUM

D-Day 1944
June 6, 1944 ✷

Paris ★
Battle of the Bulge Dec. 1944– Jan. 1945

FRANCE

GER.

Vichy ★

SWITZ.

VICHY FRANCE 1940–1942

1944

ITAL

194

PORTUGAL

SPAIN

1942

SP. MOROCCO
SPAIN

1942

Oran
Algiers
Tun

Casablanca

Vichy French in North Africa join Allies in Nov. '42

Kasserine Pass Feb. 1943 ✷

MOROCCO
FRANCE

TUNISIA

RIO DE ORO
SPAIN

ALGERIA
FRANCE

FRENCH WEST AFRICA
FRANCE

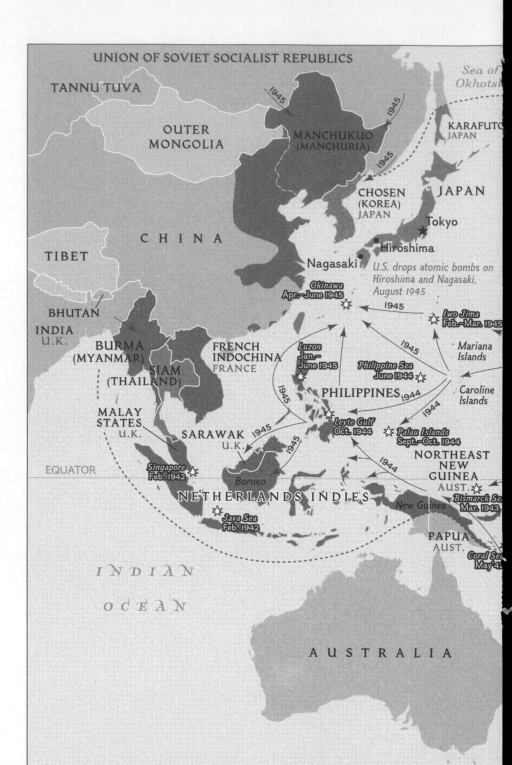

UNION OF SOVIET SOCIALIST REPUBLICS

TANNU TUVA

OUTER
MONGOLIA

MANCHUKUO
(MANCHURIA)

1945

1945

1945

Sea of
Okhotsk

KARAFUTO
JAPAN

CHOSEN
(KOREA)
JAPAN

JAPAN

C H I N A

Tokyo

TIBET

Hiroshima

Nagasaki

*U.S. drops atomic bombs on
Hiroshima and Nagasaki,
August 1945*

BHUTAN

INDIA
U.K.

BURMA
(MYANMAR)

SIAM
(THAILAND)

FRENCH
INDOCHINA
FRANCE

Okinawa
Apr.–June 1945

1945

Iwo Jima
Feb.–Mar. 1945

Luzon
Jan.–
June 1945

1945

Mariana
Islands

Philippine Sea
June 1944

PHILIPPINES

1944

1944

Caroline
Islands

MALAY
STATES
U.K.

SARAWAK
U.K.

1945

1945

Leyte Gulf
Oct. 1944

Palau Islands
Sept.–Oct. 1944

1944

NORTHEAST
NEW
GUINEA
AUST.

EQUATOR

Singapore
Feb. 1942

Borneo

1944

NETHERLANDS INDIES

New Guinea

Bismarck Sea
Mar. 1943

Java Sea
Feb. 1942

PAPUA
AUST.

Coral Sea
May 4?

I N D I A N

O C E A N

A U S T R A L I A

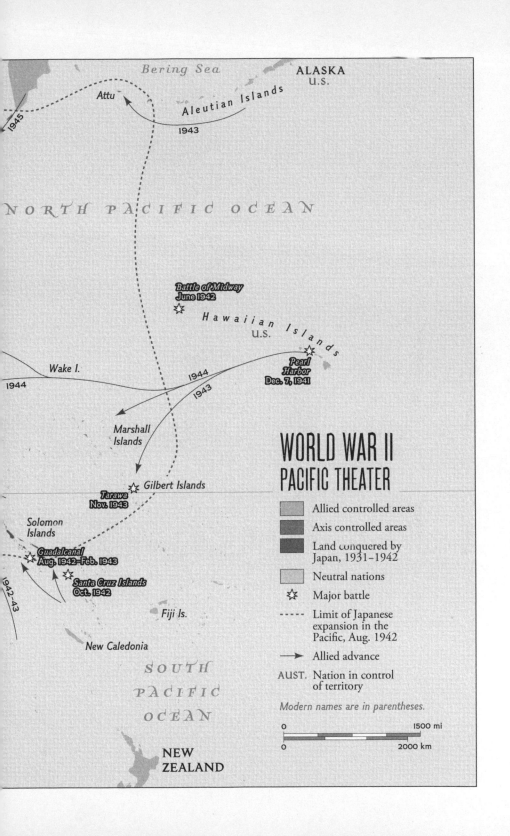

Bering Sea

ALASKA
U.S.

Attu

Aleutian Islands

1943

1945

NORTH PACIFIC OCEAN

Battle of Midway
June 1942

Hawaiian Islands
U.S.

Wake I.

1944

1943

Pearl
Harbor
Dec. 7, 1941

1944

Marshall
Islands

Gilbert Islands

Tarawa
Nov. 1943

Solomon
Islands

Guadalcanal
Aug. 1942-Feb. 1943

Santa Cruz Islands
Oct. 1942

1942-43

Fiji Is.

New Caledonia

SOUTH

PACIFIC

OCEAN

NEW
ZEALAND

WORLD WAR II
PACIFIC THEATER

Allied controlled areas

Axis controlled areas

Land conquered by
Japan, 1931–1942

Neutral nations

☆ Major battle

----- Limit of Japanese
expansion in the
Pacific, Aug. 1942

→ Allied advance

AUST. Nation in control
of territory

Modern names are in parentheses.

0   1500 mi

0   2000 km

CONTENTS

PROLOGUE

November 1943

It was a sunny day in Tehran when Winston Churchill and Franklin Delano Roosevelt arrived by air to attend the second Allied leadership summit of World War II, code-named "Eureka." Joseph Stalin, who did not like to fly, had finally agreed to a meeting with the American president and the British prime minister in the recently occupied Persian capital, which he could reach by private train from Moscow. Great Britain, the United States, and the Soviet Union had fought alongside one another for nearly two years to stem the Nazi tide that threatened Europe, yet their leaders had never before gathered together in the same room. Churchill himself later remarked that it was the greatest concentration of political power the world had yet seen.

On the afternoon of the first day, Stalin appeared at Roosevelt's door with a hearty welcome. He insisted that Roosevelt stay at the Russian Embassy in Tehran, citing a suddenly uncovered assassination plot. Polio had long since destroyed Roosevelt's leg muscles, so he was appreciatively surprised that his suite at the embassy included a newly built handicapped-style bathroom. But an atmosphere of suspicion hung over the proceedings: if Roosevelt had been expected to stay in the Soviet building all along, as the new bathroom suggested, it probably meant that he was being surveilled by Stalin's cronies. After a long chat, Stalin went away amused by the American president's cheery, casual approach to diplomacy but judged him a lightweight compared to the more formidable Churchill. Roosevelt, on the other hand, believed he could "do business" with Stalin, known familiarly between him and Churchill as "Uncle Joe."

In Tehran, the three great leaders were perfectly in character. Roosevelt was charming as always, attempting with finesse to establish favor with his Soviet counterpart. He made martinis and cracked jokes to ease the obvious tension between the other two Allies. Stalin remained quiet and mysterious, projecting an icy confidence in his crisp military uniform and epaulets. Churchill stubbornly resisted playing nice with the Russian dictator and focused conversation on the war's multiple fronts, especially the eastern Mediterranean. While Stalin insisted on a definitive date for the cross-Channel Allied invasion of France that would open a second front against the Germans, Churchill urged the American president to consider delaying the invasion slightly in favor of new operations to get at Germany through the southern Balkans. Roosevelt sided with Stalin: Operation Overlord (now remembered as D-day) would be the main event.

FDR had always been more favorably disposed toward the massive Communist state and its leader than had his British counterpart. Ever the bon vivant, Roosevelt approached Stalin with characteristic confidence in his own sparkling charisma. So when the two finally met in Tehran, it is perhaps not surprising that he found Stalin personally engaging. (Influenced by Walter Duranty's *New York Times* articles praising the Soviet regime, one of Roosevelt's first acts as president had been to diplomatically recognize the Soviet Union as a legitimate nation—against the wishes of a large number of his countrymen and his own mother.) As soon as Stalin became an ally of the United States in the war against Hitler, he was routinely portrayed in the American media as a benign, avuncular figure or as a bold, fearless leader. And yet up to this point in history, Uncle Joe—*Time* magazine's 1942 Man of the Year—had systematically killed at least 20 million of his fellow citizens.

Churchill, for his part, hated communism from its inception, and he remained distrustful of Stalin's intentions even after the Soviet Union openly avowed that it had no designs on any countries in Europe. At Tehran, Churchill was loath to allow the relationship he had carefully cultivated with the American president to be undermined by Stalin's insistence on definite plans for a second front and was put off by Roosevelt's eagerness to please the Communist leader. Stalin frequently tossed out words like "freedom," "liberty," and "democracy," in regard to such Soviet-occupied countries as Poland, prompting Churchill to recall Humpty Dumpty's conversation with Alice: "When I use a word it means just what I choose it to mean—neither more nor less."

Churchill came away from Tehran more skeptical than ever about Stalin's postwar intentions. Roosevelt, virulent anti-imperialist that he was, remained more concerned about whether Churchill's government would try to retain the massive global empire that the British had acquired over the past two hundred and fifty years. In fact, Roosevelt left Tehran thinking that he had won over Stalin. It did not seem to occur to him that the wily Soviet premier might be playing his own game.

The conference in Tehran saw the convergence of three lives that would stand above all others in the history of the twentieth century. Here, the Allies of World War II had their first opportunity to size each other up in person. True to form, they were all principled and ruthless, far seeing and personally preoccupied. The fateful intertwining of their lives that led to this moment is a story with consequences of the greatest magnitude. Together, these three men brought the world through a period of devastating conflict—sometimes with stunning courage, sometimes with brutal force. Churchill and Roosevelt would be rightly remembered for their bold leadership in crisis, but the enormity of Stalin's crimes would echo just as powerfully. For better or for worse, none of the Allies ever seemed destined for a lesser fate.

CHAPTER ONE

Winston Spencer Churchill was born November 30, 1874, in Blenheim Palace, Oxfordshire, the traditional seat of the Dukes of Marlborough, who had descended in the Churchill family name since the beginning of the eighteenth century. It was said that his mother was expecting to deliver him in London in a month's time, but that out on a shooting party she stumbled and fell, causing her to have him early, at Blenheim. It was also circulated that there was nothing premature about the birth except for premature sexual relations between his parents before their marriage.

In the summer of 1873, Churchill's mother, the exquisitely beautiful American heiress Miss Jennie Jerome of New York, was attending the annual English regatta at Cowes. There, she met Lord Randolph Churchill, who fell in love with her at first sight.[1] For his part, Churchill conceded many years afterward that while he was present at the occasion of his birth he had "no recollection of the events leading up to it."

Winston Churchill was raised as an aristocrat between the society circles of London and large country houses. His parents were friendly with the country's most important people—including His Royal Highness the Prince of Wales, the ultimate social arbiter of the day who would later reign as King Edward VII.*

---

* Except, that is, for an excruciating decade when the prince had Randolph effectively banished to Ireland for embroiling him in a scandal involving Randolph's brother George and the wife of the Earl of Aylesford, with whom His Royal Highness had also had an affair.

Churchill's father, Randolph, was a thoroughly political creature. After graduating from Oxford in 1870 with a law degree he ran successfully for Parliament. As an aristocrat he was a member of the Tory or Conservative Party—but it was the society parties (and especially their costs) that nearly did him in.

Lord Randolph was a third son—and thus his inheritance did not sufficiently provide him the style of living that his family enjoyed.* But he had also become a rising politician, with whispers he might someday become prime minister. He kept homes in London's fashionable Mayfair district, with a staff including a butler, housekeeper, chef, cooks, maids, and coachmen as well as a nanny for young Winston. Jennie had brought a significant dowry with her to the marriage, but she was running through it at great speed, ordering scores of dresses from haute couture dressmakers in Paris, some costing as much as $20,000 in today's dollars. The couple entertained lavishly, with fine champagnes and expensive dinners, followed by the best brandies and cigars.

Perhaps in keeping with her opulent social routine, Mrs. Churchill is known over the years to have had affairs with a number of prominent aristocrats, not excluding important politicians, officers of the army, and the prince of Wales himself. Indeed, Churchill's parents had a peculiar marital arrangement. At some point in the 1870s Lord Randolph was diagnosed with syphilis; his wife's affairs may have been a part of some arrangement following the diagnosis, for these were the days before penicillin and there were no effective medications. In any case, Lady Randolph Churchill's long list of lovers is, interestingly, not terribly unusual for the Victorian era.

That there was no shortage of men who came under her spell was certainly *not* surprising, for Jennie Churchill was one of the great beauties of the day and imbued with abundant personal charm as well. Lord D'Abernon caught sight of her at the Irish viceroy's ball in Dublin where "all eyes had turned on a dark, lithe figure standing somewhat apart and appearing to be of another

---

* The previous Dukes of Marlborough had at times become so strapped for cash to run their palatial estate, Blenheim, that they sold off the family jewels for more than $5 million (in today's dollars)—and, later, the splendid and (almost) priceless Sunderland Library.

texture to those around her, radiant, translucent, intense. A diamond star in her hair—her favorite ornament—its luster dimmed by the glory flashing in her eyes. More of the panther than of the woman in her look, but with a cultivated intelligence unknown to the jungle. She was universally popular. Her desire to please, her delight in life, and a genuine wish that all should share her joyous faith in it, made her the centre of a devoted circle."[2]

This was indeed a splendid tribute, however exaggerated. In any case, the Churchills spent much time apart on separate trips abroad, which assisted in Jennie's various trysts. What Randolph did on his numerous journeys history does not tell us. But we do know that it was not spending time with his son.

While his parents carried on the grand social life of the day, young Winston was left to the care of a Mrs. Everest, the nurse and nanny to whom he became greatly attached. He also became devoted at an early age to his collection of lead toy soldiers—fifteen hundred of them—that he would arrange in different imagined battles, with his infantry, cavalry, artillery all arrayed against various enemies of the Crown. To say that Churchill was an intractable child would court understatement. But his personality was certainly shaped by his parents' willful neglect of him.

As was the practice in Victorian England, children of the upper classes were sent off to boarding school at an early age. Thus when he was seven young Winston was sent to the fashionable and expensive St. George's School, near Ascot. Accompanied by no one, including his parents, he was put on a train with a handful of coins equaling less than a British pound. Admitting to himself that he was a "troublesome boy," he was bullied at the school and mercilessly beaten by the masters and headmaster.[3]

Winston's loneliness and longing for his parents became pathetic as the weeks and months droned by without a single visit. Churchill treasured both parents almost to the point of worship, recalling later in life that his mother was to him then "like a fairy princess: a radiant being possessed of limitless riches and power . . . She shone for me like the Evening Star."[4]

By now Winston had a brother, Jack, but he was barely a toddler and at any rate no company while Winston was away at school. "Please come and see me," he wrote his mother. "Come and see me soon, dear Mamma."[5] She rarely even replied. Churchill's father never wrote, although he once sent his son

Robert Louis Stevenson's *Treasure Island*. The boy immediately devoured the book and took up the habit of reading to mask the tedium and brutality of life in a private boys' school. Many years later, Churchill's own son recalled that "the neglect and lack of interest in [Churchill] shown by his parents were remarkable, even judged by the standards of the Victorian and Edwardian days."[6]

Winston was home for a holiday when Mrs. Everest noticed ugly scars and welts crisscrossing the backs of his upper thighs. Further investigation revealed the full extent of the cruelty that had been inflicted; his mother immediately removed him from St. George's and put him in a small school in Brighton. There, he began to flourish under the tutelage of Kate and Charlotte Thomson, the old maid sisters who ran the institution. His writing and elocution were vastly improved, and he was doing well even in math.

In the summer of 1887, when Winston was twelve, England was convulsed by the largest celebration in its history: Queen Victoria's Golden Jubilee. He was determined to go and begged his mother to write the Thomson sisters, granting her permission for him come to London, but she had plans of her own for the event and declined. Winston would not be put off, and he continued to plead so pitifully that his mother relented. Mrs. Everest took him to watch the old queen, wearing her glistening crown, ride by in the royal coach amid the jubilantly cheering throngs. His mother had a seat in Westminster Abbey for the ceremony but there was none for her son. Afterward, however, she took him for an outing on the royal yacht, where he met Edward, Prince of Wales, the future king of England.

The next year, Winston got double pneumonia and nearly died; he languished with temperatures exceeding 104 degrees. His doctor, who had gone down to Brighton from London, stayed by the boy's bedside for nearly a week, sending notes to Jennie and Randolph in London (they had earlier arrived separately but stayed only a few short hours). When he had recovered, Winston continued to bombard his mother with pleas for a visit. He was in a play and wanted her and his father in the audience. "Please do come. I have been disappointed so many times."[7]

In the meantime, he sought out newspapers for items about his father, who in 1886 had been named chancellor of the Exchequer. These he pasted in a scrapbook as a sort of shrine to his mostly absent parent. Randolph was busy making speeches throughout the land: the custom for politicians before the advent of radio and television. Young Winston would commit these speeches to memory, as well as statements by his father gleaned from news stories.

★★★★★

WHEN WINSTON WAS FOURTEEN his parents decided to send him to Harrow, a private school on the outskirts of London dating to the sixteenth century that rivaled its prestigious counterpart Eton. Generations of Churchills had been educated at Eton, but the boy's weak chest, caused by the pneumonia, would be aggravated by that school's location on the damp, foggy banks of the Thames.

Winston traveled to Harrow accompanied not by his parents but by one of the Thomson sisters from Brighton. Winston had boned up on questions likely to be asked on the entrance exams, but he panicked and nearly failed, leaving him as "the class dunce," to be ridiculed by his fellow students. Altogether it was not a promising start.

Winston wasn't happy at Harrow. For one thing he had to "fag" for the upperclassmen. Much like a pledge in a fraternity, he was required to shine the shoes of his "betters," run errands, and serve as a general flunky. He had trouble with his studies, particularly ancient languages, for which he found he had no natural gift. He also discovered for the first time that not being rich—as so many of his aristocratic classmates were—was a distinct disadvantage. And, once again, the parents he idolized were entirely absent.

In 1887 a calamity struck the Churchill family. Randolph, who had seemed poised to become the next prime minister of Great Britain, suddenly found all his prospects collapsed. It was his own undoing. As chancellor of the Exchequer he had objected to an item on military funding in the budget that had been submitted by the prime minister. When his objection was overruled, he impulsively wrote a letter of resignation, assuming that Lord Salisbury, the PM, would refuse to accept it. But Churchill had overplayed his hand. Salisbury was in no mood to brook insolence from one of his own Conservative Party members. The prime minister removed Churchill not only from the Exchequer but also from his position as leader of the House of Commons. He still retained his seat in the House, but he had lost his well-paying job as the nation's treasurer and would never regain it, nor any other important post. It was a crushing social blow as well, as many erstwhile friends lost interest in a man who had destroyed a promising career. Winston was still too young to understand the implications of this event, and the name of Churchill remained a household word throughout Great Britain. But as the years went by his comprehension of what his father had done began to haunt him.

After his first two years at Harrow, Winston was directed into the school's Army Class, which aimed at preparing students to enter Sandhurst, England's version of West Point. One day, while he was at home on holiday arranging his fifteen-hundred-man army of toy soldiers, his father paid one of his rare visits to Winston's quarters. Observing the precise formation of every infantry regiment, cavalry squadron, and artillery battery, his father asked him, "Do you want to go into the army?" Churchill immediately answered in the affirmative, and for years he believed that it was his toy soldiers that had prompted the question. Unfortunately, he found out later, it had been proposed because his father did not think he was smart enough to go to law school.

It took him three tries to pass the entrance examination to Sandhurst, which required proficiency in English, math, and Latin, among other subjects. The math and Latin threw him, but at length, and by dint of a terrific personal effort, he mastered mathematics and was accepted into the academy as a cavalry cadet. Churchill was delighted with himself when he wrote to his father about "what fun it would be having a horse," and also that "the uniforms of the cavalry were much more magnificent than those of the Foot."

Imagine then his shock to receive the following reply: "My dear Winston, I am rather surprised at your tone of exultation over your inclusion in the Sandhurst list."[8]

This was the nicest thing in the entire letter, and it was a long one.

Lord Randolph branded Winston's failure to get into the more competitive infantry "discreditable," further evidence of the "slovenly, happy-go-lucky, harum-scarum style of work that has always distinguished you at your different schools." His fury unabated, the elder Churchill ranted, "Never have I received a really good report on your conduct in your work." In page after page the letter goes on, beyond chiding, to recite young Winston's deficiencies of character and scholarship, concluding, "You need not trouble yourself to write any answer . . . because I no longer attach the slightest weight to anything you may say about your own acquirements and exploits." He even threatened to cut off his son financially if he failed at Sandhurst. Not the least of Lord Randolph's complaints was that Winston's going into the cavalry would "impose on me an extra £200 a year" (about $25,000 in today's dollars) for horses, servants, fancy uniforms, and equipment—which seems to be what the whole argument was about in the first place.[9]

What went through Winston's mind when he received this screed is not recorded. But the day it came, he wrote back to his father, "I am very sorry that you are displeased with me," promising that he would make it up at Sandhurst by hard work and good conduct. He signed it, "Ever your loving son, Winston Churchill."[10]

During his years at the Royal Military Academy, Churchill for the first time began to find himself. He took his studies seriously, including tactics, fortification, topography, military law, and military administration. His enthusiasm grew, although for the first months during drill he was "placed in the awkward squad," for "smartening up."[11]

As a prospective cavalryman, Winston became enthralled with horses and spent his military leaves and vacations in riding school at the Knightsbridge barracks of the Royal Horse Guards. Here also Churchill mended fences with his father when he acquired what he called the status of a "gentleman cadet." On leaves in London, he and his father visited the Empire theater, a kind of circus and vaudeville establishment. More important, his father took Cadet Churchill with him to important Conservative political parties and events, introducing him to prominent politicians and personally discussing with him the critical issues of the day. Even so, Churchill later wistfully wrote, every time he attempted a moment of true friendship, his father became offended and "froze."

In December 1894 Winston Churchill graduated from the Royal Military Academy at Sandhurst with honors (eighth in his class of a hundred and fifty) and received the queen's commission as a second lieutenant—or subaltern—in the British army. He had, as he said, "passed out into the world."[12] He was just twenty years old.

At that time, the imperial British army was composed of approximately 224,000 troops, most of them stationed halfway around the world. Threats from continental rivals such as France, Spain, or Holland had passed and danger from Germany was not yet apparent. The present job of the British army was to put down the frequent rebellions among the peoples of the empire that included nearly one-quarter of the human population of the earth. These were the nearly 500 million souls who composed—from Cape Town to Cairo, Bombay to Rangoon, Melbourne to Auckland, Khartoum to Dublin and the many points between—the mighty British Empire "upon which," it was said, "the sun never sets."

As Churchill entered Her Majesty's Service, trouble had been brewing with the Boers in South Africa, the Dervishes of the Sudan, and the fierce, ruthless tribesmen of the Hindu Kush. He had written his younger brother, Jack, who was then attending Harrow, "There is no ambition I cherish so keenly as to gain a reputation for personal courage." Over the next several years he'd have every opportunity to prove this—although in the process he earned the dubious reputation of a "medal chaser"* and "self-advertiser."[13] In this era, he appears more like a young man in a hurry, rather than a young man on the make, as he watched his father decline at a shockingly young age.

By the time Winston graduated from Sandhurst, the elder Churchill was experiencing the full effects of the illness that had been diagnosed as syphilis, including deterioration of the brain. Soon, as his son described it, the

---

* To this day the British remain such a medals-conscious people that in many publications when the recipient of certain medals is mentioned—including his obituary—abbreviations identifying those medals follow the first mention of his name.

reporting of Randolph's speeches in the *Times* dropped from three columns to two, then to one and a half, and finally to none.[14]

"Had he lived another four or five years he could not have done without me," Churchill said. "But just as friendly relations were ripening . . . he vanished forever." Lord Randolph was just forty-five years old at the time of his death, and Winston, who feared a similar fate, must have felt a nearly crushing pressure to succeed early in life.

He would not want for opportunity. In February 1895, Winston's assignment came at last: the Fourth Hussars, an elite regiment of light cavalry often used as scouts. They were scheduled to be posted to India for at least the next decade, but Winston had no intention of staying with them all that time. Although he'd taken to army life and longed to prove himself in combat, he'd begun to see the military as a springboard for a political career—as illustrious, he hoped, as his late father's, though with a better ending.

But first he needed to do something that would call attention to himself, enhance his reputation, and perhaps even gain him a promotion. When guerrillas under the well-known liberator José Martí* rebelled against Spain's colonial army in Cuba, it presented a likely opportunity to further his goal. Through his mother's (possibly romantic) connections, he sought and received from the Spanish government permission to accompany the Spanish army in Cuba as an "observer"; he also wrangled a spot as a war correspondent for the *Daily Graphic* at five guineas per letter (about $600 today), which would help him manage expenses. Having obtained leave from his regiment prior to its posting to India, Churchill soon found himself in the thick of battle on the tropical island.

Before he departed, in what must have been an absorbing experience to say the least, he took part in a champagne-fueled three-day whirlwind visit to his mother's hometown of New York City. His host was a fabulous American Irishman named Bourke Cockran, a successful lawyer and Tammany politician, as well as another of Jennie's paramours. Cockran put Churchill up in lavish style in his Fifth Avenue apartment and introduced the young British officer to all the right clubs. At one point he was received

---

* Martí was killed in the fighting several months before Churchill's arrival.

by Cornelius Vanderbilt, the railroad magnate; Vanderbilt's niece Consuelo would one day marry Churchill's cousin Charles "Sunny" Churchill—becoming, in the process, the latest Duchess of Marlborough.*

After departing from Key West on a steamer, Churchill arrived in Havana on November 20, 1895. He soon found himself at the fighting front—such as it was—in a guerrilla war. The segment of the Spanish army to which he was attached had put itself on a lengthy weeklong march in hopes of being attacked by the enemy; they were rewarded with several grueling days of sniping and minor actions before anything rising to the dignity of a battle broke out.

Churchill found himself exhilarated at being under fire for the first time. Officers and men fell all around before the Spanish prevailed and the rebel firing slacked off. Churchill took it all in with gusto. Altogether he filed five letters for the *Daily Graphic* under the headline "The Insurrection in Cuba." The Churchill biographer William Manchester notes: "They show a keen eye for detail, a gift for clarity, and a sure grasp of tactics."

But if Churchill's knowledge of tactics was firm, it was his notions of strategy that caused difficulties. He was condemned by newspapers on both sides of the Atlantic, apparently on the assumption that a mere second lieutenant in the British army had no right to comment on such weighty matters as how to proceed in a complex guerrilla war. He told the *New York World* that if the Spanish could take the towns of Matanzas and Santa Clara from the rebel forces before the rainy season, they would probably defeat the insurrection; if not, it might last another several years. The insurgents themselves, he added, were both unsoldierly and cowardly or, as Churchill put it, "well versed in the art of retreat." Furthermore it was his opinion that the United States should intervene in the conflict. Remarks like these prompted American newspapers to say that Churchill's presence in Cuba was proof that England was "throwing more bricks at the Monroe Doctrine."[15]

---

* Due to mutual infidelities, the marriage did not last. In the "small world" department, however, it is interesting to note that before she married the duke, Consuelo had been secretly engaged to New York socialite Winthrop Rutherfurd, who afterward married Lucy Mercer, who had been the mistress of Franklin D. Roosevelt.

In Great Britain some newspapers were likewise unkind, one sarcastically musing that "spending a holiday fighting other people's battles is rather extraordinary, even for a Churchill." Another prophesied that the head of the British army would "probably order him to return at once and report himself."[16]

Manchester believes that Churchill's British upbringing caused him to side with the Spanish, and that he would be biased against *any* colony that rebelled against its empire. "He had been, and in some respects always would be, a defender of established order. *Imperialism* would never be a pejorative for [Churchill]," Manchester observed.[17] Later, however, Churchill would write: "I reproach myself somewhat for . . . having perhaps done injustice to the insurgents . . . I succeeded in making out a case for Spain . . . But I'm not sure it was right."[18]

SOON CHURCHILL AND the other officers of the Hussars were aboard the SS *Britannia,* bound for Bangalore, India. During his six months of leave before departure, Churchill had used every bit of guile he possessed, as well as the not inconsiderable guile of his mother, to get out of the Indian assignment—but to no avail. Jennie had just returned from a nine-month romp in Europe, including a torrid affair with Bourke Cockran in her apartment on the Champs-Élysées. She was desperate for money so she borrowed £17,000 on her life insurance and rented a seven story Georgian mansion near London's Hyde Park.

From this base of operations, Churchill regularly sallied forth to the newspapers of Fleet Street, trying to finagle a war correspondent's job. But there were no respectable wars going on at the time, even though there was some action in South Africa and things were heating up again in the Sudan, so all responses from the papers were negative. Churchill begged his mother to lean on her widespread contacts to secure him a position anywhere but "the tedious land of India." But at length it became clear that there was nothing doing, so he packed up and left on September 11, 1896.[19]

A chance encounter would soon turn all of this around for Churchill, opening his world to new vistas and providing him with the advantage he needed to seek political office. The following summer marked Queen Victoria's Diamond Jubilee, and the aristocrats in and around London began a months-long celebration leading up to the event. One of the most fashionable occasions was a weekend party at Deepdene, the estate of Churchill's aunt Lily, the current Duchess of Marlborough, which she was hosting for His Royal Highness Prince Albert Edward. Among the other guests Churchill met an army general with the striking name Sir Bindon Blood, with whom he struck up an instant friendship.* By the time the weekend ended, Churchill had secured a promise from Blood that if the general were to get a field command in some exciting place, he would arrange for Lieutenant Churchill to be on his staff. Before long, young Churchill would take him at his word. But first India loomed.[20]

"THE WEATHER IS BEGINNING to get hot and the troop decks are awful," Winston wrote to his mother as the ship passed through the Suez Canal into the Red Sea. The voyage took upwards of a month, and Churchill used most of this dead time to improve his chess game, winning the semifinals of a shipboard tournament. When the ship reached Bombay, it was anchored offshore and skiffs were used to ferry the officers ashore. It was here Churchill had the accident that dislocated his shoulder. Five-foot swells were rolling in from the Indian Ocean, and when the boat reached the long stone dock it was nearly awash with "dripping steps and iron rings for handholds." Just as Churchill grasped a ring, the skiff suddenly dropped into a trough, jerking his right shoulder so hard it was dislocated.[†21]

---

* Sir Bindon was a direct descendant of Colonel Thomas Blood, a notorious Irish troublemaker who in 1671 unsuccessfully attempted to steal the Crown Jewels from the Tower of London.

† This injury would give him trouble the rest of his life. Most immediately, he was unable to swing a polo mallet without strapping his right arm to his side. Later, the shoulder would go out at unanticipated times—reaching for a book, swimming. It even went out once when he was making a gesture during a speech in Parliament.

At dawn the next morning the regiment boarded trains for the day-and-a-half trip to Bangalore. It was located on a plateau three thousand feet above sea level, where days were hot but nights were cool. The officers—even second lieutenants—lived "like princes," Churchill said. For a moderate price in rupees he secured a butler, a dressing boy, and a groom for his horses. Churchill and two others rented a magnificent bungalow plastered pink and white with a red-tiled roof. Shaded verandas were studded with large rounded columns entwined with purple bougainvillea. The house sat in an enclosed two-acre garden of colorful plants and flowers.

It was around this time that Churchill began to feel a need for higher education. Even though the studies at English private schools were considerably more advanced and rigorous than those in American private schools, they stopped at a point far beneath the education to be gleaned at such prestigious universities as Oxford and Cambridge. Back home in England, and to a lesser extent abroad in India, Churchill sometimes found himself embarrassed in conversations that turned toward the intellectual. He knew the arts of war and had a grasp of politics but found himself deficient in subjects such as history, philosophy, and economics as well as the rich literature of his own country.

Now, at the age of twenty-two, he was ready to learn. He asked his mother to send him books by the trunkful, and soon he plunged into the great set pieces of classical antiquity such as Gibbon's *History of the Decline and Fall of the Roman Empire* and Macaulay's *Lays of Ancient Rome*. He studied Plato and Socrates, as well as other philosophers. He read for four or five hours each day, tackling Darwin's *Origin of Species* and Thomas Malthus's *Principle of Population*. "It was a curious education," he wrote much later. "First, because I approached it with an empty, hungry mind, and with fairly strong jaws, and what I bit I got . . . and secondly, because I had no one to tell me, 'This is discredited.'"[22]

Other than reading, polo became Churchill's most fervent avocation. After the early morning drills and maneuvers there was little to do in the heat of the day but wait for the 5 p.m. polo hour, which lasted until 8:30. One of his fellow officers wrote that "if you wanted to understand Churchill, you had to see him play polo." Churchill would stay out of the pack, waiting, watching, this observer noted. Then, when he saw a chance at the ball, he would dash in—"neither deft nor graceful, but full of tearing physical energy, and skillful with it, too."[23]

Soon, the officers of the Hussars devised a scheme to become the first polo team from southern India to win the prestigious Indian Empire's Regimental Cup. The plan was to pool their money and buy the entire string of twenty-five polo ponies from the Poona Light Horse, a native regiment that was stationed in Bombay very close to the docks, where they could have their pick of prized Arabian steeds arriving from the Middle East. A large part of winning at polo depends on the horse and now the Fourth Hussars would have an advantage over other teams that had been in the country for years.

To the surprise of everyone connected with polo, six weeks after arriving in India the Fourth Hussars won the Golconda Cup in Hyderabad. Prior to the match, the game day was celebrated with an impressive display of marching drills by both native and British troops—including a procession of twenty of the maharajah's elephants hauling an enormous cannon. (The elephants saluted the reviewing stand by raising their trunks as they passed by.) Churchill played the match magnificently, even with his injured arm still strapped to his side.[24]

And, before leaving Hyderabad, Churchill managed to fall in love for the first time.

She was a Miss Pamela Plowden, "the most beautiful girl I have ever seen," Churchill wrote his mother, "and very clever." The two began to see each other and a romance developed, but it was not to be. For the first two years they wrote constantly, then Churchill let the thing fall by the wayside, even as he professed his love for Pamela. She probably would have been a good choice for Churchill, "eminently suitable," one of his biographers wrote, as the daughter of the distinguished Sir Trevor John Chichele-Plowden and a young woman of great wit and beauty. But his ambition to attain high political office apparently got in the way. Marriages were expensive; houses had to be bought, children provided for—and Churchill wasn't even paid a living wage in the service of his queen. In any case, when Pamela ultimately wrote accusing him of "lack of ardor," he responded by denying it. "Why do you say I am incapable of affection? Perish the thought," he answered and went on to express his love. But little or nothing else happened between them, and Pamela Plowden went on to marry the Earl of Lytton.[25]

IN THOSE DAYS THE BRITISH RAJ, or Raj for short, meaning "rule," was in full control in India. The English had constructed a complex civil service system to govern the hundreds of "states" on the enormous subcontinent and filled it with highly educated staff, all supported by a sizable military force of infantry and cavalry regiments strategically located throughout the country. The British had cannily included large numbers of Indians in their civil service, as well as organizing Indian military units, officered by white men. The whites, including those in the military, lived in a rarefied atmosphere compared with regular Indians. It was said, for example, that the only difference between the Bombay Club and the Bengal Club was that one excluded Indians and dogs while the other accepted dogs.[26]

India had been relatively peaceful since the Great Mutiny of 1857. After the British quelled that bloody uprising, the country saw a massive increase in British military presence, and control of the colony passed from the Honourable East India Company to the Crown. Over the next half century most of the country seemed pacified. But beneath this misleading surface India seethed. The new, more educated population felt helpless and hapless against the growing British power. Except, that is, for the fierce, ungovernable tribesmen of the North West Frontier, who recognized *no* authority other than the resolute and unsparing jurisdiction of Islam.

In the fall of 1893, an event took place that unleashed the wrath of the Pashtun tribesmen, particularly in the Valley of Swat. A British diplomat named Mortimer Durand had drawn up—reportedly over a glass of gin—a somewhat arbitrary one-page document to delineate the fifteen-hundred-mile boundary between India and Afghanistan. This became known as the Durand Line, which ran directly through the mountains where the Pashtun tribesmen lived. Each valley had its own tribe, but all the mountain people spoke Pashto, which was the official language of Afghanistan. From that day until this, the Durand Line remains the most deadly political boundary on earth.*

Soon afterward the British came and began building roads. They put up signs; they built forts and bridges and strongpoints. Presently a Muslim holy man known to the British as the "Mad Fakir" appeared in the Swat Valley urging the Pashtuns to rise up and kill the invading infidels. He appealed to their fanaticism, claiming that British bullets had no effect on those following the Islamic faith. (As proof he showed a small scar on his chest, which he said was the only result of his being shot head-on by a British cannon.) Imams and other Muslim leaders made similar pleas to tribes in surrounding valleys for jihad, or holy war.

At length, with a strength estimated at between ten thousand and fifty thousand men, the Pashtun tribesmen swarmed out of the valleys and attacked the British fortifications at the strategic Malakand Pass near where the Durand Line ran. It was a ferocious battle in which the Pashtun warriors, armed with rifles and curved sabers, nearly overran the British garrison of 2,700: mostly native troops led by British officers. Afterward, the tribesmen laid a weeklong siege of the British position and relentlessly continued their massed attacks. By the time the fort was relieved by a British column, several thousand Pashtun tribesmen lay reeking in the tropic sun. Nearly two hundred British officers and native Indian troops were also killed.

The reaction of the British Raj in India was no different than that of any colonial power facing a significant uprising. The rebellion must be put down and the rebels punished so as to deter them from future misbehavior. Thus was hatched the Malakand Field Force, designed to enter Pashtun territory and chastise the recalcitrant tribesmen. And who should be chosen to lead this punitive expedition but Winston Churchill's house party friend: General Sir Bindon Blood.

---

* For the past decade and a half, American troops have been fighting in Afghanistan against the great-grandchildren of those same Pashtun tribesmen—men who abetted Osama bin Laden and Al-Qaeda and who remain determined to restore Taliban rule in the country.

CHURCHILL WAS HOME ON LEAVE back in England when the Pashtun rebellion broke out. He was on the lawn of Goodwood, the country estate of the Duke and Duchess of Richmond, where he had gone to attend the horse races. There, he picked up a newspaper and read of the revolt, and of General Blood's assignment to lead the Malakand Field Force. Without hesitation, Churchill sent a telegram to Sir Bindon, reminding him of his promise to take Churchill on his staff if he was ever to lead a fighting expedition. Without waiting for an answer, he caught the next mail boat to India—the first leg of a seven-thousand-mile journey that would carry him back to his regiment at Bangalore, where he would still need to get permission to accompany Blood's foray.

At various ports along the way Churchill checked in with telegraph offices, but there was no reply from Sir Bindon Blood. At last, when he reached Bombay, Churchill received the word he had been waiting for. "Very Difficult. No Vacancies," Blood had wired, but he told Churchill to "come up as a correspondent, will try to fit you in." That was all he needed. His mother had finally secured a war correspondent's position for him with London's *Daily Telegraph* at £5 per story.[27]

When he reached Bangalore, Churchill's colonel indulged his lieutenant's passion to take the field. Churchill took his dressing boy and campaign kit and left that same night by rail on a five-day, 2,028-mile trip to the town of Nowshera, which was quite literally the end of the line. From there it was a long forty miles across the plains in astonishing heat, in a small, pony-pulled cart called a *tonga,* before making the steep, winding ascent to the Malakand Pass in the foothills of the Himalayan Mountains.[28] In the staff mess tent, still covered in yellow dust from his tonga trip across the plains, Churchill was acquainting himself with other officers when someone handed him a glass of whisky. He had until then confined his drinking to champagne, wine, and brandy; that "smoky taste" of whisky had always repelled him. But faced with the choice between whisky and the tepid water he "grasped the larger hope" and began a lifelong relationship with the Scottish national beverage. Later he wrote to his mother, somewhat darkly,

"By the time this reaches you everything will be over so that I do not mind writing about it. I have faith in my star—that is, I am intended to do something in the world—if I am mistaken, what does it matter? My life has been a pleasant one, and though I should regret to leave it—it would be a regret that perhaps I should never know."[29]

General Blood had been away when Churchill arrived, but he soon returned victorious after chastising the mutinous Bunerwali tribe for its part in the uprising that led to the Malakand attack. The notion of chastising involved combing through a valley where every village was fortified by large mud "castles," often heavily defended by tribesmen. Artillery would be used to reduce the structure to rubble and then the villagers' mud houses would be set ablaze, their wells ruined and water reservoirs destroyed, their stores of food taken or ruined, their cattle and goats driven off, their shade trees cut down, and every armed man they could find would be killed. The idea was to suppress the tribe and defeat them so totally and utterly that they would lay down their weapons and come to terms. This was done on a tribe-by-tribe basis with those involved in the revolt—Afridis, Swatis, Pathans, Wazirs, Mahsuds, Gilgits, Citirals, and Bunerwalis—peoples who had lived in these mountain valleys for thousands of years, constantly warring with one another and deadly dangerous to any stranger caught alone and unprotected.

The tribesmen were hideously brave, legendarily strong, notorious for their proficiency with the sword, and renowned as good shots with their long-barreled rifles or, in some cases, with the modern British bolt-action rifles they had either smuggled in from Kabul or found on the battlefield.* It was their long-standing practice to hack to death any wounded enemy they could find, and they thoroughly mutilated the dead by chopping off heads, limbs, etc.[30]

---

* In describing how accurate these mountain tribesmen could shoot, Churchill introduced the world to the term "sniper," which derived from the expression meat hunters of the day used to describe a good shot. Because a snipe is one of the most difficult game birds to hit on the wing—and meat hunters were notoriously stingy when it came to wasting ammunition—to see a man with a string of snipe over his shoulder would often elicit an expression of awe and praise: "There goes a sniper."

It was therefore the custom of the British to go to great lengths to recover any of their own wounded or dead. During General Blood's recent foray several officers had been killed and brought back for funerals and burial. It was also the custom in the regiments to auction off the belongings of dead officers and send the proceeds to their families. Thus Churchill acquired a "complete martial wardrobe," including two good horses with all their tack— one of them a big white charger—a revolver, water bottle, blanket, and so forth. It was a strange feeling, Churchill wrote afterward, to "see the intimate belongings of one's comrades unceremoniously distributed among strangers," and he admitted that he felt a pang a few weeks later when he acquired some equipment belonging to "a gallant friend I had seen killed the day before."[31]

Thus armed, the next morning Churchill joined the staff of Sir Bindon who, erect in his saddle and handsomely resplendent in immaculate khakis, led a force of twelve thousand men and four thousand animals out of the Malakand encampment and into the mountain valleys where the violent tribesmen were grinding their swords.

There were three brigades in the Malakand Field Force marching at two-day intervals, one behind the other. General Blood and his staff, including Churchill, were in the lead with the First Brigade, marching toward the Valley of the Mohmands to teach them their lesson. Along the way, however, they were compelled to pass the entrance to the Valley of the Mamunds, "whose reputation was pestilential, [so] the greatest care was taken to leave them alone."

Encamped for the night where the valley emptied out onto the plain, the First Brigade found itself being sniped at from a distance by some of the tribesmen. When the Second Brigade arrived at the same spot the next day, the Mamunds were waiting and "excited." As soon as darkness fell, the valley erupted with shots from thousands of men. The British soldiers quickly began digging shallow pits against the fire, but when morning came it was found that more than forty officers and men had been hit, as well as scores of horses and pack animals.[32] This was too much for General Blood, who ordered Second Brigade commander General Patrick Jeffreys to retaliate. Turning to Churchill, Blood said, "If you want to see a fight, you may ride back and join Jeffreys."

On September 16, 1897, the infantry, cavalry, and artillery of the Second Brigade moved into the Valley of the Mamunds in warlike formation.[33] Not an enemy shot was fired, and the villages they found seemed deserted. When they reached the far end of the valley Churchill took out his field glasses and scanned the five-thousand-foot cliffs that hemmed them in on both sides. The enemy were there, all right. Clusters of tiny figures could be seen all along the mountain wall, the sun glinting on their swords and rifle barrels.[34] Eventually the leading company of the 35th Sikhs, an Indian outfit, arrived, and it was decided they would attack a village that could be seen on the cliffs above. Two more Sikh companies would fight their way up a long spur to the left; the Bengal Lancers would remain as the rear guard.

Churchill elected to go up the mountain with the Sikhs. The party consisted of five British officers and about eighty-five Sikh infantrymen. The climbing was rough, especially as they were being shot at in regular intervals. When they reached the village they found it already deserted. The enemy fire died away. Churchill took out his field glasses and scanned the valley plain. Suddenly, no British units could be seen. Here they were, he thought, this small party alone among thousands of well-armed tribesmen watching them from up on the cliffs. "I was fresh enough from Sandhurst to remember the warnings about 'dispersion of forces,'" Churchill observed. "But like most young fools I was looking for trouble, and only hoped that something exciting would happen. It did!"[35]

The Sikh company commander, an English captain, arrived to say that the regimental colonel had ordered them to withdraw from the hill because their flanks were "up in the air," a decision that Churchill pronounced "sound." The captain told Churchill, then a junior cavalry lieutenant, to take charge of a squad of eight Sikhs and remain as rear guard until the others got down to a fresh position on a knoll below. They had waited rather nervously for about ten minutes, watching the others descend, when all hell broke loose.

"Suddenly the mountainside sprang to life," Churchill said. "Swords flashed from behind rocks, bright flags waved here and there. A dozen white smoke puffs broke from the face in front of us." From high up on the crag, figures in white or blue robes appeared, dropping down the mountainside from ledge to ledge. A shrill cry arose from many points: "Yi! Yi! Yi!"

As the entire hillside became covered in smoke, Churchill could see in the distance small robed figures descending closer in every moment. The Sikhs commenced fire but it did nothing to stem the flow of the enemy, who leaped down from terraces in the cliffs. About fifty Mamunds had now gathered in rocks a hundred yards distant. The battalion adjutant arrived, dashing under fire between rocks, saying, "Come on back now. There is no time to lose. We can cover you from the knoll." As they rose to withdraw there was a volley from the rocks, followed by screams and curses. Churchill thought the men had lain down again, which they had, except that two had been shot dead and three wounded. One, his chest torn open, was pouring blood; another "lay on his back, kicking and twisting." An officer "was spinning around" right behind Churchill. His eye had been shot out.

They resumed, carrying the wounded downhill. About halfway down they were rushed by about thirty enemy, either firing or brandishing swords. The Sikhs opened fire, breaking the charge, but the adjutant, a popular officer who was bringing up the rear, had been shot. Four of his Sikhs were carrying him when suddenly half a dozen enemy rushed out with swords, screaming. The men carrying the adjutant dropped him and ran off down-hill. Churchill turned to try and rescue him, but before he could get there the leading Pashtun had hacked him to death with his saber.

It had come down at last to man upon man. Broken bodies lay everywhere among the rocky crags. Bullets thrummed, hissed, and often made a curious sound, "like the noise of one sucking in air through pursed lips," Churchill remembered. As Churchill stormed toward the enemy figure, who awaited him with sword in hand, about a dozen more armed tribesmen dropped down from the cliffs and joined the butcher.

Suddenly aware of his recent shoulder injury, Churchill reached instead for his revolver. He carefully aimed it at the man, pulled the trigger, and fired with no result. He did it again, and yet again. He continued to approach, and the tribesman stepped backward and "plumped down behind a rock." Churchill couldn't tell if he had hit the man or not but wasn't staying around to find out.

Churchill clambered down to the first knoll, and then to the second, which was being held by a company of Sikhs. There were dead and wounded lying all around and bullets continued to rip the air. A running gunfight ensued while the soldiers struggled to carry two wounded British officers and six wounded Sikhs to safety. They left a dozen dead Sikhs and a dead British officer to be hacked to pieces by the tribesmen.

It was Churchill's first experience with mortal combat, but by no means his last.[36] Other units of the Second Brigade had lost even more heavily than the regiment Churchill was with, and casualties filled both the hospital tents and the morgue tent. "I saw for the first time the anxieties, stresses, and perplexities of war," Churchill said. "It was not apparently a gay adventure." When Sir Bindon Blood got news of the events in the Valley of the Mamunds, he sent instructions for the Second Brigade to stay there and "lay it waste with fire and sword." In a two-week cavalcade of punitive vengeance and destruction, the brigade obliterated nearly fifty villages—filled up their wells, blew down the castles, sawed down the shade trees, burned the fields, and wrecked the water reservoirs. All the while, sullen tribesmen watched from the mountains, knowing they were no match for the British on the open plain. The villages in the valley had been fairly easily demolished, but the story was different when it came to those located on the sides of the mountains. There the Pashtun resisted fiercely and for every village, Churchill said, "we lost two or three British officers and fifteen or twenty soldiers. Whether it was worth it, I cannot tell. At any rate . . . honor was satisfied."[37]

CHAPTER TWO

When word got around of Sir Bindon's depredations, the entire frontier convulsed in rebellion, including the large and very powerful
Afridi tribes farther up in the Himalaya. Finding the pull of battle
now irresistible, Churchill spent the next six months angling for a
position on the staff of Sir William Lockhart, who was given command of
thirty-five thousand men to put down the revolt. Churchill used every
resource at his disposal, including his mother. "[S]he left no wire unpulled,
no stone unturned, no cutlet uncooked," he said—but nothing was doing.
So he decided to write a book.[1]

Back with his regiment at Bangalore, Churchill began assembling the
dispatches he had sent to the *Daily Telegraph* into a workable manuscript.
Within three months he had produced a passable draft and sent it back to
England for his mother to sell, which she did with a publishing house called
Longman. *The Story of the Malakand Field Force* was received with mostly
highly complimentary reviews.* Churchill showed "a wisdom and comprehension far beyond his years," said one critic. He even received a praiseful
note from His Royal Highness the Prince of Wales, who said, "I have read
it with the greatest possible interest . . . Everybody is reading it."[2]

---

* Churchill had foolishly turned over the copyediting to an uncle who fancied
himself a writer. Unfortunately the uncle left wholesale errors in spelling, grammar,
and punctuation in the manuscript, and numerous reviewers seized on this to
criticize the book, though it mostly received widespread praise.

To his shock and delight, Churchill discovered that the small book he wrote had earned him more money in a few months than two years' worth of pay in the army. He decided to remain in the army only long enough to write about other British wars that were heating up around the world, among them, Sir Herbert Kitchener's punitive expedition to Khartoum in the Sudan.

On leave in London, Churchill began to press for an assignment with General Kitchener's army. However, as he had discovered in India, choosing his own assignment was easier said than done, especially when a reputation precedes you—and Kitchener didn't want any part of him. Through his politicking, Churchill now fully realized that he was making a lot of enemies, which would in fact become a lifelong avocation. Interestingly, this never seemed to bother him; even at this early age, his self-confidence was supreme. Nor did he seem to feel an animus toward these enemies, but instead sought to make them friends: the mark of a good statesman. He would continue to make enemies later in life, even during his greatest, most powerful days, but he always seemed to wish them well. To his enemies, this was maddening.

Through family connections he secured the command of a cavalry troop with the 21st Lancers, which was headed for Africa. His mother, an old friend of Kitchener, wrote to the general himself, but she was rebuffed. Undaunted, Jennie actually took off for Cairo to "get closer to" the sirdar, as Kitchener was known in his capacity as the head of the Egyptian army. She also brought along one Major Caryl John Ramsden, her present lover. Not only did Kitchener refuse to see her, but she returned one day unexpectedly to her suite in the Cairo Hotel to find her major in the embrace of the wife of Colonel Sir John Grenfell Maxwell, the sirdar's nephew. Her remonstrations on that occasion were so vehement they reverberated all the way back to London into the ears of the Prince of Wales, who admonished her with a note: "You had better have stuck to your old friends than gone on your expedition to the Nile! Old friends are the best."[3]

Then a great stroke of luck swung Churchill's way. The British prime minister Lord Salisbury—the same Lord Salisbury who years earlier had fired Churchill's father—summoned young Winston to his chambers. He had read *The Malakand Field Force* and was greatly impressed. Salisbury told Churchill that the book gave him insights into the military actions in India no army field report could match. He said to Churchill at the end of a half-hour audience, "If ever there is anything I can do for you, pray let me know."

Several days later Churchill asked Salisbury's private secretary if the prime minister could put in a good word for him to Lord Kitchener. The word was duly put and the response duly received: No! Even the great man himself could not move the indomitable sirdar.

Churchill had one last card, and he played it beautifully. Through an old friend of the family, he learned that Sir Evelyn Wood, the adjutant general of the army, was displeased with Kitchener for choosing his own officers over the recommendations of the War Office. The friend, Lady St. Helier, was close to Sir Evelyn, and Churchill suggested that she communicate with him the prime minister's desire for Churchill to be included in the Sudan expedition. Two days later he received a communication from the War Office attaching him to the 21st Lancers with orders to proceed immediately to Cairo. He departed the next morning with an agreement at £15 per column* to cover the war for the *Morning Post*. The War Office communiqué laconically specified that if Churchill were to be killed during the battle, "It is understood that . . . no charge of any kind would fall on British Army funds."[4]

THE TROUBLE IN THE SUDAN (or Soudan, as the British spelled it then) had begun nearly twenty years earlier, when a Muslim fanatic named Muhammad Ahmad proclaimed himself to be the Mahdi, "the chosen one," or leader throughout the Muslim world. He persuaded a sect of Islamists called Dervishes to revolt against the Anglo-Egyptian authority that had ruled them for sixty years. They in turn laid siege to various isolated Egyptian garrisons until they effectively controlled most of the outlying country, which was then a British protectorate.

---

* Roughly $2,500 in today's dollars.

Alarmed, the khedive of Egypt sought help. General Charles G. "Chinese" Gordon, a highly respected officer who had previously served as the Sudan's governor-general, answered his call. When Gordon arrived in the fortress capital of Khartoum he was appalled. Inside the fortress, situated at the confluence of the Blue and White Niles, were some seven thousand Egyptian soldiers and twenty-seven thousand civilians. Outside, laying siege, was the sixty-thousand-man Dervish army.

Gordon soon received word from the British and Egyptian authorities in Cairo that the Sudan was to be abandoned to the Dervishes, but nobody knew how to get the Egyptian troops back north without them being slaughtered. The liberal government of Prime Minister William Gladstone dithered in Parliament about sending a relief column to rescue Gordon. At last it arrived, two days too late; Khartoum had been captured and the entire Egyptian army garrison, including Gordon and four thousand of the civilian population, had been butchered.*

That was in 1885. There was much criticism of Gladstone, and when at last the Conservatives came back into power they vowed to restore British honor by sending an army to the Sudan to defeat the Dervishes and avenge General Gordon's death.

Churchill, now twenty-three years old, arrived in Cairo toward the end of July 1898. Half the 21st Lancers—about two hundred strong—had already started up the Nile, and his squadron was due to leave in the morning. A cavalry troop had been reserved for Churchill, but his delay had caused another officer to be assigned. ("Fancy how lucky I am," wrote Lieutenant Robert Grenfell to his family. "Here I have got the troop that would have been Winston's, and we are to be the first to start."†)

It was twelve hundred miles from Cairo to the Sudan, where the Dervish army waited. The troop traveled on stern-wheeled steamers up the Nile, then by rail laid down by Kitchener's twenty-thousand-man force for resupply—and at last, two hundred miles across the desert by horseback.

---

* Gordon was decapitated and his head taken to the Mahdi.
† Grenfell would be killed September 2 when the troop he was leading was nearly "cut to pieces" in the great cavalry charge at the Battle of Omdurman.

At least Churchill had friends in the 21st Lancers—classmates from Harrow and from other walks of his life—unlike his stint with the Bengal Lancers, which had been in India forever and where he had known no one.[5]

As they neared Khartoum, cavalry troops scouted ahead for the enemy. All they saw were mirages, scrub thorn, and the awful heat of the desert, which they could actually see shimmering in the distance. Soon the soldiers began to speculate that the Dervish army had disbanded. Then, on the last day of August, Churchill dined with some British friends in the officers' mess of the Sudanese Battalion. "They are all there," the officers informed him. These men had been fighting the Dervishes for a decade. The next morning Churchill's troop was riding in support of the advanced cavalry screen when people began seeing "white patches" and "gleams of light" among the mirage, Churchill said. The troopers rode forward with growing tension and excitement.

Then a lieutenant rode back and announced that the enemy was in sight.

"Where?" Churchill asked

"There, can't you see?" He pointed to a long brown smear in the desert. Others began to come back, including the squadron commander, who took Churchill to the regimental commander. The enemy was "coming on pretty fast," Churchill said. The colonel told Churchill to have a good long look for himself, and then get the word directly to General Kitchener, who was with the infantry.[6]

After confirming sight of the enemy, Churchill crossed six miles of desert, where he found Kitchener riding alone in front of his staff and the mass of infantry that made up the British force. He brought his horse in a semicircle in front of the sirdar, then came up from behind him on his right side and saluted, wondering if he'd been recognized. Kitchener nodded for him to proceed with his report and then asked, "How long, do you think, have I got?" After some rough calculations Churchill replied that he had about an hour and a half. Kitchener nodded, a signal that the conversation was at an end.[7]

Churchill had lunch with the army intelligence director Sir Reginald Wingate, who received him warmly, interested of course in the news he had brought. The mood among the staff was high, Churchill said. Nobody expected to be killed in the Sudan, he observed. It wasn't like the Great War, he wrote long afterward, where everyone expected to be killed.[8]

★★★★★

THE DERVISH ARMY did not attack that day but drew up several miles before Kitchener's host and commenced a great howl before settling in for the night. "We young men who lay down to sleep that night within three miles of 60,000 fanatical Dervishes . . . we may be pardoned if we thought we were at grips with real war," Churchill later reflected.[9]

They were up the next morning a little after 4 a.m. Churchill's squadron commander gave him a special mission to lead a six-man patrol to reconnoiter a rocky ridge called Jebel Surgham about a mile south. Dawn began to break as they reached the ridge, and at last the veil of dark was lifted, revealing "these enormous black smears" of thousands of men, "and the shimmering and the glinting of their weapons." Churchill handed a communiqué with the enemy position to a corporal with instructions to ride like the wind to Kitchener, whose reply soon came back: "Remain as long as possible and report how the masses of attack are moving."

A deadened roar, a kind of cheering sound, swept over the desert and up over the ridge, "like the sound of the sea," as Churchill picked his way down the west slope, nearer to where the Dervish army was marching. Its gigantic mass glittered with weapons—spears, lances, swords, rifles, knives, axes, and picks. The army was led by bearers of hundreds of colorful silk flags embroidered with verses from the Koran. "We see for ourselves what the Crusaders saw!" Churchill marveled.

Then a crashing boom announced the opening of Kitchener's artillery barrage, which sent scores of high-caliber shells air-bursting over the heads of the advancing Dervish army. Hundreds of men went down "in shapeless heaps, some jumping, some tumbling," leaving great gaps in their ranks and their banners. The artillery fire was constant and soon joined by the huge shells from the navy gunboats that could kill a hundred men in a single burst. By now thousands of Dervishes were dead or dreadfully wounded.

Informed by the squadron commander of incoming infantry fire, Churchill and his troop took shelter from the battle by the steep banks of the Nile. But he could see the cannon boom from the gunboats and hear the crash of the artillery batteries as they decimated "the pride and might of the Dervish Empire . . . on this, its last day of existence." Then the Maxim guns opened up—all fifty of them—each spitting out six hundred bullets per minute at its maximum rate of fire, filling the air with up to thirty thousand pieces of lead as each minute passed. The power was so overwhelming it prompted the prolific poet and Parliamentarian Hilaire Belloc to compose a bit of doggerel:

> *Whatever happens, we have got*
> *The Maxim gun, and they have not.*

Then the infantry opened fire—their twenty thousand Lee-Enfield rifles, shoulder to shoulder, with a maximum rate of aimed fire at thirty shots per minute—that would theoretically put another half a million bullets in the air during any given minute if they were firing all together, which of course they weren't. But the sheer number of deadly missiles to which the Dervish army was exposed was almost unfathomable.

Nonetheless on they came. Banners went down, and men with them. Others seized the flags and brought them forward, only to go down themselves. They got within a thousand yards of the Anglo-Egyptian lines and began to waver but were rallied by emirs on horseback and came on again. This time, their attack came to within seven hundred yards—but the withering fire was too much.

The Dervishes broke into retreat, leaving some seven thousand of their number crumpled dead or wounded on the ground. But the emirs coaxed them back into formation, still over fifty thousand strong, this time getting to within a hundred yards before they wavered and "dissolved into fragments . . . and streamed away into the fantastic mirages of the desert." Twenty thousand of their casualties lay on the ground "in heaps, like snowdrifts."

Kitchener's plan was to keep driving the Dervishes into the desert, and he now ordered the battalions to assemble for a march on Omdurman itself. It was the cavalry's job to keep the Dervishes from the city. Kitchener sent orders for the 21st Lancers to move out ahead and screen the army's march. This prospect excited the officers and many of the men, because for one reason or another the regiment had never been in battle since its inception in 1858. Wags in other outfits wondered aloud if the Lancers' motto was "Thou Shalt Not Kill."[10]

The regiment moved out at a trot and reached Jebel Surgham where, mounting a lower point, Churchill could see the entire plain of Omdurman spread out before them. Now they formed a "column of troops," with each of the regiment's sixteen troops of twenty or twenty-five men riding each behind the other, strung out for nearly a mile. "Everyone expected to make a charge," Churchill said; they had talked of little else since leaving Cairo. The trumpet blew "right wheel into line" and the entire formation swung around to face the enemy riflemen. No order was given to charge; it was understood. With a whoop everyone spurred his charger and plunged forward hell for leather at breakneck speed.

The bloody affair following the charge was measured in minutes. Churchill saw one of his troopers dragged from the saddle and hacked to pieces. The battle had broken into hundreds of personal combats. Churchill himself trotted up to individual Dervishes and shot them in the face, killing at least three. He realized his troop had broken up and that the regiment was trying to re-form about a hundred yards away. He spurred his horse out of a ditch and wheeled toward his comrades.

Now, riderless horses returned, "some spouting blood, struggling on three legs, men staggering on foot, bleeding from terrible wounds, fishhook spears stuck right through them." Churchill recalled a sergeant trying to organize his troop after the charge: "His face was cut to pieces, and as he called on his men to rally, the whole of his nose, cheeks and lips flapped amid red bubbles." Churchill shot a Dervish who had suddenly popped up from a hole in the ground. "How easy to kill a man! But I did not worry about it," he wrote later. He asked one of his sergeants if he had enjoyed himself. "Well, I don't exactly say I enjoyed it, Sir," the sergeant replied, "but I think I'll get more used to it next time."[11]

In the meantime, Kitchener's army managed to reach and occupy Omdurman before the Dervishes could reoccupy it. Now the British held the enemy's base of supply while the Dervishes were relegated to the desert wilderness. Kitchener vindictively had the Mahdi's tomb demolished and his body exhumed; the head was cut off and put into a tin of kerosene.

Word was that Kitchener planned to use it for an inkwell but was disabused of this notion by Lord Cromer, England's chief diplomat in Egypt, on grounds of offending the Muslims throughout the land.

Churchill was relieved to see the Union Jack lifted over Omdurman and Khartoum, but he felt grim upon learning of the 21st Lancers' losses—nearly a quarter of the force had been killed or wounded, as well as 139 horses. He stayed for less than two weeks after the battle, and at one point he visited the battlefield, which he described as a vast pile of "corruption," picking through the stinking dead on horseback with a friend. Corpses of thousands of the enemy were slowly being buried under the shifting sands; piles of white or brown cloth robes covered shrinking bodies, dead horses and donkeys, broken weapons, the miserable litter and junk of battle. Churchill reflected on it afterward in his dispatch to the *Morning Post*, saying that "these were as brave men as ever walked the earth. The conviction was borne in on me that their claim beyond the grave of a valiant death was as good as that any of our countrymen could make."[12]

As THE YEAR 1898 drew to a close, Churchill returned to England, staying with his mother at her rented grand mansion in London's Hyde Park district. There he resolved to relieve her of paying his £500 a year allowance (about $60,000 in today's dollars). Remaining in the cavalry was in fact costing him money, as his late father had predicted, and writing was more lucrative. He was also determined to run for a seat in Parliament—a more difficult proposition because, as he also discovered, getting a "safe" seat would entail spending more money than even his new career could afford him.

Churchill's next step was getting himself introduced to Richard Middleton, the manager of the Conservative Party better known as the "Skipper." Middleton observed that surely a seat could be found for him, providing Churchill could cough up as much as £1,000 a year to the constituents in the form of "charitable contributions." Informed that Churchill could pay only his personal expenses, the Skipper replied that Churchill would be relegated to seeking a "risky" seat or, worse, a "forlorn hope," with little or no chance of election. But, he continued, because of Sir Randolph and because of Churchill's war record, he would "see what could be done." In the interim, the Skipper steered Churchill toward making speeches in some of the Parliamentary districts as a sort of "finger into the wind" test of his popularity.

This notion momentarily paralyzed Churchill with fear. He'd never made a formal speech—not at Harrow, not at Sandhurst, and certainly not in the Hussars. But, he said charmingly, some years afterward, "In life's steeple-chases, one must always jump the fences when they come."[13]

He gave his maiden talk ten days later in the ancient city of Bath, in a little park on a hillside. It was well attended and covered by the *Morning Post*. To Churchill's astonishment, the audience cheered at lines such as "England would gain far more from the rising tide of Tory Democracy than from the dried-up drainpipe of Radicalism." To his wonder, he got an entire glowing column in next day's *Post*, just as his father once had. With this new glory ringing in his ears, he left for India to play polo, the final vestige of his military connection there. After years of fond memories he would not have missed the Indian championship for the world.[14]

AFTER ARRIVING IN BANGALORE, Churchill almost immediately boarded a train for Meerut, fourteen hundred miles distant, where the 1899 India Inter-Regimental Polo Tournament was to be held. Along the way the team stopped in Jodhpur as guests of the maharajah, to relax in luxury and practice with the finest Indian polo teams.

There, however, Churchill was overtaken by "a grievous misfortune"—he slipped on some stone steps and threw his right shoulder out again. He knew from experience that it took three weeks or more to heal, and the tournament was scheduled in four days. He tried to take himself off the team but was overruled by the vote of his fellow members. His position was the number 1 back; even if he would have tremendous difficulty hitting the ball, he could still perform a valuable role with his superb horsemanship by taking the opposing back out of the play with his own pony.[15]

After winning their way to the championship match, the Fourth Hussars found themselves facing the formidable Fourth Dragoon Guards, with Churchill himself opposing the daunting Guards number 1 back Captain John Hardress-Lloyd, later an international high goal polo player. It would be a contest measured in tremendous emotion and grit. Galloping full speed, his arm once more strapped to his side, Churchill played the finest match of his career. All afternoon, he rode Hardress-Lloyd out of the game and managed in the process to score three goals in the 4 to 3 victory for the Hussars. "You would have thought it was not a game at all, but a matter of life and death," Churchill said afterward.

BACK IN ENGLAND in the summer of 1899 Churchill failed to get elected to Parliament. He came up against a by-election in Oldham, a cotton mill city in Lancashire. In the two-seat parliamentary district, one sitting member died of pneumonia and the other submitted his resignation due to ill health, resulting in a double election. Churchill performed well, but he was dragged down by the fact that the other Conservative candidate was, in the most confounding of ironies, a practicing socialist. Besides, the only reason the Conservatives had held the seat in the first place was that the member who had died had also been the respected lawyer for the local trade union. Nevertheless, Churchill gained valuable experience on how a campaign was run, and his speaking manner improved immensely.

In the meantime, he was feverishly working on a new book, *The River War,* an account of the Sudan campaign, which was to become a celebrated success upon publication. Churchill had interviewed all of the principal players—except for the formidable sirdar, who frowned on lieutenants reexamining military campaigns in the public forum. Foremost, the young man was developing what was to become the distinct Churchillian style that readers over the world would grow to know and respect. He interspersed official reports and intelligence documents with his keen and well-honed phraseology.[16]

In the meantime, something very nasty that had been brewing in South Africa for more than a decade came to a boil. On October 8, 1899, the Boer government in Pretoria telegraphed an ultimatum to the British authorities, giving them three days to withdraw all British forces on the Boer frontiers and threatening the arrest of any who remained.* Within the hour, Winston Churchill had been appointed chief war correspondent for the *Morning Post* at a salary of £250 a month† plus all expenses, making him most likely the highest paid war reporter of the period. Within days he was aboard the steamship *Dunottar Castle,* headed for the bottom of the world.

To CHURCHILL'S GREAT LUCK, Sir Redvers Buller, who had been charged to take command of all British operations in South Africa, was aboard his ship, along with his entire staff. Nobody knew what to expect and, as there was no wireless at sea at that time, their only sources of intelligence were what could be gleaned from ports of call or from passing ships.

The British War Office had warned before they left that it might take two hundred thousand troops or more to put down the Boer rebellion, but most people thought that a gross exaggeration. Then, off South Africa's southern coast, they encountered a tramp steamer and signaled for news. A blackboard was held up from the tramp:

> *Boers Defeated*
> *Three Battles*
> *[General] Penn Symond Killed*

As the steamer faded into the mists behind, "we were left to meditate upon this cryptic message," Churchill remembered. But the mood among the general's staff was sanguine.[17]

---

* *Boer* in the Dutch language means "farmer." It also referred to any South African who was descended from Dutch colonists.
† About $30,000 in today's dollars.

But not for long. When they arrived at Cape Town a new, and less encouraging, picture soon emerged. It was true the British had defeated the Boers at the Battle of Talana Hill in Natal. But the Boers had killed the commanding general and sent his four thousand defenders reeling in retreat to Ladysmith. There, they joined the twelve thousand men of General Sir George White— who, contrary to orders to fall back until he could link up with the large force led by General Buller, instead made a stand. As a result his entire army was bottled up in Ladysmith, under siege by the Boers. The British were rushing forces from England, India, and other far-flung parts of the empire to help but, for the time being, all British plans in South Africa were disarranged.

The Boer conflict in South Africa was not new. Since the British capture of the region from the Dutch in 1806, there had been friction between Boer settlers (of Dutch origin) and British settlers. The Boers were mostly farmers, while the British set up trading operations in the coastal towns and cities. The Boers were particularly incensed when the British abolished slavery in 1834;* in response, they moved themselves and their farms en masse across the Vaal River into the Transvaal, where they set up a capital at Pretoria. There, along with other Boers in the so-called Orange Free State, they went about their farming business.

The British permitted this de facto secession until the discovery, in 1867, of vast quantities of diamonds and gold in the Boer-governed territories, which the Boers had neither the manpower nor industrial know-how to exploit. Many British settlers migrated into Boer areas, where they conducted mining operations that began making the Boers wealthy along with them. These immigrants, known to the Boers as "Outlanders"—most of them located in Johannesburg—soon outstripped the local population in size. Before long, the Outlanders began demanding the right to vote.

The Boers just as adamantly refused them this privilege, leading to an incident known as the Jameson Raid, in which a large band of volunteers from the British sectors made a failed attempt to take over Johannesburg

---

* From the time of emancipation, there had been constant friction between the British government in Cape Town and the Boers over the Boers' treatment of the blacks in their employ, which was often little different from slavery.

and rally the Outlanders into revolt. Tensions continued to escalate until the Boers' ultimatum of 1899 triggered an actual war.

The Boers were grossly underrated by the British. Their army consisted of more than sixty thousand Mauser-armed "commandos"—mounted riflemen, some of the finest shots on earth—who had been well trained under the generalship of such Boer luminaries as Paul Kruger and Louis Botha. As well, because of their newfound wealth and connections with Germany, the Boers were equipped with an array of the latest Krupp artillery and U.S. Maxim guns, including a new fast-firing weapon known as a "pom-pom" that shot 1-inch-diameter exploding bullets like a cannon shell.

Churchill, of course, insisted on going to the most dangerous places to report for the *Morning Post*. That would have been Ladysmith, except that location was closed to him due to the Boer siege. The nearest he could get was the last station up the rail track—a tent city called Estcourt—where he encountered an array of old friends, including chums from Harrow, and Reggie Barnes, his polo teammate from India who had been shot earlier. There was little to do in Estcourt but sit and wait for an army of Boers to surround and capture them. With a force of twelve thousand enemy in the neighborhood, all the British could muster up was about a thousand infantry and cavalry, a couple of artillery pieces, and an armored train. Bad odds, but Churchill and his fellow troops were confident in the inherent superiority of the British military.[18]

Churchill had been in Estcourt about a week when opportunity to get closer to the war offered itself in the form of an excursion in the armored train. As he put it: "Nothing looks more formidable and impressive than an armored train, but nothing is in fact more vulnerable and helpless."

Captain Haldane was the officer in charge of the armored train that morning. It was used as a reconnaissance tool to travel the fifteen miles or so from Estcourt to Chieveley, the last station before Ladysmith that the Boers had not wrecked. The train consisted of half a dozen open cars that were protected by sheets of iron plate, with the engine and tender in the middle. Along for protection were two companies of infantry and a dozen sailors with a six-pound naval cannon. At 5:10 a.m. on November 14, 1899, they steamed out of Estcourt. Despite his misgivings about the train,

Churchill said he went along as part of his duty to the *Morning Post* and also "because I was eager for trouble." It found him soon enough.

The train had no sooner reached Chieveley without seeing enemy activity when, from the woods atop a hill only six hundred yards away, Boer soldiers began to emerge. They wheeled out three field cannons and immediately opened up on the train. Shrapnel burst overhead, maiming and killing soldiers in the open-top cars. There were sharp explosions from the front of the train. Bullets from rifle fire clanged against the iron sides. The engineer, who had reversed directions, picked up speed to more than 40 miles an hour, and they were soon careening downhill into a sharp curve. There, the Boers had placed a large boulder on the tracks, and the train hit it head-on. The first three cars were derailed, tumbling over and killing many of the soldiers inside. The first car was knocked off the tracks entirely; the next two obstructed the tracks ahead. The Boers kept up a constant fire at the wrecked train, including steady booms from one of the fast-firing Maxim pom-pom cannons.

At the moment of the crash, everyone in Churchill's car, which was behind the engine, was hurled violently to the floor, some badly injured. Churchill scrambled up the side of the open car and dropped to the ground, hoping to find a way to get the train moving again. The engineer, bleeding from a shrapnel wound to the head, sprang from the cab and sought shelter behind the wrecked cars, complaining that its wasn't his job to get into gunfights with the Boers. Churchill calmly informed him that no man was ever hit twice in one day, that he would be rewarded for gallantry, and that he needed to use the engine to shove the wrecked cars off the tracks. Churchill's manner was so steady and calming that the engineer, a Mr. Wagner, wiped the blood off his face and returned to the engine—and, Churchill said, "thereafter obeyed every order I gave him."*[19]

It was agreed that Captain Haldane would coordinate a covering fire against the Boers while Churchill would see to clearing the tracks—an extremely dangerous business. An enemy shell put the British naval gun out

---

* A decade later when he was home secretary, Churchill was able to fulfill his promise when he saw to it that Mr. Wagner received the Albert Medal, the highest civilian award for gallantry in the realm.

of the fight and another set the engine ablaze. All the while Churchill exposed himself outside. Seemingly oblivious to the hail of bullets, he called for volunteers to help move an overturned car and dashed back and forth from the engine to the wreck, shouting orders. The engine gave a mighty push to clear the tracks, but the derailed cars jammed together and ground to a halt; Churchill ordered the engineer to loosen them up by moving backward, but the coupling chains were too short. The enemy fire kept up. Longer chains were found and installed. The car directly ahead was cleared from the track, and the forward car was only partly obstructing their escape. The engine moved forward but the foot plate jammed on the derailed car and again things came to a halt. For seventy minutes they struggled to free the engine amid the horrible clanging, banging, explosive fire of the Boers.

At length, the obstacle was removed. Haldane directed that wounded would be placed on the engine and the coal tender. Uninjured infantry retreated by walking on the lee side of the engine, away from the fire, and back to Estcourt. Nearly forty wounded soldiers were jammed into the engine and coal car; the dead were left alongside the tracks. The enemy fire actually seemed to increase as the furious Boers realized their quarry was escaping.

Churchill was on the train, but by the time he noticed that the driver had outpaced the infantry outside they were three hundred yards behind, once more at the mercy of the Boers. Churchill told the driver to cross a bridge and wait on the other side while he went to get the beleaguered infantry. As he hurried back down the tracks, he saw figures on horseback "with dark flapping clothes and slouch hats," riding toward him with rifles leveled. When they fired, Churchill heard the whistling bullets pass on both sides of him. He flung himself into a rail cut but it gave no shelter. He began darting down the cut, hoping for the best, when ahead a lone rider came toward him. The large Boer pulled up short and, shaking his rifle, ordered him to surrender. Churchill reached for his Mauser pistol, only to discover he'd left it in the engine cab. He was trapped and made a prisoner.[20]

CHURCHILL AND ABOUT FIFTY other prisoners were made to march to the Boer capital of Pretoria, a three-day trip by foot and train. Along the way Churchill's personal captor gave him his hat to help against the rain.* The officers were imprisoned in a former school building, enclosed by a ten-foot-high fence and constantly surrounded by ten heavily armed guards. Churchill was miserable. A man of action, he now had nothing to do.[21]

Churchill insisted to the Boer command that he was not a combatant but a war correspondent and should be released. "We are not going to let you go, old Chappie," he was told. "We don't capture the son of a lord every day." Churchill responded by writing letters to the Boer authorities, pleading this case. But his own newspapers back in London did him in, running stirring pieces on his heroism at the battle of the train. "[Churchill] needs to be guarded and watched, as he is dangerous to our war," ordered the Boer commanding general Petrus Jacobus Joubert. "Otherwise, he can do us a lot of harm. In a word, he must not be released during the war."

Churchill reproached himself for going back from the train to see about the others. In the Boer prison, "hours crawl by like paralytic centipedes. Nothing amuses you," he wrote. "I certainly hated every moment of my captivity more than I have hated any other period in my whole life."[22]

The day after Churchill's twenty-fifth birthday on November 30, Captain Haldane informed Churchill that he and another soldier—a tough sergeant major—intended to escape. Churchill immediately signed on. The sergeant major was dead set against this but was overruled by Haldane, who felt that Churchill's gallant behavior at the train overcame any objections to his joining in the escape.

The plan turned around getting over the wall at a particular spot in the back of the prison yard that sometimes attracted less attention from the guards than others. At nightfall, Haldane went to scout the potential escape hatch, only to find it too dangerous because of the alertness of the guards. The sergeant major encountered the same difficulty. When Churchill arrived

---

* As Churchill found out years later when Boer officials visited London, his captor was none other than the new prime minister of the Boer republic, the legendary Louis Botha.

for surveillance, he saw an opening when a guard whose back was turned began lighting a cigarette. On impulse he scrambled onto a ledge, leaped to the fence, and began scaling it. At one point he thought the jig was up when his coat became entangled with barbs on the top, but he managed to shake free and dropped down into the garden of an adjoining house.

Churchill could see people in the house and hid in shrubs alongside the prison wall. A fellow officer walking along the wall inside the prison—an accomplice to the escape—was startled to hear a cough from Churchill. "They cannot get out," he murmured. Churchill digested this powerful information, then responded, "I shall go on alone."[23]

Wearing a dark woolen suit and a Boer-style slouch hat, Churchill spotted a garden gate and made a break for it, exiting onto the street. When he saw a guard nearby, he stifled the urge to run and continued walking. After a hundred yards, he concluded he was past the second hurdle, free in Pretoria. The streets were full of Boers but not one paid him any attention. He crossed a bridge and was in the suburbs, where he sat on a small bridge and contemplated his predicament. He was alone in enemy territory with the nearest safety three hundred miles away. He knew no one to ask for help, spoke none of the language, had no map or compass, and no money he could spend because English pound notes would raise suspicion. All he had, in fact, was the constellation Orion to point him roughly in the right direction, so long as the nights were clear; walking around in daylight was out of the question.

He found a rail track and followed it. All rail bridges were heavily guarded, but he found ways around them. He realized it would probably be impossible to walk three hundred miles without being spotted, so he resolved to hop a freight train and hope for the best. Presently he saw the "great yellow headlight" of an engine, and as the train passed he jumped aboard an open car.

It contained sacks of coal and Churchill burrowed in, worrying whether he'd been seen, whether the train was headed in the right direction, and a hundred other important questions before finally falling asleep. When he woke up, he concluded he must leave the train before daybreak in order not to be discovered among the coal bags during unloading. He leaped off and wound up in a ditch. He found water and drank, then headed for a copse of trees to wait out the day until another train came along. A large vulture soaring overhead became his unsettling companion for much of the day. He had brought a bar of chocolate to eat, nothing else.

By late afternoon hunger closed in on him. Churchill, never a strong man of the cross, began to pray "long and earnestly." Near dusk he walked toward some hills because he had noticed that trains—especially the long ones—slowed dramatically while climbing a grade. The vulture followed him. He hid behind rocks and bushes and waited for a train, but none appeared. He had been there more than six hours, on the verge of despair. He once more considered his situation and decided to walk—at least to put ten more miles between him and Pretoria. To avoid bridge guards and Boer strongpoints, he slogged through a swamp, waist high in water, swam streams, climbed rocks, and kept Orion in position to lead him to the Portuguese-held coast where the British housed a consulate. He finally saw a train, but there were too many people around to safely board it. He plodded on until he reached the veld, the great rolling plain of South Africa. Ahead he saw lights and fires, thinking they belonged to "Kaffirs,"* who might be friendly toward Englishmen and might give him a warm meal and "a dry corner to sleep in."

The lights he'd seen were much farther off than Churchill had thought. After walking an hour and a half they were still in the distance. About 2 or 3 a.m. he arrived at a working coal mine with several outbuildings and houses; the fires drove the engines that mined the coal. Churchill saw nothing behind him that would lead to safety, and he determined to take a chance that the occupants of the houses were British Outlanders running the mine.

He knocked on a door and a window above flew open with a flood of Dutch. He felt a shock of consternation but had the presence of mind to answer that he'd had an accident and needed help. Presently the door opened and a tall stern-looking man stood in the doorway and said, in perfect English, "What do you want?"

---

* A term used for blacks in South Africa now considered highly derogatory.

Churchill began lying. He told the man he was in the Boer army, fell off a train, and had dislocated his shoulder. He was invited in and ushered to a small dining room, where he sat at a table. The man, clearly suspicious, inquired further about the rail accident.

"I think," said Churchill, "that I had better tell you the truth."

"I think you had," the man replied very slowly.

"I am Winston Churchill, war correspondent for the *Morning Post.*" He blurted it all out: his capture, his imprisonment in Pretoria, his escape, and that he needed help to get to the frontier.

After a long pause, the man said, "Thank God you have come here." It was, he said, the only house for twenty miles where Churchill would not have been handed over to the Boers. "We are all British here. We will see you through," his host, a Mr. Howard, informed him.*

FOR THE TIME BEING, Churchill's rescuers decided to hide him in the mine until a plan for his escape could be organized. Thus, in the wee hours of the morning he was lowered into the darkened, rat-infested coal pit to await word of his fate. He stayed there nearly a week.

After years of war reporting, Churchill had by now become a correspondent of worldwide repute. The wire services had picked up stories of his escape from Boer newspapers and broadcast them to the ends of the earth. But after five days, the heat was off, and various news reports had him captured in points all along the frontier. The hunt had moved on, and he was allowed to leave the coal pit late at night for long moonlit walks in the freshening breezes of the veld.

At last a plan evolved that chilled Churchill to his bones, for he would now have to rely on others to see him through instead of his own burgeoning self-confidence. He had wanted no more than a pony, a revolver, some food,

---

* For obvious reasons, Churchill omitted the surreptitious aid he'd received from the miners when he wrote his contemporary account of his escape in the *Morning Post,* and in fact he went to great lengths to disguise what really happened in order to protect his abettors.

and a guide to take him to the Portuguese border—but instead, his rescuers planned to move him there in an open railcar filled with huge bales of sheep's wool being sent by a Dutch farmer who was in on the scheme. All turned on how thorough a search would be made of the contents of the car on the Boer side of the border.

Wedged into a small recess between the wool bales, Churchill was given food, water, tea, whisky, a revolver, and wishes of good luck. The trip was expected to take sixteen hours; in fact it took almost two nerve-wracking days. At every stop for coal, water, passengers, shunting, and so on, Churchill expected the tarpaulin to rip and angry Boers to discover his hiding place. In London the newspapers reported: "With reference to the escape from Pretoria of Mr. Winston Churchill, fears are expressed that he may be captured again before long—and if so, may probably be shot."

At daybreak, the train lurched and rattled toward Komatipoort, the last checkpoint on the line before reaching Portuguese territory. It waited there for three hours, Churchill said, with lots of shouting in Dutch. He knew they were searching the train. It was only a few hundred yards to the frontier, and he considered jumping out and making a run for it. But ultimately he thought the better of it.

At length the train pulled forward, and within a short time Churchill peered out from behind his wool bales to behold the uniforms of Portuguese police. He was so excited he began to shout and fired his revolver into the air "as a *feu de joie*." He was free.

He left the train and made his way through the streets to the British consul, who (after first mistaking him for a fireman or deckhand off one of the ships) provided him accommodations, new clothes, and a fashionable dinner "with real tablecloth and real glasses." That night, he arranged passage for Churchill on a steamer bound for Durban, South Africa, and a hero's welcome.

Word of his escape had preceded him as Churchill disembarked from the steamer; British flags adorned the harbor at Durban, bands and wildly enthusiastic crowds jammed the dock and wharves. The mayor, a general, and an admiral greeted him and the crowd swept him up on their shoulders.

"I was nearly torn to pieces by kindness," Churchill said, as he was carried to the town hall. He was implored to make a speech, which he did. Baskets of telegrams from all corners of the world arrived with congratulations and blessings.

Winston Churchill had experienced his first taste of greatness—but he did so with a certain charm and humility. Upon discovering that the newspapers had greatly exaggerated his role in the armored train fight, he felt embarrassed, but he showed a mature understanding of it. "I became for the time quite famous," he wrote, adding, "The British nation was smarting under a series of military reverses . . . and the news of my out-witting the Boers was received with enormous and no doubt dispropor-tionate satisfaction."

All of this lavish attention produced the inevitable backlash from the press, which began to question Churchill's motives and even his creden-tials. "The question occurs, what was he doing in the armored train?" complained the *Phoenix*. He wasn't a soldier, the newspaper went on, so he had no business in the train, and whoever invited him had "over-stepped his duty"—or if Churchill went about without permission, he was an undue burden to the commanding officer. The *Daily Nation* called him dishonorable, and the *Westminster Gazette* accused him of playing a double game by claiming to be a news correspondent and then fighting and escaping.

General Sir Redvers Buller, who remained disconcerted by the reverses suffered by the British army and the so far successful enemy siege of his army at Ladysmith, grilled Churchill at length over conditions in the Transvaal, then asked if there was anything he could do for him. Churchill replied that he would like his lieutenant's commission back and volunteered for a position, for no pay, with the South African Light Horse regiment commanded by Colonel Julian Byng. This was granted, and Churchill became Byng's assistant adjutant.*

---

* Colonel Byng was a descendant of Admiral John Byng, who was infamously executed by firing squad on the deck of a ship, following his court-martial convic-tion for failing to follow the general orders of the British fleet.

Meanwhile, Churchill still retained his job with the *Post*. This profoundly infuriated "the old colonels and generals at the 'Buck and Dodder Club,'" who telegraphed Churchill, "Best friends here hope you will not continue making an ass of yourself."

The focus of their scorn was a series of dispatches the *Morning Post* had published under Churchill's byline, in which the young lieutenant maintained that "the individual Boer, mounted in suitable country, is worth from three to five regular [British] soldiers." As if that were not bad enough, he also predicted that an army of as many as a quarter million men would be necessary to put down the rebellion. Both of these contentions were ridiculed as absurd, and Churchill himself was accused of being "infantile" by the incensed field officer class. In fact he was right, and in the end an army of more than half a million was needed to defeat the Boers—a manpower ratio of 5 to 1.

CHURCHILL'S FIRST ACTION AS an actual soldier in the Boer War was among the most dangerous of his career: the legendary Battle of Spion Kop, in Natal.

The battle was a consequence of General Sir Redvers Buller's attempt to relieve the British army at Ladysmith, with reinforcements he'd recently received totaling about twenty-five thousand infantry, artillery, and cavalry. Part of Buller's force, which was engaged in a long right-flanking swing around the Boer positions, had observed a tall, flat-topped hill with a commanding view of the immediate territory through which the British needed to march. Churchill's division commander sent one of the brigades to take the hill and hold it at all costs, which was where the trouble lay.

Spion Kop was a steep hill—a mountain, actually—about fourteen hundred feet high, with a fairly flat top "about the size of Trafalgar Square," as Churchill described it. These three acres were now crammed with more than two thousand British infantry on the sweltering rocky ground. The Boers had watched the British advance with growing alarm. On the morning of January 24, 1900, they found the Englishmen in control of the summit and determined to eject them.

The Boer force, which was considerably smaller than the British contingent, was well armed to enfilade Spion Kop with rifle fire. Worse for Sir Redvers's infantry, the Boers employed their extremely accurate Krupp-made artillery to sweep every foot of the table-topped plateau with shells, dropping at the rate of about sixty a minute. The Boers had cut their fuses to explode on contact so that the shells landed on the rocky surface, which sent deadly rock fragments tearing into men's flesh. This horrific pounding went on all day until an afternoon attack by the Boers was repulsed by the sorely tested British riflemen at great cost to both sides.

That afternoon, Churchill and a companion cavalryman arrived at the base of the mountain to find a veritable village of hospital tents and wagons tending to hundreds of mutilated British soldiers. They tethered their horses at the base of Spion Kop and climbed its boulder-strewn rear until they reached the top and encountered an exhausted and demoralized Colonel A. W. Thorneycroft, who had assumed command after the brigade commander was killed by Boer artillery. Taking stock of the terrific fire to which the troops were exposed, Churchill and his friend decided to return to the division staff and report the situation to the commanding general.

"Our tidings did not cheer him," Churchill said of the general's reaction upon learning of conditions at Spion Kop. But he told Churchill to return to the hell-blasted hole with orders to Thorneycroft that fresh troops would be sent up later that night and for him to hold on.

Churchill returned to the mountain after dark. He wandered for a long while over ground "thickly dotted with killed and wounded" before finding the colonel, who was in the process of ordering a retirement from the plateau. Churchill tried to convince him to countermand his decision in light of the general's orders, but to no avail. Lieutenant Churchill and the colonel left the hill just as the reinforcements were arriving. Again, Churchill gently beseeched the colonel to return to the summit, but again he was rebuffed, and next day the Boers retook Spion Kop. It was an embarrassing British defeat, with upwards of three hundred British officers and soldiers killed and more than a thousand wounded or taken prisoner, which Churchill deemed a "military crime."

When the first vanguard of Buller's army finally rode into the bedraggled streets of Ladysmith after Spion Kop, the British army there had been reduced to eating horses and mules and was "starving as slowly as possible." Churchill helped break the siege, and he dined that night on the last bottle of champagne and—instead of horsemeat—the last dray oxen in the now relieved army's possession.

Churchill remembered the days that followed as containing "the most happy memories of my life." There were still numerous skirmishes to be fought with recalcitrant Boers, camping out under the stars, riding the length of the country and taking in its "wonderful air and climate." It was not always the safest occupation, however, as Churchill learned late one afternoon when riding past a hill that, as an experienced officer, he felt gave off sinister emanations.

He had arranged a few months earlier for his nineteen-year-old brother Jack to join him in the South African Light Horse. As they rode together in a cavalry column, he had a premonition and remarked, "We are much too near those fellows," just as shots rang out from the crest of the hill. The cavalrymen quickly galloped to the crest of a hill of their own and, after stashing their horses safely behind it, lay down and proceeded to engage in a gunfight with the surprisingly numerous Boers.

Suddenly Jack grunted and backed off several feet. Churchill discovered his brother had been shot in the calf by a bullet that missed his own head by inches. He managed to get Jack off the firing line and into a wagon headed for the hospital at Durban, where a surgeon operated to remove the bullet. It was there he learned to his jaw-dropping surprise that a brand-new hospital ship had just entered the harbor, organized and directed by none other than his and Jack's own mother, Jennie, who had raised a subscription fund by throwing parties and balls in London to equip it with the finest medical staff and nurses. In a stunning coincidence, Jack became its first patient.

Jennie invented a grand time for herself in South Africa, attending all the luncheons, dinners, and military balls that behind-the-lines living offered. She was forty-five and in the full flower of her beauty and charm: still slender and fair, though it was said she dyed her hair now. Before she left she announced her engagement to Lieutenant George Cornwallis-West, a handsome and well-connected but impoverished British officer the same age as her son Winston. It scandalized her friends, but she replied, "I don't care, I'm having fun!" Churchill's reaction is lost to history. But in years afterward (and before her divorce) he frequently visited his mother at Salisbury Hall, a large estate in Surrey.[24]

With the retreat from Ladysmith and Natal, the Boers thought the war was over, and the two Boer republics sought to formally end the conflict through negotiations. But the British entertained no such notions and determined to press on through the Orange Free State to the Transvaal and capture Pretoria, then dictate terms of their own. Churchill thought this a bad idea and said so in print, angering many in both South Africa and England. He was a conciliatory person by nature and persisted in the hope that "a generous and forgiving policy be followed."

In any event, the British took their time making their way toward Pretoria, allowing the Boers to catch a second wind and reorganize to carry on the fight. This time it would be guerrilla style, with the Boers acting as peaceful farmers and then violating their neutrality oaths by sneaking out for night raids against British positions. The British retaliated, as they did in India, by burning Boer farms and herding the Boers' wives and children into concentration camps where they could be fed and sheltered. Unfortunately, not enough attention was paid to the latter, and an inordinate number of women and children died of disease from unsanitary conditions and malnutrition.

Churchill, in the meantime, had secured a position on the staff of the army marching on Pretoria, which nearly cost him his life.

While on a cavalry patrol, Churchill and a troop of mounted infantry scouts encountered a wire fence and dismounted to cut it. Just then a large number of Boers appeared from behind a small hill and began firing at them. Everyone jumped to his horse, but when Churchill reached his mount the animal began rearing and plunging because of the gunfire. When he tried to spring into the saddle it slipped and wound up under the horse's belly. The horse then galloped away, leaving Churchill alone to face the approaching enemy. The Boers had sighted him and were firing right at him, so he did the only thing he could think of, which was to run for his life. With bullets whizzing all around him, Churchill suddenly saw one of the scouts pass by ahead of him. "Give me a stirrup!" he shouted. The man reined in his horse and Churchill instantly swung up behind him. They galloped away to safety. As Churchill put it, he had "thrown double sixes again."

The Boers had cleared out of Johannesburg ahead of the British army, and four days later out of Pretoria as well. Churchill rode into the city along with his cousin the Duke of Marlborough, who was on the staff of Churchill's friend General Sir Ian Hamilton. The Boers were leaving town on a long train with rifles bristling from every window. Churchill went first to the officers' prison camp, where the imprisoned men burst out in wild cheers at the sight of him. The Boer guards threw down their weapons, and the Union Jack was run up the flagpole. For Churchill, it was the culmination of his duties with the army. He secured his release and went to Cape Town, where he would take a steamship home. The Boer War would drag on for two more years, "shapeless and indefinite," before the final British victory was declared.

Back in England in the fall of 1900, Churchill returned to the cotton mill town Oldham, where he'd been defeated for Parliament the previous year. This time he was greeted by great throngs of mill hands and mill girls, enthusiastically shouting his name. He gave a speech describing his escape, in which he mentioned the name of the engineer on the armored train where he was captured. Someone shouted, "His wife's in the gallery!" to the general elation of the crowd. This was to be a "khaki election," meaning that the issues turned on martial events—namely, the Boer War. The Conservatives were returned to office with a great majority, and Winston Churchill was swept along with the tide. He was twenty-six years old and at last in the House of Commons from which his father had attempted to guide the British Empire.

He also discovered there was money to be made giving speeches. The world still savored the details of his escape from Pretoria, and after his English tour was concluded he went to America and spoke to eager audiences in Boston, New York, Baltimore, and Philadelphia. When he was done, Churchill had accumulated a £10,000 war chest with which to face his ever complicated world.

CHAPTER THREE

Around the time that Winston Churchill was battling Pashtuns in India, Dervishes in the Sudan, and the Boers of South Africa, Joseph Stalin was engaged in planning a Russian bank robbery, one of many that he staged. The act was an effort to raise money for Stalin's mentor and boss Vladimir Lenin, the father of Soviet communism.

The banned Russian Socialist Party had recently split into two distinctly different factions. Lenin's branch, the Bolsheviks, wanted immediate action to overthrow the czar—violently if necessary. The opposing Mensheviks wanted a more peaceful revolution by working within the system. Lenin, who was then in self-exile in Finland, needed money to aid the Bolsheviks. So Stalin engineered the robbery of a stagecoach full of rubles that was being brought under armed guard from a Russian post office to the state bank in the Georgian capital Tiflis (now Tbilisi), in the Caucasus between the Black and Caspian Seas.

Stalin was then twenty-eight years old and the leader of a large gang of Communist-oriented criminals in Tiflis. This included young girls and boys who spied, ran errands, and performed other Faginesque duties for the innovative political system they hoped would lead them out of poverty into a brave new world.[1]

The robbery, which newspapers at the time described as a terrorist act, became a major story worldwide because as many as forty people were killed during its commission. The rubles, stacked in Russian bank notes worth today more than $3 million, were contained in a horse-drawn coach escorted by five Cossacks* on horseback, as well as another coach containing various bank officials and armed guards. Stalin had managed to penetrate the bank through a clerk he knew and was able to determine exactly when the shipment would arrive. As the caravan approached the crowded town square of Tiflis, a pretty young girl gave a signal to a man reading a newspaper on a bench, who put the paper down as a signal to the other gang members, armed with pistols and homemade bombs.

Stalin apparently did not participate in this robbery directly, preferring to be the mastermind rather than an actor. His deputy was a quasi-psychopath named Simon "Kamo" Ter-Petrosian, Stalin's friend and protégé and an accomplished murderer and master of disguises. Today he had chosen to arrive at the scene on a horse, dressed in the red uniform of a Cossack captain (complete with a large curved saber and tall bearskin hat). When the caravan entered the square, Kamo rode past it and came up behind. At this, two of the girls and a number of the robbers drew out their bombs, pulled the fuses, and rolled them under the coaches.

What happened next became the subject of widespread discussion by Tiflilinos until the day they died. An earthshaking roar shattered every window for half a mile around, toppled over chimneys on buildings and houses, and knocked people anywhere nearby to the ground. The last carriage containing the guards and bank officials exploded, hurling people and parts of people into the air. The bombs aimed at the first carriage, which contained the money, exploded instead beneath the horses, disemboweling most of them. Gunshots rang out and more bombs were thrown; people in the crowded square ran screaming into the streets, while others lay torn asunder by the bombs or bullets. Panic and utter confusion reigned. It had all happened precisely as Stalin had planned it.

A number of the robbers rushed at the first carriage to grab the money. But just as they reached it, one of the two lead horses somehow managed to scramble to its feet and bolted through the square and down the hill

---

* A warrior caste of Slavic Russians skilled in horsemanship who served as cavalry guards to the czars.

toward the river, dragging the carriage, the money, and the dead horses along with it. Some of the participants got cold feet at this point and ran off, but several others chased after the horse. One of them got close enough to hurl a bomb under its belly, blowing the animal apart. Unfortunately, the bomb thrower was too close to the explosion himself and was flung into the air, landing on his head on the cobblestone street.

Another robber reached the carriage and grabbed two large moneybags containing the rubles. They were so heavy, however, that he could barely stagger off with them as the authorities began arriving at the scene in alarming numbers. Just as the man was about to drop the loot and run, who should come riding into the smoky chaos but Cossack Kamo in his bearskin hat, driving a stolen phaeton.* He seized the money and cantered off past the palace of the viceroy to a location where female members of the gang sewed the money into a mattress. This mattress in particular had been stolen from the director of the Tiflis Meteorological Observatory, where Stalin had once worked checking thermometers and barometers. Thus disguised, the money mattress was returned to the director's residence: an unlikely place for the authorities to look.

No one was ever arrested for the crime. Rumors circulated it had been the work of various Socialist or anarchist organizations, which had begun conducting terrorist-type activity with increasing frequency since Lenin came on the scene. Lenin's brother had been executed by agents of the czar; the experience made Lenin recoil from achieving socialism by peaceful methods, declaring that, instead, "We shall take a different path."

However, in order to maintain a quasi-legitimate image, the local Socialist Party had forbidden the kind of bloodthirsty mayhem featured in Stalin's bank robbery, resulting in Stalin's expulsion from its membership. He didn't care. Two days later, he left Georgia forever, taking his wife and young son with him to Baku, the sprawling, violent oil boomtown on the Caspian Sea.[2]

The robbery money had to be laundered through banking systems in various countries before at last reaching Lenin in some marketable condition.

---

* A light, four-wheeled horse-drawn carriage.

But the feat was enough to make him conclude that Stalin was "exactly the kind of man I need"—which, a decade later, would place his loyal follower in the rarefied upper reaches of Soviet communism.[3]

JOSEPH STALIN WAS AS DIFFERENT from Winston Churchill as it was possible to be. Where Churchill was outgoing, straightforward, and enjoyed the limelight, Stalin was shadowy, secretive, and devious. In fact "Stalin" (in English, "man of steel") wasn't actually his name. He was born Josif Vissarionovich Dzhugashvili in 1878—four years after Churchill's birth. He used numerous aliases and physical disguises in his youth to throw the Russian czar's secret police off his trail. And he certainly wasn't descended, as Churchill was, from peers of the realm; his father was a violent, drunken, shoe cobbler who deserted his family in a remote town in Russia's Caucasus Mountains. Stalin didn't play polo or go to cocktail parties, nor was he on speaking terms with such notables as His Royal Highness the Prince of Wales. He was lucky as a youth to find an ass to ride along a mountain road, and the most important personage he likely knew growing up was his village priest in the Russian Orthodox Church.

While Churchill at an early age was publishing books and newspaper stories involving himself and would even go on to write his autobiography, Stalin spent nearly as much energy removing any mention of himself from published accounts (and the idea of an autobiography was out of the question). For nearly forty years after he came to power, there was only one official story of Stalin's life; it was very thin, and often untruthful.

He ran the Soviet Union with an iron hand, and anyone who differed with him did so at his own peril. A saying was attributed to Stalin: "When one man dies it is a tragedy; when a million men die it's a statistic." Compared with Churchill and Roosevelt, Stalin probably had more in common with Adolf Hitler, who had once aspired to be an artist; Stalin in his youth sought to compose romantic poetry. But both instead became revolutionary dictators who murdered vast populations of their own countries—and of other countries as well.

After World War II broke out and Hitler stabbed Russia in the back, Stalin partnered up with the United States, Great Britain, and other Western Allies against Nazi Germany, which was defeated in no small measure by the mighty armed forces of the Soviet Union. But no sooner had the war ended than Stalin became the West's most implacable and dangerous enemy.

JOSIF DZHUGASHVILI WAS BORN in the village of Gori, in a two-room cottage lit by an oil lamp in the shadow of the Caucasus Mountains. His mother, Ekaterina (known as "Keke"), was the daughter of serfs* (a legitimate social caste until Czar Alexander II abolished the institution a decade and a half earlier). Ekaterina had married a local cobbler Besarion "Beso" Dzhugash-vili, a descendant of wild mountain tribesmen not dissimilar from the Pashtuns Churchill had battled in the Hindu Kush. Beso's business prospered for a while, and he even took on apprentices. But when their first two children died of illness he sought consolation in wine. By the time Josif was born, Beso had become a full-fledged alcoholic whose violence—especially toward his son—was deplorable.

Unlike Winston Churchill's father, who ignored him, Beso's treatment of young Stalin was such that when the noise of his father's drunken singing announced his impending arrival, Josif would ask if he could go to the house of a friend until his father went to sleep. Once Beso threw him across the room so viciously there was blood in the boy's urine for a week. A childhood friend recalled that the father's behavior taught the boy "how to hate people."

Keke enrolled her son in a church school, hoping he would grow up to be a priest, while Beso slipped further into squalor and self-mortification on rumors of Keke's infidelities. Stalin's mother had a rather loose reputation around town (perhaps understandable, considering the degradation of her

---

* A form of legalized slavery under which peasants were bound to feudal nobility to till fields, build roads, and perform household chores. They had more rights than African slaves, but it was still a fairly miserable existence.

husband, whose business had gone sour along with the wine). To say that she was a prostitute would be inaccurate—although Stalin in later years once referred to her as a "whore." But there is historical evidence that she sought favors from wealthy or powerful men in her village in exchange for sexual reciprocity.[4] Eventually, Beso left Gori to work in a shoe factory in Tiflis; to observe that Stalin had a miserable childhood fraught with viciousness and chaos would be an understatement.[5]

This circumstance might have been made more bearable by the clannish violence that hung over Gori in those days. Brutal street fights between males of all ages were not only condoned, they were sanctioned, making it seem as if the town were populated by maniacs. On important Georgian holidays—including Christmas—males beginning with young schoolboys would swarm through the streets setting on friends and enemies alike with fists, teeth, kicking feet, and gouging fingers, egged on by the older men. When this began to wear itself out, the teenagers would start fighting, then the young men, followed well into the night by the old men, all of it fueled by a river of wine of which even the youngest would partake. It was said that Stalin jumped right into the mayhem, which had been a ritual in Gori as far back as anyone could remember. Even in his youth, Stalin was evidently no stranger to the routine brutality he inflicted on the Russian people years later.

When he was fourteen, Stalin's mother put him in a boarding school in Tiflis with the goal of turning him into a priest. It was no mean feat arranging for a child to be appointed to the Orthodox Theological Seminary, but it has been suggested by more than one historian that Keke accomplished this by having an affair with a local priest in Gori.

The school was a severe environment, ruled by monks who prohibited students from reading anything secular, including newspapers, magazines, and novels. Greek and Latin were the mainstays of the curriculum. Violators of the myriad rules were sentenced to a dark hold, or "hole," for days at a time. It was this atmosphere of repression and harsh discipline that turned Stalin into a Socialist; at least, that's what he declared to the interviewer Emil Ludwig in 1931: "I joined the revolutionary movement when fifteen years old," he said, "in protest against the outrageous regime and Jesuitical methods prevalent at the seminary," adding that the monks' "principal method is spying, prying, worming their way into people's souls, and outraging their feelings." One of his biographers wondered whether it became Stalin's desire to "outdo" these so-called Jesuits, rather than recoiling in revulsion at their methods, "which placed its peculiar stamp on Socialism as interpreted by Joseph Stalin."[6]

Whatever his motivation, Stalin joined a Marxist group at the seminary when he was sixteen, but he soon broke off to form a rival group of his own: apparently, the beginning of his desire for political leadership. There was only a single copy of Marx's *Das Kapital* in Tiflis, but members of Stalin's group went to the library and took notes from it. Soon, Stalin was caught at the seminary with unauthorized reading material in his possession and sentenced to spend hours in the hole.[7]

There were many revolutionary movements in Russia's history during this period. But in 1898, the empire was convulsed when the Russian Social-Democratic Workers' Party was formed, based on Marxist teachings. Like Christ, the party had been born in a stable, in Minsk, with Lenin presiding. But for these atheists, it was the party that would be their messiah: all powerful, giver of all things to all people, and the source of all goodness and righteousness in the world.

Still at the seminary but now twenty years old, Stalin had become a member of another Marxist circle in Georgia called Group Three. After reading an article by Lenin he declared that "I must meet him at all costs." He would not meet his hero for another eight years. But a few months after encountering his writing, in May 1899, Stalin was expelled from the Tiflis Orthodox Theological Seminary. He was on his own.[8]

Shortly thereafter, Stalin obtained a position at the Tiflis Meteorological Observatory, where he recorded weather data. He spent his spare time running an underground printing press for the Social-Democratic Workers' Party, organizing strikes and demonstrations by local factory workers. Following a wave of these strikes the government authorities began a serious crackdown, arresting many of the revolutionaries. At this point, Stalin quit the Meteorological Observatory and went "underground," becoming a full-fledged Socialist revolutionary.

Stalin's style of revolution was far more violent than that of many of his contemporaries, and not only because of his inclination to provide strikers with clubs and brickbats. His notion of Socialism ran to acts of violence against his fellow revolutionaries as well, in an effort to consolidate control of the local party for himself. In so doing, he employed the methods with which he was culturally familiar. The German historian Jörg Baberowski explains it this way: "Stalin and his comrades-in-arms brought into the party both at the center and edges of the empire the culture of violence of the Caucasian periphery, the blood feud and archaic conceptions of honor."[9]

By now, Stalin had become a fanatic of the Socialist creed. He declared that Marxism was not just "some theory of socialism," but instead that "the revolutionary proletariat alone is destined by History to liberate mankind and bring the world happiness." He added, however, that this would not happen before "many storms, many torrents of blood. Blood, death, and conflict were essential," during "the struggle to end oppression."[10] For him, it seemed, the path was clear. And he was more than right about the results being bloody and decisive.

In 1902 Stalin either was forced out of Tiflis after many party squabbles or left under his own steam. Whichever the case, he landed in Batumi, an important oil industry city on the Black Sea, using the alias Comrade Soso. In due time, Socialist worker strikes and demonstrations began to break out in Batumi. The Rothschilds' oil refinery was set afire, employers were shot dead, and the city became awash with Marxist propaganda, from slogans painted on walls and fences to pamphlets and even newspapers.

At one point Stalin had an affair, his first recorded, with the married landlady of one of the many apartments he stayed in during this time. She later spoke of his "tender attention and thoughtfulness."

A major incident occurred in March of that year, when workers led by Stalin stormed a prison containing many of their comrades who had been arrested during the demonstrations. Russian soldiers opened fire, killing thirteen workers and injuring many more. Stalin was at last arrested, dressed this time in the burka and veil of a Muslim woman.

In jail awaiting trial, he pleaded with his mother and others to swear that he was in Gori during this period and had had nothing to do with the disorders in Batumi. Keke duly produced a petition—obviously written by someone else—asserting that her son was "the breadwinner for himself and his mother, and had neither the time nor the occasion to participate in conspiracies or disturbances." This did not impress the authorities, and a year after he was arrested Stalin was sentenced to exile in Siberia.

THE TRIP FROM BATUMI TO SIBERIA took four months. Stalin and the other prisoners were placed in leg shackles and taken via steamship up the Black Sea and the Don River to Rostov-on-Don. Next, they boarded boxcars on the Trans-Siberian Railway for the three-thousand-mile trek across the Urals to Irkutsk in Siberia. From there it was fifty miles farther north by oxcart to the remote and forbidding Novaya Uda, a collection of ramshackle houses, stores, taverns, a church, and a wooden fort for protection against Mongol tribes. It was bitterly cold in November—but still, this was only *southwestern* Siberia, near Lake Baikal on the border with Mongol China, and nothing like the terrible Siberian gulags a thousand miles to the north, where Stalin later sent his exiles to toil and die in the salt and gold mines at the Arctic Circle.

In the czar's Siberia, exiles were not required to work. In fact, the government gave them a monthly allowance for clothes, food, and rent for a room in one of the peasant hovels. As Stalin's biographer Simon Sebag Montefiore puts it, there was "little to do in Novaya Uda except read, argue, drink, fornicate, and drink more—these were pastimes for locals and exiles alike."

Stalin read when and what he could. Whenever he could scrape up the money, he caroused in the filthy taverns with exiled criminals, who were a class apart from the political exiles—or so many Socialists believed. Stalin preferred the criminals, because they were easier to get along with and also because they were, well, criminals. According to Montefiore, his behavior was among the worst of any of the political exiles. Immediately upon arrival, he began breaking rules and became, in turn, "a reckless seducer, procreator of illegitimate children, serial feuder, and compulsive troublemaker."[11] He wasn't there long before he decided to escape, but he tried and failed three times in 1904 for want of proper clothes and poor planning.

Later on in Communist Russia, much was made of Stalin's fabled escapes, during which he was said to have fallen into icy rivers, nearly perished in blizzards, been hunted down by the czar's secret police, and set upon by wolves and bears. In truth, he got to the rail depot in Irkutsk by hopping a ride on a local peasant's horse-drawn sled. Using a fake ID and money provided by his mother, he bought a ticket on the Trans-Siberian and found himself back in Tiflis within two weeks, having read a Russian translation of Carlyle's history of the French Revolution in his spare time on the train.

Stalin's timing could not have been better. Czar Nicholas II gave revolutionaries across Russia an opening when he foolishly picked an argument with the Japanese in order to expand his Eastern empire. The Japanese turned it into a fight by executing a sneak attack against the Russian Far East Fleet at Port Arthur in Manchuria before war was formally declared (eerily presaging their unannounced Pearl Harbor attack thirty-eight years later). The infuriated czar ordered his grand Baltic Fleet to sail halfway around the world to avenge the outrage, only to have it soundly defeated by superior Japanese naval tactics and gunnery. Moreover, in Manchuria the Japanese inflicted a series of humiliating defeats on the Russian army and were near to winning the war when U.S. president Theodore Roosevelt intervened to broker a settlement. The consequent Treaty of Portsmouth ended the war in 1905 but resulted in serious repercussions on the czar's domestic front. Eighty thousand Russians were dead, much of the home fleet was at the bottom of the Sea of Japan, nothing had been gained, and Russian international prestige was at an all-time low. Even the czar's royal friends and those in his peerage were turning against him.

But czars being czars, Nicholas II could not simply wait for some "next election" to exit the national stage, and his children weren't old enough to succeed him should he abdicate. It was at just this moment that the Russian people, including the Social-Democratic Workers' Party, chose to rise up and claim what they said was theirs.

It might have been a propitious moment but it wasn't. Disunited, the fractious revolutionaries were at the height of their squabbles about ideology. A great march was held on a Sunday to the czar's palace at St. Petersburg to protest all manner of inequities, including low wages, high taxes, national and religious persecution, land reform, fishing rights, and political repression everywhere. The marchers got too close to the palace, however, and the czar's troops opened fire. Several hundred protesters were killed, touching off a widespread "revolution" that ultimately went nowhere (at least at that time) though it shook the regime to its core. "Bloody Sunday" set off a chain of strikes and stoppages through the country, prompting the historian Stephen F. Jones to quip, "Everyone from palm readers to prostitutes went on strike." Socialist councils, or "soviets," arose in nearly every city of the realm. Their committees were run by an equal number of "workers" and "intellectuals," or educated Socialists. Within a few months, nearly a hundred and fifty political assassinations were committed in Georgia alone. Nationwide, the number exceeded three thousand.

In retaliation the czar's Cossacks in Tiflis raided a student meeting, killing sixty children but no revolutionaries. No bank was safe, and bombers and arsonists plied their violent trade. In desperation, the czar promised the people a Duma, or Congress, as well as a constitution and rudimentary bill of rights. This seemed to satisfy most of the people, and the largest strikes and protests drifted to a close.

However, the Bolshevik branch of Socialists under Lenin not only continued their violence, they stepped it up, assassinating government officials and factory managers on an unprecedented scale and fomenting strikes and demonstrations throughout the country. Like all revolutionaries, the Bolsheviks were conspiratorial and secretive. They had to be: their party was banned, and if the local police or the Okhrana—the czar's secret police—discovered them they would be arrested and exiled to Siberia (or worse). So they existed in shadow communes, preaching the mighty shibboleths of socialism, atheism, and free love. There were of course women involved; Stalin in fact had a gang of armed girl students under his control, as well as the band of Faginesque street urchins who acted as spies and informants. With all the unrest and the terrible humiliation of the war with Japan still cloaking the land, Russia seethed.

Because of his previous arrest, Stalin was well known to the Okhrana, which was actively looking for him. He managed to elude capture by moving from apartment to apartment, usually occupied by women he knew; tips from fellow party members kept him posted and on the run. But now Stalin decided he was too hot a property in Tiflis, and it was time to move on. In 1906 he went to Baku, the violent, booming oil city on the Caspian Sea, to find out what kind of trouble he could stir up there.

As it was, there was plenty of trouble, as Stalin soon found out; Baku was in the midst of a murderous religious and sectional convulsion that left the streets reeking with thousands of corpses. Armenians killed the Muslim Turks, and vice versa. Caucasian Socialists (Stalin included) killed extortion victims who wouldn't pay up, loyalists of the czar, traitors, and whoever else threatened them. And as usual it was everybody against the Jews. Even the mostly Jewish Mensheviks, who eschewed violence, began arming themselves. Stalin wound up for the first time presiding over a heavily armed gang of mostly Muslim thugs who engaged in robberies, extortion, and protection rackets to raise money for the party. By his side as the gang's number one hit man was Stalin's faithful friend Kamo, the erstwhile "Cossack captain" of the Tiflis bank robbery. They assassinated people when they deemed it necessary and were accomplished arsonists. These outfits were called battle squads, but they operated more or less as armed terrorist organizations—even though terrorism was forbidden by the party. There was no social morality to contend with here, only the expediency of laying groundwork for the revolution. Murdering rich people or government officials was a way of destabilizing the regime and was considered, basically, all in a day's work.[12]

Stalin located a printing press and began distributing Socialist propaganda. He organized study sessions for the semiliterate workers to absorb the tenets of Socialism and, should they prove able and trustworthy, shape them into secret cells numbering three or five for further exploitation for the cause.

Strangely, contributions to the party came in from beyond the proceeds of extortion and robbery. Upper-class citizens (Marx's "bourgeoisie") often opened their wallets to the revolutionaries: doctors, lawyers, merchants, and factory owners who secretly hated the czar, as well as less well-off sympathizers including shopkeepers, academics, students, and the clergy. Lenin characterized these people as "useful idiots"; come the revolution, most of them would be killed or exiled to the slave mines of Siberia.

It was at around this time, in early 1905, that Stalin started a feud with the Mensheviks, whom he reviled. The Bolsheviks and Mensheviks now openly vied for power in the factories and the mines. Debates between the two factions were held before the wretched workers. After one of these Stalin declared, "Lenin's outraged that God sent him such comrades as the Mensheviks! Who are these people anyway? Martov, Dan, Axelrod are circumcised Yids. You can't go into a fight with them and you can't have a feast with them."[13] It has come to light that Lenin's grandfather was a Jew—but he himself professed to be an atheist.

In April of the same year, Stalin challenged a Menshevik leader, a man named Isidore Ramishvili, to a debate at the manganese ore mining town of Chiatura before a gathering of several thousand miners. He won the debate handily by letting the Menshevik speak first; the man droned on in a lengthy oratory. Then Stalin took the stage, employing a folksy style like the American firebrand Huey Long. He spoke in this populist tone for no more than fifteen minutes. Observers said it was a magnetic, stirring speech that had the miners on their feet in cheers.

IN THE SUMMER OF 1906 Stalin got married. His new wife, the former Kato Svanidze, was a dressmaker in a Tiflis clothing salon; he had known her as a fellow traveler of the revolutionary set. Despite his seemingly endless string of girlfriends and mistresses, Stalin seemed genuinely taken with the beautiful Kato, and by all accounts he was gentle and kind to her. For her part, she was aware that his first allegiance was to the party, and that he was a notorious womanizer and gangster who specialized in bank robbery and extortion. But his ideas and style fascinated her. She was, of course, Ortho-dox, and Stalin had become an atheist per revolutionary dictum, so diffi-culties arose in finding a priest to marry them. At length, one was procured who agreed to perform the ceremony, but only at two o'clock in the morn-ing. The reception and honeymoon were held in the bride's apartment.

Eight months later, in March 1907, Stalin's first child was born: a son named Yakov. Stalin, at that time disguising himself as a Turk by wearing a fez on his head, continued his subversive activities in Baku while Kato tried to make do at home: a rented room in a "squat adobe cottage on an oil field." The robberies continued—banks, trains, stagecoaches—and enormous sums of rubles were taken in. But Stalin, if nothing else, was a conscientious thief; not one penny went to himself or his wife for luxuries, or even essentials. He began to style himself sanctimoniously as a sort of Russian Robin Hood, who stole from the rich to give to the poor, in this case, to Lenin, who was far from poor but who professed to stand for the masses who were in fact poor.[14]

In the same spring that his son was born, Stalin at last fulfilled his wish to meet Lenin, whom he so adamantly admired. The noble-born estate holder and so-called Father of Communism had convened a Bolshevik conference in St. Petersburg, and Stalin was selected as a representative from the Caucasus. On reaching the city, however, Stalin and other comrades from the far-flung reaches of the empire were startled to hear that the czar's agents had gotten word of the meeting and arrested most of the important members of the soviet, including Leon Trotsky (formerly Lev Bronstein), the Jewish intellectual who had become one of the most prominent sup-porters of supposedly moderate socialism and had split from Lenin while writing for the newspaper *Iskra*.

Eventually, Stalin's group was given money for a train ride to a village in the mountains of Finland where, disguised as teachers, they would see the great man preside over the conference. "Imagine my disappointment," said Stalin afterward, "when I saw the most ordinary man, below average height, in no way different from ordinary mortals."[15]

He remained in awe of Lenin, however, as he heard him speak. At one point Lenin invited him to give his opinion of how Socialist organization was going in the Caucasus. Later, the two clashed over whether the Bolsheviks should participate in the coming elections to the czar's Duma, which had been formed to redress the people's grievances. Lenin was for it but Stalin arose to disagree. In the end Lenin told him to draw up a resolution stating his position.

The conference was in its second day when a series of riots, uprisings, and other revolutionary acts spread from Moscow to other cities, including Tiflis and Baku. The workers in the cities and the peasant farmers in the countryside were in open revolt, an ongoing aftershock of the Bloody Sunday massacre two years prior.

The conference hurriedly disbanded in a shambles, and Stalin caught the next train to Tiflis, where an army lieutenant general named F. F. Griaznov (nicknamed the "Butcher of Tiflis," "General Shithead," etc.) was wreaking havoc on anyone remotely associated with the revolt. Many innocents were swept up in the Cossacks' dragnet as they marched through the city and into the countryside, burning, shooting, hanging, lancing, and sabering the terrified citizens. The same was happening in Baku and other Georgian towns and cities. Anything resembling rebellion was crushed. This time the czar meant business. But by now the country was in chaos and on the verge of civil war.

Stalin threw himself into the fray with unabated fervor. As angry mobs marched through the streets he was seen atop a coach denouncing the czar's concessions of a constitution and Duma for the Russian people, branding them "a negation of the people's revolution." He pressed Marxists to revolt. "Smash this trap and wage a ruthless struggle against liberal enemies of the people," he urged, meaning the Mensheviks and anybody else who would accept the czar's compromises. Concessions, Stalin believed all of his life, were a sign of weakness. If the people only pushed harder, the government would collapse and socialism would prevail.

But the people did not push harder, and the revolution of 1905 collapsed in a bloodbath of Cossack repressions. Tens of thousands were killed. Thousands were executed and thousands more were imprisoned or exiled to Siberia. For his part, Trotsky dismissed it as a mere "dress rehearsal," like great theater.[16]

Stalin now went back underground with his gang and continued robbing and extorting. By now he had grown his famous black mustache as well as a scruffy beard. And he had taken to wearing a Caucasian overcoat (for "from the Caucasus") and beat-up black hat, which earned him the sobriquet the "Man in Black"—or simply, to friends and foes alike, the "Caucasian." Stalin was not a tall man, but he was very thin; with his pockmarked face, large ears, and piercing hazel eyes he held a frightening aura for some. He spoke little and acted shifty, as though he was hiding a knife or a gun.

He also redoubled his intrigues against the Mensheviks, setting a pattern of behavior he would employ for the rest of his long and violent career. He wrote scathing letters to the party leadership about specific members, accusing them of misdeeds that were demonstrably untrue. It was the old divide-and-conquer strategy, coupled with an utter paranoia that they were employing the same methods against him.

Stalin now concocted a plan to assassinate General Griaznov. Working with the hated Mensheviks, a joint crew of revolutionaries dressed as workmen were painting railings around the viceroy's palace when the general's heavily guarded carriage emerged from the gates. As it passed, they dropped their tools and produced bombs, which they tossed into the general's lap, blowing him into half a dozen pieces.[17]

Despite an earlier quasi-agreement at the Fourth Socialist Congress in Stockholm that the bank robberies should be banned because they were giving Socialism a bad name (there was no FDIC or equivalent so the people simply lost their savings), the holdups continued unabated in Georgia, thanks to Stalin and his like-minded gang. The Mensheviks had outvoted the Bolsheviks on this one, but Lenin looked the other way because he needed the money. Stalin's gang—now known as the Outfit—apparently even indulged in piracy by hijacking a mail steamer on the Black Sea that was delivering workers' payroll from port to port.

THEN TRAGEDY STRUCK Stalin's young family. Kato, alone and miserable all day with their baby and frightened that Stalin would be arrested as he carried out his revolutionary activities, took ill. She began losing weight. Stalin paid little attention at first, and was generally away from early morning to late at night. The heat of the Baku oil fields and a meager diet made things worse. Her family back in Tiflis got word that Kato was sick and wrote her husband, asking him to bring her home. But Stalin dallied, and by the time he got her there it was too late.

Kato's illness has been variously diagnosed as stomach cancer, typhus, or tuberculosis. But in any case, on December 5, 1907—just seventeen months after their marriage—she died in intense pain, hemorrhaging blood and simply wasting away. She was twenty-two. Stalin got back just in time for her death. He was devastated, attested to by a photograph taken of him looking down into her casket. She might have died anyway, but his failure to seek treatment after she became seriously ill was abhorrent. Stalin was almost always absent: to a dedicated party man, the party always comes first. Kato's family took in baby Yakov while Stalin returned to Baku to resume his revolutionary activities.

AMONG THE DUTIES that kept young Stalin away from his wife and son was the Fifth Socialist Congress in London, which met in the summer of 1907. There Stalin first met Trotsky, who would become his most bitter enemy. Stalin, the young terrorist and committed Bolshevik, loathed the well-known Menshevik at first sight, and Trotsky returned the favor. Each man thought himself the savior of the party's future, and even at this early date they were already on a collision course. Everybody with Marxist views was there—Bolsheviks, Mensheviks, Social Democrats, Social Revolutionaries, and the like. Trotsky was said to have arrived "in a blaze of glory, eclipsing even the god Lenin." That alone was enough to warrant Stalin's ire, let alone the fact that he was Jewish. (Stalin had recently written in reference to the Jewish-dominated Menshevik party that it "would not be a bad idea" for the Bolsheviks to organize a pogrom—or massacre—to deal with them.)

To many, Trotsky was a great hero. He had previously been convicted of sedition and exiled for life to Siberia. In 1902 he escaped, traveling hundreds of miles on a hastily crafted reindeer sled, acquiring a brave reputation and his new surname in the process. Now, like Lenin, Trotsky would have to live in European exile until the revolution arrived. A return to Russia at this point would mean death.[18]

The Mensheviks renewed their calls to disband Stalin's terrorist-like battle squads. But the Bolsheviks, Lenin included, would have none of it. Lenin formed his own secret party-within-a-party to keep the robbery money coming in. Worse, many of the leaders of these squads became common criminals who kept most, if not all, of the loot and disported themselves dishonorably.

Stalin, of course, was not among this cohort and kept up his work organizing robberies and assassinations. But in 1908 he was arrested for revolutionary activities and banished for a mere three years to the dismal Siberian town Solvychegodsk, which contained some two thousand residents and five hundred exiled Socialists. They spent their days and nights as before: reading, arguing, drinking, fornicating, and drinking more—all at government expense.

In June 1909, Stalin escaped again and returned to Georgia, where he remained at large until March 1910, when he was once more rearrested and eventually sent back to Solvychegodsk to serve out his three-year sentence in exile. He stayed at the house of an attractive young widow, Maria Kuzakova, with whom he fathered a son, Konstantin, who grew up to be a prominent producer and executive in Soviet television. When Stalin later came to power, Maria was moved to a nice apartment in Moscow. And although he never knew his father, during the years of rampant repression and executions Konstantin appealed to Stalin to spare his life. In his file there is a protective note: "Not to be touched—Stalin."

His exile officially ended, Stalin, who was not permitted to live in St. Petersburg or any large city, chose the town of Vologda in the northwest of Russia, from which he promptly departed for St. Petersburg under a false passport. Three days later he was again arrested by police, who had been watching him, and returned for another three years' exile, once more in Vologda.

After the failure of the 1905 uprising, the squabbling factions within the Socialist umbrella agreed to stop arguing and work together to produce another, more productive revolt. Lenin publicly assented to this, but privately he had no intention of keeping his word. In 1912 he carried off a brazen coup, declaring that the Bolshevik wing would be the sole representative of the Russian Social-Democratic Workers' Party. This faction would be led by an all-powerful, all-Bolshevik central committee on which Lenin, personally, reserved a place for Stalin to serve.

In February 1912 Stalin again escaped Vologda for St. Petersburg, where on Lenin's orders he was charged with making certain that as many Bolshevik delegates as possible were elected to the new Duma. This brought Stalin in contact with Vyacheslav Molotov, the sinister up-and-coming Soviet foreign minister during Stalin's reign, and the namesake for the infamous gasoline-fueled "cocktail" that became so popular in the revolution of 1917. The two men campaigned for a Bolshevik victory.

This venture did not last long, however. Knowing that arrests usually came after dark, Stalin did not return to his room to sleep but spent his time in all-night bars and cafés, which nearly wore him out. But soon the police caught him yet again, and this time he was banished to the forbidding snowbound Narym region of Siberia, littered with swamps and dense forests. It was autumn, and Stalin contrived to escape before the harsh winter set in. He did so, and even without legitimate credentials he managed to reach Cracow, Poland, for a meeting of the Bolshevik Central Committee and a visit with his mentor Vladimir Lenin, who had begun to call him the "Wonderful Georgian." Afterward, Stalin repaired to Vienna where, in postal conversations with Lenin, they refined the sort of studied cruelty that would be necessary to make the next revolution, as well as its aftermath, successful.

Lenin had sent Stalin specifically to Vienna to write a lengthy paper studying the definition of nationhood among the peoples of Europe, a subject that had been troubling him. This opus, filled with fifty-odd pages of mostly double-talk that Stalin himself referred to as "rubbish," was published in the St. Petersburg *Prosveshcheniye,* the Socialist Party's sociological journal. Nevertheless, the publication sent Stalin's stock in the party soaring. It was believed that he had developed an ability to identify, analyze, and clarify complex issues unique to the establishment of Marxist socialism, which was undergoing constant iterations as its adherents tried to refine and reflect on the philosophy of the world's greatest thinker.

It was during this period that Stalin became Stalin, by name and reputation. Stalin inveighed against the Jewish Bund (union), which was trying to establish a Jewish national identity, as well as the dangers that presented to a Socialist revolt, for many Mensheviks were Jews. He signed his position paper *Marxism and the National Question*. For the first time, Stalin—meaning "man of steel"—was using his name to political effect (much in the fashion of Molotov, which translates to "man who smites with hammer," but who was born Vyacheslav Skryabin). These two men changed their names as they sought to change the world.

An ulterior motive of Lenin's for sending Stalin to Vienna has been suggested by the historian Frederic Morton in his splendid *Thunder at Twilight: Vienna 1913–1914*. Morton speculates that Lenin viewed Stalin as a kind of "diamond in the rough," a Georgian yahoo who needed a "finishing school" in the persons of the wealthy and sophisticated Alexander and Elena Troyanovsky (who, while stationed near the top of Viennese society, were also prominent party members in good standing because they, too, had done some time in Siberia).

Stalin stayed with the Troyanovskys more than a month but the diamond in the rough refused to be polished; perhaps he was simply unpolishable. He had arrived in Vienna right at the beginning of carnival, Vienna's gayest social season, which occupies the month before Lent, in a third-class train carriage wearing crude peasant boots, a coarse overcoat, and carrying a peasant's rough wooden suitcase. Stalin partook in none of the festivities, shunning the nightly parties and dinners, including the annual labor union ball and one at the local insane asylum known as the Lunatics Ball.[19]

He tramped the seediest streets in Vienna, drinking tea and researching his scholarly paper on nationalism. It was there that he had a face-to-face encounter with his soon-to-be archrival Trotsky, who was sitting in a tearoom in conversation with a comrade "when suddenly," Trotsky recalled afterward, "without knocking at the door, there entered from another room a man of middle height, haggard, with a swarthy grayish face showing marks of smallpox. The stranger, as if surprised by my presence, stopped at the door and gave a guttural grunt which might have been taken for a greeting, went to the samovar and filled his glass with tea, and went out without saying a word."[20]

At length, when Stalin had finished his mission in Vienna, the "city's charm and the Troyanovskys' chic" notwithstanding, he boarded a third-class railcar with his essay tucked away in his wooden suitcase. He chugged out of Vienna "a grim virtuoso wearing the mask of a clod."[21]

IN THE SPRING OF 1913, the czar's police and courts caught Stalin at a "charity" concert that was actually a fund-raiser for the party; he had attempted to escape wearing a woman's dress and wig but the police were not deceived. Stalin was clearly a dangerous revolutionary, and this time the government was not fooling around. A czarist court sentenced him to four years' exile in a tiny godforsaken village in Siberia's Arctic Circle. Here, the temperature in winter could reach 100 degrees below zero. The short summers were plagued by swarms of bugs, and a dull constant sun shined twenty-four hours a day, like a bare lightbulb in a prison cell. The flat, featureless landscape remained snow-covered as far as the eye could see, and suicide was not uncommon among the inmates. Stalin had used up all his money and therefore could not buy proper winter clothes, food, vodka, or other essentials. He took to writing begging letters to friends, including the Alliluyev family, into which he would marry in the not too distant future. Escape, if not impossible, was extremely dangerous, so the Man of Steel settled down to wait out the sentence of his exile and occupied his days (and, in the summers, nights) by ice fishing for his dinner. A nonconformist as usual, Stalin got into trouble with his hutmates because whenever it was his turn to do the dishes he simply put them on the floor and let the dog lick them clean. After some weeks of this he was forced to live in another hut.[22]

Meantime, the Great War of 1914 had sucked Russia into its vortex, and the Motherland was on the verge of defeat two years later when somebody realized that thousands of Siberian political prisoners might be more useful as soldiers. Among these was thirty-seven-year-old Joseph Stalin, who was sledded, floated, trucked, and railroaded out of Siberia to the nearest army induction station. Here, he was pronounced unfit for duty, due to an arm that had been withered in a childhood accident and a limp he incurred when Lenin had tried to show him how to ride a bicycle.

Better still, rather than return him to Arctic hell, the kindly authorities concluded that Stalin could serve the remainder of his sentence in the town of Achinsk, from which good judgment told him not to escape—at least not while the First World War was still going on. He wrote to a friend: "I swear to you on the life of my dog that I will serve out my term. At one point I thought about leaving, but now I've abandoned that idea and abandoned it for good." In any event, it was there that the revolution found him.[23]

During this period Lenin and the Bolsheviks had not been idle. In fact, the entire Bolshevik deputation in the Duma had been put under arrest for opposing the war. Lenin had watched these events unfold from his places of exile in Switzerland and Germany.

In February 1917 a revolution broke out in the czar's capital of St. Petersburg, sparked by the revolt of the local army garrison, which didn't wish to be herded into the trenches to be slaughtered at the hands of the ferocious Germans. After setting fire to their own barracks buildings, the soldiers burned down the police stations and other seats of power and declared solidarity with the Bolsheviks. This touched off an astonishing wave of sympathy at almost every level of society, save the so-called royal class.

The czar abdicated and was later arrested and sent with his family beyond the Urals, never to return. A provisional government was formed by the Duma in hopes of keeping some kind of democracy in place. Red flags and ribbons sprang up everywhere until the entire city was engulfed in a sea of red. Delirious Russian throngs marched the streets, arm in arm and singing the French revolutionary anthem "La Marseillaise," which they had adopted because the czar had forbidden any Russian revolutionary music whatsoever.

When news of these terrific events reached Stalin in the burg of Achinsk, he caught the St. Petersburg–bound Trans-Siberian Express and made his way to the home of his friend Sergei Alliluyev, a former railway worker and professional party agitator who had sent Stalin money while in exile. Agitators were inciting crowds, and people daily marched in the streets shouting slogans. But Stalin chose not to be a part of those activities. Instead he threw himself into writing editorials in *Pravda,* the official party newspaper; at night, he told hair-raising stories of his experiences at the North Pole to Alliluyev's daughters, including teenage Nadezhda (or Nadya), a high school student who listened to these adventures with rapt attention. Stalin would also read to them from the great Russian writers—Chekhov, Pushkin, Gorky—while smoking a pipe, giving off the impression that he was truly a man of the world.[24]

This was a time of great uncertainty and confusion in Russia. Much of the chaos was inspired by the German enemy, which had financed Socialist revolutionary foment in hopes of knocking Russia out of the war. Elements of the Russian army and navy were in open revolt over the dreadful conditions at the front; a recent offensive in Galicia had cost the Russians nearly half a million soldiers. The provisional government and Duma were attempting to keep order, with mixed results. Soldiers and sailors were killing their officers and desertion was rampant. There were cries everywhere of "Stop the war!" In St. Petersburg, the Mensheviks and several other Socialist groups organized the Petrograd Soviet, which became very powerful very quickly, hauling before it members of the former czar's administration for trial and punishment.

Against the likely wishes of Lenin, who had yet to show his face in Russia, Stalin threw in his lot with the Petrograd Soviet, apparently on the theory that "if you can't beat 'em, join 'em." In his *Pravda* editorials Stalin, in typical Bolshevik style, urged all democratic groups to come together to run the country, while also sanctioning a continuation of the war on the grounds that too much sacrifice had been made to enter into a dishonorable and costly surrender.

In the middle of this political upheaval Stalin found the time to fall in love. The object was the fifteen-year-old Nadezhda Sergeevna Alliluyeva, in whose family's apartment Stalin had been residing. The favor was returned by the gregarious, mature student, who found the now graying Bolshevik revolutionary, twenty-three years her senior, both exciting and irresistible. When her parents at last figured it out they were aghast and—even though they considered Comrade Stalin a friend—tried to end the affair on grounds that Stalin's personality was prone to violence. But she would not be shaken. In fact, it would be a dark hereditary mental affliction of Nadya's that would bring the affair to tragedy.

It was Easter Sunday when Lenin and a number of other self-exiled revolutionaries at last arrived in Russia via a secret German-armored train from Switzerland, loaded with German gold to boost a Russian revolution. They were met by the tempestuous cheering of Socialist throngs. Lenin, who had worried about getting a cab because it was Easter, immediately startled the crowds by declaring there would be no supporting the provisional government and no supporting the war. Socialist revolution was immediately at hand, he avowed. The Bolshevik cells must rise up across the land and become Red Guards, seizing power in the country. Lenin promised that his revolution would be "peaceful," but that was the furthest thing from his mind. Stalin instantly changed the course of his *Pravda* editorials to parrot Lenin's preachings.

About the same time, the former Menshevik Leon Trotsky arrived on the scene. Hated by both Lenin and Stalin, Trotsky nevertheless held enormous sway within the party. Lenin decided to court his old enemy by suggesting to Trotsky that he become a Bolshevik and agitate for the revolution. Trotsky told Lenin to change the name of the Bolsheviks, which Lenin refused to do. Trotsky nevertheless became a kind of quasi-member, asserting that he was an equal co-leader with Lenin. Things were happening quickly now, and former alliances shifted.

The newly reconstituted Bolsheviks attempted to assemble a Bolshevik-riddled army machine-gun regiment, along with a band of heavily armed sailors who had recently mutinied and executed 120 of their officers (including several admirals) to participate in a large "solidarity" demonstration in St. Petersburg on July 4, 1917. In fact, the demonstration was designed to turn into a coup that would give Lenin total power. But the event was put down by large numbers of loyal army troops who had been hastily called back from the front.

After this defeat of the Socialists, the provisional government issued arrest warrants for the Bolshevik leaders, with Lenin and Trotsky topping the list. Lenin escaped but Trotsky was thrown in jail. Lenin, in hiding, felt he should leave St. Petersburg and enlisted Stalin to spirit him away. As Lenin's train rolled out of sight, Stalin stood watching it for a long while, absorbing the fact that he was, by default, in control of the Bolshevik Party.

His leadership did not last long. Lenin, hiding in a shack in a countryside hayfield, was soon sending political slogans, propaganda, and other double-talk for the Bolshevik Central Committee to employ. What none of the Socialist groups realized, however, was the growing weakness of the provisional government. As Bolshevik cells began rising up all over the empire, a colossal amount of looting took place. The palaces of princes, dukes, viscounts, earls, landowners, and business magnates were raided, and priceless heirlooms were soon being peddled in the streets; dealers in antiquities, fine arts, and jewelry sellers did a land-office business. At length, after endless arguing and counterarguing over the course of weeks, a secret time for the mass uprising was set: October 24. Despite the fact that this date was supposed to be secret, it was already rumored all over St. Petersburg.

The post office was seized, as were the central telephone exchange, the state bank, the main railroad station, and the bridges into town. Lenin sneaked back into the city, disguised with a wig and fancy women's makeup, his trademark goatee shaven clean. "He looked like a Lutheran priest," said one old Bolshevik. Lenin declared that the provisional government no longer existed. Democracy in Russia was dead.

At dawn on October 25, Bolsheviks, including disgruntled members of the Russian army and navy, laid siege to the provisional government's seat of power: the czar's Winter Palace. The siege lasted throughout the day and into the next, when the final troops occupying the palace—

a women's battalion and something less than a platoon of military cadets—surrendered.

The Bolsheviks proceeded to loot the czar's last home. Precious items were taken and fine wines consumed. According to the first sergeant of the women's battalion, which had been charged with defending the palace, the drunken Bolsheviks then "hunted women down, raped them, and threw them from the upper stories of houses into the street."[25]

Except for the women soldiers, there was surprisingly little bloodshed. The leader of the provisional government, Alexander Kerensky, fled the city. A new day had dawned but the ghastly horrors of the twentieth century were just beginning to throb over the vast Russian Empire.

STALIN WAS NOW IN QUASI-LEGITIMATE power, meaning that the police could not arrest him, for the police had been killed or driven away. But it was not the kind of power with which he felt comfortable. All these years since he had first gone underground as a Bolshevik, Stalin had been used to life on the run—hiding in people's apartments, printing Socialist propaganda leaflets and newspapers, getting arrested, escaping, planning robberies and murders, dodging the police, using disguises and aliases. Now, here he was, almost forty years old and an upstanding party member with credentials, able to walk the streets without fear. He missed the shadows. It was maddening. Sitting in a restaurant gave him the heebie-jeebies. He always sat with his back to the wall, facing the door. Loud, unfamiliar shouts made him cringe. Now he could walk in the sunshine in a public park, eat out, maybe take in a movie. It was going to take some getting used to.

During these perilous times, two enormous events would convulse Russia. The first was the Great War with Germany; the second was the imposition of the Bolshevik will over the people, which became known as the Red Terror.

Lenin was adamant that the war must be stopped, no matter the consequences. He used a radio address to decree that the commander in chief of the Russian armies must be removed for failing to negotiate an armistice.

A "detachment" was subsequently dispatched by Lenin that same day to the army's general headquarters, led by a Bolshevik naval ensign. Upon arrival, he made a speech calling on soldiers to revolt and surround the general. They did, and then murdered him on the spot.

THE REVOLUTIONARIES FACED many urgent political questions: How can we stop the war and on what terms? Who would lead the country now that the czar was gone? How would the citizens of the cities be fed? How will everyone get back to work? Though Lenin was interested in solving these problems, he saw with ruthless and inescapable insight that the main problem was hanging on to his power, no matter what.

Opposing socialist parties were then allowed within the soviet, but Lenin saw to it that their members were given unimportant posts. The Bolsheviks moved their headquarters to Moscow, where they formed a secret security force of thugs, drunks, sadists, and killers known as the Cheka to combat "counterrevolutionaries." It was nothing more than an execution squad of extraordinary size and power. The Socialists also changed the name of their group to the Communist Party, shortening a very long acronym.

At first the Cheka killed those thought to be enemies of the revolution; then they began killing people who simply might be, or might become, enemies, including aristocrats, business owners, bureaucrats, industrialists, army officers, professors: Marx's wretched bourgeoisie. Then they began killing people for no reason at all, except to show that they could do it: to prove that men had no rights whatsoever and that their very lives were served only at the pleasure of the party.

The Cheka killed millions; the favorite method was a shot to the back of the head or neck while the victim kneeled. When there were mass executions, the condemned were lined up in front of graves they themselves had dug and either fell or were pushed in after the fatal shot. Stalin underlined a passage in his copy of Marx that he kept in his library: "There is only one way to shorten and ease the convulsions of the old society and the bloody birth pangs of the new: revolutionary terror." Beside it, Stalin wrote: "Terror is the quickest way to the new society."

United States president Woodrow Wilson, a former college administrator, sent the Communists a congratulatory telegram expressing sympathy with the Russian people for "casting off the yoke of autocracy." The Soviet Congress composed an ungracious reply in which it promised to overthrow the United States government and liberate the American people from "the yoke of capitalism." Indeed, it went on to threaten worldwide revolution that would establish Communism as the only true political system.

In the big Russian cities—Moscow, Petrograd—people were starving because the entire distribution system, a capitalist one, had been disrupted. It was determined by Communists that the kulaks—the better class of farmers—were hiding their grain and other foodstuffs from revolutionary confiscation. The Cheka opened a land-office extermination business, and soon the kulak class was almost entirely wiped out in the new Soviet Union.

Stalin was sent to Georgia to make sure its grain and oil were getting into the Soviet pipeline. He had a private train to transport and house him, along with his typist, Nadya Alliluyeva, who would soon be his wife.

In Georgia, Stalin was basically a supply officer, but he established himself as a sort of general, affecting a costume consisting of a light-colored tunic with a leather belt, high polished boots, and a military cap with a polished bill. He immediately picked a fight over military authority with Trotsky, who was running the Bolshevik army. Both appealed to Lenin to have the other recalled. For his part, Trotsky considered Stalin a "clerk" and "a stooge for Lenin."[26]

AT THE SAME TIME THAT THE Cheka was wiping out entire classes of people, peasants and others rose up to begin a genocide of their own. Soon the country was in the throes of a civil war that eventually organized itself beneath the banners of Red (Communists, Socialists) and White (capitalists, democrats, free traders, czarists). Generals from the former Russian military led these armies, which killed far more savagely than those of the world war.

In the meantime, the czar and his entire family—four young daughters and a son—who had been under house arrest in the Urals were taken to a filthy cellar in their home in the town of Ekaterinburg. There, they were murdered by gunfire on orders of the Bolsheviks. Their bodies were set on fire and thrown down a well. Thus was Lenin's "peaceful" revolution exposed. When some Mensheviks raised the proposition of outlawing capital punishment, Lenin had replied, "Nonsense. How can you have a revolution without shooting people?"

In October 1917 the Russian army had effectively ceased fighting the Germans. Five months later, in March 1918, the Communist government signed the humiliating Treaty of Brest-Litovsk, surrendering to Germany. This act, freeing more than a million German soldiers to bolster the huge German attack against the Allies on the Western Front, ceded to the Germans large portions of the former Russian Empire including the Baltic states, Ukraine, and parts of Georgia. The Communists got them all back in November when the Central Powers collapsed, but it did buy the Bolsheviks time to organize their army and begin fighting the Russian Civil War. Before it was done, some 60 million Russians who had lived under the auspices of the Romanov dynasty found themselves under German or Turkish control. Stalin was not involved in these proceedings.

The Russian Civil War wore on for three years, horrifying the world. More than 3 million soldiers were killed in clashes between the White and Red Armies. An additional 5 million citizens died of murder or starvation during the famine caused by the war. In late 1918 a dozen nations of the Allies—the United States included—sent troops into Russia's northern ports. The initial goal was to secure munitions being produced in Czechoslovakia, as well as to try and reestablish the Eastern Front that the Bolsheviks had abandoned. In the end they stayed until 1920, fighting on the side of the White Russians, but without much success. There was little that 175,000 British, Czech, French, Japanese, Australian, Canadian, Polish,

Italian, and U.S. troops could achieve against 3 million soldiers of Lenin's Red Army.

All but the most personal private property was confiscated. Land, factories, and businesses became the property of the state. It was illegal to own a weapon, even for hunting to feed one's family. The party began laying plans for how to distribute essentials such as food, medical care, and education and to advance transportation, foreign relations, and the military. Beyond complicated, their new world would require a vast new bureaucracy that the country was unprepared to provide.

In the summer of 1918 Lenin believed that the Bolshevik Party's hold over the Russian people was insufficient. The czars had ruled since the year 1547, and revolutionary fervor had abated. People began asking themselves what was to happen next. For Lenin and Stalin this was not good news, mainly because the people might want a say in the matter or even a democracy. So it was decided to bring them all under total control by unleashing what became known as the Red Terror.

Those members of the royalty, aristocracy, or peerage who were not already slain or had escaped into Europe were now hunted down and killed. It was the same with the remaining bourgeois class, hundreds of thousands more of whom were marked for death, along with their families. The Cheka—the Bolsheviks' brutal counterrevolutionary force—was efficient in eliminating these unfortunates. Most were dispatched quickly in groups by a shot to the back of the head, hanging, or strangulation with wire. They were then buried in mass graves dug by those in the forced labor camps.

Others were put to death in more shocking ways: a carnival of perversion so breathtaking as to be almost unbelievable, except for the many files that recorded it. Condemned men, women, and children were incinerated in furnaces or flayed alive, their skin made into clothing. Others were fiendishly dunked into vats of boiling water. Crucifixions were commonplace, especially for members of the clergy. One appalling practice was to tie naked people to stakes in the cold of the Russian winter and douse them with water until they became human icicles; another was to seal naked prisoners into barrels studded with inward-pointing nails that would then be rolled around for sport until the victims died from shock or loss of blood. Some were sealed in casks with rats that eventually ate them; others were thrown through holes in icy lakes to drown or boiled in tar or melted lead.

It was Stalin's and Lenin's aspiration for the terror to cow the entire Russian population—not only wiping out entire classes of people but, while they were at it, most of the rival revolutionary parties. To justify this butchery, Lenin in particular relied on what he said were the teachings of Karl Marx, offering a quote attributed to Marx following the failed Socialist uprising in Vienna: "There is only one way in which the murderous death agonies of the old society and the bloody birth throes of the new society can be shortened, simplified, and concentrated—and that way is revolutionary terror." Joseph Stalin concurred with all of this, and was complicit in it.[27]

When the civil war finally ended in 1922, the Russian people were prostrated, which is just what Lenin (and Stalin) wanted. Lenin had never tried to prevent a civil war, because he was convinced it would be the only way the Communists could consolidate absolute control over the country. The Communists began to ease the food shortage and soon the people—many of them, at least—began to feel grateful to them: a sad and frightening syndrome that would permeate the country throughout the existence of the Communist regime.

Stalin, whose role by now was as a bureaucrat of variously important diktats and a chief flunky of Lenin, would pace the floor of his study sucking on his pipe, trying to grasp the enormity of the thing he'd inherited. One by one, he had eliminated his rivals through power plays, sleight of hand, and in some cases murder; now, much of the power was in his hands. Only Trotsky remained a threat, and a weak one at that. He could deal with him later. For now, he had to form a vision, a picture, of how the world would look once things were in place. The mighty state would contain "a single bank, a single economic plan, a peasantry organized on collective farms. There would be ruthless discipline, ruthless punishments, gigantic resources concentrated in the hands of the state, a huge industrial economy and a huge army above which would be a pyramid of lesser leaders, and atop which would stand the Supreme Leader, himself!"[28]

Once again, the killing began in earnest. Hundreds of thousands were executed as enemies, or potential enemies, of the state; millions were enslaved in the gulags of Siberia. Lenin, for example, sent a telegram ordering local revolutionaries in the city of Penza to hang "no fewer than one hundred" of the wealthier farmers suspected of hoarding grain. In the end, five hundred were hanged; others were woefully tortured. It has been estimated that for the next twenty years an average of a million Russian people a year were executed by the Communist regime, which, for much of that time, would be headed by the dictator of the Union of Soviet Socialist Republics: Joseph V. Stalin.[29]

CHAPTER FOUR

Franklin Roosevelt grew up in Hyde Park, New York, on the bluffs overlooking the Hudson River about a hundred miles north of his more famous cousins the Theodore Roosevelts, on Long Island's Oyster Bay. Franklin went to school at Groton—in many ways the American equivalent of Churchill's Harrow. Although he didn't struggle academically, as Churchill had done, Roosevelt's grades were about average, as they remained after four years at Harvard. He seemed, in fact, about average in most things—"superficial," some said, except for his exquisite charm and tall, handsome good looks as he grew older.

Roosevelt married, had children, and lived the life of the wealthy Yankee patrician, becoming a scratch golfer, an elegant horseback rider, an accomplished yachtsman, and a dead-eye hunter and fisherman. He worked for a New York City law firm and served New York as a state senator and the country as an assistant secretary of the Navy. He summered at the family's home on Campobello Island in Canadian New Brunswick, on the Bay of Fundy off the coast of Maine, where he dreamed of advancing his career in politics. Then, out of the blue, Roosevelt was struck with what most everyone called a great tragedy, from which almost no one expected him to recover.

Infantile paralysis, or polio, had become a new scourge in the early twentieth century. It arrived in epidemics during the summer months, usually striking children, but often adults as well. By 1908 scientists had identified the infectious virus that caused polio, but doctors nevertheless remained baffled as to exactly how it spread or how to treat it. In 1916 in New York

City alone, some seven thousand polio deaths were recorded. Districts outside New York began to quarantine city-dwelling youngsters. In the ensuing years the epidemics came and went; Roosevelt was concerned for his five children and kept them on Campobello Island for the summers, where the disease had yet to appear.

By the end of the summer of 1921 Roosevelt had arrived on the island from New York City on the oceangoing yacht of the wealthy investor Van Lear Black. After taking the children for a sail in the family's sailboat *Vireo,* he led them on a romp through fields to swim in a warm pond on the other side of the island. When he got back to the cottage, Roosevelt was suddenly exhausted; his legs ached and he felt a fever coming on. At thirty-nine years old, he was healthy, fit, and vigorous and thought it was a cold.

He went to bed and his wife, Eleanor, took his temperature, which had risen to 102 degrees. He smiled it off saying he'd be all right in the morning. He wasn't. When he got up to go to the bathroom, one of his legs gave way and he fell. He managed to struggle up and complete the task, but afterward his legs became numb and hard to move. He thought he had a cramp and tried to work it out but it only grew worse.

Eleanor sent for a doctor on the mainland, and when he arrived he diagnosed a bad cold. Roosevelt began to suspect that something serious was afflicting him. He repeated over and over to his friend and political adviser Louis Howe, who was seated at the foot of the bed, "I don't know what's the matter with me, Louis. I just don't know."[1]

Another doctor was sent for, an eighty-four-year-old surgeon who was vacationing nearby. His diagnosis was that Roosevelt was suffering from a blood clot that had settled in the spinal cord. He prescribed a massage. The pain was exquisite, but Roosevelt endured it. Soon he realized he had no feeling in his legs; he was paralyzed from the waist down. His temperature soared to 107 and he became delirious. It seemed he might die.

After a week the temperature began to subside; he found he could move his toes slightly on one leg. At last a Boston specialist in infantile paralysis was summoned, who examined Roosevelt and gave his own diagnosis: polio.

The specialist thought there was a chance for a full recovery, which sometimes happened. But, on the other hand, the legs might remain paralyzed. This was something of a relief for Roosevelt, who had thought he would likely not survive. It was nevertheless a frightening prospect to lose the power of his legs and become, in the parlance of the day, a "cripple." Much later, Eleanor remembered that the look on Franklin's face as he contemplated this fate was not unlike his expression when he learned the Japanese had attacked Pearl Harbor—"strained and tired" but "completely calm."

All they could do now was wait until the disease had run its course. But the waiting was taking a pathetic toll. Roosevelt had always been an active person—some might say superactive. Aside from the offices he held, he was on the boards of various colleges and charities and deeply involved in Democratic politics—he planned to be governor of New York, and he aimed to be president of the United States. Now, here he lay: half paralyzed and bedridden while the world turned without him.

His mother, Sara, arrived, fresh from a summer abroad in Italy. She hadn't been told of her son's condition until she got off the ship, because of fears she would have worried all across the Atlantic. When she walked into his room in Campobello after the long journey by train and boat, she found her son sitting up in bed, freshly shaved. "Well, I'm glad you're back, Mummy, and I got up this party for you,"[2] he said, smiling broadly.

It was vintage Roosevelt: the sheer definition of an indomitable spirit. Over the years he coped with his affliction, always hoping for some miraculous cure. Polio was a terrible, lifestyle-altering disease for sure, one that would have sent lesser men into invalidism. Roosevelt overcame it to be elected governor of New York and president of the United States. He was not always a fair man, nor a truthful one; he was a politician, after all. But even to his enemies he was cheerful in all weathers, courteous, and polite. He loved a good joke and a good drink. And in his time he transformed American society in ways that affect us greatly today.

FRANKLIN DELANO ROOSEVELT was born January 30, 1882, at Springwood, his parents' estate at Hyde Park. His mother, Sara, nearly died giving birth and was told she should not make another attempt to do so. Franklin was raised as an only child, although he had a half brother, twenty-eight years his senior. James "Rosy" Roosevelt was by then married to an Astor and living in New York City, sired by Franklin's father and his late wife.

Franklin's father, James Roosevelt, was the epitome of a New York Knickerbocker society country squire. His Dutch ancestors had been among the original settlers of the colony, and his family had owned land along the spectacular setting of the Hudson River valley for generations. Over time many of the old Dutch families erected a series of fabulous mansions for a hundred miles along the high bluffs of the Hudson, and eventually James purchased one of these in which to raise his family.

James inherited money from his father, who'd made it in the Caribbean sugar trade. After college, he embarked on a grand tour of Europe, taking time off to fight with Giuseppe Garibaldi's revolutionary army in Italy. In time, he became a successful businessman in his own right, owning substantial interests in coal mines, railroads, and steel mills and serving them in a variety of positions, mainly as president, vice president, or member of the board of directors. His politics were Democratic—but not the radical midwestern variety, nor the Tammany Hall Irish bunch in New York City. His Democrats were for low taxes, small government, sound money, and free trade. James was also a prominent horse breeder, raising gaited trotters for the racetrack. As young Franklin grew up, James taught him to ride, hunt, and fish, and he was idolized in his son's eyes.[3]

Sara, likewise, was a devoted figure in young Franklin's life. She was a member of the equally wealthy and society-connected Delano family that lived nearby. Although Sara's father had made his fortune smuggling opium to Chinese addicts, it was generally understood that he was merely a successful shipping company owner who dealt in the Far East trade.

James's wife, and Rosy's mother, Rebecca, had died in 1876. Four years later, at the age of fifty-two, he met the twenty-six-year-old beauty Sara—who was also his sixth cousin—at a party for their mutual cousin Theodore Roosevelt, who had just graduated from Harvard. They were married that same year. Two years afterward, following a lengthy honeymoon in Europe, she gave birth to Franklin at Springwood, his father's thousand-acre estate of farm fields and forests with majestic views of the river.

Nearly every year the family went to Europe for several months. Once, when Franklin was only three, they almost didn't make it back. They were sailing from England on the *Germania* when two days out they encountered a fierce storm. Heavy seas were tossing the big liner like a toy when suddenly an enormous wave crashed over the ship, causing her to broach. The lights went out and water filled the companionways. "We seem to be going down," James Roosevelt remarked.

The wave had caused the ship to founder, washing a seaman overboard, ripping away half a dozen lifeboats, and tearing away the bulkhead of the ladies' reading room, which was right above the Roosevelts' cabin. One woman was flung across the room where her dress caught on a coat hook, leaving her dangling until other passengers came to the rescue.

"If he must go down, he's going down warm," declared Sara Roosevelt, wrapping a mink coat around the child. Water was sloshing around on the cabin floor when Franklin spied his favorite toy floating in it. "Mama, Mama," he cried, "save my jumping jack!" She did, as the ship miraculously began to right itself. The captain had been knocked unconscious in the chartroom but resumed command and they returned to Liverpool for repairs. It had been a very close call for the future president of the United States.[4]

As he grew up, Franklin was given a series of governesses and tutors who taught him classical languages and French, mathematics, and literature. The idea of someone of Roosevelt's social class attending public grade school was out of the question. It has been said of the wealthy English that the men become either grand sportsmen or, if they are not athletically inclined, collectors of everything under the sun. Franklin Roosevelt, although he did become a fine sailing yachtsman, seemed to fall into the latter category. It started with stamps.

When Franklin was ten, an uncle passed on a collection that had once been his mother's, which was extensive enough to make it the envy of most adult collectors. Roosevelt himself famously enlarged it for the rest of his life until he had millions of specimens, some near priceless. He also began collecting birds' eggs, until he had assembled under glass the eggs and nests of every type of bird in the Hudson River valley. He then felt compelled to collect the birds themselves and began begging for a shotgun so he could take specimens and mount them as John James Audubon had done for his magnificent series, *The Birds of America*. Franklin's mother was horrified, saying he was too young. But James bought him a fine small-gauge double-barrel shotgun, admonishing him never to shoot birds during their mating or nesting seasons, and to take only one bird of a species.

Over time, Franklin acquired a specimen of every bird in Dutchess County, and he acquainted himself with the rudiments of taxidermy. Before he reached his teens more than three hundred stuffed birds graced the large glass-front cabinet in the living room of Springwood; some were good enough to be included in exhibits at the Museum of Natural History in New York. He remained an ardent birder until he died, having given up killing and mounting the creatures for spotting them with his binoculars and including them in his "life list."[5]

From the age of four Franklin took daily morning rides with his father around the estate to check up on things and enjoy the healthy air. His father usually rode one of his prize trotters and Franklin tagged along on Debbe, a sturdy Welsh pony. James also rode in the Dutchess County Hunt, a foxhunting steeplechase that led across miles of farm fields, fences, and other obstacles, the riders in their colorful "pinks" behind a gaggle of yipping foxhounds. Franklin was too young to ride in such a dangerous and exhausting exercise. But one day when he was a little older, watching the hunt from afar, he could stand it no longer; he jumped on his horse and gave chase. He arrived right at the time of the "kill," only to be publicly ordered home by his chagrined father, who berated him afterward more for having his horse in a lather than for his disobedience.

In 1890, James Roosevelt had a heart attack that left him a semi-invalid until his death at the end of the decade. In that era, doctors knew little about heart ailments, other than to urge the patient to avoid stress. This posed a substantial problem for Franklin, who was told never to do anything that might upset his father. So anytime he got hurt he would hide the wound; if something unpleasant occurred, he would keep it to himself and try to be cheerful. He and his mother conspired to make as quiet and tranquil a home for his father as possible.

The following year, when Franklin was nine, James (despite his illness) took possession at Campobello of the *Half Moon*.* He himself had designed the boat, a broad-beamed fifty-one-foot-long, two-masted, gaff-rigged schooner, after commissioning it from a Maine boat builder two years earlier. It came with a captain and three-man crew, but when James and, later, Franklin were aboard, they became the captains, respectively. Sailing could be a tonic for James, as long as the waters were reasonably calm and the winds light. It was a tonic for Franklin as well, though he frequently preferred a good hard sail in frisky breezes and white-capped seas.

When he was sixteen, Franklin was given his own small yacht, a sleek twenty-eight-foot racing sloop that he named *New Moon;* he enjoyed sailing it among the fickle tides of the Bay of Fundy. Seamanship ran in his family's blood, and soon Franklin began collecting sailing prints from all over the world. In time, he became an accomplished sketcher of sailboats. He also collected models of full-rigged ships. By the time he got to the White House he had amassed hundreds of these, many of which were put on display there. One of his favorite sayings during the Great Depression and, later, during the war years was: "When you're at the end of your rope, tie a knot and hang on."

Taught by James, young Franklin was soon a master yachtsman with all the necessary seafaring skills: navigation, seamanship, weather forecasting, maintenance, and repair. Some years, James would have the *Half Moon* brought down to the Hudson, where Franklin loved to navigate it along the difficult stream with its tricky currents and rocky obstacles. The family also had a handsome varnished twenty-six-foot iceboat that they would sail when the river froze.

---

* Named in honor of the ship that the English explorer Henry Hudson, in the service of the Dutch East India Company, sailed into New York Harbor in 1609.

In 1893, when Franklin was eleven, his parents took him to Germany for several months, where the elder Roosevelt intended to "take the waters" (then thought to be useful in the treatment of heart disease) in the mineral baths of Bad Nauheim. While there, young Franklin and a tutor, a Mr. Arthur Dumper, embarked on a bicycling trip through the surrounding towns and villages. They managed to get themselves arrested no fewer than four times by the strict Teutonic constabulary for crimes ranging from "picking cherries by the roadside" to "riding bicycles at night," which was forbidden by the fortified city of Strasbourg. Mr. Dumper, fluent in German, was able to get them off for these offenses. But in the end they were fined five marks (about $5) for the death of an errant goose that had inadvertently run its silly head into the spinning spokes of Mr. Dumper's bike and got its neck wrung. Nor did they get to keep the goose.

At one point Franklin's parents enrolled him for six weeks in a German school, where he recalled years later that, even so early on, the new kaiser's penchant for militarism had infected even the children. Every schoolboy was expected to learn map reading and military topography.*[6]

ONCE BACK AT HYDE PARK, Franklin prepared for his entrance into Groton. The boarding school, a recently created private Episcopal institution in Massachusetts, was run by the eminent Endicott Peabody, an educator with innovative but inflexible ideas about how boys should be brought up.

The Grotonians slept and studied in stark, puritan nine-by-six-foot cubicles. Pictures, photographs, or other decorations were strictly forbidden, with only a curtain for privacy. Down the hall was a common washroom, where the inmates greeted the day with group ice-water showers. Peabody, a stern taskmaster who loathed "loafing," "lying," and "snobbery," in that order, prized athletic ability over scholarship. Football, which in

---

* During both world wars, Roosevelt told this story to emphasize the Germans' penchant for military aggression.

that day was an extremely brutal pastime, was his passion.* All of this was a bewildering, frightening, even horrifying experience for the sons of American society's millionaires—young Franklin Roosevelt included.

Peabody did not subscribe to corporal punishment as a means of keeping order. Instead—and certainly worse—he permitted, and even encouraged, the older students to administer punishments of their own when a boy got out of line. Such punishments ranged from "bootboxing," in which the offender was forced into his small, airless coffin-like footlocker where he kept his boots, while the others beat upon it with their fists. The worst of the punishments was called "pumping" (or what is now known as waterboarding, a procedure that has been branded as torture by many in the U.S. government). Following the evening prayers, Peabody would solemnly march out early; an announcement would then be made that the upperclassmen "wanted to see" an erstwhile troublemaker outside the chapel auditorium—immediately. After being admonished for his crimes the boy was then seized by the huskiest punishers (usually football players) and rushed to the cellar, where he was held upside down under a large gushing water faucet until it produced in him the terrifying sensation of drowning. Often, if the offender wasn't sufficiently repentant the first time, the procedure was repeated.

Peabody had forbidden "fagging" (the practice in British private schools of Winston Churchill's day whereby underclassmen were virtual slaves to the older boys). But bullying existed at Groton, and young Franklin got his share of it. He never mentioned this in letters home, possibly for fear of upsetting his father. In fact, he was so good-natured about the bullying that the other boys soon left him alone.

Franklin was a slender, somewhat awkward youth, generally unfit for football or even baseball. But he earned a varsity stripe for being the manager of the baseball team. His biographer Geoffrey Ward writes that Roosevelt was so embarrassed about his inferior athletic ability as an adolescent that as

---

* In 1905 alone there were eighteen deaths and upwards of two hundred injuries, making a case for football's banishment. But Franklin's cousin President Theodore Roosevelt stepped in to "save" it by brokering a deal among all schools playing the game to clean up its rules and ban or penalize dangerous formations and practices.

an adult "he felt compelled to lie about it," claiming he'd been "quite a boxer" at Groton, and also that he'd broken his nose twice on the football field.

Politics in those days was generally considered an unworthy calling by the society classes. But Peabody believed strongly that Groton men should change that impression for the better and become involved in government service. "If some Groton boys do not enter political life and do something for our land, it won't be because they have not been urged," he said. To that end, Peabody introduced an obligatory debating class. The subjects up for discussion ran the gamut from international to national to local affairs, and the debates were spirited. Franklin once took on the subject of a transpacific canal through Nicaragua, a project dear to his father's heart, owing to the fact he had made heavy investments in the company aiming to build it.*[7]

As rector, Peabody continually preached to the students on the subject of "impurity," by which he meant sexual activities of any description. He warned them to conduct themselves with only the highest rectitude around girls. Franklin took Peabody's confirmation class, which was held after school in his home; in 1898, after turning sixteen, he was confirmed into the Episcopal Church. He also became a member of the Groton Missionary Society, which did good works with the elderly and the poor and conducted evening services in churches around the county. Franklin soon became the society's organist, and he managed to negotiate a quartet of hymns out of the instrument, which by his own admission were "pretty fair."[8]

In summertime, the Groton Missionary Society put on a charity camp at New Hampshire's Lake Asquam, where Franklin taught swimming, canoeing, and sailing to poor boys from Boston and New York. It was his first real exposure to the squalor bred by life at the bottom in the nation's large cities and was undoubtedly an absorbing experience for both the campers and the Groton boys on the "faculty." It was also one of the ways Peabody sought to eradicate the snobbery he so much despised among the well-to-do.[9]

---

* Ironically, it was James Roosevelt's cousin Theodore who, as U.S. president, nixed the Nicaraguan canal for one through Panama. James's investment was lost, although by that time he was dead.

That same year, the Spanish-American War broke out. Franklin in his later years liked to boast that he and a fellow Grotonian tried to run off and join the armed services, but according to biographer Ward this, too, seems to have been a fabrication. It is Ward's opinion that Roosevelt as an adult recounted the so-called adventure of his youth not as it was but "how he wanted it to have been." His cousin Teddy, however, did in fact go off to the war with his famous Rough Riders and charged up San Juan Hill—a feat that propelled him into the governorship of New York that same year and later to the White House itself.

By 1899, Franklin's final year at Groton, he had come a long way from the bewildered, frightened boy who'd entered the school four years earlier. He was tall—six feet one inch—and fine looking. His grades were middling but he had developed a rhetorical flair and manner that could make him seem warm, suave, and prepossessing, although some classmates characterized him as contrary, artificial, and insincere. He was made a prefect—a high honor—and put in charge of helping the younger students, who seemed to look up to him.

In the spring, Franklin won a starring role in the senior class play, W. S. Gilbert's *The Wedding March*. But he turned bitterly against Endicott Peabody after failing to be selected as a senior prefect, the school's highest honor. During Easter vacation his mother tried to comfort him over the perceived slight, but to no avail. All his life, he was fiercely loyal but also had a long memory—and those who went against Franklin Roosevelt did so at their peril.

At graduation he was awarded the Latin Prize, then headed for Harvard. "I can hardly wait to see you," he wrote his mother, "but feel awfully to be leaving here for good." And then he was gone.

FRANKLIN SPENT THE SUMMER before Harvard at the Roosevelt compound on Campobello, where he played endless rounds of golf and sailed his father's new yacht *Half Moon II* (the original *Half Moon* had been destroyed two years earlier in an unexplained explosion while being towed up the

Hudson). Roosevelt also attended the teas, parties, dinners, and dances that formed the social life of the island's elites.

His father, James, was not faring well with his heart condition. He was well enough to ride a new horse given to him by Sara but had to be assisted in mounting it by the stable hands. He took only one long trip on *Half Moon II,* when the family sailed up the Bay of Fundy to New Brunswick. But it made him so tired that Sara feared the strain was too much.

Worse, a scandal developed in James's family that was deemed by some relatives as the proximate cause of his death. James's son Rosy had produced a grandson by his wife, the former Helen Astor. Three years older than Franklin, he was known as "Taddy," and though he was a half nephew to Franklin, he and his younger sister were treated more like cousins. It was in him where the scandal lay.

From an early age Taddy was "different" than other children. It was as if he were born under the wrong star. He was almost hopeless in schools, including Groton, where he continually embarrassed Franklin with his peculiar behavior. Somehow he managed to get into Harvard, where he was promptly expelled for failing to show up for classes. Following the death of his mother, he was set to come into a huge Astor inheritance when he reached his majority—but in the meantime, he proceeded to squander his considerable allowance on whisky and women in New York's infamous Tenderloin district.

Informing his father that he intended to spend the summer on a sailing cruise with a friend, Taddy instead continued his self-destructive tendencies by marrying a Hungarian hooker and sometime dancehall girl named Sadie Messinger and moved into an apartment on the Upper West Side. When his father got wind of this development, he found that Taddy had lied about his age on the marriage license and promptly contacted his lawyers. Armed with two attorneys, Rosy appeared at the door of Taddy's apartment threatening to have the marriage annulled, and a large row ensued.

The upshot was that the newspapers had found out about the marriage, and the tabloids went into convulsions of spurious rectitude. A blizzard of unseemly headlines announced the union of the scion of the Roosevelt and Astor families to a known prostitute.

Everyone was scandalized, but none more than James, who prized his privacy and family name above all else. Reporters arrived at his office wanting a statement. The sordid headlines continued. James had two mild heart attacks and seemed to be growing weaker. Franklin wrote his mother from Harvard, "I do not wonder that it has upset Papa, but although the disgrace to the name has been the worst part of the affair, one can never again consider [Taddy] a true Roosevelt. It will be well for him not only to go to parts unknown, but to stay there and begin life anew."*[10]

On December 8, 1900, about a month after the scandal broke, James Roosevelt died, and Franklin and his mother Sara began a lifelong closeness that rivaled that between Winston Churchill and his mother Jennie after she became a widow. Sara remained well-off, with an estate of many millions. She was forty-six and still a handsome woman. But now, in what would soon become a bone of contention, she focused nearly all of her vast energy and emotion on her only son.

At Harvard, Roosevelt and a roommate occupied a four-room suite in Westmorly, an exclusive residence hall apart from the shabby rooms on Harvard Yard where most of the students lived. It was luxurious only in comparison with where he'd lived at Groton. But he and his roommate furnished it nicely, gamely adorning the walls with Groton team photos and pennants and other mementos of the old boarding school. Sara took a house near the campus to be close to him.

Like many of his former Groton classmates, Roosevelt settled at Harvard for a "gentleman's C" so far as scholarship was concerned. Instead, he concentrated on his social life and on getting to know as many people as he

---

* In fact, Taddy was shipped down to Florida where he lived under an alias, until moving back to New York, where he repaired automobiles for a living. He never used his large inheritance and cut off all communications with his family, except to inform the Astors that on his death the money should be given to the Salvation Army. Sadie had long since moved out, and when he died in 1958 Taddy left $5 million to the Salvation Army.

could, possibly as a prelude to a political career. His one ambition seemed to be getting chosen for the *Crimson*, the school newspaper. He was, and he became its editor after three years of apprenticeship.

In the summer of his freshman year Franklin and his mother sailed once more to Europe, unwilling to bear the memories of Campobello or Hyde Park without James. They spent time in Germany, Switzerland, and Norway, where they met the German kaiser, who was vacationing there on his yacht, the *Hohenzollern,* surrounded by half a dozen warships of the imperial German navy. Franklin and his friend Frances Pell were invited to go aboard, along with some other passengers. Sara, watching through binoculars, was thrilled when the kaiser turned to look as her son passed by with the tall and beautiful Frances on his arm. Afterward, Franklin returned with a pencil he had stolen from the emperor's desk that was "authentically dented by the imperial teeth."[11]

In Paris in early September, newspapers carried the story of the shooting of President William McKinley by an anarchist at the Pan-American Exposition in Buffalo, New York. Later that week, the Roosevelts sailed for home. Aboard ship, on September 14, they received word that McKinley had died of his wound. It was shocking news—the more so for the Roosevelts, because Franklin's cousin Theodore was now president of the United States.

Back at Harvard, Roosevelt languished in a kind of academic malaise, getting by but mostly working on the *Crimson*. He did, however, enroll in a famous course by visiting professor Frederick Jackson Turner on the history of America's westward expansion. Turner speculated that since the first expansion had ended about 1890, the United States would likely become more like European countries, locked in their borders with heavy class conflicts and strained economic growth: the very conditions that Franklin Roosevelt encountered when he was sworn into the U.S. presidency at the height of the Great Depression.

Also at Harvard, Franklin engaged in various charity programs, in one instance raising several hundred dollars for the wives and children of the South African Boers, whom Winston Churchill was presently fighting. Many of the Boer women were being held by the British in concentration camps to keep them from supplying their husbands in the Boer army.

Franklin's chief regret at college was in not being elected into Porcellian, Harvard's most exclusive eating club—possibly, in the estimation of his biographer Frank Freidel, because of the scandalous behavior of his nephew, Taddy. But his bitter reaction to the slight provides a window into his provocative political career.

FOR MORE THAN A YEAR Franklin had been seeing a beautiful, prominent Bostonian girl named Alice Sohier. But when he informed her that, being an only child himself, he wanted at least six children she turned him down. "I did not wish to be a cow," she remarked much later, following her divorce from her husband after having two children.[12]

Whether this left Roosevelt on the rebound is open to speculation but, shortly after the Sohier romance ended, he accidentally ran into his second cousin Eleanor Roosevelt on a train, an event that developed into a life-long marriage.

Eleanor was not unattractive, but she characterized herself as "plain." She was certainly the product of an unhappy childhood. Two years younger than Franklin, she was the daughter of the alcoholic Elliott Roosevelt, Franklin's godfather and TR's brother, who was killed in a drunken accident in 1894 when Eleanor was nine years old. Her mother, no paragon of parenthood, had died from diphtheria two years earlier. She had once told her only child, "Eleanor, I don't know what's going to happen to you. You're so plain that you have nothing to do but be *good.*" As Roosevelt biographer Alonzo Hamby put it, "He had not the slightest understanding that he had proposed to an emotional train wreck."[13]

Orphaned Eleanor went to live with her maternal grandmother, whose alcoholic daughter heaped further abuse on the child. She had no playmates and was plagued by depressions. This Cinderella-like existence ended in 1899, when, at the age of fourteen, Eleanor was sent off to the exclusive Allenswood boarding school near London. There, she came under the supervision of its headmistress, Madame Marie Souvestre, a charismatic nonconformist freethinking lesbian.[14]

Mme. Souvestre took a special interest in her American charge and developed in Eleanor a sense of self-worth where before there had been only self-doubt. On summer trips to small towns in France and Italy, Eleanor was exposed to social classes beneath her own and taught by Mme. Souvestre that these ordinary people had worth and self-respect, just like the well-heeled socialites to whom she'd always been exposed. Eleanor stayed at Allenswood until her grandmother called her home to make her debut on her eighteenth birthday. By then she had absorbed the knowledge and many of the attitudes of Mme. Souvestre and carried these in her persona, though the scars of her earlier childhood also remained.[15]

Sara was thoroughly shocked when she heard the news of Franklin's engagement. She expected that he would seek romance and marriage among the very top girls of society, and Eleanor, though certainly nowhere near the bottom, was more in the middle than the top. Sara immediately spirited Franklin away on a lengthy Caribbean cruise, but it did little to chill his ardor toward his cousin.

They were married on March 17, 1905, at an Episcopal service in New York City (the Right Reverend Endicott Peabody presiding), in range of the din of the St. Patrick's Day parade. Among the several hundred fashionable guests was the uncle of the bride President Theodore Roosevelt, who gave his niece away in the absence of his deceased brother.

Sara, for her part, had decided to take Eleanor under her wing, for she knew what a wretched childhood she had endured. Eleanor "knew she had a ghastly childhood," said a younger cousin, "but she didn't realize how ghastly it was." At the same time, there was a friction that would endure from then till Sara's death, hinging on the attentions that Franklin would divide between the two women. Since James's death in 1900, Sara had come to rely on Franklin for comfort and affection—and she wasn't about to surrender those special treatments, marriage or no marriage.

Thus, when the couple returned from their honeymoon, a nearly four-month grand tour of Europe, they were taken by Sara to an Upper East Side town house—near her own and furnished completely by her—to begin their married life. Franklin studied law at the Columbia Law School. On May 3, 1906, a daughter, Anna, was born. Sara decided that her son's town house was too small and commissioned the construction of two adjoining six-story town houses—one for her and one for Eleanor and Franklin—on Sixty-fifth Street between Park and Madison Avenues. Their house, once more, came with all the furnishings, causing Eleanor to complain to Franklin later that she "did not like to live in a house that was not in any way mine, one that I had done nothing about. And which did not represent the way I wanted to live."

But Sara continued to dominate the lives of her son and daughter-in-law, creating holiday plans, hiring their servants for them, and buying clothing for their children. Their family continued to expand. By 1910 their children numbered three, and would have eventually been complete at six—the very number that Franklin had told Alice Sohier he wanted in his family—but for the tragic death of a son, Franklin Jr., who died of illness in 1909. (Coincidentally, perhaps, there were six children in Theodore Roosevelt's family, the cousin whom Franklin idolized and emulated.) For her part, Eleanor once told her daughter, Anna, that "sex was a wife's burden to bear."[16]

Franklin was mostly bored by law school, and in fact he never received his doctor of law degree from Columbia. In his last year, he took and passed the New York Bar exam and left before graduating. He soon joined the Wall Street "white shoe" firm of Carter, Ledyard & Milburn as a $10-a-week clerk handling mostly small claims, wills, deeds, and the everyday mundane traffic of a novice attorney. In the meantime, he became heavily involved in the New York Yacht Club, while plotting a run for the New York State Senate in Hyde Park.

It was an uphill venture because the town's district was fairly solidly Republican. But Roosevelt wasn't about to shed his father's Democratic politics for the GOP, even if his venerated cousin TR had ridden it into the White House. Traveling in a bright red Maxwell touring car, Roosevelt barnstormed his largely rural district, kissing babies, giving speeches, and glad-handing farmers, shopkeepers, and immigrants, all of whom he loudly proclaimed to be "my friends." It was a lifestyle well suited to Roosevelt's "confident extraversion" but anathema to Eleanor's "puritanical insecurity." She stayed home in Hyde Park and minded the children while he tooled around in his fire-engine-red convertible.[17]

Roosevelt ran on a platform that was more or less progressive for the day: opposition to the big-city machine politics of Tammany Hall and to bomb-throwing labor unions, and a pledge to bring honesty and economy to the state government. He was elected with 52 percent of the vote.

★★★★★

ROOSEVELT QUICKLY ASSUMED LEADERSHIP of a group of twenty-one Democratic state legislators to block the candidacy for U.S. senator of a Tammany Hall–backed political hack.* Along with their Republican colleagues, the votes of the twenty-one so-called insurgents were enough to derail the nomination. It was a bold action on the part of Roosevelt and the others, who stood to lose a lot regardless of the election's outcome. The Tammany machine would not refuse to stoop to violence, fraud, or slander to ruin those who got in its way.

Yet somehow, buoyed by his articulate arguments and conciliatory manners, Roosevelt managed to dodge the Tammany bullet. In the end the insurgents failed to wrest power from the machine. They set a precedent not only in New York but in cities and states across the country. A note came from cousin Theodore: "Just a line to say we are really proud of the way you have handled yourself." To Franklin, it meant the world.[18]

Roosevelt spent much of his time in Albany working on bills that would benefit his mostly rural farm constituents in his Hyde Park district. And he did get on board with a bill to increase safety measures in state factories following the dreadful Triangle Shirtwaist factory fire at New York City's Washington Square that had killed 146 workers, most of them women.

In 1912, Roosevelt had genuine fears that he might not win reelection. He had continued his fight with the Tammany regime and its leaders had long memories. However, he rode to victory on the coattails of both Woodrow Wilson, who was running as a Democrat, and his cousin Theodore, a Republican who was running for a third term on the platform of the new

---

* In the days before the Seventeenth Amendment of 1913, most U.S. senators were elected by their state legislatures, not by popular elections.

Progressive Party. TR lost but the split in the Republican Party ensured a Democratic victory.

During the insurgency Franklin Roosevelt came to know an experienced newspaperman named Louis Howe, described by one of Roosevelt's biographers as looking like "a medieval gnome." Howe was a diminutive, asthmatic, afflicted, chain-smoking wretch in shabby suits and stained shirts who often repelled people by his appearance and his politics. But Roosevelt recognized in him a canny political adviser, and in time he became indispensable. Howe was frequently to be found in the Roosevelt household, sometimes even living there. Eleanor tolerated him because she had to—but to Sara he was an abomination.[19]

In March 1912 Roosevelt gave a speech in Troy, New York, one that in hindsight supports the premise that even then he was toying with the idea of socialism. Speaking to a group called the People's Forum, Roosevelt defended a notion that the "liberty of the community, rather than the liberty of the individual" should be foremost in a society. He made an analogy to the fact that many farms in New York (and in all of New England as well) were barren, and the farmers gone to the Midwest. This Roosevelt attributed to the fact that many farmers simply "wore out the land" by not using lime and fertilizers. "These early farmers," he went on, "gave no thought to the liberty of the community," and concluded with the notion that "the time is not far distant when the government of the State [of New York] will rightly, and of necessity, compel every cultivator of land to pay back to that land some quid pro quo."[20]

"That little phrase [liberty—or rights—of the community], which might seem innocent to the unwary," began a running argument a hundred years later in the opinion pages of the *Wall Street Journal,* "is the essence of every totalitarian system in history from Hitler to Mao to Stalin." The writer went on to say, "The Nazis even had 'The Common Good Comes Before the Individual Good' inscribed on the rims of their silver coins," and concluded indignantly that "there is no possible way to increase the liberty of the community while diminishing the liberty of the individual. Phrases like that are an excuse for the power hungry."[21]

Roosevelt, of course, would have been horrified to be compared with monsters such as Hitler, Mao, and Stalin, who didn't even exist in his world at the time. But the speech does give some insight into Roosevelt's mind-set—especially in light of what he set into motion twenty years later with his New Deal programs, which gave the state powers few had ever dreamed of except in wartime.

With Woodrow Wilson newly in the White House, many political appointments were being handed out in Washington. Roosevelt hoped in particular to become assistant secretary of the Navy. Given his interest in the sea, and the fact that his cousin Theodore had used the same position as a springboard to propel himself to the governorship of New York, the job seemed an ideal fit. It was a tough, demanding post, because the assistant secretary in fact ran the department day to day, and the Navy was spread out all over the world. But there would also be perks, such as the magnificent yachts *Dolphin* and *Sylph* that the service kept for dignitaries.

While in the lobby of the capital's Willard hotel on the morning of Inauguration Day 1913, Roosevelt encountered Josephus Daniels, Wilson's new Navy secretary. The two men had met before at the Democratic National Convention the previous summer. Now Daniels came right to the point. "How would you like to come to Washington and be assistant secretary of the navy?" he asked.

"It would please me better than anything else in the world," Roosevelt replied. He seemed to live a charmed life—at least for now.

CHAPTER FIVE

T he opening of the 1901 Parliament was both splendid and somber. Queen Victoria had died a few weeks earlier and her son His Royal Highness Crown Prince Albert Edward was now His Majesty King Edward VII. It was he who opened the ceremony, which he described as "a moment of national sorrow," as the country continued to mourn the death of his mother.

These were somber times for other reasons as well. The Boer War ground relentlessly on, piling up casualties in excess of fifty-five thousand (including more than ten thousand killed) and dragging in soldiers from more than a dozen British colonies, as well as the bulk of the British army.

It was a divided political house too, with the conservative Tories, the party of Churchill's father, still in charge. They were led by the venerable Lord Salisbury (Robert Cecil) and his top cabinet, including Arthur J. Balfour and Joseph Chamberlain. The opposition were well represented also, with such names as Edward Grey, Herbert Asquith, and Richard Haldane destined for prominence when the world erupted into war early in the next decade. Inside the House of Parliament, these men renounced their opponents in speeches that would have resulted in duels in older times, but off the floor most of them remained the best of friends. Because it cost money to become a member of Parliament, almost all were from the upper classes and knew one another socially. When they spoke on the floor they always used the phrase "the Right Honourable Gentleman" to describe their opponents.

With this in mind, Churchill prepared to give his "maiden speech," which was the custom for newly elected members. He was preceded, however, by the Liberal Party, in the person of a man who would become a principal figure in his political life until the end of the Second World War. This man, a Welshman from a coal mining district, was David Lloyd George, whose piercing progressive oratory would for the next quarter century alight on the ears of Tory politicians as a relentless din. Today, the Tories would get their first taste of it when the Right Honourable Gentleman from the opposition gave his speech.

The burning issue, of course, was the Boer War. Lloyd George lit into it right off in the process of introducing an amendment. He accused the British army of committing atrocities: of prosecuting a war "against women and children," of barn burning, and other unsavory acts. Citing the high casualty rate, he fumed that those parliamentarians who voted to continue the war were guilty of manslaughter. He called the British peace proposals ridiculous.

When his turn came Churchill, at the urging of an older member, said to clucks of laughter: "Instead of making his violent speech without moving his moderate amendment, the Right Honourable Gentleman had better have moved his moderate amendment without making his violent speech." He then proceeded to make his own moderate speech regarding the war, defending the army by pointing out that the Boers were conducting guerrilla war by day and returning to their own homes by night, where they were given sustenance by their wives and other family members. He closed by referring to his father and "a certain splendid memory, which many honourable members still preserve."[1]

The reaction was generally favorable, with light applause. Churchill was then hustled off to the House bar, where he received the appropriate lubrications. The tone of his speech had been independent, annoying some Tories, but certainly not very pleasing to the Liberals either. The speech set Churchill somehow apart and presaged his stormy relationship with the British House of Commons.

Churchill associated with a group of several younger Tory members, including Lord Hugh Cecil, Ian Malcolm, Lord Percy, and Arthur Stanley, which often dissented from the party line. They called themselves the Young Hooligans (a play on "Hughligans" à la Cecil) and every so often invited—or were invited by—one of the older, more conservative Tories to dine together. In all of 1901, Churchill made twelve speeches in the House, gave more than thirty paid lectures, played polo twelve times, spent fourteen days hunting (steeplechase), two days shooting, and eighteen days abroad on holiday. For a while he had a splendid time. But more and more he found himself disagreeing with the Tory leadership on issues such as tariffs versus free trade, home rule for Ireland, the budget, labor unions, and any number of smaller matters. At last, in exasperation, he wrote his mother in 1903, "I am a Liberal in all but name."[2]

Though he continued to sit on the Tory side of the House, Churchill in his speeches began insulting his party's leadership. He even picked a public fight with the prime minister, prompting other members to walk out of the speech he was making. He was going through a crisis of conscience, terrified of leaving the party where his father had made himself a household name. But he simply could not seem to help himself. As his biographer William Manchester put it, "He was going through the political equivalent of a divorce suit, and approaching the brink of a breakdown." In the midst of this tumult, Churchill once stood to begin a speech and fumbled for words, then went completely silent, looking around for notes that did not exist, because he carefully memorized all his speeches. Finally he sat down, put his hands to his face, and sobbed, saying, "I thank the honourable members for having listened to me."

On May 31, 1904, with little ado, he crossed the floor and sat with the Liberals. The first person to welcome him with a heartfelt handshake was David Lloyd George, even though Churchill had once gladly referred to Liberals as prigs and filthy toads. Now, his former Tory colleagues regarded *him* as "the filthiest of all toads": a traitor.

Nevertheless, his future was now brighter. Churchill swore he'd changed parties on principle, and not the other way around. Lo and behold, his prediction of a Liberal victory in Parliament came true in the next election of 1906. The Tories were swept from power and Churchill was poised to join the new government.

Over the next eight years Churchill rose upward in the Liberal government in a number of capacities, including becoming president of the Board of Trade and, later, home secretary. In these offices he remained a stalwart liberal—a radical, even—amazing his friends and infuriating his enemies. He was involved in labor union strikes and tariff disputes; he pushed for a welfare state—minimum wage, health insurance, old-age pensions; and he backed a contentious effort to defang the House of Lords by removing its veto power over bills produced by the House of Commons. He was mute on women's suffrage and, of all things, favored the prohibition of alcohol.

CHURCHILL HAD BEEN IN his new position as undersecretary of state in the Colonial Office a short while when, at a dance, his mother introduced him to tall, nineteen-year-old Clementine Hozier, a beauty who asked, "How do you do?" During what has been somewhat tackily described as "a pregnant pause," Churchill, then twenty-nine years old, replied not at all, but instead simply stood and stared until she excused herself. After this unpromising encounter, both went their separate ways for the next four years.

Four years later, in 1908, she and Churchill met again at a dinner given by her great-aunt that neither wanted to attend. Clementine had just returned from a day of giving French lessons and was tired, and Churchill "claimed it would be a great bore." Her mother scolded her into going in deference to the kindness of the aunt, who had financed her debut. He, who remained in his bath even as the dinner hour approached, was chastised by his private secretary Edward Marsh, who reminded Churchill that it was this selfsame aunt, Lady Jeune St. Helier, who had interceded with army chief Sir Evelyn Wood to get Churchill on the Omdurman campaign, which sealed his fame as a war correspondent.[3]

Clementine and Winston were seated next to each other, it turned out, and this time he opened the conversation by asking if she had read *The Life of Lord Randolph,* Churchill's popular biography of his father. When she replied that she had not, he asked whether if he sent a copy she would read it. She agreed, but the copy never arrived, "which made a bad impression on me," she wrote years later.[4]

Churchill, however, must have seen something in Clementine that he had missed in other women and was evidently impressed the few times they had met. He asked his mother if she would invite Clementine to a small party at Salisbury Hall. This time, he courted Clementine exquisitely. But, in what at first seemed a misfortunate coincidence, Clementine and her mother were off next day to a six-week tour of Europe. This, however, gave Churchill—by now a master of the English language—the decided advantage of courting her in letters.

When she returned from her European tour, each was clearly smitten with the other. Churchill's cousin Sunny, the Duke of Marlborough, graciously invited Clementine and a few other guests to a party at his magnificent Blenheim Palace. Churchill proposed by a lake during a ferocious rainstorm, and she accepted.

The wedding was held a month later in St. Margaret's Church, Westminster, on Saturday, September 12, 1908. Among the guests were David Lloyd George; Ian Hamilton, Churchill's friend and mentor from Indian army days; and Sir Bindon Blood. As a testament to British "political civility," presents were received from A. J. Balfour, Joseph Chamberlain, and Ian Malcolm—Tories all. The king sent a gold-handled walking cane. Best man was Hugh Cecil, Churchill's old friend from his days as one of the Tory Hooligans. Presiding over the service was J. E. C. Welldon, Churchill's headmaster at Harrow (much as Endicott Peabody had performed the Roosevelts' wedding).[5]

Few women have been so abruptly pitchforked into the kind of political hay wagon that Winston Churchill drove. Clementine must have gotten a whiff of this when, mere minutes after the wedding services ended, she noticed her husband and Lloyd George in an animated political conversation in an enclave of the church.

Their honeymoon began at Blenheim and ended in Venice, where Churchill was furiously revising chapters of a book he was writing on Africa. During the course of the European tour she discovered her new husband wore delicate and expensive pink silk underpants, while she wore cheap cotton chemises. A month after the wedding she was pregnant.

Three months later the new couple moved into a house on Eccleston Square. Clementine gave birth to a girl, Diana. There would be four more children over the next thirteen years: Randolph, 1911; Sarah, 1914; Marigold, 1918; and Mary, 1922. Not all of them turned out as Churchill would have wished—but that's true in many families, if not most.

Churchill was almost constantly on the go in his positions with the Foreign Office and afterward the Board of Trade, which put something of a strain on the marriage. They loved each other unswervingly all through the years, but once when he was in Paris, Clementine wondered if there were other women in his life and in a fit of jealousy she wrote him a note to this effect. After pledging total fealty he wrote: "We do not live in a world of small intrigues, but of serious & important affairs . . . You ought to trust me because I do not love & will never love any woman in the world but you."[6]

Unlike her husband, Clementine was highly sensitive to anything she perceived as a political slight. Churchill chose to confine his opposition to the House of Commons and, to Clementine's dismay, retained among his friends many staunch conservatives with whom he ate, drank, and gambled in London's various gentlemen's clubs.

His government salary was now about $500,000 in today's currency, but the family had many expenses: servants, stables, entertainments, clubs. As a result, Churchill never felt "wealthy," as were so many of his friends. He had also put on weight, and with it he became somewhat stooped. He had plenty of work to do but was not playing polo on a regular basis or getting other forms of heavy exercise as he did in the army. Still, life was good.

In 1911, Prime Minister Asquith named Churchill the first lord of the Admiralty, which he later described as "the four most memorable years of my life." The British fleet was the pride of the nation and the envy of the world. For more than a century it had stood between England and the threat of invasion. It was the principal instrument of England's imperial conquests, and by the early twentieth century it was the most powerful naval force in the world, enforcing British rule over an empire upon which the sun never set.

The most important development in the fleet's history was the ongoing construction of the Dreadnought-class battleship, the first of which was commissioned in 1906. Unlike previous ships of the line, the Dreadnoughts carried all big guns—12-inchers at first, which got larger in successive models. They were fast, starting with a speed of about 21 knots—23 mph— and carried foot-thick belts of steel at the waterline and main decks. When the first Dreadnought slid down the ways into the waters of Portsmouth Harbor all previous battleships worldwide became obsolete.

When Churchill took office, he found himself dead in the middle of a major arms race with Germany; its kaiser was determined to match the size and strength of the British fleet. Upon Churchill's arrival at the Admiralty, the Germans had pulled to within one ship of equaling the number of British Dreadnoughts at ten apiece. At the same time, Germany's ally Austria-Hungary had acquired four Dreadnoughts of its own that surpassed British naval supremacy in the Mediterranean. British naval policy called for a 2:1 ratio, and Parliament—struggling for funds to pay for social pro- grams—plunged ahead anyway with a new eight-ship program to outstrip the German menace.

As the Germans continued to build their powerful battleships, Churchill increased his warnings to the Asquith government that the kaiser was planning a war. But the prime minister was skeptical. Europe was enjoying a second "era of good feelings"—some called it the Gilded Age, or in France the belle epoque. The industrial revolution was in its most mature aspect. It was a period of luxury ocean liners, electric lights, telephones, automo- biles, and empires—except, of course, at the bottom, where the coal miners and mill workers, dissatisfied with their lowly lot, dwelled. Nevertheless, it was an age where it seemed almost everyone was in their place and either had money, or was making it, or at least had the opportunity to do so.

Churchill summed up the great advances in technology this way: "Every morning when the world woke up, some new machinery had started run- ning. Every night while the world had supper, it was running still. It ran on while all men slept."

These technological advances were not limited to creature comforts. It was also a time that saw breathtaking improvements in military weapons:

the development of high-explosive gunpowder, rapid-fire rifles, and of course machine guns. Certainly the most important were the advances in long-range artillery with enormous destructive power that now could be sited miles from a battlefield. The dawn of the century also foretold the advent of the airplane and submarine as potent military weapons.[7]

THE FIRST INKLING THAT A WAR was brewing came around the turn of the century, when others noticed that Germany was building up a tremendous military force. But the matter reached much further back than that, to the year 1888, when an alarming turn in international politics developed as the new kaiser, Wilhelm II, ascended the German throne.

In fact, the stage had been set several decades earlier, when the new kaiser's father, under the tutelage of that master of statecraft Prince Otto von Bismarck, began to assert the power of his native Prussia to unite the twenty-five loosely governed Germanic kingdoms and principalities into a Greater Germany, which created the largest and most powerful state in Europe. This new Germany soon began subduing her neighbors—Denmark (1864), Austria (1866), and France (1871). The Prussian conquest of France had caused the most trouble, because Germany demanded and seized two longtime French provinces, Alsace and Lorraine, which changed the Franco-German border and incited a horrific outrage from what was left of the French aristocracy down to the last peasant and goatherd.

One of the most remarkable aspects of diplomacy leading to World War I was the intimate relationship between the rulers of the belligerents. It began in 1837 when Victoria of England, granddaughter of George III (who had been king of England during the American Revolution), assumed the throne. She and her husband, Prince Albert, a German, had nine children. Upon her death in 1901, her son Prince Albert Edward became England's King Edward VII. His son—Victoria's grandson—became King George V when Edward died just before World War I.

Victoria's granddaughter married Czar Nicholas II of Russia, and another of her sons was wed to the czar's aunt. Her eldest daughter married the

German kaiser Frederick, and their son became Kaiser Wilhelm upon his father's death. Thus, when war broke out England's George V, Russia's Nicholas II, and Germany's Wilhelm II were all cousins, directly or through marriage, each of them descended from England's Queen Victoria.

When the new kaiser Wilhelm took over Germany, one of his first acts was to fire Bismarck. Seized by various fits of pique and jealousy, he commenced to harass his neighbors by creating a series of international "incidents." In particular the kaiser resented the nations England, Holland, France, and Spain, which early on had colonized nearly all of the desirable areas of the earth for their imperial coffers. England, for example, had taken India while also occupying Egypt and the best parts of southern Africa; France held much of the north of the so-called Dark Continent. All that was left by the time the Germans got there were parts of equatorial Africa: a steaming, unhealthy, and fetid place, prone to native uprisings and not very prosperous for raw materials or anything else. The Germans seized them anyway, to their ultimate regret, and then tried to muscle in on the profitable French possessions in North Africa.

Wilhelm appointed himself an admiral, as well as a field marshal, and ordered that the military uniform would henceforth be the official dress at court. Though he could be cranky, the kaiser was not stupid, and when he was shown a Gatling gun—a forerunner of the machine gun—he insisted that it be incorporated into the German army's infantry battalions. In the meantime, the British army was still talking about the advantages of the cavalry charge, while the French spoke of the "spirit of the bayonet."

As the years went on, the kaiser continued to bully and threaten his neighbors. The building of his Dreadnoughts and the huge increase in the German army alarmed the capitals of Europe. Churchill spoke out against Germany's armaments buildup but was told by the prime minister to tone it down for diplomacy's sake.

Meanwhile, for security purposes the French created what had been Bismarck's greatest nightmare: a dual French-Russian alliance under which each would come to the other's aid in the event they were attacked by Germany. This, among other things, meant that if hostilities broke out, the Germans would have to fight a two-front war, a huge and ominous development. The alliance nevertheless allowed Germany to trundle out its old complaint of being "encircled" by enemies, a claim it had first employed under Frederick the Great at the beginning of the Seven Years' War.

The kaiser was not only highly vexed at the French for this startling diplomatic coup, but his behavior toward England became rooted in one of the world's worst motives for troublemaking: jealousy. Britain, with its great empire and matchless fleet, remained exalted in the eyes of nations. Germany, according to the historian Martin Gilbert, "united only in 1870, had come too late, it seemed, in the race for power and influence, for empire and respect." The kaiser was determined to rectify this situation by building the most powerful military machine on earth. Germany, he declared, must have its "place in the sun."

The international incidents created by Germany throughout the first decade of the new century and into the second continued to disturb diplomats and caused the French to rearm themselves. The kaiser was apparently spoiling for a war and, as Churchill put it, "all the alarm bells throughout Europe began to quiver."[8]

In 1905 Germany's chief military strategist, Count Alfred von Schlieffen, drew up a war plan predicated on the notion of France's alliance with Russia. It assumed the Russians would be slow in mobilizing their army, so upon the outbreak of war the Germans should move swiftly to attack and defeat the French with a lightning strike through Belgium, violating its neutrality. They would then turn east to meet the Russian threat. In Schlieffen's mind it was to be another Cannae.

Meantime, in southern Europe, that most turbulent of regions, war broke out around the end of the first decade between the Ottoman Turks and the Balkan states in a squabble for territory, hegemony, and nationality. By the eve of World War I the fighting had settled down but tensions ran extremely high. The Austrians considered the Balkans part of their empire, but the Russians also considered them within their sphere of influence because the Balkan peoples were fellow Slavs with common linguistic and cultural traits—or so the Russians said.

Thus, if war broke out between Russia and Austria—which was a German ally—both France and Germany would be dragged into the fray by treaties.

The Schlieffen plan would then be set into motion, violating Belgium's neutrality, which England, bound by a decades-old treaty to protect the commercial seaports on the east coast of the English Channel, had guaranteed to uphold. All the major powers were aligned against one another.

The tinderbox sparked on June 28, 1914, when a deranged nineteen-year-old Bosnian-Serb anarchist shot and killed Archduke Franz Ferdinand, the Austrian heir to the Hapsburg throne, and his wife who, against all good sense and advice, were parading through the streets of Sarajevo, Serbia, in an open motorcar.

The furious Austrians (whom Churchill described as Germany's "idiot ally") quickly concluded that this was a case of "state-sponsored terrorism" by the Serbs. In due time, they delivered a twelve-point ultimatum to the Serbian government, for which they had sought and received the blessings of the German kaiser. He fully understood that this could bring down the wrath of Russia, France, and England upon his spiked helmet. But he was convinced that a German victory would at last solve the problem of his country's "encirclement" by enemies.

The Serbs acceded to every Austrian demand but the last, which was a virtual takeover of their country (and even *that* they suggested be put to international arbitration). The implacable Austrians nevertheless declared war and began bombarding the city of Belgrade from gunboats on the Danube.

At this startling development, the kaiser's cousin Czar Nicolas II of Russia (they traded telegrams headed "Dear Willy" and "Dear Nicky") ordered a partial mobilization of his army, hoping the Austrians would reconsider their actions when confronted with the prospect of having to face the giant Russian bear on the field of battle. The Austrians did no such thing, however, but like a typical bully when confronted they ran back into the protective arms of the kaiser, who was beginning to see that things were getting out of hand. German military leaders, however, advised their kaiser to tell cousin Nicky that if he did not cease mobilizing the Germans would have no choice but to do likewise, and war would inevitably follow.

The Russians for some reason believed this to be a bluff and refused. In the face of continued Russian mobilization, both Germany and Austria-

Hungary also mobilized their armies. On August 1, 1914, Germany declared war against Russia, and two days later, citing the Franco-Russian alliance, against France as well. The Schlieffen scheme was immediately set into motion, and the German army began invading Belgium.

On August 3, Britain issued its own ultimatum demanding that Germany respect Belgium's neutrality. The Germans responded that the British treaty was "just a scrap of paper" and the ultimatum expired at eleven the next night, prompting British foreign secretary Sir Edward Grey to make his melancholy pronouncement: "The lamps are going out all over Europe. We shall not see them lit again in our lifetime."

Churchill had been playing bridge with friends at his residence in Admiralty House on a Saturday night when he was handed a telegram saying that Germany had declared war on Russia. He immediately gave his cards to a friend and walked over to Number 10 Downing Street, residence of Prime Minister Herbert Asquith.

He informed the PM it was his intention to mobilize the British fleet, which would entail calling up more than forty thousand naval reservists and putting all ships on a war footing. He had been expressly forbidden to do this that same morning by a cabinet vote—but now, with a German declaration of war against France imminent, he was given tacit approval to go ahead.

Churchill had established a naval division of infantry consisting of some fourteen thousand officers and enlisted men, complete with a silver-instrumented marching band. A flier himself for nearly two years, Churchill sent the fledgling Royal Naval Flying Corps, which he had nurtured into a valuable arm of the service, out looking for German submarines.

He seemed to be having the time of his life—but this did not always sit well with the seasoned navy officers at the Admiralty. By tradition the first lord, though nominally in charge, was a political appointee who in practice was a kind of financial liaison between the Admiralty and Parliament. He was supposed to leave the military aspects to the professional sea lords, of whom there were seven. Churchill was having none of that. He did his best to get along with the admirals, and constantly sought their advice. But in the end Churchill—a cavalryman who had never risen above the rank of captain—assumed vicelike control of the British navy and the tactics it would employ to meet the present danger.

Churchill knew that the new German battle cruiser *Goeben* was operating in an area where the French were bringing infantry troops across the Mediterranean from their colonies in North Africa, and that the French troopships would be virtual sitting ducks for the powerful German squadron. He ordered the British admiral commanding in the Mediterranean to immediately take steps to shadow *Goeben* with his own powerful squadron and—should the cruiser attempt to attack the French—to intervene and sink her. It was a bold and in fact illegal move for Churchill to make without knowing for sure that Germany had declared war on France. But as was his practice, Churchill acted decisively, incisively, even impulsively, on the strength of his own egotistical convictions. Mercifully when the British Mediterranean warships hove into view, the *Goeben* fled toward Turkey, saving Churchill from responsibility for having started a major war. But he would not always be so lucky.

Once war was declared, Churchill stewed over what the German fleet was planning to do. He boasted in a speech in Liverpool that "if they do not come out and fight . . . they will be dug out like rats in a hole." The next day, unfortunately, a German submarine found three British battle cruisers off the coast of Holland and sank them within an hour, one after the other, taking the lives of 1,459 British sailors. Churchill had already ordered these ships to be withdrawn for fear of submarines but it was too late. Not only that, but in the days following the Liverpool speech the Germans had indeed come out—only they were submerged. Four British capital ships, including two Dreadnoughts, were torpedoed and sunk in Scapa Flow, the main British naval base in the Orkney Islands far to the north in Scotland.[9]

Next, a part of the German High Seas Fleet steamed across the North Sea and along the east coast of England, bombarding British ports without so much as a shell being lobbed against them. Five hundred civilians, including many women and children, were killed. Another German force under Admiral Maximilian von Spee cruised the Atlantic and Pacific north and south, sinking dozens of British commercial ships. A British squadron under Admiral Sir Christopher Cradock (using older, slower, and weaker ships) engaged von Spee off the coast of Chile. Cradock's force was wiped out, including the admiral himself, by the German raider force, which continued its depredations.

Parliament now began questioning Churchill's competence and calling out "What's the navy doing?" Lord Kitchener, now running the War Office, predicted that if the Germans decided to invade England the navy would be unable to stop them. Clearly in the minds of most in the House of Commons, it was time for someone's head to roll. The head selected, however, was not Churchill's but that of the first sea lord, Admiral Prince Louis of Battenberg. A German who had married a daughter of Queen Victoria, he had become a naturalized British citizen and been an upstanding British naval officer for forty-five years. He had just learned that his son, a British infantry officer, had been killed in France when the ax fell on him most unfairly because of his German name, upbringing, and accent. Churchill, an old friend, had the onerous duty of informing Prince Louis of the decision of the liberal cabinet—news that he received "with great dignity." Later in the war, because of increased anti-German feeling, the king suggested that Louis relinquish his German titles and change his name to something more Anglo-Saxon sounding. He became Sir Louis Mountbatten, a surname since written starkly across the annals of British history. For its part, the British royal family changed its name as well, from the House of Saxe-Coburg and Gotha to the House of Windsor, which it is known as to this day.

It was a shameful episode for England that such a loyal subject and military servant as Prince Louis was embarrassed and relieved from his duty by a witch hunt of trumped-up rumors of disloyalty—mostly contained in anonymous letters to the editor—but in any case the war had to go on. A replacement for the first sea lord needed to be decided upon, and the name that kept recurring was the former occupant of that position: the mercurial, contentious, and now retired Admiral John Arbuthnot "Jacky" Fisher, the naval genius who from 1904 to 1910 promoted and oversaw completion of the great Dreadnought fleet now protecting England.

Ever since Churchill took the post of first lord, he had cultivated Fisher's friendship and was high on the idea of his nomination. Others, however, weren't so sure. Both men were unpredictable, impulsive, and volatile, and some foresaw a clash. For his part, the forty-year-old Churchill was keen to have the seventy-four-year-old Fisher aboard, with all of his vast naval experience. As one of Churchill's friends explained it later, "There was a magnetic mutual attraction between these two and they could not keep away from each other for long." Churchill later wrote that he was "never in the least afraid of working with him, and I thought that I knew him so well . . . that we could come through any difficulty together." Nevertheless, the friend warned Churchill, "You are no doubt prepared for the squalls ahead."[10]

During the first weeks of the war, the Germans crushed their way through Belgium and across France toward the ultimate prize: Paris. But on its doorstep, they were halted. One of five German armies failed to meet its mission and was cut off by a French army hastily pulled together by moving soldiers from the city to the battlefront in convoys of Paris taxicabs. The British had sent its expeditionary force of about one hundred thousand professional soldiers—the "Tommys" of Rudyard Kipling's imagination—into the fray. As the German drive stalled, they fought a series of vicious running battles in the north of France and into Belgium to prevent the Germans from seizing the channel ports that were the lifeline to England. This was the so-called Race to the Sea.

Afterward, the war settled down to opposing lines that ran from Ypres, in southwest Belgium, to the Swiss border nearly five hundred miles away. The opposing armies began to dig in. Trench warfare bogged down the war for the next four years and killed almost 8 million soldiers on both sides, including more than seven hundred thousand British: the "flower of its youth," the poets said.

Churchill was appalled. He had visited the front a number of times, including when he had personally endeavored to save the Belgian port Antwerp with his vaunted naval brigade. This occurred in the early days of the war, before the German setback at Paris. As early as 1906, Churchill had warned that Antwerp was a critical strongpoint in case of a German attack and should be defended at all costs.

Scarcely two weeks into the war, in the face of the German onslaught, the king of the Belgians had pulled his battered five infantry divisions into the fortresses outside Antwerp and defied the two German corps of ninety thousand men for the next three months. The Belgian action removed these men of the German First Army from the Schlieffen plan's critical right wing, which failed to take Paris. However, daily blasting of the Belgian forts by German high-explosive artillery was slowly reducing them to heaps of brick dust. The crisis came to a head on August 30 when the Belgians let it be known they were moving their government, documents, and valuables to England. The British ambassador wired that Antwerp would fall in a matter of days.

Kitchener was now thoroughly alarmed that if Antwerp fell other channel ports would as well, opening the door for a German invasion of England. The prime minister was away, but Kitchener and the British foreign minister, Lord Grey, summoned Churchill to an emergency meeting. Churchill suggested sending in the Royal Marines, as well as six thousand inexperienced men of the Admiralty's Naval Division, to help relieve Antwerp. He volunteered to go there himself and survey the situation, reporting back by phone and telegraph.

Churchill headed for Antwerp on the next boat, but not in the role of a noncombatant "observer," as had been intended. Instead he seized personal command of not only his brigade of naval forces but the Belgian troops as well, the king of the Belgians notwithstanding. "He dominated the whole place—the King, ministers, soldiers, sailors," wrote a friend to Prime Minister Asquith. "So great was his influence that I am convinced that with 20,000 British troops he could have held Antwerp against almost any onslaught."

The arrival of Churchill's Allied troops heartened the embattled Belgians, soldiers and citizens alike—and when the Germans again attacked, the Royal Marines threw them back. An Italian war correspondent spotted Churchill watching the battle standing on a parapet "in a rain of shrapnel . . . enveloped in a cloak and wearing a yachtsman's hat and tranquilly smoking a long cigar.

"It would not be easy," continued the correspondent, "to find in all Europe a Minister who would be capable of smoking peacefully under that shell-fire. He smiled and looked quite satisfied." The "bucking up" that Churchill gave the Belgians, according to Asquith, encouraged them to "give up their idea of retreat . . . and to hold Antwerp as long as they can."[11]

The Germans, however, continued their assault and their shelling with huge 17-inch howitzers mounted on railcars. The guns lobbed 1,500-pound shells—"the size of a full-grown hog"—that atomized the thick masonry forts. At last, Churchill threw into the forward trenches his six thousand half-trained and untested "stokers, sailors, scholars, and musicians" of the Naval Division. This force included the Oxford-educated Rupert Brooke, the most well-known young English poet of his day and a brand-new lieutenant, who, after watching the fighting for more than a week, was inspired to write this famously patriotic verse:

> *If I should die, think only this of me*
> *That there's some corner of a foreign field*
> *That is forever England.**

The Germans were not to be denied. A large relief force of British soldiers was on its way to reinforce Antwerp but was held up by heavy German opposition. By the time reinforcements arrived the situation had reversed itself. With the Belgian army "in complete exhaustion and imminent demoralization," the British commander, a lieutenant general who had taken over from Churchill, ordered a general retirement to the inner line of forts and then evacuation by sea.

The retirement itself was a nightmare of slogging through the besieged and bombarded city of Antwerp that was, according to Brooke, "like several different kinds of hell; the broken houses and dead horses lit by an infernal glare. The refugees were the worst sight. The German policy of frightfulness ["terror" in today's language] had succeeded so well that out of that city of half a million, not ten thousand would remain."

---

* Six months later Rupert Brooke was dead, slain not by a bullet but by an infectious mosquito that bit him on the way to Gallipoli, where he very likely would have been killed anyway.

Brooke goes on to describe the horrors brought by the bombardment—things on fire or blown to bits, bodies in the street, old men weeping, terrorized women and children. "It's queer," he wrote, "to think one has been a witness to one of the greatest crimes of history. Has a nation ever been treated like that?"[12]

The answer, of course, is that throughout history a great many nations have been treated that way, from the depredations of Alexander the Great to the Sack of Rome. It's just that Rupert Brooke was not there to witness it. His compassion for the Belgians had quite remarkably turned him away from the skepticism of his socialism and atheism into an altruistic young Englishman, willing to fight and die for what many suddenly believed was the noblest cause since the Crusades. The war had a similar effect on a great many young English intellectuals and members of the wealthy classes, who were soon fighting and dying in extraordinary numbers on the fields of France and Flanders.[13]

Contrast this with the feelings of another young patriot on the German side, a twenty-five-year-old struggling artist and sometime political activist named Adolf Hitler. On the day Germany declared war, he was among the huge throng gathered in the Munich town square to celebrate. A subsequent enlargement of a photograph taken that day pinpoints Hitler, grinning and passionate-eyed and "overpowered by stormy enthusiasm," as he wrote in his book *Mein Kampf (My Struggle)*. "I fell down on my knees and thanked Heaven from an overflowing heart," he wrote, "for granting me the good fortune of being permitted to live at this time."

Hitler was not unlike the millions of raw recruits, many mere schoolboys, who crammed the German recruiting stations at the beginning of the war. Unlike Rupert Brooke, who saw his duty as a champion of the abused Belgians, Hitler wrote to his landlord that he actually "hoped to get to England." As his biographer Ian Kershaw bluntly points out, "The war made Hitler possible."[14]

The unhappy withdrawal from Antwerp and its capture by the Germans was widely reported in the press. The Conservative newspapers immediately blamed Churchill, although he was not in charge then and had nothing to do with its capitulation. His friend and frequent correspondent Violet

Asquith, daughter of the prime minister, called it "a savage and venomous campaign." The press questioned why Churchill—whose title was first lord of the Admiralty—was in Antwerp in the first place, conducting an infantry operation. "We suggest to Mr. Churchill's colleagues that they should quite firmly and definitely tell the First Lord that on no account are the military and naval operations to be conducted or directed by him," one paper admonished.

In retrospect, it turned out that the stubbornness of the Belgians and the British at Antwerp was responsible for the Germans' failure to quickly end the war by taking Paris. The British Official History of the war described the Allied resistance at Antwerp as having a "lasting influence on operations" by keeping the ninety thousand German troops occupied there, and not joining the German First Army in the critical Battle of the Marne where it was defeated. But this conclusion was reached only in retrospect. Churchill shouldered the blame for the loss of Antwerp through the rest of the war, gaining a reputation for being impetuous.

ONE OF THE THINGS CHURCHILL had seen at Antwerp, however, convinced him that the war was being fought the wrong way. Both sides had entrenched themselves along this impossible line from the North Sea to the Swiss Alps, with a hellish no-man's-land in between. With combined artillery and machine-gun fire, attacks to break the line were rarely successful, and the casualties were horrendous. Every day, the Germans made their line stronger, with their defense "in depth"—meaning that once attacking troops overran the first line, the exhausted and depleted soldiers then faced a second line, equally strong, and a third, and even a fourth. Churchill feared it would soon become impregnable, and the Allies would bleed themselves white trying to crack it. (There were a million British casualties in the first three months of the war.)

However, he had a plan, and he sent it in a letter in early 1915 to Prime Minister Asquith, who thought it had merit. Both Churchill and Maurice Hankey, secretary to the war cabinet, reached the conclusion that an attack on the German ally Turkey at the Dardanelles—the narrow stretch of water from the Aegean Sea that led to the Black Sea—would permit the Allies to conquer Constantinople, the Turkish capital,* and knock Turkey out of the war. Kitchener signed on to the idea almost immediately, after receiving an urgent request from the commander of the Russian army begging for an Allied attack on Turkey to draw off Turkish armies that were threatening a breakthrough in the Russian Caucasus.

Churchill envisioned a purely naval operation, using a number of obsolete battleships to force the strait and bombard Constantinople into submission. With Turkey out of the war, Allied forces could get at Austria-Hungary through the "back door" and cause Germany to fight a three-front war.† But Churchill's first sea lord Jacky Fisher insisted on including a seventy-five-thousand-man expeditionary force to land on the Gallipoli Peninsula at the northern end of the strait to overcome and secure a series of Turkish forts that lined the sides of the strait with dangerous artillery.

The battleship fleet, which also included ships from the French navy, attempted to force the Dardanelles in March 1915, but the Turks had mined the strait and several vessels were sunk. Another Allied attempt was turned back by fierce gunfire from Turkish shore batteries aimed at smaller boats attempting to clear the mines. There was a great deal of indecision on the part of the British naval command. Part of it was due to the severe penalties imposed in peacetime by the Admiralty on captains losing their ships. The very idea of having one's ship damaged or sunk was enough to deter some commanders from going into harm's way; the British admiral at the Dardanelles was apparently one of these. After more foiled attempts and a spell of bad weather, Fisher recalled the ships and the mission was scrubbed.[15]

Churchill was bitterly disappointed at the navy's failure to force the Dardanelles—and at Fisher for calling off the effort—but did not attempt to override the first sea lord. The war cabinet, and various committees of

---

* Now renamed Istanbul.

† Turkey had no warships to match Great Britain. It had ordered two Dreadnoughts that lay in British shipyards when war broke out and the British confiscated them.

the departments, dithered about what to do next. Kitchener was against dispatching the seventy-five-thousand-man army corps on the grounds that it was unsound military principle to divide one's forces (and in any case he could not spare any men from the Western Front). At last, it was decided that a British infantry division, a number of detached brigades and battalions, and a large force of Australians then training in Egypt for the Western Front would be diverted to invade Gallipoli. The French contributed eighteen thousand infantrymen to the enterprise. The hope was that they could quickly clear the peninsula of Turkish opposition, which would allow the naval assault to proceed.

First Sea Lord Fisher then got cold feet and sent around a secret paper saying he was now against the plan to send troops. But it was too late. Too many people had signed on, and the grim war machine had been set into motion. A rift developed between Fisher and Churchill just as many (including the king) had predicted: two iconoclastic personalities now created high-powered friction. Churchill thought Fisher was becoming senile, while Violet Asquith, a perceptive political observer in her own right, thought he was mad.[16]

By now the Turks were fully alarmed at the Allied attempts to force the Dardanelles. They brought a sizable army to defend the peninsula including a canny German adviser named Otto Liman von Sanders, who thoroughly understood the magnitude of the problem. Thus the Allies were given a hot reception when the invasion force arrived.

The Gallipoli Peninsula is ringed by high clay cliffs that the soldiers ascended with great difficulty, only to be met at the top by withering machine-gun fire punctuated by enormous artillery barrages. As a result, none of the five landing parties reached their objectives that first day. As had quickly developed on the Western Front in France and Belgium, modern weaponry dictated that the Gallipoli soldiers dig in: at first by scraping out shallow holes to escape the gunfire, which in time turned into an elaborate trench system. A deadly stalemate ensued as the Allies threw in more men, only to incur more casualties. The Germans sent more machine guns, the Turks sent more men. It soon got back to Britain that the situation was critical.

At this, Fisher began going around to members of Parliament blaming Churchill for the mess—never mind that it was his idea in the first place to land troops. But Churchill's name had become so identified with the enterprise that everyone, including the press, gave him ownership of it. Fisher resigned, publicly, putting Churchill in a precarious situation. Almost simultaneously, because of dissatisfaction over the course of the war, the political parties organized into a "National Government," a coalition of Tories and Liberals. The Tories, however, had never forgiven Churchill's defection from the party and were anxious for a reason to have him step down. This was it. Churchill's friend Asquith was still prime minister, but the pressure to fire the first lord was too great. It was either that or lose the coalition. Asquith sent Churchill a little red box containing a note in which he had asked every minister to place his resignation in his hand.

Churchill was magnanimous in his reply, but it was a crushing blow. For four years, he had dedicated his whole being to the Admiralty, developing the naval flying service, recruiting the Naval Division that at that hour was playing its part in the Gallipoli battle, crafting each year the naval estimates, and building Dreadnoughts and all manner of other ships. He was also instrumental in the development of tracked armored "land ships," which would later become known as tanks.

He had been a minister, one of the elite, a man of great substance and respect. Now, like his father, he was forced to resign in disgrace. He told his friend Violet Asquith that for a few hours his thoughts were suicidal; then they turned merely to sorrow. Years later, his wife told one of his biographers she actually thought he'd die from grief.[17]

CHAPTER SIX

Rotten times lay ahead for Churchill in the wake of his resignation in the fall of 1915. The weeks and months passed indifferently while he contemplated his fate. He and Clementine had rented a country farmhouse in Surrey along with his brother Jack and sister-in-law Gwendoline (or "Goonie"), yet black despair hovered around Churchill like a pall. Then one morning he wandered into the garden to find Goonie at her palette and easel, paintbrush in hand. "I would like to do that," Churchill remarked, and Goonie happily lent him her paints.

He took to it immediately, and in typical Churchill style he ordered the finest accoutrements of artistry and sought someone to instruct him. This turned out to be a neighbor, the painting master Sir John Lavery. Soon, Churchill was painting morning, noon, and night. As one of his biographers has written: "He discovered, as other sensible people have done, that painting is not only the best of hobbies, but a sure refuge in time of trouble—for while you are painting you can think of nothing else."[1]

Painting became a restorative tonic for Churchill, and he excelled at it for the rest of his life, turning out canvas after canvas of bright, colorful oil landscapes around the Surrey countryside. Most he gave away to friends, but one in particular startled the British art world. In

1925, a three-man committee of the most prestigious figures in British art awarded a prize for the best anonymous painting by an amateur. Churchill had submitted "Winter Sunshine" and had won first place. Not only was the committee astonished that the work was made by an amateur, but imagine the members' surprise when they discovered who had painted it!

THE PRESS HAD A FIELD DAY with Churchill's resignation. Both scorn and approbation were heaped upon him. He remained convinced that the Dardanelles operation would have been successful if the original fleet had tried harder to get through, and that it could be successful still if more Allied troops were sent to Gallipoli to turn the flank of the Turkish army. If Turkey had been knocked out of the war, it would have been a terrific blow to the Germans and a huge boon to the Russians; it might have postponed or even averted the Communist takeover and perhaps the Russian Revolution. But all of the plans suggested were, in the end, rejected—and at last it was decided to evacuate the army from Gallipoli, a most dangerous undertaking. At this decision, Asquith resigned as prime minister; his place was taken by David Lloyd George.

The Dardanelles-Gallipoli adventure ended in January 1916, ten months after it had begun. By then the Allied armies there had swollen to nearly half a million; roughly half of these became casualties. It was the most conspicuous British defeat of the war.

Jacky Fisher's Iago-like role in Churchill's downfall was disgraceful. But he was an old man, and some said off his head. Nevertheless, Churchill felt stabbed in the back. "I am finished," he told Violet Asquith when they met in a corridor of the House of Commons a day after he resigned. "What I want above all things is to take some active part in beating the Germans. But I can't—it's been taken from me."

But it hadn't, actually. Churchill retained his reserve membership in his old army regiment and, after it became apparent that the Tories intended to block any further political role he might play in the war effort, he requested that he be sent to the fighting front. In the autumn of 1915, as the last soldiers were preparing for evacuation from Gallipoli, Churchill was recommissioned with the rank of major, with orders to report to army headquarters in France.

There, he was received warmly by the British army's commander in chief, General Sir John French, who took him to dinner and explained the general war situation. Next morning, French asked Churchill what he would like to do. When Churchill replied that "I will do whatever I am told," French replied, "Will you take a brigade?"

Churchill was delighted. It was a huge leap from the rank of major, which is a mid-level staff position, to brigadier general in charge of five thousand infantry with artillery, cavalry, and all the rest.[2] He answered that he "would be proud to do so," adding that he wanted to learn firsthand about trench warfare. French arranged for him to be attached to the "best school of all—the Guards," and taken personally by the commander of the Guards Division to the Grenadier Battalion, where he was introduced to the colonel (who was the only surviving officer of the battalion since it had arrived in 1914) and his staff.[3]

That, however, was the end of warm welcomes. The next day, as they were walking toward the frontline trenches on "a darkening plain in an icy drizzle amid the red flashes of the guns," the battalion colonel said to Churchill rather curtly that the battalion was "not at all consulted in the matter of you coming to us." Churchill replied that he didn't know himself where he'd be sent, but he thought it would "be all right." They walked on.

The battalion adjutant broke another long, icy silence by telling Churchill that they "had to cut down" his baggage, which included in addition to boxes of fine cigars, cases of brandy, and tins of fancy food from Harrods and Selfridges a bathtub complete with a boiler for heating the water—and, of course, his painting gear.[4] The adjutant went on, "We have found a servant for you," who was carrying a spare pair of Churchill's socks and his shaving gear. "We have had to leave the rest behind."

It was pitch-dark when they reached battalion headquarters near the frontline trenches. Churchill was given a choice of where to sleep: a stuffy cubbyhole occupied by four Morse code signalers or "a sort of pit" that was two hundred yards away and knee-deep in water.

The headquarters itself was located in "a pulverized ruin" called Ebenezer Farm,* where they were offered food, tea, and condensed milk, but nothing stronger, because the colonel ran a "dry" headquarters, much to Churchill's surprise and indignation. He had always warmed himself with liquor on cold wintry nights. He turned down the water pit in favor of the signal office, and as they stumbled back in the dark, "the bullets, skimming over the front line, whistled drearily," he wrote later. "Such was my welcome to the Grenadier Guards."[5]

Within a few days Churchill had won them over. He asked the colonel to let him accompany him on his twice-daily visits to the trenches: two- or three-hour ordeals in which they "slid or splashed or plodded together through snow or mud . . . where no one was ever dry or warm"—nor, he might have added, safe. He was jolly in the face of fire, because, like them, he'd been there before. What they didn't understand was that he relished it, thrived on it, had been brought up gnawing on a different bone.

Churchill suggested to the colonel that he could better understand the conditions in the trenches if instead of living at battalion headquarters he might live with the companies in the line at the very edge of no-man's-land (and where the rules about alcohol were also greatly relaxed). He was forty-one years old, going pudgy, still baby-faced, a former minister in the government, and it had been a long time since he'd stood the rigors of outdoors warfare. Remarkably, he stood them cheerfully and well. He was not at all astonished at the huge rats that inhabited many parts of the trenches, and he actually claimed they performed a useful duty eating corpses.† When the second in command went on leave, Churchill was invited to take over

---

* Ebenezer Farm was the site, three years later, of a blood-drenched battle when a brigade of the famed U.S. 42nd Rainbow Division, under Brigadier General Douglas MacArthur, attacked and ejected a German stronghold there that had overrun the British line during the huge and final German offensive of March 1918.

† The rats were so voracious they quickly devoured the bodies of the dead before they could be buried. The army trucked in hordes of street cats from Paris and dumped them into the trenches, but the rats ate them too. The war ground on.

his duties, a request Churchill felt was "one of the greatest honours I have ever received."[6]

Stationed on the front, Churchill even found a few times when he could set up his easel and paint. Little did he know that in the enemy lines not far from his position there was another amateur artist painting scenes across no-man's-land: Lance Corporal Adolf Hitler.*

By now Churchill was thoroughly in his element. Comfortable with the hazards, easy with the men, everyone seemed to warm to him. He often crept out at night and into no-man's-land to check the barbed wire, reconnoiter trails, or look for signs of enemy penetration. He was dazzled, he said, "by the bright eyes of danger." He was older and a stabilizing figure, out in the mud and slime and rats of the trenches. He shared with the men his bounty of food and brandy that arrived from Clementine on almost a daily basis. He wrote to her: "I am very happy here. I did not know what release from care meant. It is a blessed place."[7]

Several days later, Churchill had a terribly close call. He was about to enter his two-man dugout after running an errand when a sergeant stopped him. "Sir, don't go in there," the sergeant told him, and explained that about five minutes after Churchill had left an enemy artillery shell had penetrated the roof and exploded, decapitating the other occupant. Luck, chance, destiny were all the same thing, Churchill mused. The incident confirmed in his mind that the universe was dominated by a "superior power."

CHURCHILL NEVER GOT HIS infantry brigade. His political enemies were utterly antagonistic, and now they had serious power again. After the Gallipoli disaster, Prime Minister Asquith had been obliged to form a wartime coalition government in the summer of 1915, and the Tories turned their ire on the man they still regarded as a traitor to the party. Instead he was

---

* Though neither artist ever rose above the category of "talented amateur" (or in Churchill's case "exceptionally talented amateur"), Winston Churchill's paintings today fetch upwards of $2 million at art auctions—whereas the best of Hitler's work goes for around $100,000.

promoted to lieutenant colonel and given a battalion, the 6th Royal Scots Fusiliers: eight hundred Scottish lowlanders, many of them miners. With the battalion came a hint that, if he performed well for a year or so and wasn't killed, he might get the brigade and another promotion. The battalion was stationed at the line in the ruined Belgian town of Ploegsteert, which the men called "Plug Street." It was a highly dangerous place, being as it was part of the giant Battle of Ypres (which the men called "Wipers"), where the fighting had been bitter and nearly continuous since the early days of the war.

At the beginning, Churchill was resented. The old commanding officer was well liked and the men couldn't understand why a prominent politician had been sent there to lead them. But, as he had in the Guards, Churchill won them over in time. He hadn't been in the military for seventeen years—but he remembered enough of it to put his own stamp on the 6th Royal Scots Fusiliers, whose regiment had been born 237 years earlier.

First he conducted a war on lice, delivering of himself a scholarly dissertation on the history of the louse from ancient times on, and how it affected the morale of the men. Baths were scheduled, heads shaved, clothing deloused. In due time, the battalion was rendered liceless. He made the men sing while they were marching to and from the front on grounds that it abated fatigue. (All most of them knew were church hymns, so at first they sang those.) He supervised the building of defenses—of parapets and traverses and such—with the keen eye of a graduate of the Royal Military Academy at Sandhurst. Morning and night he was in the trenches, inspecting, improving, learning. He told wonderful stories to the men of historic battles that the battalion had fought, summoning up the stylish rhetoric of his ancestor the Duke of Marlborough. The men loved it. He ordered his officers always to smile during enemy artillery barrages or when in actual combat. "If you can't smile, grin," Churchill told them. He believed it had a "pleasing effect" on the men.

All the while, his fertile mind was churning with ideas about how the war could be won. Unlike most officers and practically all the men, Churchill truly loved being in a combat command. He understood more than most the queer psychology of the battlefield, which is one thing to men in line and quite another to somebody looking at a map back at headquarters. It had to be endured to be believed—the bizarre proximity of the armies, sometimes only two hundred yards apart, where men on both sides could hear their enemies laughing or cursing or smell their cooking across the rot and stench of no-man's-land. Compared with the impersonality of an artillery barrage or the sniper's bullet, this lent a strange intimacy to the war.

But as the days passed Churchill began to feel he was being underused. His battalion was only a tiny cog in the gigantic wheel of war, which at its apotheosis would see 68 million men under arms on both sides. (Before it ended, nearly 10 million of these would be dead.) It was the greatest event of his lifetime, Churchill believed—and here he was, mired in the mud and the blood of the trenches.

From that perspective he saw, for example, that futile infantry charges only kept the coffinmakers in business; that German planes ruled the sky, and that Britain desperately needed an effective air policy. Above all others, Churchill had been responsible for the development of the tank, and now that it was in field trials it had become an underfunded political football. He understood firsthand that conscription was a necessary evil to fill gaps in the understrength battalions, now that volunteerism had dried up. But the draft was another political hot potato. And the navy—once *his* navy— was moribund and lacking initiative. Unless something was done, he felt, the Allies would lose the war.

He went on leave to London in April, and he astonished everyone by calling for a return to the Admiralty of his old enemy Sir Jacky Fisher. The present administration of the navy didn't know what it was doing, Churchill suggested, and that at least Fisher did. He was lampooned in the press.

When he returned to the war he found that his brigade had been so shot up by German artillery it was merged into another division, and that the brigade commander had moved on. Churchill did not get the promotion. He decided it was time, after half a year on the Western Front, to return to England and to Parliament, where he retained his seat but, thanks to the Tories' eternal venom, held no role in government. His fellow officers at the front gave Churchill a farewell lunch at which every one of them spoke of a sense of "personal loss" at his going.

★★★★★

CHURCHILL BIDED HIS TIME. He secretly became Lloyd George's personal adviser on the war, for if the Tories found out there would be hell to pay. In the meanwhile, he began earning handsome fees writing magazine and newspaper pieces for the London press barons Lords Northcliffe and Beaverbrook. These monies easily outstripped the financial vacuum created when he lost his ministerial seat in the government.

By the summer of 1917 Lloyd George felt strong enough to defy the Tories in the coalition government and named Churchill as minister of munitions: at that time, a most critical position. In typical Churchillian fashion, he stormed into his ministry and soon began sweeping changes that would vastly improve the efficiency, quality, and quantity of the tremendous array of weaponry with which the war was fought. Moreover, a blue ribbon committee of the House cleared Churchill of any mismanagement regarding the Dardanelles campaign, laying the blame mostly on Admiral Fisher, where it belonged.

Churchill's leadership at munitions was so effective that the press seemed for the time being to forgive his past transgressions. By the following year he was named secretary of state for war, meaning that, with limitations, he would run the whole shebang—including his pet project the tank, which had at last proven its merits on the battlefield.

The system Churchill had set up at munitions created an easy and efficient resupply of artillery shells and bullets for individual weapons, which allowed the British to respond effectively to German attacks in early 1918. By March, the German ranks had swollen by more than a million men following Lenin's sudden Bolshevik coup and the surrender of Russia. They launched a last-ditch offensive along the Western Front. The German strategy was to split the British and French armies, capture the channel ports, and bring a swift end to the war before the Americans could arrive in force.

After initial successes the German attack stalled, in large measure because of Churchill's reforms. Churchill was frequently at the fighting front and, as his duties also included overseeing the air force, he began flying across the English Channel to consult and inspect. This of course terrified Clementine almost to distraction—all the more because she was pregnant with the couple's fourth child, who would be named Marigold.

The German army was now bleeding to death from Allied counterattacks and unable to hold on to its gains. Slowly, but ferociously, the Germans began to give ground when pressed by the British, French, and now American forces, who fought bravely but without the skill of those who had been at the front for years. In British lines, it was rumored that the Germans had established a "corpse factory," which turned dead bodies into tinned can food for their soldiers, whose rations had been cut almost to starvation level because of the continued British blockade of German ports.

By November 1918 the Germans had had enough and called for a ceasefire, or armistice, that became a de facto surrender. Against the advice of the American commander, the German armies were allowed to return to their homes unescorted and German territory was mostly unoccupied. It has been argued that this oversight allowed for the rise of Hitler and the Nazis, who convinced the people that their armies were never defeated but "stabbed in the back" by cowardly politicians in Berlin.

The victorious Allies divided up German colonies and changed the face of the Middle East. The kaiser abdicated to Holland and a democracy was installed to govern the country. Steep reparations and territorial losses were inflicted on Germany, which fueled the resentment and breakdown of democracy that marked the Hitler years. Large parts of France and Belgium had been utterly destroyed, and their restoration in some cases went on into the 1960s. (Farmers plowing in the area from that day to this uncover live artillery shells or other unexploded munitions, which on average have killed several persons a year for a century.)

Not content with this undisputed victory, Churchill's antipathy toward the Bolsheviks was such that he successfully argued for British and other Allied troops to intervene in Russia, which was undergoing a civil war after the deposition of the czar and the Communist takeover of the government. Here was where a split with the prime minister began. Lloyd George had had enough of war, and he also had a rebellious situation on his hands in Ireland, whose Irish Republican Army had taken advantage of Britain being so deeply involved in the war and was able to organize a formidable force of its own.

Lloyd George dealt with the Irish problem by sending British soldiers who'd been at the front to quell the Irish rebellion. These became the hated "black and tans," so named for the uniforms they wore. Churchill continued to agitate for British troops to save Russia from Communism, but the prime minister viewed that country's vast expanses as the kind of place where troops, money, and everything else could simply vanish without a trace. In 1921, in order to get Churchill off his back, Lloyd George transferred him to the Colonial Office, which had no responsibility for intervention in Russia.

Ever restless, Churchill as minister of the Colonial Office began meddling in the Middle East, a term he officially institutionalized by organizing the Cairo Conference. In March 1921 Churchill summoned all the British military and civil leaders across the Middle East to determine what was to be done with this seething, exotic, Islamic vastness. For generations, the Middle East had been ruled from Constantinople by the Ottoman Empire, which after World War I was no more. When Turkey surrendered, it left a great vacuum in the region: a jumble of deserts, mountains, oases, towns, and cities, superimposed on a mostly Islamic culture of numerous tribes and sects, many of which were at war with one another.

For the British, the main issues were the security of the Suez Canal and the stupendous quantities of oil in the Persian Gulf region, as well as a promised homeland for Jewish peoples in the Palestine territory.

With T. E. Lawrence, the famous Lawrence of Arabia, as his adviser, Winston Churchill was intimately involved in redrawing the map of the entire region, creating Iran and carving out Iraq and Jordan as separate principalities and establishing relations (for the purpose of controlling British oil interests) with Saudi Arabia and its ruling families. Also within his bailiwick was overseeing enforcement of the 1917 Balfour Declaration—so named after the British foreign secretary Arthur Balfour, which guaranteed Jews land along the river Jordan. In fact, it can be safely said that—except for Iran and Iraq, which in the late 1970s were overthrown by radical Islamists and a strongman dictator, respectively—Churchill had an indelible and lasting hand in creating the Middle East as we know it today.

DURING THIS PERIOD, Churchill's life was buffeted by good fortune in finances and tragedy from deaths in the family. He had further increased his income by contracting to write a book on the war, *The World Crisis,* which ultimately stretched to three large volumes that earned him more than a million dollars in today's money. Not only that, but a small fortune fell into his hands by way of a bequest of his deceased great-grandmother: all told, nearly £57,000.* This prompted Clementine to gush that the windfall felt "like floating in a bath of cream," and to inquire whether she should pay off the substantial household bills that had piled up. For his part, Churchill purchased a Rolls-Royce and went on a gambling spree in Monte Carlo.

Historically, Churchill's finances had always been a burden and a mess. Whenever he received any substantial sum of money he tended to use it as security to borrow a larger sum. This process was repeated until his financial situation was a tangled web of debts that constantly had to be paid off—often robbing Peter to pay Paul—after which he would spend the living daylights out of the proceeds.

Amid these fluctuations of monetary fortunes, personal tragedy struck Churchill on June 29, 1921, when Jennie Jerome Churchill died at the age of sixty-seven. She had fallen down some stairs and broken her ankle, which became infected and was amputated above the knee. A sudden hemorrhage killed her. Churchill for a while was inconsolable; not only was he devoted

---

* Upwards of $2.8 million in today's dollars.

to her as a mother, but over the course of his life she had used all her connections (and personal charms) to bestow upon him social, political, and professional cachet.

On her death, Churchill inherited both Jennie's trust fund from his father's estate and her family's trust in the United States. Together they totaled £54,000 ($2.7 million today). However, these were what are now known in the United States as a "pass-through," meaning that Churchill could use the yearly income they produced during his lifetime but not the principal, which would go to his children. Nevertheless, it was a windfall, bringing in about $100,000 a year in today's money.

Now, for the first time in his life, Churchill could relax to some extent, knowing that he had a meaningful amount of capital investments that— even if they wouldn't bring in enough to support his extravagant lifestyle— would ensure a steady income that could be supplemented by his writing and government salary.

In the summer of 1921 another tragedy occurred. Churchill received an urgent message from Clementine to come immediately to Kent, where he had rented the family a home by the seaside. Two-and-a-half-year-old Marigold had tonsillitis and an alarmingly high fever—this was a half decade before the development in 1928 of penicillin and other antibiotic drugs. He arrived just in time to watch his daughter die.

"She said, 'so tired, so tired,' and closed her eyes," Churchill recalled, worried that Clementine herself "would die in the violence of her grief."[8]

Although Churchill never allowed personal sorrows to stand in the way of service to his country, we can only imagine that the loss of his beloved mother and young daughter in such a short span of time must have wounded him deeply—perhaps, for the rest of his life.

WITH THE END OF THE GREAT WAR, the political winds in England began to shift, and Churchill's political prospects shifted with them. In fact, a great social upheaval was under way; many of the men who had fought were no longer content with the stern, class-driven society of the prewar days, from which they had been hurled into the bloody trenches of France and Belgium. This also was true of the millions of British servants—male and female—and other menial workers who had joined the war effort. One anecdotal sign of it lay in a bit of doggerel in a song often chanted in the streets following the Armistice of 1918:

> *What shall we be . . .*
> *When we aren't what we are?*

The two traditional parties, Tory and Liberal, were now joined by a third entity: the Labour Party. Composed initially of members elected by the working class and the labor unions, it soon became loosely associated with the same Socialist movement that had overthrown the Russian government. By the early 1920s, the Labourites had forced the Liberal Party into a coalition government and, by the election of 1922, had eclipsed it by some 142 votes to 62. The Liberal Party was, in fact, dying, and would be gone as a political force before the decade was done.

Overshadowing both of these parties by a sizable majority of 345 votes were the Tories, who were now squarely back in power. This was bad news for Churchill in more ways than one—not only was he out of government but he had lost his seat in Parliament. Shortly before election day Churchill became ill and had to enter the hospital, causing his race to lose momentum. "In the twinkling of an eye," he said, "I found myself without an office, without a seat, without a party, and without an appendix." It was beginning to look as though the promising political career of Winston Churchill had at last come to an inevitable and inelegant end.[9]

Over the next two years he ran three times in three different districts, and he lost every race. Part of the problem was his implacable hatred of Socialism, which he ridiculed as "government of the duds, by the duds, and for the duds." Whenever Churchill gave speeches to regain his office, the Socialists made sure he was greeted with jeers, obscenities, spittle, and rock throwing. All of this, of course, was reported in the newspapers. Thus reviled by both the Tories and the workingmen, Churchill had to hire a private detective to accompany him on campaign trips.

OVER THE YEARS, Winston and Clementine had often discussed acquiring a country estate as so many of their aristocratic friends had. Now, in the fall of 1922, they decided to take the plunge. Chartwell was an eighty-acre property in Kent, about thirty miles from London. Featuring a redbrick manor house dating to the time of the Crusades, it was set on a magnificent high rise of ground that looked over the district's celebrated Great Weald.

During the previous century, the owners had added garish Victorian features ill-suited to its original, simple architecture. Churchill first described it as "dreary," overshadowed by giant trees with bricks that were "slimed in green." He complimented the old part of the manor as "floored and raftered with solid oak" but condemned the newer, which, he said, "was weary of its own ugliness so that the walls ran with moisture, and creeping fungus ran down the cracks and crevices." But Winston had a vision of how the property could be remade, and he purchased it for £5,000 against the wishes of his wife, who took a disliking to the property immediately upon seeing it. It was the one disagreement in their marriage about which Clementine felt Winston had simply been dishonest with her.[10]

During his time out of office, Churchill devoted himself to Chartwell and began building an impressive series of ponds that fell off in the distance from the high ground of the manor house. These he populated with black swans. He hired an architect to modernize the place, rearranging the house around a marvelous library and writer's study. The grand dining room saw a "dazzling succession of lunches and dinners" with parliamentary and world leaders, as well as the greatest intellectual minds of the day. There was a vast wine cellar and a special room for Churchill's prized Cuban cigars.

Over years of weekends Churchill learned to work with his hands, and he became a more than adequate brick mason and carpenter. He collected a variety of farm animals, as well as butterflies that he netted himself and placed in a special mesh wire house. He raised fruit, vegetables, and flowers.

He lived well, but nearly always on the edge: in the distance, the world of politics always beckoned.[11]

Churchill began to realize that the Liberal Party was doomed. He looked at Labour, and even on a lark applied for membership in the bricklayers' union but was blackballed. In time it became clear that his future lay with the Tories, where he remained hated—so that, too, seemed an impossible contradiction. Churchill's problem was that as a young minister he often had overplayed his hand to the consternation of his peers, and he had done so repeatedly during the coalition government when many of his counterparts were Tories.

Just as it seemed that he had shut himself out entirely, he went on a forgiveness campaign with those conservatives with whom he remained on friendly terms, including F. E. Smith, the Earl of Birkenhead, and a mysterious young Irishman, Brendan Bracken, who was building a British newspaper empire. Churchill began making conservative speeches in various political districts to test the waters. In 1924, two years after losing his seat in Dundee, he won a solid majority of the vote in the Epping district of Essex. He returned to Parliament to become, in the future, the greatest Tory of them all.

Not only was he back in office, but the new Tory prime minister, Stanley Baldwin—like Churchill, a Harrow graduate—made Churchill chancellor of the Exchequer, an office that corresponds roughly to the U.S. secretary of the treasury. He "lit up like a gigantic lightbulb" and grasped Baldwin's hand. "I still have my father's robes as Chancellor," Churchill cried. "I shall be delighted to serve you in this splendid office!"[12]

One of his first new rituals in office was having an early morning chat with the prime minister, who lived at Number 10 Downing Street, right next door to the chancellor's residence. For the next five years, there was never a quarrel or harshly spoken word between them. Churchill's yearly budgets were introduced with a majestic lucidity—the best of them, according to the biographer Paul Johnson, "since Gladstone's golden age and never equaled since."

His first budget, in 1925, however, was far from his best. Churchill astonished almost everyone by recommending that the nation go back to the gold standard with the high, prewar parity. It had been pointed out to him that this would make the pound sterling so strong that Britain's exports—mainly raw materials such as coal, or second-tier raw materials such as cotton cloth and steel—would suffer from being too expensive. But supporters argued it would make London the world's financial center once more and spawn a host of highly technical industries in electronics, airplanes, and automobiles that would create more employment.

The plan was soon met with more skepticism when coal company owners tried to cut wages for the nation's 1.2 million miners, because the gold parity had caused a downturn in exports. A mine strike ensued, followed in 1926 by a much dreaded general strike, in which all labor unions refused to come to work. This caused vast disruptions to British commerce and daily life. No buses ran, no newspapers were printed. Truckers refused to haul, and strikers from steelworkers to bricklayers shut down most of Britain's economy.

A general strike had been a topic of much apprehension since the turn of the century. It had been threatened but never called—and now that it was upon them, the English people seethed and spread their fury between the strikers and Winston Churchill.

Churchill for his part admirably shouldered the blame and as chancellor of the Exchequer took charge of the situation. He served as strike mediator, organized food trucking convoys escorted by armored cars from the military, sent police and troops to put down violence in trouble spots, and with unrestrained relish even published a government newspaper to provide information about the strike and other issues.

In the end, the miners trudged back to work under a settlement negotiated by Churchill, who had threatened mine owners with a government-mandated minimum wage. Other labor unions followed suit, prompting the writer Evelyn Waugh to declare, "It was as though a beast long favored for its ferocity had emerged for an hour, scented danger, then slunk back into its lair." Churchill was once more the smiling hero of the government.

Economist John Maynard Keynes savagely condemned Churchill, as did the owners of low-production industries. But history seems to have vindicated him for putting the nation back on the gold standard—not least because it generated a spurt of high-tech industries in the 1930s. As historian Johnson points out, on the eve of World War II this development spurred the production of the Spitfire fighter plane, as well as the Lancaster bomber, radar, television, and high-compression Rolls-Royce aircraft engines: all achievements that would give Britain the edge when it was most critical.

Beginning right after the First World War, Lenin, and later Stalin, had begun exporting Marxist provocateurs to England and other nations, often in the form of secret agents that pandered to workingmen with a mind toward the overthrow of governments. Churchill was among the first to recognize this and sound the alarm. "Of all the tyrannies in history, the Bolshevik tyranny is the worst," Churchill said. Communist revolution in Great Britain, he said, would "mean the extinction of English civilization."

IN THE 1929 GENERAL ELECTION the Tories were overwhelmed by the Labour Party. Churchill retained his seat in the House of Commons but he no longer held a cabinet position. In spite of his foresight regarding the fate of the Liberal Party, Churchill found himself out of power once more. He used the occasion to embark on a tour of the United States by railcar. By then he had amassed a small fortune from his writings that he'd invested with the Wall Street firm E.F. Hutton & Co. Along the way he gave speeches, one of them ominously warning that Germany, which was becoming unsettled, angry, and unstable, had twice as many youths of military age as France. In California he met and became friends with such movie stars as Charlie Chaplin and Victor McLaglen, fished off of Catalina Island (he caught a 188-pound swordfish), and visited the press lord William Randolph Hearst at his $30 million castle at San Simeon.

Crossing the continent once more, Churchill listened to a radio in his private car that carried news and hourly stock market updates. In Washington he visited President Herbert Hoover, and he toured the Civil War battlefields of Gettysburg and Antietam. He was in New York's Plaza

Hotel on October 24, 1929 ("Black Thursday"), when the stock market crashed and began its low, long slide to fractions. Churchill, who was now fifty-four, had believed his investments would leave him financially stable for the remainder of his life. But even though he was not completely wiped out, any hope of that kind of monetary independence was gone. On the night of the crash, Churchill attended a formal dinner at the Fifth Avenue mansion of the financier Bernard Baruch, along with a host of bankers and Wall Street investors. One of them rose and lifted his glass to Churchill, addressing the other guests as "friends and former millionaires."[13]

The next week Churchill sailed for home, only to be greeted there by what for him was appalling news. The British viceroy of India, Lord Irwin (later to become Lord Halifax), had recommended self-rule for India. And Stanley Baldwin, leader of the Tories, had agreed. To Churchill, this was one of the great heresies of a lifetime.

For three hundred and fifty years, English colonization had amassed a British Empire that governed more than 400 million people and nearly a quarter of the earth's land surface, including colonies, dominions, commonwealths, mandates, protectorates, and so forth. It had made Great Britain fabulously wealthy until the First World War came along and wiped out the treasury surplus. It had also created many great personal fortunes for men of trade, and produced a vast foreign service system to govern these far-flung reaches. The crown jewel, of course, was India; its teeming millions kept the cotton mills of Manchester and other industrial towns humming and furnished the tea that was the foundation of that peculiarly British custom.

Of late, however, there had been unrest and violence among the Indian people, a majority of whom were Hindu but about 30 percent of whom were Muslim. The Raj came under heavy fire. It had educated the higher caste of Indians, who now demanded freedom to form their own government and make their own laws.*

---

* For two thousand years Indian society had been governed by a caste system, ranging from upper-class Brahmins, who were the intellectuals and priests, to Untouchables, who took out the garbage, with a variety of castes and subcastes in between. These were absolute. The caste you were born into was your lot in life.

Mohandas Gandhi was an Indian Hindu lawyer and activist who had begun a movement of civil disobedience and boycott of British goods in India that threatened to disrupt the smoothly running Raj. In the face of these continuing problems, the viceroy reluctantly concluded that the situation was not going to get better, and the wisest course was to give the subcontinent dominion status within the empire, meaning that it would become self-governing.

Churchill, who had served in India as a young army officer, was vehemently opposed to this proposition and attacked it with a fury "that was almost demented." It was another of his tangents that seemed bound to cause him trouble, going against the leader of his party in such a fashion. His first salvo was an article in the *Daily Mail* in which Churchill described the Indian Raj as "upon the whole the finest achievement of our history."[14]

The Indian continent, he continued, was "rescued from ages of barbarism, internecine war, and tyranny" and "prey to fierce racial and religious dissentions and the withdrawal of British protection would mean the resumption of medieval ways." Branding the very notion of home rule for India as "fantastic," Churchill went on to remind his readers that England "had a responsibility" for the welfare of the country's 350 million—60 million of whom were Untouchables who lived in the utmost squalor.[15]

Churchill called Gandhi, whom he had once met, "a half-naked fakir," and in speeches throughout England in 1931 he reiterated his warning of a bloodbath in India if the British pulled out. Baldwin, who liked Churchill personally, reached out to make him stop, but Churchill seemed to redouble his efforts, creating a breach that could not be healed.

In the summer of the same year, the Labour government collapsed and formed a coalition with the Tories and Stanley Baldwin. But by now there was no room for Churchill in the government, and the feeling was mutual. Never a "team player," he told his son Randolph he wanted no part of a party that was trying to give up India. Churchill maintained his "safe seat" in Essex, but retired to Chartwell to paint, build, enjoy his family, and chase butterflies.[16]

Always in need of money, at the end of 1931 Churchill and Clementine sailed to the United States where he was to write and give lectures—a trip that almost became the end of him. On December 12, on his way to a dinner at Bernard Baruch's, he was crossing Fifth Avenue and momentarily forgot that Americans drive on the right side of the road. He failed to look to the right and was immediately struck hard by a car that dragged him fifty feet and left him in a heap in the cold street. A crowd gathered. Although bleeding heavily from a scalp wound that cut to the bone, Churchill reassured the distraught driver of the car that it was not his fault, that he had failed to look before crossing. An inch or so either way and the accident could easily have been fatal.

A taxi took him to nearby Lenox Hill Hospital, where the staff refused to admit him without proof of payment. Clementine was phoned, and she rushed in with a New York detective who had been assigned to protect Churchill. In addition to the scalp gash, he was cut badly on both thighs and had two broken ribs that were especially painful. Ever a man to turn a buck, as soon as he was able Churchill propped himself up in bed and began scribbling "My New York Misadventure," which ran on the front page of the *Daily Mail* and garnered him the equivalent of nearly $50,000 in today's money.[17]

Outwardly Churchill tried to appear as if the ordeal of the accident was over. But from Clementine, his friends knew otherwise. Brendan Bracken took up a collection to buy him a car, which he thought might cheer Winston up. They got him a sleek, expensive Daimler. Some were waiting at the rail station when he disembarked from the train singing "For He's a Jolly Good Fellow." Churchill smiled but his eyes filled with tears. He bowed his head and sobbed.[18]

CHURCHILL NOW WAS ENTERING what has been popularly described as his wilderness years: the near decade when he continued to be an elected member of Parliament but remained out of government office, even when

TOP LEFT: Sir Randolph Churchill, in line to become the British prime minister, disgraced himself and lost the chance, prompting young Winston to go into politics. BOTTOM LEFT: Winston Churchill's mother, Jennie Jerome, of a wealthy American family, was one of England's great beauties and used her considerable charms to prod powerful men into helping her son. ABOVE RIGHT: Lieutenant Winston Churchill, a champion polo player with his regiment in India, distinguished himself in his first battle.

LEFT: Franklin Roosevelt's mother, a member of the prominent Delano family, devoted herself to her son's career and personal life after the early death of her husband. RIGHT: Roosevelt's father, James, shown here with Franklin (about two), was a wealthy industrialist whose health seriously declined in Franklin's youth.

Franklin as a senior at Groton School, where "waterboarding"
was among the prescribed punishments for misbehavior

TOP LEFT: Joseph Stalin as an Orthodox Catholic seminary student in 1894
BOTTOM LEFT: A remarkably handsome police mug shot of Stalin, who was frequently
arrested for Communist activities ABOVE RIGHT: Stalin's mother, Ekaterina, who
endured the brutish, drunken behavior of Stalin's father until he deserted her when
her son was fourteen. Stalin ostracized her when he became the Soviet premier.

LEFT: Winston Churchill (right) walks with future prime minster David Lloyd George on Budget Day, 1910. RIGHT: Churchill, first lord of the Admiralty, with Admiral Jacky Fisher, first sea lord, who stabbed Churchill in the back over the Gallipoli operation

LEFT: At his family home at Campobello, Roosevelt sits with Eleanor in August 1904, three months before their engagement. ABOVE: Lucy Mercer (circa 1915), who became Roosevelt's mistress and eventually the love of his life

TOP LEFT: Leon Trotsky, a prominent Communist who soon became Joseph Stalin's rival
BOTTOM LEFT: Russian revolutionary Vladimir Lenin, who became the father
of communism in the Soviet Union ABOVE RIGHT: Stalin wears his civil war uniform
as a member of the Revolutionary Military Council of the Republic in 1919.

TOP: In the garden of Stalin's dacha, Svetlana Stalin sits on the lap
of the murderous Lavrenty Beria, who headed the NKVD—the Soviet
secret police—while Stalin works at a table in the background.
BOTTOM: Stalin carries daughter Svetlana in the mid-1930s.

the Tories came back to power. It gave him more time to write, of course, and his productivity was astonishing. He finished the three-volume history of his great ancestor the Duke of Marlborough, as well as contracting to write his *History of the English-Speaking Peoples,* for which he received an advance from the publisher Cassell of nearly $1 million in today's money. He also wrote numerous popular histories on subjects great and small (usually ghostwritten by his secretary for a set percentage fee) as well as scores of magazine and newspaper articles. He became, in fact, one of the most popular writers in England.

Churchill lived at Chartwell with his painting and bricklaying, his farm animals and gardens. He even built a heated swimming pool. He described his life there as idyllic, "with my happy family around me . . . at peace within my habitation." It might well have been so, especially in retrospect (these reflections were written twenty-five years later). But it was also a period of dark angst for a man so accustomed to having power. According to the biographer Roy Jenkins, there was "a sense of political impotence, of his talents wasted, of time passing him by." There also may have been periods of the "black dog," or depression, and of drinking too much.[19]

During his visits to Parliament in this period, Churchill never desisted in his rants against the government promising India autonomy, until 1935, when the House at last passed an India home rule bill. By then he had taken up a new subject that was fraught with far more danger and controversy: the rise of Adolf Hitler and the Nazis and the rearming of Germany.

In 1925, when Churchill was in the midst of writing his multivolume history of World War I, *The World Crisis,* there appeared in print a book by a failed thirty-six-year-old Austrian artist and former corporal in the defeated German army: Adolf Hitler. Written while he was in jail for trying to overthrow the democratic government, *Mein Kampf* was Hitler's blueprint for the Nazi takeover of Germany and the restoration of its rightful place in the world order. Within a few years the book would be a staple in nearly every German home.

While the Allied-sanctioned Weimar government tried to break Germany out of its economic depression, astronomical monetary inflation, and dangerous Communist agitation, Hitler began organizing his Brown Shirt military order along the lines of Mussolini's Fascist Black Shirts, which had taken over Italy. Hitler's speeches were filled with vitriol for the Allies, who had defeated the Germans, with special attention given to Germany's Jews who, according to Hitler, were either behind the "sabotage" of the German army in 1918 or behind the Communists—or both.

As they gained seats each year in the Reichstag, Germany's parliament, the Nazis were likewise gaining strength in membership and secretly building a large military force in direct violation of the Treaty of Versailles. Hitler seized power in 1933, vowing to overturn the humiliating treaty. His first overt act was to march an armed force into the Rhineland between France and Germany, which had been demilitarized under the treaty.

The Allies did nothing, prompting Churchill to warn the House of Commons: "Five years ago, all felt safe; five years ago all were looking forward to peace . . . Five years ago to talk of war would have been regarded not only as a folly and a crime, but almost as a sign of lunacy."[20]

It was too true. Not just in England, but in the lands of *all* the Allies, a spirit of profound exhaustion had languished with respect to the idea of another war. The prestigious Oxford Union debating society voted 275 to 153 a motion "that this House declines under any circumstances to fight for King or Country."

The verdict was not surprising. By this point, a rash of British war poets, novelists, and memoirists had depicted the squalor of the trenches and the horrors of the war so vividly that it stamped a lasting impression not only on their contemporaries but upon an entirely new generation. They read and recoiled from the poetry of British army lieutenant Siegfried Sassoon:

> *The rank and stench of those bodies haunts me still*
> *And I remember things I'd best forget.*

Or Lieutenant Edmund Blunden:

> *The shell struck right in the doorway . . .*
> *There were six men in that doorway.*

Or Lieutenant Wilfred Owen:

> *But someone still was yelling out and stumbling*
> *and floundering around like a man in fire or lime.*

Or the anonymous barracks ditty, "The Bells of Hell":

> *The bells of hell go ting-a-ling-a-ling*
> *For you, but not for me.*

Or Wilfred Owen again:

> *If you could hear, at every jolt, the blood*
> *Come gargling from the froth-corrupted lungs, . . .*
> *My friend, you would not tell with such high jest*
> *To Children ardent for some desperate glory*
> *That old lie:* Dulce et decorum est
> Pro patria mori.*

They had read Robert Graves's tales of dead men shot to rags hanging and rotting in the barbed wire, and of the utter futility of war in the German author Erich Maria Remarque's celebrated *All Quiet on the Western Front.* Such impressions were nearly universal from the writers who had served in the war, and they completely overwhelmed naive notions of patriotism and glory as penned by young Lieutenant Rupert Brooke, who had served with Churchill's navy battalion at the very beginning of the war.

---

* "It is sweet and good to die for your country." Published posthumously.

Patriotism, international outrage, even self-preservation were no longer ideals held by a majority of British citizens in the years following World War I; these sentiments influenced even the military budgets of the House of Commons. Parliament was especially stingy, given the horrid economics of the Great Depression years. But Churchill sought to moderate what was understandable with what had become an alarming new reality: a vengeful and aggressive Hitler, backed by a quickly rearming Nazi-run Germany, had become a world threat.

He sounded the warning in speech after speech. Intelligence indicated in 1933 that Britain was slipping dangerously behind Germany in airpower. Churchill may have overplayed his hand when he described London as "the greatest target in the world: a kind of tremendous, fat, valuable cow, tied up to attract the beast of prey." He predicted that in a prolonged bombing attack, great parts of the city would be destroyed, and that thirty thousand to forty thousand people would be killed or wounded. He wasn't far off the mark. But he was not only making people nervous; he was making them angry. His enemies called it "scaremongering."[21]

Baldwin himself, the prime minister, thusly regaled a colleague of Churchill's: "When Winston was born, lots of fairies swooped down on his cradle bearing great gifts—imagination, eloquence, industry, ability—and then came a fairy who said, 'No one person has the right to so many gifts,' and gave him such a shake and a twist that he was denied judgment and wisdom. And that is why while we delight to listen to him in this House, we do not take his advice."[22]

Churchill kept giving advice anyway—especially after Hitler felt strong enough to take over Austria, which was expressly forbidden by the Treaty of Versailles, in 1938. Again, the Allied nations did nothing. Hitler obtained six Austrian infantry divisions on his side. The Nazis then demanded that all German-speaking countries be combined in a union, or Anschluss, with Germany. Because Czechoslovakia's Sudetenland had many German speakers its turn came next.

Churchill continued his eloquent harangues, hoping to kindle a spark in the cloak of apathy that lay across Britain like a London fog. Despite his efforts, the people remained war-weary, depression-weary, and warped in a kind of lethargy as colonial possessions began to agitate for their freedom and the Exchequer struggled to refinance its obligations and pay its debts. Under such circumstances the very idea of another war with Germany was so dreadful as to be unspeakable—even with the likes of Winston Churchill's oratory. And so the world turned.

IN 1937 STANLEY BALDWIN HAD RETIRED. Neville Chamberlain, with his stiff wing tie, bowler hat, and bumbershoot, took his place. Hitler had made threatening moves against Czechoslovakia, citing the German-speaking population; leaders from England and France went to Munich for a conference with Hitler to see what could be done. In the end, there was nothing. Hitler promised it would be the end of his aggression in Europe, Chamberlain swallowed it, and he returned famously waving a piece of paper for reporters at the airport and proclaiming there would be "peace in our time."

Churchill was furious, and he gave perhaps his best speech yet, in which, among other things, he asserted that "Britain has now sustained an unmitigated defeat." He predicted that the Germans would soon swallow up the rest of the country: "Czechoslovakia now recedes into the darkness . . . All the countries of Central and Eastern Europe will make the best terms they can with the triumphant Nazi power." And once they had been absorbed, "Hitler would begin to look westward."

It all played out just as Churchill had predicted. On March 15, 1939, Hitler marched into Prague and took over the country, with its forty well-equipped infantry divisions and the giant Skoda armaments works.

With his dire warnings now seeming prophetic, Churchill was back in favor at home. But events abroad were now moving swiftly to a conclusion. Mussolini, declaring that democracy was dead, invaded and took Albania; Hitler began to threaten Poland, which Britain and France had guaranteed against German aggression. Britain ineffectually tried to enlist the Soviets in an alliance against Germany. But Hitler got there first with the German-Soviet nonaggression pact, which also provided for the Nazis and the Communists to divide up Poland between themselves.

On September 1, 1939, Hitler invaded Poland, and two days later Great Britain and France declared war on Germany. In just over a month, the Nazis and the Communists gobbled up Poland. There now ensued a period of inactivity known by journalists as the Phony War, while Hitler and Stalin digested their Polish prey.

Britain was now not only alarmed, it was at war. Chamberlain took Churchill into the government, giving him back his old job as first lord of the Admiralty. He was now nearly sixty-five years old, and he looked it. He had put on weight and gone bald; years of drinking and smoking cigars had taken their toll. But he flew into the Admiralty with almost supernatural energy that continued, electrifying and unabated, all through the next most difficult years of his life.

CHAPTER SEVEN

By 1921 Stalin was rapidly assuming control over the Communist Party in Russia as Lenin's health began to deteriorate. Problems began three years prior, in the summer of 1918, when Lenin was leaving a factory in Moscow, and a young woman stepped up with a Browning pistol and fired three shots at him. One missed, but the other two knocked him to the ground, one bullet lodging in his neck and the other in his collarbone.* Lenin refused to go to a hospital for fear of more assassins, so he was taken instead to the Kremlin, where doctors decided it would be too dangerous to remove the bullets. They remained in his body the rest of his life.

In May 1922 the fifty-two-year-old Lenin suffered a major stroke that left him partially paralyzed and his speech distorted. He slowly managed to overcome these afflictions but remained mostly invalided and isolated, while Stalin, now forty-three, consolidated power in his new position as general secretary of the new regime.

Soviet politics in those times involved a web of intrigue not seen since the bewildering days of the Borgias. One of Stalin's protégés tried to explain why it was so easy for members of the party to change their views, or to betray each other. "For the party's sake," he said, "you must . . . force yourself to believe that white is black." All of this nefarious behavior had begun to

---

* She was Fanya (Fanny) Kaplan, a disgruntled twenty-eight-year-old Jewish member of a rival socialist group. Four days later, after interrogation by the Cheka, she was executed.

instill in Stalin's peasant mind a healthy kind of paranoia. He always saw himself as a survivor, but never by accident. There were always enemies to be dealt with.[1]

As he recovered, Lenin began to fear that Stalin was setting himself up to replace him, and the leader's feelings for his trusted protégé began to change. He confided to his wife that Stalin was "not intelligent," and that, being a Georgian, he was "Asiatic," a pejorative. Lenin also had begun to have political disagreements with Stalin, and his first notions of removing him from power began to take shape.[2]

Stalin continued maneuvering against anyone he considered competition. He became aware that Lenin distrusted him, but he persisted in his subservient manners, waiting for the other shoe to drop. It did, soon enough, in the autumn of 1922, when Lenin quietly embraced Stalin's archenemy Leon Trotsky as the future leader of the Soviet Union. Stalin had been secretly informed of this union, however, and was thoroughly alarmed. Knowing he could not stand up to a Lenin-Trotsky combination, Stalin took measures to head it off.

Then Lenin's health took a turn for the worse, and his doctors demanded complete rest. Stalin seized on this diagnosis to seal Lenin off forever. Just before Christmas of 1922, he carried a resolution to the Bolshevik Central Committee assuming "personal responsibility for the isolation of Comrade Lenin." There would be no more meetings. Friends and family were forbidden to discuss politics with the leader. Stalin took personal authority over correspondence to and from Lenin, who remained uninformed of this act of treachery.[3]

The plan did not work out as Stalin had hoped. Lenin's wife allowed her husband a congratulatory phone call to Trotsky, whom he wished to thank for a vote in the Central Committee that he had championed: government control of all international trade. When Stalin learned of it he was furious and made a serious mistake—he personally berated Mrs. Lenin, who immediately ran to her husband in tears. An angry Lenin composed a letter to Stalin breaking off all relations.

Cooler heads prevailed, including, interestingly, that of Trotsky. When informed of the situation, Trotsky slyly—and for his own inscrutable reasons—informed one of Stalin's allies that he was "against liquidating Stalin" but insisted that Stalin be made to write a strong letter of apology to Mrs. Lenin, which of course, recognizing his mistake, Stalin did.

Now Lenin wrote another letter, a part of his last will and testament, which was to be read to the Soviet Congress after his death. In it, he assessed both Stalin and Trotsky vis-à-vis their fitness to lead the Soviet Union. Lenin stated that, in his opinion, Trotsky was "the ablest person" on the Central Committee but was boastful and vain. Stalin, on the other hand, "had concentrated immense power in his own hands, and I am not sure that he will always succeed in using that power with the requisite caution."[4] This was a serious indictment indeed, considering the horrors that Lenin's own great power had visited upon the Russian people in recent years.

Lenin dragged on, living now in a rehabilitative medical facility away from Moscow and deteriorating by the month. In March 1923 another stroke rendered him unable to read, write, or speak, which came as a great relief to Stalin. But then, miraculously, throughout the summer, Lenin began to improve; he was able to walk again and his speech came back. In October he was well enough to visit Moscow. This terrified Stalin, who feared he would damn him in a speech before the General Assembly.

But Lenin did not make a speech anywhere. Once in Moscow, he paid a visit to several offices, then merely asked to be driven around the city, returning afterward to his quarters in the countryside. There, he went into convulsions and began to die. The end came January 21, 1924; he was fifty-three years old. As luck would have it (for Stalin, anyway), Trotsky was out of town, recovering by the Black Sea from a serious bout with influenza.

This left Stalin, general secretary of the Assembly, to make the funeral arrangements for the man all good Communists considered a god. Stalin decided to have a glass-front sarcophagus built, in which Lenin's embalmed body in its casket could be viewed in the Kremlin's Hall of Columns, then rest in perpetuity in a glassed-in mausoleum in Red Square—sacred, monumental, imperishable.

In Communism, as envisioned by Karl Marx, all men were to be equal. "From each according to his ability. To each according to his needs," is an oft-used Marxian slogan. But some men were more equal than others, it was quickly learned, and Joseph Stalin was the most equal of them all. Despite the pleas from Lenin's widow, Stalin suppressed her husband's last will and testament, in which he had warned that Stalin might not use his power "with requisite caution." Coming as it did from the official god of the party, this document could have been the kiss of death for Stalin had it been read openly before the Central Committee. So Stalin simply ordered it sealed and stashed away.

The cause of Lenin's death, like everything else in the Soviet Union, was made a state secret, although it was put out at the time that he had died of arteriosclerosis. This gave rise to a wave of speculation, including rumors of his being poisoned by Stalin, for no sooner had Lenin paid a visit to Moscow than he went into convulsions and died. Stalin, certainly, had his reasons—and, as one of the more modern Russian historians pointed out, he was "absolutely ruthless." Others (physicians among them) speculated that Lenin was a victim of lead poisoning from the two bullets that remained in his body, the theory being that tiny particles had leached out into his system and killed him. But the most likely cause of Lenin's death was a massive cerebral hemorrhage. This was the conclusion of a consortium of doctors in the 1990s. He had already had several strokes, and his father had died young of a brain hemorrhage. In any case, the Communist world was convulsed in grief.[5]

Stalin envisioned that all good Russians would make the pilgrimage one day, much like the hajj to Mecca made by Muslims, to gaze on Lenin's countenance in his glassed-in tomb.* He ordered biochemistry professors from a Moscow university to perform the embalming operation, one that would last forever.† Stalin would arrange a grand, fine send-off for the Father of Communism, the man who had created their brave new world.

---

* Lenin's wife visited the tomb frequently over the years, once remarking plaintively to a friend, "I am getting old, but he is just the same."

† Lenin's remains have lasted nearly a century and still look remarkably good, according to all accounts. In the 1930s, responding to an American newspaper's assertion that the figure in Lenin's casket was actually a wax doll, Stalin had the glass sarcophagus opened and the body of the leader manipulated in such a way as to show it really was him.

Stalin himself would make the final oratory, and the best thing about it was that Leon Trotsky wouldn't be there. Trotsky had been preparing to take his rightful place in the funeral ceremony—Moscow was a two-day train ride—when a telegram arrived:

"The funeral takes place on Saturday. You cannot get here on time. The Politburo thinks that the state of your health makes it essential that you go to Sukhumi. —Stalin."[6]

Lenin's funeral, in fact, wasn't held until Sunday, but now the big show would all belong to the general secretary, Joseph V. Stalin.

FOR THE NEXT FOUR YEARS, Stalin and Trotsky conducted a protracted antler dance of insults private and public, published in various Communist press organs, memorandums, or in speeches made to Communist associations. Trotsky often sided with the Mensheviks. He criticized Stalin and the Bolsheviks for not democratizing the power in the government, running it instead like a dictatorship. Another difficulty posited by Trotsky—who advocated a Communist world revolution—was that if such a thing ever took place, the Russian Soviet would in likelihood be diminished by the larger entity. For all his blather about pure international Marxism, Stalin was content with holding absolute concentrated power over the huge expanse of Russia. That was hard enough to control, and he didn't want to have to report to any greater authority.

Trotsky dominated the debate in such Communist organs as *Pravda*. But behind the scenes Stalin continued to concentrate his power, eliminating any prospective rivals and promoting toadies until it was he above all others who could call the tune in the Secretariat—which, in turn, controlled the Communist Party. Slowly, the vibrant Trotsky was squeezed out.

In 1926 Stalin had Trotsky removed as chairman of the Military Council, the highest Red Army post in the Soviet government. On the heels of this action came a merciless purge of Trotskyites in the army. At the Fifteenth Party Congress, Stalin refused to let him speak, so Trotsky set up an underground press and handed out broadsheets of his remarks to his fellow

Communists as they exited the meetings. Shortly afterward, Trotsky was expelled from the Central Committee.

In 1927, Stalin came into the cutting room where the brilliant Russian director Sergei Eisenstein was finishing his renowned film of the Russian Revolution, *October: Ten Days That Shook the World*. Stalin demanded to know if Trotsky was in the picture. When the answer was yes, Stalin "said categorically that the picture must not be shown with Trotsky in it." And out Trotsky went.[7]

Trotsky, however, continued writing and speaking out against what he considered to be Stalin's perversions of Socialism—but he overplayed his hand. In 1928, he found himself expelled from the Communist Party. Instead of relenting and begging forgiveness, he did the opposite and was publicly banished to Kazakhstan, a remote Asiatic province near Mongolia almost two thousand miles from Moscow. Stalin's men came to Trotsky's apartment in the Kremlin and carried him, kicking and screaming, to the train station. The journalist Karl Radek, who was awaiting his own train to Siberian exile, remarked pithily upon Trotsky's awkward arrival: "Moses led the Jews out of Egypt. Stalin led them out of the Politburo."[8]

Trotsky stayed in Kazakhstan only six months, but even there he coughed up a cascade of anti-Stalinist literature. At that point, the Soviet leader could have simply had him killed. But a greater plan was turning in Stalin's paranoiac mind. He had already begun envisioning a monstrous scheme to seal the fate of vast numbers of perceived enemies when the time came, and Trotsky was shaping up to be the perfect foil.

Stalin felt confident that Trotsky would never cease publishing his contrarian literature, nor making heretical speeches. After all, now that Lenin was gone, Trotsky was the most visible revolutionary in the world. So instead of killing him Stalin had Trotsky permanently banished from the Soviet Union and sent him abroad. In good time, Stalin could accuse Trotsky of counterrevolutionary activity, then link his own enemies to Trotsky whenever it was convenient and put them on trial for treason. From now on, Leon Trotsky would be bait for one of the most bloodthirsty episodes in Russia's Communist history.

As it turned out, moving Russia and its far-flung empire from a demand economy to a command economy proved to be a stupendous task. The majority of Russians were peasants—basically slaves until 1861, when they were freed by Czar Alexander II. Now, they were mostly subsistence farmers on small plots of state land, or land leased from noble landlords. Under communism, the idea was to place them in enormous "collectives," or communes, in order to streamline agricultural production. Their produce, mostly grains and corn, would belong to the state, which would distribute much of it to bakers in Moscow and other cities, sell most of the rest abroad for cash, and then remit some amount back to the peasants for their own use.

There was much resistance to this from the peasants, especially from the kulak class, which had risen above the peasant class so as to have more than one cow, or a field of goats, or a hired hand. These, Stalin found, were the real troublemakers, and he lit upon a simple but highly consequential solution: to "break [the kulaks'] resistance, to liquidate them as a class, and to replace kulak production with production from collectives and state farms."[9]

This simple-sounding order resulted in the horrific deaths of as many as 7 million Russian kulaks between late 1929 and 1932. The repulsive Cheka had been replaced by an organization known as the OGPU, which was supposed to be an improvement, and *was,* in its own peculiar way: it was even *more* thuggish and murderous. Kulaks were executed by the hundreds of thousands. Soon the definition of "kulak" began to enlarge into anyone the OGPU thought needed executing. And the OGPU painted with a very large brush.

Countless millions more peasants were hauled off into giant concentration camps, where many were worked to death in menial labor jobs, toiling with picks and shovels to build great dams and other hydroelectric projects, as well as roads, canals,* railroads, government buildings, city housing, and

---

* It has been estimated that at least one-third of the one hundred thousand workers digging the White Sea Canal died on the job.

an endless host of state-run factories turning out everything from tools and tractors to trolleys and tanks.

All of this upheaval was heartbreaking. A typical peasant house was little more than a couple of rooms to keep out the cold and a few possessions for eating, sitting, and sleeping. But a home, even one such as this, was a man's castle, and the kulaks fiercely resisted the government's bulldozing their hovels and moving them into the vast collective housing from which they were to toil away. A mere sixty years earlier, when they had been serfs, they'd at least often had a benevolent master landowner who looked after them—if for no reason other than to keep them productive and reasonably happy. But now, some 60 million peasants had suddenly become slaves of the state: a faceless, uncaring behemoth.

In the meantime, as it became apparent that Moscow needed the resources and manpower of all other countries under its control, Stalin focused his attention on establishing the International Communist Party in nations throughout the world. For a while, communism became surprisingly popular in England—not so much among the working classes, as had been anticipated by Marx, but in the upper classes. Many of those who attended such elite institutions as Eton and Harrow, Oxford and Cambridge were drawn to Soviet communism. (During World War II, a number of top British agents and foreign service officers selected from the so-called public schools and universities turned out to be Soviet spies.) The Communist Party was well established in France. It thrived in Germany between the wars until Hitler crushed it. Communism became so entrenched in Spain that a civil war was fought over it. The party sprang up in South and Central America—and, of course, in the United States as well.

The Communist Party USA was established in 1919, following the collapse of the old American Socialist Party. Immediately, it began to be identified with workers' movements and unionization. Anarchists and radical leftists gravitated to it; at one point, it was said to contain two hundred thousand members. But over the next two decades interest seemed to sag, at least among the working classes. Adherence to the Soviet line was seen by most Americans as "foreign," and "un-American," although some intellectuals, academics, writers, and theatrical people still subscribed to its ideology.

In 1929 a Lithuanian-born American founder of the Communist Party USA, Jay Lovestone (born Jacob Liebstein), traveled to Moscow, where he had the temerity to inform Joseph Stalin that because of something he termed "American exceptionalism," organizing a large Communist movement in the United States would be impossible. Stalin reacted with a temper tantrum during which he excoriated this "heresy of American exceptionalism" and threw Lovestone out of the party.*[10]

In the mid-1930s, things began to get out of hand. Word got back to Stalin of the extreme bloodshed and chaos his collectivism order had caused—so he simply denied it. Writing in *Pravda* of the "dizzying success" of collectivization, Stalin explained that any excesses were the fault of overzealous subordinates, adding that, "One cannot implant collectives by violence; that would be stupid and reactionary." In the meantime, hearing of continued peasant resistance to collectivization in the face of a poor crop year, Stalin hit upon a novel solution: to simply withhold vast amounts of the peasants' own harvest that was languishing in the state's grain elevators until they saw the error of their ways. This resulted in the great famine beginning in 1931, in which another approximately 10 million peasants perished while lurid reports of cannibalism leaked out.[11]

Around that same time, Stalin received two famous visitors in the form of the Irish playwright George Bernard Shaw and a companion, Lady Astor, an American-born member of Parliament. Shaw, a lifelong socialist, decided that the diminutive Stalin looked "like a cross between the Pope and a field-marshal," while Lady Astor, a staunch antisocialist, demanded of the Russian dictator, "How long are you going to go on killing people?" Stalin appalled the outspoken aristocrat by coolly replying that it would go on "for as long as necessary."[12]

Always curious about "the competition," Stalin had asked Lady Astor about the political situation in England. She replied that "[Neville] Chamberlain is the coming man." When Stalin asked, "'What about Churchill? [this was after the India debacle] her eyes widened. 'Churchill?' she said. She gave a scornful little laugh and replied. 'Oh, he's finished.'"[13]

---

* This appears to be the first mention of the expression "American exceptionalism."

As it was with the collectives, so it went with Stalin's vaunted "five-year plans." Stalin had told the world that the Soviet Union would revert from an agrarian society to an industrialized nation by the end of the 1930s. These were vague promises without many benchmarks and much room for "walking back." But indeed, the Communists' effort to industrialize the country was impressive. The rationale for all the deaths and suffering associated with this reverted directly to Marx's original manifesto that urged brutal pragmatism.

Yet there was also tremendous waste associated with these projects. The Russians had little or no experience constructing modern factories and infrastructure and were highly distrustful of any outsiders who did. Nor had Russian workers yet adapted to operating modern machinery, so there was a great deal of costly trial and error. The logic of Soviet communism imposed catch-22 conflicts. If workers reported that a project was not going well or efficiently, they were subject to being branded troublemakers or counterrevolutionaries. On the other hand, if they did not report such difficulties, they could be accused of treason! It was maddening.

Stalin personally justified his ruthlessness this way: "We are fifty or a hundred years behind the advanced countries. We must make good this distance in ten years. Either that, or they will crush us."[14]

★★★★★

MANY TEACHERS, SCIENTISTS, authors, artists, and other "intellectuals" had been murdered during the terrors of the 1920s and '30s or banished to forced labor camps. But education in the Soviet Union was given primacy in Stalin's Russia. At the time of the 1917 October Revolution, fewer than 30 percent of the population was literate. By the mid-1930s, on Stalin's orders, that figure was improved to almost 90 percent. But the nature of education had vastly changed. In fact, it was somewhere between training and indoctrination. Stalin's opinion on the subject boiled down to this: "Education is a dangerous weapon, whose effects depend on who holds it in his hands, and at whom it is aimed."[15]

Math and science were stressed above all else in Stalin's Russia, as engineers would be highly necessary for the industrialization program. Also, doctors would be needed, so medicine was stressed. Reading was taught to the extent that it complemented the latter. Subjects such as history, literature, philosophy, and the social sciences were treated as suspect and mostly closed out. In their place, a new curriculum was introduced, watched closely by the secret police. The overarching themes of these new subjects were dressed in Communist ideology and infected with so many falsified facts and statistics as to be ludicrous to modern Western scholars.

The goal of Stalin's education establishment was to turn out as many right-minded communists as possible, who would serve the state with unquestioning loyalty. Those who fell by the wayside through lack of intelligence, behavioral problems, or mental issues were sent to the labor camps. Teachers lived in constant fear of being exiled or worse. The entire enterprise was conducted with a quivering, wearying tension.[16]

This did not apply, however, to Stalin's children, of whom there were now three: two boys and a girl. They were tutored privately. Most Russians did not even know that Stalin had children, let alone a wife. Yet in 1921 Stalin's second wife, Nadya, had given birth to their son Vasily, who was joined in the Stalin's Kremlin household by Yakov, Stalin's fourteen-year-old son by his first wife, Kato, who had died when the boy was only nine months old.

At first Stalin seemed to warm to the boys, taking them in the summers to his dacha, a lavish vacation home outside the city near the Moskva River (which the Communists had expropriated from a rich bourgeois industrialist). It was a pastoral spot in Chekhovian country that was once home to the old imperial gentry. There, Stalin was frequently joined by his old friend and political ally the *Pravda* editor Nikolai Bukharin, who often arrived with his tame gray fox on a leash and his artist's box of canvases and paintbrushes. They drank and sang late into the night.

But as the boys grew older Stalin was generally harsh and distant, demanding of them stern rigors because they were his sons and were expected to set a disciplined example for the country. Neither boy was capable of it, and both came to bad ends as we shall see.

Then, in 1926, Nadya presented Stalin with a daughter, whom they named Svetlana. She became the apple of her father's eye. He took her everywhere with him and carried her in his arms or on his shoulders, even when she was a teenager. Photographs show her with many of the most famous Communists of the day—and some of the most dangerous—in garden settings where Stalin often held informal meetings. Svetlana came to a better end than her brothers, but she had to renounce and repudiate her upbringing to do it.

Nadya's suicide has been the subject of much speculation. What is known is that schizophrenia ran in her family, and she had terrifying mood swings. She wanted to be in the party and contribute to the cause but Stalin—who was raised in the old way, in which women were subservient, silent, and obedient—was opposed. Nadya covertly enrolled in a college to learn, for some reason, fiber chemistry. There, other students talked in hushed tones of the current state terror, of executions and mass murders and people being herded into forced labor camps. When she told Stalin of this he dismissed it, and a rancor ensued. They argued more as time passed. After one particularly unpleasant quarrel in November 1932, Nadya left a dinner party and returned to the apartment in the Kremlin, where she shot herself fatally in the head with a British Walther revolver.

Her death affected Stalin intensely, and he brooded in between fits of rage. He sought reasons where there was little evidence. She had been reading a book that might have set her mind off; he blamed three of her friends for somehow being involved in the suicide. (And, indeed, sixteen years later he had them all arrested and imprisoned for "knowing too much about the death of Stalin's wife.")[17]

From then on, various tutors, companions, and security personnel provided by the state supervised the children. One can surmise that their upbringing was not the easiest or the most fulfilling.

Nadya suspected Stalin of having dalliances with other women—particularly in his office, a hundred yards across Red Square, from which he often did not get home until late at night. It was rumored that Stalin had affairs with various women, from simple peasant workers to former aristocrats, and that in some cases he even married them, which would make him a bigamist. One engaging report came from the noted British travel writer Rosita Forbes, who recounted in her memoirs of interviewing one of "Stalin's wives," whom she described as a plain factory worker in a cramped, dilapidated cottage in Moscow. "She was pale with hair falling around her neck" amid a "perpetual smell of cabbage soup," a "glaring electric bulb hanging by dusty wires," and a "pathetic electric saucepan in which scraps of meals were cooked on the living room table."[18]

Many of these accounts are interesting, but there's no solid proof of any of it. Communists were not required to obtain marriage licenses, so there are few records on file for proof. There was other gossip, but little hard evidence, because Stalin wrote his own biography—and indeed the entire history of the Soviet Union—the way he wanted it to be told, under penalty of death. Others might have had suspicions or even proof but revealed it at their peril. In the end, it's not hard to surmise that Stalin, with all his fearsome power, could have had his way with just about any Russian woman he wanted who valued her life. And he probably did.

WELL INTO THE 1930S STALIN continued to solidify his power until he became unquestionably the ultimate dictator of the Soviet Union. The final triumph over his perceived enemies was embodied in the infamous Moscow Show Trials. In these, thousands of high-ranking Communist intellectuals, and much of the higher officer corps of the Soviet army, were arrested and tortured by the NKVD (which had replaced the OGPU) until they confessed to "crimes against the state." These included such charges as treason, sabotage, conspiracy, terrorism, attempting to overthrow the Soviet state, and plotting to assassinate Stalin. For these crimes, they were publicly tried and sentenced to death or lengthy prison sentences. Stalin's pretext for the show trials was the murder in 1934 of the Leningrad Communist boss Sergey Kirov. Moreover, millions of ordinary Soviet citizens were either killed or imprisoned as Stalin's lust for power and vengeance swept the land.

The trials began in the early 1930s in the shadow of the colossal failures of the first five-year plans. Stalin's paranoia had convinced him that a whole array of people, including many old friends from Bolshevik days, were scheming against him with a mind to bring down not only him but the Soviet state as well. Stalin intended to strike the first blow. A new criminal code had been authorized in the late 1920s with just this in mind, including all manner of provisions for trying and penalizing cases of treason.

In the first trial, more than fifty coal mining engineers were hauled before a tribunal for everything from "sabotage" to "supporting capitalism" to "opposing the state." Prosecution was led by Andrey Vyshinsky, a longtime Communist Party apparatchik who later became the Soviet minister of foreign affairs (equivalent to the U.S. secretary of state). His watchword became "Give me a man and I will find the crime." The accused were subjected to brutal tortures and threats against their families until twenty pleaded guilty. Others who had confessed recanted their confessions; still others refused to confess at all.

Held in the Kremlin's enormous Hall of Columns, or the House of Unions, the trials were witnessed by tens of thousands of Communist Party members (daily attendance was obligatory on a rotating basis). Almost a hundred "carefully chosen" foreign journalists covered the proceedings. Aside from the rigged confessions, testimony included accusations by subordinates of deliberate slowdowns or machinery malfunctions; fake letters and documents were also produced. The verdict was a foregone conclusion. All were found guilty. Eleven were sentenced to death and thirty-eight were sent to prison for up to ten years. Mining engineers were at a premium in Soviet Russia at the time, however, so many of the prison sentences were commuted or greatly reduced.

The purpose of the trial was to put a terrifying fright into everyone involved in the vast industrialization and modernization of the Soviet Union. Based on this standard it was a success.

Other show trials followed. These were merely the prelude for Stalin's Great Purge of 1936–38, which focused on the old Bolshevik Party that had clustered around Lenin and Stalin after the revolution of October 1917 (including Stalin's longtime friend Nikolai Bukharin, who was shot by firing squad and his wife put in a forced labor camp). The principal charge was that they conspired with Trotsky, or Hitler, or right-wing conspirators, or at least *somebody,* to overthrow or betray the Soviet Union. All were tortured and "confessed."

Two old Bolsheviks, Grigory Zinoviev and Lev Kamenev, had also been longtime friends of Stalin who, he perceived, had gone astray. They agreed to confess, provided they received a personal assurance from the entire Politburo that their lives and the lives of their families would be spared. When time came for the personal assurances, who should be their guarantor but Stalin himself, who agreed to their conditions, telling the men, "That goes without saying." Then he had them shot anyway—along with most of their families.[19]

Bukharin, Stalin's old drinking and singing companion who had been with him from the outset, wrote an almost daily series of letters to the boss, some of them nearly incoherent with apprehension and grief. He confessed his sins, claimed to have understood the reason for these mass murder purges—and actually *agreed* with it. Stalin's answer was Sphinx-like. At first nothing. He let him sweat it out over the months until his turn came. In the last days Bukharin asked to be given a fatal dose of morphine in his cell instead of a bullet to the brain. But even this was denied him. He asked to see his wife for a final time. No dice—she had already gone to the labor camps.

Another of those executed was an old Bolshevik named E. S. Goltsman, who was convicted in part on evidence that he had conspired with Trotsky during a speech by the latter at Copenhagen's Hotel Bristol in 1932. A week after Goltsman's execution, a Danish newspaper revealed that the hotel had been demolished in 1917. One is left with the impression that this inconvenient fact, had it been introduced at the trial, wouldn't have mattered a bit.

The trials continued week after week, until nearly all the old Bolsheviks who had formed the party during and after the October Revolution had been liquidated. In fact, of the nearly two thousand delegates to the 1934 party congress, half were arrested and many sent to the firing squad. The military fared no better. Three out of five field marshals were arrested, tried, and executed, as well as thousands of lesser grade officers.

Toward the end, there were so many defendants that the courts could not handle them. Stalin then set up a series of "tribunals" all over Russia: a trio of party men with nearly limitless indictments were restricted by

Stalin's edict that a trial should last no more than ten or fifteen minutes. Tens of thousands were condemned and liquidated through these proceedings, before at last the members of the tribunals were themselves liquidated, as was the head of the secret police, his successor, and, eventually, his successor as well. Stalin even liquidated his own longtime bodyguard. Some people thought, privately, that Stalin intended to kill everyone in Russia.

Almost all arrests were made after midnight. The NKVD would ride in dark cars to the address of the suspect (all addresses in Russia were known to the police). He, or occasionally she, would be arrested before their terrified family and taken away, never to return. Residential buildings in Moscow and other large cities generally featured a single room to live in with a communal bathroom on each floor, where other families could hear the loud knock of the NKVD and the order to "open up."

The next morning, according to the historian Edvard Radzinsky, everyone's eyes would be averted from the unfortunate family while they used the communal bathroom. After a few days they would be moved out, and a short while later a new family would arrive.

After the trials were over Trotsky at long last was singled out for special attention. He had been living with his wife in Mexico City, where he had escaped several botched assassination attempts, until one of Stalin's agents drove an ice ax into his head in 1940.

Stalin's show trials made for some good literature ranging from Arthur Koestler's powerful novel *Darkness at Noon* to George Orwell's satirical *Animal Farm*—but these were Western publications. The arts under Stalin were brutally suppressed, and creative expression was channeled entirely through the state, overseen by commissars, or party operatives, who saw to it that art, literature, and music were strictly directed at the masses to glorify the revolution and its aims. The Western left—British, American, French, etc.—generally approved of the Soviet depredations as necessary evils to achieve the promise of the Socialist dream. But they were mostly unaware of the extent of the killing.

Much of the information disseminated to the American people about Soviet Russia in that era came from Walter Duranty, the *New York Times'* bureau chief in Moscow. Duranty, a one-legged, womanizing, drug-using,

Eton/Harrow-educated Englishman, ignored—apparently deliberately—a majority of the ritual killings and other sufferings during the early Communist terrors and famines. He described the Soviet Union from the early 1920s to the show trial period in the 1930s in mostly glowing terms. Obtaining interviews with Stalin, Duranty painted a rosy picture of the Soviet leader in thirteen stories in the *Times* that ran in 1931. He compared him as "benevolent" in the fashion of Ivan the Terrible, and contended Stalin was bent on helping the millions of Russian peasants out of poverty. The profiles did not turn Stalin into a world figure of the stature of a Churchill or Roosevelt—but they took the edge off of a shadowy character many people saw as an ogre and a monster. There is evidence that Soviet agents provided Duranty with women and luxuries that were rare in the Soviet Union in the 1920s and '30s. Duranty's stock response when another reporter or visitor brought up the wholesale murder associated with the Communist regime was "You can't make an omelet without breaking eggs."[20]

In 1932, Duranty won a Pulitzer Prize, which was said to be a critical factor in President Franklin Roosevelt's decision to recognize the U.S.S.R. diplomatically, which happened the following year.* A few well-established newsmen at the time spoke out against Duranty, but it wasn't until the 1960s that the breadth of his misrepresentations became known. In 1990, in response to a book by S. J. Taylor that exposed Duranty's misreporting, the *Times* itself repudiated him in a piece charging that his articles were "some of the worst reporting to appear in this newspaper."

The elimination through the show trials of so many high-ranking Communists tightened Stalin's iron grip on the country almost to the breaking point—but did give some relief to his ever gnawing paranoia. It also gave some new meaning to the king's soliloquy in Shakespeare's *Henry IV*: "Uneasy is the head that wears a crown."

---

* Roosevelt's diplomats received assurances from Soviet representatives that large U.S. debts run up by the Russian government in World War I would be repaid, and that the Soviets would stop sending agents to infiltrate the U.S. government and stir up trouble. As soon as diplomatic recognition was accomplished these assurances evaporated.

★★★★★

LIFE IN SOVIET RUSSIA in the 1930s was not always bad, other than the vague sense of dread that the state might someday come calling. According to historian Radzinsky, who lived through it, most people went about their business feeling that they were part of a brave new world. In the cities, each street corner contained loudspeakers on a light pole that blared out propaganda and occasional instructions from dawn to dusk. Stalin had decreed that great parks be built around Moscow and elsewhere, where sports—most especially soccer—could be played. The Russians were crazy about soccer, which, like other Europeans, they referred to as "football." Matches drew huge crowds and rivalries were fierce. Sometimes too fierce: if the local club lost, "it became a matter of life and death."

Enormous billboards were everywhere in the cities. On streets, in parks and stadiums, heroic pictures of Stalin and Lenin were accompanied by slogans or advice. "[Stalin] had created a country of collectives. Everything was collective. You worked collectively, lived collectively in a communal apartment, enjoyed your leisure collectively, perhaps on a collective excursion into the countryside. Holidays were collective—Miners' Day, Construction Workers' Day, Metalworkers' Day. Every profession had its own holiday, so that on that one day its collectives could drink and frolic to their hearts' content and—most important—all together."[21]

The people ate simply: borscht—a kind of beet soup—was a staple, as were stews, potatoes, cabbage, and bread. They drank beer and prodigious amounts of vodka, which could be easily distilled from potatoes. Stalin initially concluded in the 1920s that the manufacture of spirits should be phased out because alcohol was an affliction caused by the "duress of capitalism." The theory was that Russians would be so happy under communism they would not need liquor. This did not work out well. Moonshiners were soon setting up shop all over the country, though if apprehended they were apt to be shot as "enemies of the state."[22]

Russian authorities from the reign of Ivan the Terrible had been trying to stamp out moonshining, with little success. Stalin's luck was no better. The moonshiners defied him, and by one estimate there were at least a million stills in operation. As the writer Kevin Kosar puts it, "Stalin himself drank heavily and soon came to realize the folly of his teetotal fantasy." Stalin soon ordered the state to begin producing alcoholic spirits.*[23]

By the late 1930s so many millions of people were in the labor camps that they posed a formidable workforce for major projects. Stalin's great push was for infrastructure: dams, canals, roads, airports. It had come up in a Supreme Council meeting that many of these people were eligible for early release, but Stalin overturned that notion with a summary order. "All will serve the full sentence." He needed this vast slave army for his prodigious projects. Scientists, engineers, intellectuals, writers, musicians, and artists were long suspected to be counterrevolutionaries by nature, and enormous numbers of them had been sent to the labor camps. Stalin realized the waste of talent and so had the scientists and engineers, at least, isolated and given better food, private quarters—even women—to keep them comfortable while plying their various fields of talent for the state. One of Stalin's favorite sayings was "Be happy in your work."

One of the most dire consequences of Stalin's purge of so many talented army officers was that the upstart fascist Adolf Hitler, who was assembling an offensive military machine of prodigious dimensions, became an even greater threat to the depleted Soviet military. Despite the fact that both Soviet communism and German fascism were monolithic political systems thriving on the cult of a dictator, they were natural enemies, abhorrent as a mongoose is to a cobra.

From his lofty perch in the Kremlin, Stalin had kept a wary eye on Hitler as he first reoccupied the demilitarized Sudetenland, then corralled Austria into Greater Germany, and in 1939 went after Czechoslovakia while the British and the French sat by and watched. Stalin understood that Hitler wanted to give the Germans "breathing space" with these expansionist policies, but he didn't want Russia to be a part of it. Just how far Hitler intended to go couldn't be guessed. Poland was certainly on the list, Stalin assumed, as well as the Baltic states, and he could never be sure that Russia wasn't too.

---

* It has been estimated that about 25 percent of Russians drank illegal moonshine, which was about half the cost of government liquor.

One thing for certain was that the German military might—on the ground, in the air, and on the seas—had sprung up with alarming alacrity from utter devastation following the First World War, and Russia couldn't match it. It was clear to Stalin that even if he started a Soviet buildup at once, all indications were that he would never be able to catch up. He knew he needed to buy time, and was wondering how that might come about, when a gift dropped into his lap. The gift was Joachim von Ribbentrop, who arrived in Moscow in August 1939 to conclude a mutual nonaggression pact with the Soviet Union.

The treaty was a godsend for Stalin, the groundwork of which was laid by the Soviet foreign minister Molotov and his German counterpart von Ribbentrop, whose prewar diplomatic machinations would have put Machiavelli to shame. Molotov had actually first sought to secure from Britain and France a mutual defense pact against Germany—but at the time, the two democracies deeply distrusted Stalin and his secretive, authoritarian state.

The Nazi-Soviet pact at first caused understandable confusion among the Communist underworld in Europe and the United States. The party's news organ the *Daily Worker,* for instance, went overnight from trumpeting Nazi Germany as the U.S.S.R.'s archenemy to praising it as Russia's best friend, leaving many Red operatives and fellow travelers collectively shaking their heads.

Still, the treaty met Stalin's purpose. He doubled and redoubled again his armaments output, putting factory after factory under military supervision. Not only that, but a codicil of the pact arranged for the Soviets to divvy up the spoils when the Nazis invaded Poland. Likewise, it allowed the Soviets to gobble up the Baltic states, which they eventually did, one by one. Still, Stalin was less than ready in 1941 when Hitler broke the agreement in a vast surprise attack all across Russia's Western Front. But by then the pact had bought Stalin time that was not just precious but priceless.

Stalin knew that a war between the two totalitarian states was inevitable. He was determined to attack Germany first. Hitler beat him to the punch in June 1941 with Operation Barbarossa. After the fierce campaign in Greece and the Balkans, the Nazis reassembled their horrendous military machine at the Soviet border and began flying reconnaissance missions to discover where the Russian army and air force were located. The Soviets formally complained about these flights, and Hitler's government apologized, explaining that the German pilots sometimes got lost.

Evidence began to pile up that the Germans were planning to attack Russia; Stalin's response was to put his head, ostrich-like, in the sand. Churchill personally warned Stalin when Ultra intercepts indicated unmistakable preparations for an attack. A famous Soviet spy in Japan sent a warning that was likewise ignored. Soviet intelligence submitted report after report that got nowhere. Even German deserters gave the exact time and place. Stalin simply refused to believe that Hitler would attack him while England still hung on in his rear. He convinced himself that the warnings were a capitalist trick to draw the Soviet Union into a war with Hitler.

When the blow fell on June 22—ironically, nearly the same date that Napoleon launched his career-ending march on Moscow in 1812—it fell heavily. Stalin had so imbued his staff and ministers with the idea that the Nazis would not go to war with him that the Soviets responded lamely when reports began coming in of Nazi armies crossing Russian frontiers and Nazi planes bombing Russian cities. Stalin at first instructed his foreign minister Molotov—who had his name on the Nazi peace pact—to get in touch with Ribbentrop. But all the lines to Berlin were down. Finally Marshal Georgy Zhukov, Stalin's closest military adviser, convinced the boss that Russia was indeed under a full-scale attack by the Germans.[24]

Stalin declared that the enemy must be "crushed," then retired to his dacha in a catatonic breakdown for nearly a week before collecting himself. He used the occasion of his recovery to solidify absolute power in the Kremlin, making himself the "Supreme," the one and only leader of the military.

The fighting became furious and vicious as the Russian resistance stiffened. Stalin's orders were to fight to the last man, and many did just that, dying with the name of their leader on their lips. By July 2, eleven days into the blitzkrieg, 2 million Russian soldiers had been killed. Hundreds of thousands of others, including Stalin's son Yakov, a lieutenant in an artillery brigade, were taken prisoner and shipped back to Germany as slave laborers. Since Stalin had sent an edict to all soldiers that surrendering would cause "serious problems" with the prisoner's family, he was at first infuriated to learn of Yakov's capture and was reported to have said, when asked, "I have no son."*[25]

Horrible atrocities were inflicted upon Russian civilians, in particular women, who were raped in countless numbers—often being shot afterward. Homes were looted and burned, pets and farm animals were killed.

The Germans got to within twenty miles of Moscow before Stalin's armies brought them to a halt. Officials had convinced Stalin that the city needed to be evacuated and measures were taken—files and archives burned, extra trains running night and day. The body of Lenin, which had been on display under glass since his death in 1924, was packed up to be moved. But even as Lenin's corpse left on a special train, at the last moment Stalin decided not to go. He defied everyone who pleaded for his safety and went to his office at the Kremlin, where one could hear the rumble of artillery and tanks fighting to the death. Miraculously, the Russian army held on until the snows and freezing weather stopped the Germans cold for a time.

Leningrad (formerly St. Petersburg—home to the czars) was subjected to a German siege that lasted nine hundred days. The electricity and the water for a million people were cut off; toilets would not flush, and the weather turned freezing. People were starved, reduced to a diet of cat meat and cannibalism. Before it was over, an estimated eight hundred thousand civilians would be dead.

An enormous German push was made in the south against Stalingrad (known as Tsaritsyn until 1925), which was key to Caucasus oil and Ukrainian wheat that the Nazis sorely needed. Again, Stalin ordered that his army fight to the last man, and they very nearly did. But then Stalin did what he did so well in the war: he suddenly produced brand-new divisions, one after the

---

* The author could find no direct evidence that Stalin said this, but in fact when the Germans contacted him trying to trade Yakov for a captured Nazi general Stalin refused, saying no lieutenant is worth a captured general. Yakov apparently committed suicide after two years by deliberately walking in a dead zone. A guard shot him in the head.

other, that he'd had training beyond the Urals. They came with the battle-proven T-34 tank that Stalin's factories had been turning out by the thousands after he had moved them entirely beyond the reach of the enemy.

By the winter of 1941 the German blitzkrieg had been halted. Big battles would rage in Russia after 1941, and 1942, and 1943. But the Russian winter had taken its toll on the invaders. So, too, had Russian cooperation with the British. Even though Stalin continued his futile demands for Great Britain to invade France and start the vaunted "second front," the munitions, planes, and other war matériel sent to him by Churchill were invaluable during those first crucial months after the Germans attacked. Soon, a far greater pipeline of supplies would open to Stalin. The Japanese attack on Pearl Harbor at the end of 1941 brought the United States into the war as an official ally.

On June 28, a week after Hitler launched Operation Barbarossa, Roosevelt sent his troubleshooter and right-hand man Harry Hopkins to Moscow with a letter to Stalin. For his part, Hopkins found himself enthralled by the Man of Steel, who looked upon the United States as a misbegotten den of thieves and exploiters ripe for conversion. "No man could forget the picture of the dictator of Russia," Hopkins wrote, "an austere, rugged, determined figure in boots that shown like mirrors, stout baggy trousers, and a snug fitting blouse. He wore no ornament, military or civilian. He's built close to the ground, like a football coach's dream of a tackle. He's about five feet six, about a hundred and ninety pounds. His hands are huge, as hard as his mind. His voice is harsh, but ever under control. What he says has all the accent and inflection his words need."[26]

Hopkins did not mention that Stalin's face was disfigured by smallpox scars, that he had a withered left arm and a clubfoot that caused him to walk in a kind of roll. Perhaps Hopkins didn't want to detract from the heroic figure he had just portrayed, for Stalin was to be an important ally in the coming years.[27]

The official letter was addressed to "My Dear Mr. Stalin" and expressed the "great admiration all of us feel in the United States for the superb bravery displayed by the Russian people in defense of their liberty." It went on to offer all available assistance for war materials.

Stalin did not answer Roosevelt's letter formally but sent his reply through Hopkins with an effusion of flattery, honoring Roosevelt, the government of the United States, and the people of the United States as kindred spirits who shared Russia's hatred of Hitler and Hitlerism. And he said the thing that Churchill had been praying for: "The one thing that could defeat Hitler, and perhaps without firing a shot, would be an announcement that the United States was going to war with Germany." Stalin added that he would "welcome American troops on any part of the Russian front." Finally he told Hopkins he was "confident that the Russian army could withstand the German army," but that they would need American supplies.

He would get them in spades.

CHAPTER EIGHT

From his first days in Washington, Franklin Roosevelt delighted in his position as the assistant secretary of the Navy. It was a post he'd coveted ever since his cousin Theodore used it as a springboard to win the governorship of New York, and from there the presidency: a powerful job with magnificent perks and a lot of press exposure. Josephus Daniels, the secretary, was a hands-off boss and allowed young Franklin, for all intents, to run the department.

Roosevelt faced a colossal task, especially after the First World War broke out in Europe. American ships were dispatched in the far-flung reaches of the world, many of them woefully out of date; some of them harked back to the days of the Spanish-American War. For three tense years the United States stayed haughtily out of the ever consuming conflict. As an adviser on politics and other matters, Roosevelt had brought to Washington the gnome-like newspaperman Louis Howe.

In 1915 a German submarine sank the British ocean liner *Lusitania*, killing 1,198 passengers and crew including 128 U.S. citizens. Many Americans, including Roosevelt's cousin Teddy, felt strongly that the United States should enter the war on the side of the Allies. But President Woodrow Wilson scotched that idea shortly afterward when he gave a speech declaring, "There is such a thing as a man being too proud to fight. There is such a thing as a nation being so right that it does not need to convince others by force that it is right."

This was soothing news to the ears of midwestern farmers' sons, Polish factory workers, Irish laborers, and others who would be called upon to do the fighting; it was also getting on to an election year and Wilson knew it would play well with the isolationist crowd.[1]

Roosevelt was disgusted, and he continued to preach preparedness and expansion of the Navy at every opportunity. But Wilson's noninterventionist policy kept the military in shackles throughout the early years of the war. Since early childhood, Roosevelt had spent a great deal of time in the countries that were now at war; he believed that a German victory would be a disaster for Europe and, ultimately, for the United States.

In the meantime, the Roosevelts had moved into a house on Washington's N Street, near Dupont Circle, owned by Roosevelt's aunt; there were four children by now. As in New York, they were swept up in the city's society world that contained a mix of high-placed administration figures and members of Washington's elite old guard (known as "cave dwellers" for the large homes they owned in Georgetown, as well as their plush apartments along Connecticut Avenue and other fashionable thoroughfares).

Roosevelt soon found himself a member of Washington's swankiest clubs: the Metropolitan for in-town dining and parties, and the Chevy Chase for dress balls and golf. Eleanor felt uncomfortable in this highly charged social atmosphere, which, unlike the society scene in New York, often demanded extensive knowledge of diplomatic and national affairs. She found that she was required to give dinners and other entertainments for a variety of muckety-mucks, including senators, congressmen, ambassadors, and cabinet members.

What with all this, plus four children and another on the way, Eleanor felt she had need of a social secretary. The person she chose for the job was herself a fringe member of Washington's high society: the tall and lovely twenty-two-year-old beauty Lucy Mercer.

Work at the Department of the Navy was not all sweat and toil for Assistant Secretary Roosevelt. With his excellent knowledge of boats and seamanship, he soon made himself comfortable among the high-ranking officers of the fleet, often taking the wheel of a destroyer or other warship in an impressive display of helmsmanship.

Roosevelt in his mid-thirties cut one of the most handsome figures in Washington, walking every morning to his office near the White House. Young women would often stop and stare, eager to get a glimpse of the dashing politician smiling, laughing, or simply looking pleasant. It was said that at dinners, parties, or balls he flirted shamelessly but no one—even his eagle-eyed, wicked-tongued cousin Alice Roosevelt Longworth, who lived around the corner—had suspicions of any impropriety on Franklin's part. His was the ideal marriage: an attractive, attentive wife and a handful of lovely and precocious children, backed by money and power.

But there *was* in fact something very inappropriate going on in Roosevelt's life that was headed toward calamity. He and Lucy Mercer, the young woman Eleanor had hired as her social secretary, had fallen in love.

Exactly how or when it happened is lost to history; Lucy had worked in the Roosevelt household for a couple of years before people began to notice. But by the spring of 1916 the affair was full-blown. As assistant secretary of the Navy, Roosevelt had the authority to use the former presidential steam yacht *Sylph,* a sleek, luxurious 125-foot cruiser. During the summers, while Eleanor was away with the children at Campobello, Roosevelt organized weekend yachting parties along the Potomac and into the Chesapeake Bay.

Lucy Mercer was frequently a guest on these adventures. Many people (as well as the Washington gossip columnists) assumed she was involved with the handsome Englishman Nigel Law, who served in the British consulate. In fact, Law was a great friend and running mate of Franklin, and on these yachting occasions and elsewhere he assumed the role of what in less polite society was known as a "beard"—a man who posed as Lucy's boyfriend, which he was not.

On one festive occasion, Roosevelt's yacht party cruised down to Hampton Roads, where the U.S. Atlantic Fleet was stationed. There, his guests, including Lucy and Law, boarded the battleship *Arkansas* for a "splendid luncheon" with the commanding admiral. This was followed by a review honoring the assistant secretary of the fleet, which steamed past while a Navy band played such gay tunes as "Alexander's Ragtime Band" and other favorites of the day. A girl like Lucy Mercer could hardly fail to be impressed with the power and authority of Franklin Roosevelt.[2]

Lucy was a kind of "almost" society girl—meaning, in effect, that she didn't have any money. Her father was a Mercer of Carroll County, one of the oldest families in Maryland; his ancestor was a signer of the Declaration of Independence, and so they had some pull in the swing of things. Carroll Mercer married Lucy's mother, the lovely Washington socialite Minnie Norcup, after her divorce from an Englishman who was principally known about town for squandering half her fortune. Mercer would squander the rest.[3]

In 1891, Mercer fathered Lucy, and then went off as an Army captain, eventually to the Spanish-American War. There, and afterward, he claimed to have been a member of TR's Rough Riders—but in truth was consigned to the commissary corps, procuring food and forage. When he returned to Washington, Carroll polished off the remainder of Minnie's money in spectacular fashion, then drank himself to death, leaving his wife and daughter to fend for themselves.[4]

Minnie, mortified, employed her skills as a decorator to earn enough to keep them from poverty. But it was said as well that, as with Winston Churchill's mother, Minnie Mercer bestowed her charms on a number of wealthy Washington gentlemen who reciprocated generously.

There is no doubt that the matter between Franklin and Lucy was a genuine love affair and not merely the kind of romantic fling in which, according to Alice Roosevelt Longworth, many politicians and administration men took "little summer wives" while their spouses were off with the children to beach or mountain vacation homes.[5]

Roosevelt's sexual relationship with Eleanor had always been strained—and according to her son Elliott it had stopped altogether when she bore her last child. Her daughter, Anna, put it more bluntly, quoting a conversation in which her mother disclosed to her that the birth of John Roosevelt "was the end of any marital relationship, period." Anna added that Eleanor had once confided that sex was "an ordeal devoid of pleasure."[6]

Nevertheless, Eleanor was sometimes consumed by jealousy and suspicion over Franklin's flirtatious attitude toward women. But she never realized what was taking place right under her nose. She'd always considered herself ordinary, and, even before her marriage, revealed to a relative that she didn't see how she could keep the dashing, gregarious Franklin, with her "plain looks" and awkwardness in conversation.[7]

Worse, a number of Eleanor's friends and acquaintances—even her relatives—not only were aware of Franklin's affair with Lucy Mercer, but were accomplices and facilitators in it. When Nigel Law was called back to England, Franklin's longtime friend from Harvard days, the wealthy Bostonian rake Livingston ("Livy") Davis stepped conveniently into the beard role. Eleanor despised Davis's drinking and lascivious behavior but never suspected he had also become a facilitator for Franklin and Lucy's affair.

Nor did she suspect that their friends Edith and William Eustis had abetted the affair by inviting Franklin and Lucy to weekend house parties at Oatlands, their magnificent country estate near Leesburg, Virginia. Least of all, perhaps, did Eleanor suspect her own cousin Alice of encouraging the relationship. Alice had spotted the couple when they were out for a country drive and confided to Franklin that she had seen him motoring with a "lovely girl."[8]

"Yes," he replied, "isn't she lovely."[9]

Roosevelt, at thirty-four years old, was highly sought after, from Washington's highest society doyennes to office girls at the Navy Department. It may not be surprising, given his stagnant marital situation, that he took a mistress; post-Victorian morals were even lower than Victorian-era morals, and having a woman on the side, as Alice Longworth so pungently pointed out, was not especially uncommon in the Washington of that day. What Roosevelt ultimately intended to do with the mistress was another question, fraught with scandalous and earthshaking possibilities.

Alice invited the couple to quiet dinners at her luxurious five-story town house on Dupont Circle—and she fostered the relationship in other ways. For her day, Alice was a forward sort of woman who smoked cigarettes and drank in public; she was married to the lascivious Nicholas Longworth, the Speaker of the House of Representatives. She was also the daughter of the formidable Theodore Roosevelt and, as such, she was an influential power in Washington society. Beyond that, Alice was also regarded as the most passionate gossip in Washington. "If you can't say anything nice about somebody," she often quipped, "come right here and sit by me."

As the affair was carried on, Roosevelt was buffeted between his job at the Navy Department and the never-ending Washington social whirl that included Eleanor whenever she was in town. This meant dinners and other social gatherings at the homes of such dignitaries as Henry Cabot Lodge, Henry Adams, Charles Hamlin, and Theodore Roosevelt himself, where they would mix and mingle with ambassadors, cabinet secretaries, legislators, and other denizens of official Washington. The couple also found themselves welcome in the homes of many of Washington's "cave dwellers," who tended to regard them as Roosevelts rather than Democrats.[10]

The Roosevelts' social activities compared favorably with those of Winston Churchill, except that while the Roosevelts associated mostly with politicians, high-ranking administrators, and wealthy swells, the Churchills' world was composed of princes, dukes, counts, and other powerful men who'd made fortunes from the British Empire.

Both lives contrasted markedly with the social scene in Joseph Stalin's Soviet Union, where there were no royals, elected legislators, or wealthy swells, because the Communists had killed them all. Cocktail parties were unknown in Stalin's Russia, as were grand balls. There were, of course, country houses to visit, built years earlier by wealthy bourgeoisie who had since been liquidated or sent to forced labor camps by the revolution's turns of fortune. There were dinner parties in the Soviet Union, of the banquet sort, but they tended to be somber affairs where conversation was usually confined to party business. At these events, vodka or no, people generally minded their tongues if they knew what was good for them.

★★★★★

OFFICIAL DUTIES CARRIED ROOSEVELT to naval bases in the far-flung reaches of the world. He even donned a sidearm for a horseback tour of U.S. Marine positions in the island country of Haiti, which had been convulsed by murderous bandits.* And that was where war found him. A telegram from the War Department called Roosevelt urgently back to Washington. President Wilson had given the German ambassador his passports and was apparently contemplating asking Congress for a declaration of war against Germany.

After the outrageous *Lusitania* sinking in May 1915, the Germans had rescinded their policy of unrestricted submarine warfare against unarmed ships on the high seas for fear of provoking the United States into war. But in early 1917 the German staff convinced the kaiser to reinstate the policy in hopes of starving Great Britain and France out of the conflict before the Americans could join it. Accordingly, German submarines sank four U.S. transports during the early months of 1917. To Roosevelt's consternation, however, even that wasn't enough to propel President Wilson onto the warpath.

Finally, an intercepted telegram from the German foreign minister to his ambassador in Mexico became the last straw. This shocking document proposed a military alliance between Germany and Mexico if the United States should enter the war. Under its terms, Germany promised, if victorious, it would help Mexico recover Texas, New Mexico, Arizona, and other territories lost at the conclusion of the Mexican-American War in 1848. (For reasons known only to the Germans, California was not included in the bargain.) The revelation was widely publicized in the newspapers and so enraged the American people that Wilson at last felt he had enough political capital to join the war he had consistently promised to keep the United States out of.

America's entry into World War I was a colossal enterprise involving the induction, training, and transport of nearly 4 million men across the

---

* The Wilson administration was alarmed by the idea that the Germans might seize Haiti, and from there would be able to threaten the Panama Canal. Thus, U.S. Marines were sent in to secure the country.

Atlantic Ocean to the battlefields of France and Belgium. Franklin Roosevelt's Navy, of course, was responsible for the latter, as well as security along the coasts from German submarines. It was also involved in a wide variety of wartime enterprises across the globe—including the laying of a giant minefield against German submarines in the North Sea that was Roosevelt's brainchild.

As soon as war was declared, TR counseled his cousin Franklin to join the military as a fighting man; he himself had done this when the Spanish-American War broke out, which he credited for boosting him to the presidency. Franklin tried to join up, only to be discouraged by Secretary Daniels as well as by the president himself on the sensible grounds that the Navy needed its highly competent administrators to stay in their positions and not risk their lives on the fighting front. Roosevelt demurred in his quest to become a military hero but determined to raise the matter again in the future.

In the summer of 1918, Roosevelt went to the fighting front in France on a tour of inspection; he managed to get himself close enough to come under enemy artillery fire. He toured the American battlefield, some of it on foot, at Belleau Wood shortly after the fighting ended. In his diary, he wrote of walking amid "rusty bayonets, broken guns, emergency ration tins, hand grenades, discarded overcoats, rain-stained love letters, crawling lines of ants, and many little mounds, some wholly unmarked, some with a rifle stuck bayonet down in the earth, some with a helmet, and some, too, with a whittled cross with a tag of wood or wrapping paper hung over it and in a pencil scrawl an American name."[11]

Roosevelt was treated as a high-level American dignitary. In London, he met Lloyd George and Churchill, and in Paris he chatted with Georges Clemenceau, the French prime minister. Somewhere along the way he contracted influenza, the current strain of which could be deadly. He was put aboard the liner *Leviathan*,* more dead than alive. When the

---

* Formally the *Vaterland,* a luxurious 1,300-passenger German liner seized by the Americans at the beginning of the war and later converted to a troopship carrying up to 14,000 soldiers at a time.

ship docked at New York, he was carried ashore on a stretcher and sent by ambulance to his mother's town house in the city. Eleanor came up from Washington to care for him. She changed his bedclothes and bedpans and spoon-fed him for days. Then, while unpacking his suitcases, she made a terrible discovery: a packet of love letters to Franklin from Lucy Mercer.

This produced a crisis in the Roosevelt household of breathtaking dimensions. For Eleanor it all came back: the time she'd burst into tears before a cousin saying she would never be able to hold Franklin, because "he's too attractive."[12]

When Roosevelt had gained enough strength to absorb the shock, Eleanor confronted him with the evidence and, finding it undeniable, Roosevelt confessed all. According to family accounts, Eleanor offered a divorce and Franklin accepted. Their daughter, Anna, remembered her mother saying years later that she'd asked Franklin to take the time to think it over. There were, of course, the children to consider, but also the social disgrace. A divorce would be fatal to any future political career.[13]

Sara somehow got into the discussion and was appalled, especially at Eleanor's offer to give Franklin his freedom. There had never been a divorce in either branch of the Roosevelts, she noted, and the shame would bring ignominy to both families. Sara informed a torn and distraught Franklin that if he should divorce his wife and abandon his family, not one penny of the great Roosevelt fortune would come his way—including income from her own trust, which she so liberally had thus far bestowed. In other words, divorce meant not only dishonor to his family, the possible alienation of his children, and the end of his political career, but reduction from the upper reaches of society to the middle class. Roosevelt's personally inherited trust from his father's estate was $5,000 a year—somewhere between $55,000 and $75,000 in today's money, certainly not enough to retain the lifestyle to which he was accustomed.[14]

Roosevelt may have been in love, perhaps desperately. But he was pragmatic enough to see that divorce was a dead end. How and what he told Lucy Mercer we do not know, but soon afterward she married the fabulously wealthy Winthrop Rutherfurd, a widower with five children. But that wasn't the end of the story between Franklin and Lucy. That played out until the very end, and she was present—though unseen—at all four of his presidential inaugurations.[15]

AFTER THE ARMISTICE ON NOVEMBER 11, 1918, Roosevelt went to Europe once more, to wind down the Navy's presence and bring the sailors back home. This time, Eleanor went with him. They had come to some mutual understanding that she would henceforth be his helpmate, so to speak, as well as the mother of his children. She excelled in both these realms and they became, in the esteem of the Roosevelt biographer Frank Freidel, "the greatest husband-and-wife political partners in American history."

Among the divvying up of whole sections of the globe under the Treaty of Versailles, which officially ended World War I, Woodrow Wilson managed to secure passage of an alliance called the League of Nations, which the president had himself conceived and believed would put an end to future wars.

Homeward-bound on the liner *George Washington,* Wilson summoned Roosevelt to his cabin and sold him on the idea of the League of Nations, which even then the president saw imperiled by a Republican Senate that would have to ratify it. Wilson told Roosevelt that if the United States rejected the organization it would "break the heart of the world." The young assistant secretary of the Navy did not need much selling. He was keen for the idea and signed on.

The president liked Roosevelt immensely and saw a great future for him in Democratic politics. And his prospects seemed very bright in the year 1920, when he found himself on the national Democratic ticket as the vice presidential candidate with Ohio governor James Cox.

It was a bad year for Democrats, however. There were shortages of almost everything, even after the war ended. Inflation, labor strikes, and waves of race riots swept the country, along with increasing fear of Bolshevism exported from Lenin's Russia. In fact, there was already a nascent Communist movement in the United States, principally in the labor unions and characterized by bombings and assassinations. Known as the Red Scare, it hit close to home for the Roosevelt family on the eve of one of his trips to Europe.

After a nearby dinner party, Franklin and Eleanor were rounding a corner leading to their house when a huge explosion erupted across the street on the front porch of the home of the U.S. attorney general A. Mitchell Palmer, who had been conducting a highly publicized series of federal raids against Communists and other agitators. The explosion not only tore off the front of the Palmer home but blew up the bomber as well, hurling body parts along the block, including a severed collarbone chucked onto the Roosevelts' lawn and brought in next morning to the breakfast table by eleven-year-old James Roosevelt.* Republican Warren G. Harding won the election by a landslide, sinking Wilson's dream of American leadership in the League of Nations, as well as Roosevelt's hopes for an easy rise in his political status.

Roosevelt was nevertheless well placed politically. His eyes had been on the governorship of New York, but his friend Al Smith was currently serving in that capacity and demonstrated no signs of departing. So Roosevelt went back into his old law practice and bided his time. Other opportunities arose, including the U.S. Senate. But Roosevelt, who had bigger fish to fry, thought that was something of a dead end.

Then came the summer of 1921 and the polio epidemic—and the fateful trip to Campobello Island. After the fever had subsided and Roosevelt's paralysis became clear, Sara, who had taken charge, decided it was vital to move him back to New York City. A special train car was arranged and he was taken by boat, on a stretcher, to the mainland and hustled aboard before any press people could see his condition. Various doctors were summoned to examine him, and various pronouncements were made regarding the possibilities of his recovery. Roosevelt remained stoic through it all and waited for the time that he could begin a program to rehabilitate himself.

---

* Eight other bombs exploded at about that same hour in other American cities that night.

First, he set a goal to walk on crutches. But even before that, a pair of steel braces weighing fourteen pounds had to be fabricated for his lower legs, because the muscles were so damaged as to be insupportable without some kind of buttress or stay to prop them up. Sara lobbied for him to settle into Hyde Park and live in comfort the life of an invalid. But between the exhortations of Eleanor and Louis Howe (who, much to Sara's chagrin, had come to live with the family) as well as Franklin's own indomitable personality and love of politics, he became determined to make himself well enough to seek public office.

By early 1922 Roosevelt was moving around on the crutches. It was painful, but he endured it, spending hours trying to exercise and strengthen his withered muscles. These efforts were to no avail. To his doctors he said little about the pain, though he told one that a corset he was forced to wear "almost cut me in two." In time he learned to stand, for nearly an hour at a time, and to get up stairs by hauling himself backward, painfully grappling hand over hand along the rail. By 1923 he was well enough to go to Florida for a fishing vacation aboard a chartered house-boat, where he strapped himself into the fighting chair because his flaccid legs alone could not give him enough purchase. He caught fish weighing up to forty pounds.[16]

Subsequently, Roosevelt acquired his own houseboat jointly with a friend. He spent the next three winters aboard it, fishing and swimming in the warm salty Florida waters that he believed were therapeutic for his legs, and enjoying luncheons, cocktails, and dinners with friends and acquaintances. The talk usually began with fishing but soon led to politics. Eleanor was seldom along on these trips, as the houseboat didn't provide the level of privacy she required.

Then Roosevelt discovered Warm Springs, Georgia, a run-down spa on Pine Mountain about an hour south of Atlanta, where the water that flowed from the limestone was extremely buoyant and a constant 88 degrees Fahrenheit. After several weeks, Roosevelt said he could feel a tingling in his toes and was soon able to walk around in the water without braces. It was a transformational experience, and Roosevelt ultimately purchased the entire property, which included an old hotel and cottages.

Using loans and much of his own fortune, he began renovations and expansions in an effort to turn Warm Springs into a modern complex for the treatment of polio victims.

In 1927, Roosevelt announced the formation of the Warm Springs Foundation, in which he became "the doctor and physio-therapist, all rolled in one." Most of the polio victims were children, who arrived from all points of the country. The reputed success of the Warm Springs treatment led droves of journalists to report one of America's great human interest stories. For Roosevelt, Warm Springs was a terrific restorative tonic both physically and mentally. But still he had his eye on politics.[17]

EVEN THOUGH HE NEVER TRIED to keep his affliction a secret, Roosevelt keenly attempted to keep the extent of his paralysis from the public eye. It was his notion that if people knew how crippled he actually was, they might get the impression he was enfeebled, or feel sorry for him. When photographers and newsreel cameramen wanted pictures, Roosevelt insisted on being posed while he was standing with the aid of a walking cane, or sometimes on crutches, or in the pool of the springs where he was "as graceful as a seal." But never in his wheelchair, or being carried, as he sometimes was, from place to place, or being helped in and out of automobiles.

Photographers and reporters in those days were far more accommodating than today, and the pictures and stories were nearly all to Roosevelt's liking. He also purchased a convertible car to drive around the property, equipped with special hand controls, which was on-limits for photos with Roosevelt at the wheel. "He had perfected so effective an illusion that most Americans did not recognize until after his death that he was a paraplegic," wrote biographer Freidel.

Seven years after being struck by polio, Roosevelt had also become the voice of foreign affairs for the Democratic Party. Whether at Warm Springs or Hyde Park, he wrote frequently for *Foreign Affairs* and other scholarly magazines, mainly criticizing Republican presidential incumbents. One of his peeves had become the maintenance and expansion of a large navy, which he had once promoted as assistant secretary but now claimed was of no real use except against an expansionist Japan—and, like Winston Churchill, Roosevelt maintained that Japan was at present a sincere and enduring ally of the United States and the other democracies.

In 1928, broadcasting for the first time over national radio, Roosevelt gave the Democratic presidential nominating speech for his friend Governor Al Smith of New York. It was an elegant speech praised by the *New York Times* as "the address of a fair and cultivated man." But Smith, a Catholic, never stood a chance against Herbert Hoover and the exuberant Republican prosperity he claimed for the 1920s.[18]

Smith then turned his attention to persuading Roosevelt to run for governor of New York—but astonishingly Roosevelt refused. He made excuses that he needed more time to strengthen his legs, and also that his financial situation was now unstable because of loans made to the Warm Springs Foundation. Both were true. But the reason Roosevelt demurred was one of the most prescient, profound, and pragmatic political assessments in American history.

After the Democrats lost the election of 1920 when he was on the ticket as vice president, Roosevelt had remarked at the time that he didn't believe a Democrat could win again "until the Republicans had led us into a serious period of depression and unemployment." He pointed out that after every war there comes a spirit of "materialism and conservatism," and that the people would not vote out a Republican administration so long as "the wages are good and markets are booming." In other words, even if becoming governor of New York was to be his springboard to the presidency, now was not the time, Roosevelt felt.

It didn't matter. The Democratic state convention of 1928 nominated him anyway, by acclimation. He could hardly turn it down.

Republican newspapers immediately began to play up Roosevelt's infirmity, but he countered this by touring the state in his chauffeured convertible, rising to give speeches from the backseat with his winning smile and sunny disposition. For his part, Al Smith chimed in, "A governor does not have to be an acrobat."[19] Given the prevailing political winds, Roosevelt was not given much chance of winning. But on election night it turned out he'd emerged victorious by a slim 25,000 votes out of 4.2 million cast.

With a Republican legislature there was little Roosevelt could do to move progressive legislation. But one thing he accomplished in his first year as governor was to prove he was his "own man." Smith, having lost the presidential election and considering that he was responsible for putting Roosevelt in the governor's mansion, tried to dictate policy in the office by fiat. Roosevelt would have none of it. He fired several of Smith's closest aides and proceeded to run things his own way.

Roosevelt proved to be a talented administrator. But nothing could have prepared him for the calamity that broke toward the end of his first year in office. On October 24 the stock markets, which had been fired up for months, began an ominous decline. The following week—October 29, 1929, Black Tuesday—the markets collapsed with a stupendous sell-off, marking the start of the Great Depression.

Roosevelt was slow to grasp the ramifications of what was happening, let alone what was going to happen. He knew that prices were falling, factories were laying off workers, banks were failing, the stock market was continuing to shrivel, farmers were going broke, and hungry people were begging in the streets. But into the end of 1930 he favored pay-as-you-go relief programs despite the fact that there was no pay to go with.

As the Depression deepened and the suffering became more widespread, figures emerged showing that some 10 percent of New York families were on the verge of starvation. Roosevelt persuaded the legislature to enact the Temporary Emergency Relief Administration, installing as its director the brilliant and immensely able Harry L. Hopkins. Hopkins persuaded the legislature to go into the red with loans in order to provide an average of $23 a month per impoverished family ($326 in today's purchasing power): enough to stave off catastrophe. Roosevelt's views had now swung a hundred and eighty degrees from his opinion that relief should be a matter of private charity to the conviction that in the present circumstance only "massive federal intervention" could save the country.[20]

In the months leading up to the presidential election of 1932, Roosevelt concentrated on educating himself on the problems that were facing the

United States—namely the Great Depression, which had only worsened. In Washington, Hoover insisted that recovery was just around the corner. But millions remained unemployed, prices remained deflated, rents went unpaid, factories and retail stores stayed closed.

Roosevelt began assembling around him what would later be called his "brain trust." These were talented men with knowledge of economics, many of them with academic backgrounds: Adolf A. Berle of Columbia Law School, Rex Tugwell of the Wharton School, as well as Harry Hopkins and others. Roosevelt would pick their minds for the new ideas he was sure were needed to ease the pain of the Depression and ultimately lift the country out of it.

ROOSEVELT UNDERSTOOD THAT THE timing was perfect to run for president. The irony was that he had nearly refused the governorship a year before. The depression he had sought to sweep the Republicans out of power had come, but faster and with a fury he never could have wanted or predicted. By the early 1930s the country was in despair and there was no end in sight.

Before he could run, however, Roosevelt had to obtain the nomination of his party, and that was no sure bet. For one thing Al Smith, who had felt betrayed by Roosevelt for cutting him off in Albany, was almost surely going to try again for the White House. For another, some publications were questioning Roosevelt's fitness for the presidency because of his ongoing health problems; others were critical of him because as governor he had never dealt with the ongoing corruption of New York City's Tammany Hall political machine. Roosevelt was doing all he could to play down health issues, and Tammany was a sore subject, owing to the fact that he had needed (and received) its votes in the past gubernatorial election. Nevertheless, to head off this criticism, he signed a bill authorizing the legislature to conduct an investigation. What they found was atrocious.

Graft, payoffs, and just plain stealing were so rife they included even the chief law enforcement officer of New York, as well as the immensely popular mayor Jimmy Walker, who allegedly had stolen nearly a million dollars.

Faced with criminal charges, Walker resigned and fled to Paris with his Ziegfeld Follies girlfriend, where he lay low until the danger of prosecution had passed.

The Democrats' rulebook in those days put up an immense hurdle for anyone hoping to run for president; fully two-thirds of the delegates had to agree on a single candidate. This forced the prospective nominees to embark on ferocious delegate-gathering campaigns in which the odds seemed to change daily, if not hourly. Roosevelt's people worked feverishly to keep delegates pledged to him from wavering, while Smith and other potential candidates labored just as tirelessly to snatch them away.

With Roosevelt chain-smoking on the telephone in the Albany state-house, a raucous Democratic Convention in the heat of Chicago's summer nominated him by a hairsbreadth on the fourth ballot during the second day of voting. The next morning, despite the fact that he distrusted flying, Roosevelt boarded an airplane for Chicago and rode to the convention hall in an open convertible, waving to the throngs who lined the streets and cheered as he passed by. To deafening applause, Roosevelt took the podium to state his program for a different America: "government economy, Pro-hibition repeal, regulation of securities sales, self-sustaining public works, reforestation, a reduced tariff, a voluntary crop control program, refinancing of home and farm mortgages, and federal relief." This was the basis of Roosevelt's New Deal.[21]

All that the hapless Hoover and the Republicans could promise was more of the same, which was intolerable. In his campaign, Roosevelt did some-thing that few presidential candidates did at that point: he courted the vote of the "forgotten man," meaning the working (or, in this case, nonworking) man. For the first seventy years of the republic, voting was restricted to property holders or taxpayers; as a result, most candidates aimed their speeches at the affluent classes. Women had been given the vote only a decade earlier, and no one was sure of the psychology necessary to win them over. Hoover campaigned on the inane slogan "A chicken in every pot and a car in every garage."

Roosevelt campaigned on his New Deal, a shotgun of possibilities aimed at defeating the Great Depression. But he also talked about the rights of men, of men's economic rights: "the right to make a comfortable living." These were not privileges guaranteed by the Bill of Rights, but Roosevelt made it sound that way. For his part, Hoover retaliated by calling Roosevelt's proposals radical and collectivist—all but accusing him of being a Socialist, if not a Stalin-style Red. The Democratic philosophy was "the fumes of the witch's cauldron which boiled in Russia," Hoover charged. But in the end the Republican's efforts came to naught.[22]

Just as Roosevelt had predicted a decade earlier, it took a depression to sweep the Republicans from the White House. When the returns came in, Roosevelt had piled up 23 million votes to Hoover's 16 million, carrying forty-two states and winning 472 electoral votes.

Roosevelt had been listening to the returns in New York's Biltmore Hotel. When by 11 p.m. it was clear that he'd won, Roosevelt cited his campaign manager Jim Farley and his longtime adviser Louis Howe as "the two people in the United States, who more than anybody else, are responsible for the great victory." Howe had opened a bottle of sherry he'd put away twenty years earlier and toasted Roosevelt: "To the president of the United States!" About 2 a.m., when Roosevelt finally got back to his mother's house on East Sixty-fifth Street, she greeted him at the door, crying, "This is the greatest night of my life!"[23]

All over America people danced and paraded in the streets, singing the Democrats' campaign song "Happy Days Are Here Again."

ROOSEVELT SPENT THE NEARLY THREE months before his inauguration in a seemingly endless round of meetings, trying to decide what his administration would look like. The next big question was how it would deal with the Great Depression that was gripping the nation ever more tightly every day.

By the time of the election Americans, to their horror, had witnessed more than three thousand bank failures. Depositors, both wealthy and working class, were lining up outside banks each morning in hopes of withdrawing their savings before the institutions closed their doors. This ongoing run on banks of course resulted in more bank failures, until the entire financial system was in peril.

Soup kitchens sprang up in most cities to feed those with no money to buy groceries. Many of them were living in what had been branded "Hoovervilles": rough tar paper shanties on the outskirts, built by rent eviction victims. There were ever increasing protest marches, large and small, and violence often broke out in farming communities where prices had fallen well below wholesale (especially when bank representatives arrived to seize a mortgaged property). Numerous bank agents were mobbed, tarred and feathered, and beaten—and at least one was found murdered in Iowa. There was talk of lynch mobs.

The largest protest was the so-called Bonus March, which had occurred the previous summer. Nearly twenty thousand World War I veterans and at least as many others marched to Washington demanding early payment of a service bonus that Congress had voted them. The crowd, including a cadre of agitators, set up a Hooverville on the edge of the city and conducted ever more violent protests until they were ejected by the U.S. Army.

Edward O'Neal, president of the Farm Bureau, testified to Congress that if conditions did not change there would be revolution in the countryside within a year. John Stimson, head of the Farmers Union, echoed that prediction when he told the Senate Agricultural Committee that "the biggest and finest crop of little revolutions I ever saw is ripe all over this country right now." Meantime, Communist agitators toiled diligently at their nefarious occupation.[24]

Given what had happened in Russia a decade earlier, Hoover was alarmed enough that he'd considered declaring a national emergency. But after meeting with advisers, he sought help from Roosevelt, whose statements on "sound money" (meaning no deliberate inflation), Hoover felt, might calm the nation. But Roosevelt demurred, claiming he did not wish to become involved in governing until he officially became president. In fact, sound money was about the last thing on Roosevelt's mind; he instead consulted his own advisers for solutions to the predicament.

One of these, the renowned economist Rex Tugwell, told reporters (without first clearing it with the boss) that he was for sound money and balancing the budget, albeit "through a drastic increase in income and inheritance taxes." He also suggested borrowing, which would increase the national debt, hovering then at a reasonable $22 billion. (By contrast, today's debt is a staggering $20 *trillion*.) "There is just one thing to do," Tugwell said in a socialistic frame of mind. "Take incomes from where they are and place them where we need them."[25]

This interview, which drew nationwide attention, nearly panicked the wealthy and upper middle classes, which already believed taxes were too high. It also caused Roosevelt to become peeved at Tugwell for going public with such a radical plan. Suddenly disinvited to what was now being dubbed the "Little White House" at Warm Springs, Tugwell rested indignantly on his moral principles, convinced that at least he'd been honest about it.

There seemed no end to ideas about how to dig out of the Depression. Some, including publisher William Randolph Hearst, promoted a national sales tax to raise money for public works projects while keeping the budget balanced. The British economist John Maynard Keynes stuck his nose in it during a trip to the United States. He agreed with Tugwell that massive government spending was the way to normalcy but, unlike Tugwell, he didn't care about a balanced budget. Instead of taxing and spending, Keynes promoted taxing and *borrowing* and spending. This notion horrified the financial world, but most people had stopped paying attention to those types after the crash of '29.

There were ever more crackpot schemes, including one proposed by a mysterious self-proclaimed engineer and floor polish salesman in Manhattan's Greenwich Village named Howard Scott. He asserted that engineers should take over the entire U.S. manufacturing system and set it to work on a highly accelerated, twenty-four-hour production schedule. There would be commensurately high wages that would allow the workers to purchase the produce of the factories. Not only that, he wanted to abolish money, including gold, and replace it with measurements of energy such as joules and ergs. He dubbed his system Technocracy and embarked on a PR campaign to explain it at Manhattan's posh private clubs and over national radio networks. Engineers instead of politicians, Scott declared, would run the country. At its peak, Technocracy had half a million members in California alone.

The novelist and Socialist Upton Sinclair called Technocracy "the most important movement which has shown its head in our time," but the critic H. L. Mencken dismissed it as "worse than communism." Scott's idea was a rage for a while, but in the end nobody really understood how it worked, if at all. By the end of the decade Scott was exposed as a fraud and his movement fizzled out entirely.[26]

Roosevelt listened to many such schemes, plots, and plans. But he played his cards very close to his vest as he sat in Warm Springs, smoking, smiling, and nodding while a stream of visitors offered their theories about how the country should be run. Huey Long got a taste of Roosevelt's noncommittal personality when he went in to discuss Depression relief in Louisiana. Afterward, the firebrand senator and prospective presidential candidate was heard to say: "He says 'Fine! Fine! Fine!' But Joe Robinson goes to see him the next day and again he says, 'Fine! Fine! Fine!' Maybe he says 'Fine!' to everybody."[27]

IN EARLY FEBRUARY, with Inauguration Day barely a month away, Roosevelt embarked on a leisurely cruise off Florida aboard Vincent Astor's luxurious yacht *Nourmahal.* Stopping in Miami, the president-elect boarded a convertible for a motorcade that would take him to the Bayfront Park, where he was to deliver a speech and meet with Chicago's mayor Anton Cermak (who was there to beg favors, having stalled in delivering critical Illinois delegation votes to Roosevelt at the convention the previous summer). After making his speech, Roosevelt was in the process of listening to someone who wanted him to read a lengthy telegram when shots suddenly rang out.

Standing on a soapbox in the crowd about ten yards away was a man firing a pistol. He was an Italian anarchist named Giuseppe Zangara, who later told police that he "hated the rich and powerful." He was hoping to kill Roosevelt, he said, but a woman put her hand on his arm and spoiled his aim. The bullets instead struck Mayor Cermak and four others. Roosevelt was utterly calm in the face of the gunfire. The Secret Service wanted to speed away, but Roosevelt ordered them to put the wounded Cermak into his car and rush to the hospital. Cermak died a few weeks later, and Zangara was tried, convicted, and sent to the electric chair the following month. Roosevelt gained a kind of hero status, having achieved such a narrow escape from assassination.[28]

Two weeks later, on a cold gray day on the Capitol steps before a crowd of a hundred thousand, Roosevelt took the oath of office on March 4, 1933. The ceremony was administered by the old waterboarder Endicott Peabody (despite his having voted for Hoover). Roosevelt wore a morning suit and a silk top hat. He was all smiles for his wife Eleanor and mother Sara—and also for Lucy Mercer Rutherfurd, who had been quietly spirited to the event from her sister's house in Georgetown in a black Secret Service limousine to watch the proceedings at a discreet distance.[29]

In his inaugural address over national radio, Roosevelt spoke to the people in a now familiar voice, radiating strength and patrician authority.

"This is a day of national consecration . . . The only thing we have to fear is fear itself . . . We must move as a trained and loyal army . . . I assume unhesitatingly the leadership of this great army . . . The people of the United States have asked for discipline and direction under leadership. They have made me the instrument of their wishes. In the spirit of the gift, I take it."[30] He set the leisure classes to quaking when he continued with a spiel of liberal ideology, singling out the "unscrupulous money changers" who "fled from their high seats in the temple of our civilization," and called for an "end to speculation with other people's money."

It was an uplifting talk, given to a people desperate for someone to tell them what to do. Banks were still closing daily, and the bankers were just as afraid as the workers and white collar employees who also were being let go. There was no money to pay doctors or lawyers, just a great unwinding, a downward spiral in which the entire fabric of the country seemed to be coming apart. Roosevelt told his listeners not to take counsel of their fears, that help was on the way, that soon there would be work. Soon there would be happy days.

Before the inauguration Roosevelt visited the mighty Wilson Dam on the Tennessee River that had been completed nearly a decade earlier. He was in the company of Senator George Norris of Nebraska, who had championed dams on the river for years but saw his bills vetoed by Republican presidents Coolidge and Hoover.

Also present in the party were a gaggle of reporters. Gesturing from the top of the dam toward the vastness of the Tennessee River Valley, Roosevelt promised Norris that his vision would now come true on a grander scale than he had ever imagined. A series of dams built by the U.S. Army Corps of Engineers would alter the geography of the river forever, prevent disastrous flooding, and supply cheap electricity to hundreds of thousands of poor rural residents of the seven states through which the river coursed. This, of course, became the legendary Tennessee Valley Authority, or TVA. Roosevelt's enemies would use this initiative as a way to accuse Roosevelt of following a socialist—even a communist—agenda, as it coincided with the vaunted hydroelectrification of the Soviet Union under Stalin. The president laughed this off with characteristic aplomb. "I'll tell them it [the TVA] is neither fish nor fowl, but whatever it is it will taste awful good to the people of the Tennessee Valley."[31]

Confronted with what historian Roy Jenkins called "the most formidable threats to face any president since Lincoln," Roosevelt selected a cabinet of mostly reasonable men that has been characterized by more than one historian as "uninspired." At the Treasury Department was Henry Morgenthau Jr., son of a prominent Jewish family from New York City and a friend and neighbor of Roosevelt's at Hyde Park. He served in all four of Roosevelt's terms, but late in the war he came under fire for initiating a scheme to bomb postwar Germany back to the stone age and turn its remaining population into shepherds and subsistence farmers. Cordell Hull of Tennessee became secretary of state, and, like Morgenthau, served for twelve years. As an administrator Hull was strangely inert—which suited Roosevelt just fine, since he intended to conduct most foreign policy from the White House. Roosevelt chose Henry Wallace, a Republican and a farmer, as secretary of agriculture. The acerbic Harold Ickes became secretary of the interior. A Chicago radical, Ickes would go on to become Roosevelt's main attack dog when the White House did not wish to sully its hands by trying to discredit someone's reputation. For secretary of labor, Roosevelt named the mild-mannered Frances Perkins, who had served in that capacity for him when he was governor of New York. She was the first woman ever appointed to the U.S. cabinet.

Roosevelt soon began writing legislative bills, a lot of them. They all passed because the Democrats held both houses of Congress. The odds faced by the country were daunting. Unemployment had risen to its highest; in Flint, Michigan, it was a staggering 80 percent, and in parts of Massachusetts it was actually 90 percent. The first of the bills that Roosevelt wrote to combat these problems was emergency legislation closing all U.S. banks for four days, allowing some breathing room from the breathless withdrawal panic of the moment and restoring some confidence in the banking system.

Alongside the Banking Act, Roosevelt suddenly ordered by executive fiat to take the United States off the gold standard. This was shocking to many. America had been on the gold standard either officially or unofficially for more than a hundred years, a process whereby money was pegged to the price of gold, then currently fixed at $20.67 per ounce. Paper money was redeemable in gold at that rate. Because of the Depression and the bank failures, vast numbers of Americans were standing in line at banks to turn their paper money into gold before the bank either closed or ran out of gold or paper money became worthless. On the day after Roosevelt's inauguration, the Federal Reserve Bank of New York ran out of gold. Roosevelt, after consulting his economic advisers, declared that the gold standard was "suspended." This did not really work, for people continued to demand that banks redeem their paper money for gold. So several months later Roosevelt announced that it would be illegal for people to keep gold, and that henceforth it would not be honored as currency.

Most citizens then began going to the banks to exchange their gold for paper money at the rate of $26.33 per ounce (the price had risen since Roosevelt took office). Then, when the government had accumulated almost all the gold in the United States in a depository at Fort Knox, Kentucky, Roosevelt got a bill through Congress raising the price of gold to $35 an ounce, causing many people to become incensed that they had been cheated.

Just as Churchill was controversial for putting Great Britain back *on* the gold standard eight years earlier, Roosevelt was criticized by skeptical economists who warned that going off gold would lead to runaway inflation. That turned out to be untrue. What it did do was allow the government, through the Federal Reserve, to pump a tremendous amount of money into the economy to fuel Roosevelt's grand-scaled New Deal programs.

A little more than a week after his inauguration, in what turned out to be a brilliant gimmick to sell his policies, Roosevelt broadcast the first of his famous "fireside chats" on national radio. He explained to Americans why they should accept and welcome the bank holiday and the relief from the gold standard. His voice, disembodied and mellifluous, seemed perfect for radio, and millions gathered around their sets for his broadcasts. Somehow, even though his tone and inflection were unmistakably patrician, Roosevelt managed to convince people that things were getting better, and that he was on their side.

Next came a blizzard of legislation creating an astonishing number of new federal agencies. One was the Civilian Conservation Corps (CCC), which provided jobs for idle young men to work in forests and national parks. It paid just a dollar a day and was run by the Army, but the men had three squares a day and a dry place to sleep. A quarter of a million people signed up within a few months, and the program ran until war broke out almost a decade later.

The Agricultural Adjustment Act (AAA), created to avoid the terrible years of harvest surpluses that caused prices to plummet, actually paid farmers *not* to grow certain staple crops such as cotton, wheat, swine, and tobacco. It continues today, which demonstrates how difficult it is to get rid of an entitlement program.

To the delirious delight of many and the furious consternation of others, the process of repealing the Eighteenth Amendment outlawing the sale of alcoholic beverages was begun under Roosevelt's signature, signaling the end of Prohibition.

As promised by Roosevelt, the Tennessee Valley Authority was cranked up, and the defense budget was cut by more than a third. This last prompted the Army's chief of staff Douglas MacArthur to become embroiled in such a heated confrontation with the president, he said, that as he stormed out he threw up on the White House steps.

The National Industrial Recovery Act (NIRA), designed to eliminate "cut-throat competition," was passed toward the end of Roosevelt's first hundred days in office. Symbolized by a picture of the Blue Eagle, its insignia was posted on the doors of businesses that agreed to pay employees a "living wage."

Finally, there was the Public Works Administration (PWA), a part of NIRA that was run by Harold Ickes. It was responsible for putting many Americans to work on such projects as the Blue Ridge Parkway, Boulder Dam, New York's Triborough Bridge, scores of federal courthouses, schools, and other assets valuable to the country.

These were the essentials of the New Deal that was supposed to bring a return to American prosperity. By the end of a historic first one hundred days in the Oval Office, June of 1933, Roosevelt had fulfilled many of his biggest campaign promises. Some of it worked—but most of it didn't, if prosperity was the sole arbiter.

CHAPTER NINE

In June 1933, with an astonishing range of legislative accomplishments under his belt and the long, hot Washington summer drawing near, Roosevelt repaired to Campobello for much needed recreation. There, he could enjoy being with his children, who were growing up quickly or already grown. The polio, of course, had severely curtailed his athletic activities such as golf, tennis, fly-fishing, and riding; he spent most of his spare time with his stamps and other collections. Occasionally, he would be helped aboard his sailboat and enjoy being captain for a while. But these old pastimes were not what occupied Roosevelt's mind anymore. Now, politics and governing drove him. He held lengthy conversations with Louis Howe and others, counting House and Senate votes and discussing who was wavering, or who was vulnerable to which emoluments, or who was having an affair with so-and-so's wife.

When he returned from vacation, Roosevelt startled many people—particularly Republicans—by announcing that the United States would now officially recognize the Soviet Union, being the last major world power to do so. Relations had been broken off during World War I, when the Bolshevik Revolution destroyed the czarist government and Lenin made a separate peace with the Germans. They remained in a void throughout the 1920s, after the Soviets refused to pay the U.S. debts from the old government, seized American property in Russia, and attempted to subvert the U.S. government by lending support to American Communists.

Roosevelt, however, felt it was time for a change. It was said that he had been heavily influenced by the now discredited reporting of Walter Duranty on Stalin's Russia in the *New York Times*. Other reasons given were that he hoped a formal relationship would serve American interests in the Pacific, assuming the Russians could help limit the Japanese expansionism that was threatening to engulf all of Asia.

Quiet talks were held throughout the summer and into the fall. At last, a "gentleman's agreement" was reached between the Soviet representative and Henry Morgenthau. The Russian minister promised his country would deal with the repayment of the old debt and cease trying to subvert and propagandize the American people. Roosevelt appointed as ambassador William C. Bullitt, who was given a cordial and happy reception when he reached Moscow.

The good relationship did not last long. No sooner had Bullitt arrived than Stalin opened the first of his Great Purges that horrified the world. Moreover, the Soviets reneged on the promise to deal with Russian debts and brazenly continued to support the American subversion and propaganda efforts.[1]

Meanwhile, for many of his old friends and associates Roosevelt remained a "traitor to his class" as his policies and his prose publicly excoriated banking and financial magnates. His tax legislation, just as Rex Tugwell had promised, had hit the wealthy the hardest. His top income tax bracket of 63 percent in 1933 rose to more than 90 percent a decade later.

For his part, Roosevelt had come to romanticize "the people," by which he meant the working and lower middle classes. They, he had come to believe, were the backbone of America—and, not incidentally, the people who had elected him. He was determined to be their champion, and to give them better lives. The rich—though he remained one of them—could fend for themselves, and he had cut himself adrift from their values.

By the end of 1933 it appeared the New Deal might be working. Unemployment was down from 15 million to 11 million. Those banks that had regained stability remained open. There seemed to be some progress in industrial output and prices were slightly higher. Hope was that the worst was over.

The trouble, though, was that rather than a steady rise upward the economy had lurched forward, then hit a kind of plateau in which it remained stuck through 1934, 1935, and 1936. The depression remained, leaving many millions of Americans stranded in the direst poverty and despair. In fact, the New Deal seemed to be coming apart.

For one thing, the agriculture bill was not working as planned. It was mostly the big farmers who could take land out of production and get money for it. Most of the little farmers didn't own their land and were subject to eviction. The Supreme Court seemed determined to take apart NIRA program by program, finding that the president had exceeded his authority. The program itself was too complicated and contradictory, and nobody seemed to know how to fix it.

Nevertheless, Roosevelt plunged ahead with what he called "a Second New Deal," which created the Social Security Administration to ensure that people would not starve in old age. All workers and employers were charged a tax for social security "insurance" that would be payable monthly beginning at age sixty-five. It remains with us today in a complex system that has been amended multiple times over the years. The taxpayers' money goes into what Roosevelt called a "trust fund," which it is not; in fact, the money is invested in U.S. government bonds with the Treasury Department.

Roosevelt once again stoked the notion of class warfare by getting Congress to pass the Wealth Tax Act, which sought to punish very wealthy people. He also went after large estates by assessing punitive taxes. It taxed any income over $50,000 at 75 percent, and quickly became known as the "soak the rich act." He stirred up more rancor with an act that forbade holding companies from owning any public utility. It was later repealed by Congress.

Adding to the nation's misery, a drought of biblical proportions struck the Midwest. Huge portions of farmland in a dozen states dried up and blew away in gigantic dust storms. Anything that was planted died. Farmers were soon unable to pay their mortgages and were forced off their land. A steady stream of these unfortunates, known as Okies, headed west for California, which became the subject of John Steinbeck's powerful 1939 novel *The Grapes of Wrath*.

Roosevelt toured the devastated states by train, promising government help. He got Congress to pass a mortgage relief act making it difficult for creditors to evict a farmer and repossess his property. The Supreme Court threw out the act, but it was rewritten and stood for nearly fifteen years, after which it expired.

Eleanor Roosevelt, in the meantime, had become an immensely popular personality in the press and on radio. She wrote a daily syndicated column called "My Day" and appeared weekly on the air. She had also developed what most historians agree was a lesbian relationship with a newspaper reporter named Lorena Hickok. The two had known each other for about five years after Lorena interviewed Eleanor at the governor's mansion in Albany. The relationship turned into an affair just as Roosevelt took up residency in the White House. Lorena quit her job with the Associated Press and moved into a room on the second floor next to Louis Howe. As for Eleanor and her husband, they occupied separate bedrooms with a large study in between. Their marriage had been unalterably estranged by his affair with Lucy Mercer, but Eleanor still provided diligent help to Franklin by becoming "his eyes and ears politically." As she put it in a letter to Hickok, "I realize F.D.R. is a great man & he is nice to me but as a person I am a stranger & don't want to be anything else."[2]

Whether this was her first lesbian affair is uncertain. But Eleanor did have a close association with a lesbian pair, the women's suffrage activists Esther Lape and Elizabeth Fisher Read, who remained partners for life. In fact, Franklin built a stone cottage at Hyde Park for Eleanor and the two women, as well as a factory building where they started a furniture-making business in 1928. The two women lived there full-time, and Eleanor came and went as practicality dictated. When the furniture-making enterprise closed, Eleanor remodeled the larger factory into Val-Kill Cottage, where she and Lorena stayed. Then Franklin was elected president and, of course, Eleanor's presence was required in the White House.

The nature of the relationship between Eleanor and Lorena came to light in the late 1970s, when a writer named Doris Faber was researching a book at the FDR Presidential Library and found herself sifting through cartons containing thousands of steamy love letters between the two women. Shocked, she discovered that Hickok had willed the correspondence to the library with the stipulation that they remain sealed until ten years after her death, a period that had expired. Faber, understanding the shock that would arise if the letters were made public, tried to have the library reseal them but the curator refused.

Lorena Hickok had grown up, poor and abused, in the Midwest. She had quit home when she was fourteen, getting by on hired jobs until somehow she taught herself journalism and signed on as a reporter on the *Minneapolis Tribune,* later joining the AP. She was rotund, homely, smoked cigars, and cussed up a storm. But she was also smart and humorous, and Eleanor clearly found something endearing in her (and, judging from the letters, something physically attractive as well).

Franklin was said to have discovered what was going on and feared that the press would expose the affair. According to one source, he was overheard to shout at Eleanor in their joint bedroom study, "I want that woman kept out of this house." Instead, Eleanor simply kept Lorena out of his sight, which was not difficult given that Roosevelt was confined to a wheelchair.[3]

WHILE THE AMERICANS and other Western nations floundered under the worldwide Great Depression, Germany, under Hitler's leadership, actually seemed to be pulling out of it. In the 1932 elections the people elected a plurality of Nazis to the German Reichstag, which named Hitler chancellor in 1933. Three months later, the day after Roosevelt took office, Hitler rigged a vote forcing the hand of Paul von Hindenburg, the aging president of the Weimar Republic. After Hindenburg's death the following year, Hitler named himself Führer (leader) of the German people. He pledged to rid the nation of the burdensome Treaty of Versailles, which had caused so much economic woe.

Hitler promised the Germans they would be a great power again, and he set about making vast infrastructure projects, such as autobahns (superhighways), under his system of National Socialism. He also secretly began a program to rebuild Germany's military, based around two potent weapons that were developed during the First World War: the warplane and the tank. In the meantime, he launched what was at first a verbal crusade against the Communists, who were sponsored by Moscow, and against the Jews, whom he saw as Communists, disloyal to German values, and incompatible with Germanic heritage. These last outrages were received with indignation by Americans of all descents.

Nazi thugs liquidated all other political parties and seized control of the German military and the economy. They also began depriving Jews of their civil and property rights, and began systematically beating them in the streets. Some of this activity was captured in newsreels shown in the United States, including in the White House.

On March 7, 1936, Hitler marched a division of infantry into the Rhineland, a sector of the Rhine River in western Germany, in a direct violation of the Treaty of Versailles. The Allies dithered and did nothing. Roosevelt was in the full swing of his reelection campaign and warned in a speech in Philadelphia that "the world cannot trust a fully rearmed Germany to stay at peace." At the time, it was a bombshell declaration.

This was a far cry from Roosevelt's original stance vis-à-vis the Nazis. Shortly after becoming president, he had publicly embraced Great Britain's proposal for world disarmament, except for a nation's basic self-defense force.* Fifty-four nations were currently meeting for this purpose in Geneva, and the crafty Hitler agreed that Germany would attend. Roosevelt's hope against hope, like that of Cordell Hull's State Department, was that Hitler's bellicose rhetoric was mostly bluster, and that eventually he would settle down and join with the peaceful nations of Europe. Roosevelt also worried that taking a stronger international stance against Nazism might rile the powerful isolationist lobby in the U.S. Senate that he needed to pass his Second New Deal legislation.

Privately, however, Roosevelt told the French ambassador, "The situation is alarming. Hitler is a madman and his counselors, some of whom I know personally, are even madder than he is. France cannot disarm now, and nobody will ask her to."[4]

When it came to public diplomacy against Hitler, Roosevelt found himself caught up in a dodgy high-wire act of his own design. The conversation with the French ambassador clearly reveals that Roosevelt feared another devastating war could be started by the Nazis. But during his reelection

---

* Interestingly, this would have included, at the suggestion of U.S. Army Chief of Staff Douglas MacArthur, whose antipathy toward airplanes was well known, a ban on all warplanes and aircraft carriers.

campaign he had to contend not only with isolationist senators but also with voters who, following the horrors of World War I, were firmly against any more European entanglements. Therefore, after his Philadelphia warning against a rearmed Germany, Roosevelt "pivoted" with his famous "I Hate War" speech in upstate New York. In it, he recounted his experiences in 1918, when he had visited the fighting front in France as assistant secretary of the Navy. He told of the American graves he'd seen, as well as the blood and bombs, grieving widows with hungry children, and whole cities leveled into rubble. He concluded with the powerful declaration, "I hate war!"

The people believed him, including the isolationists, and on November 3, 1936, Roosevelt was reelected president for a second term by a landslide. He won every state but Maine and Vermont, which as they had four years earlier remained staunchly Republican.

For their part, the Nazis sent Hitler's minister of culture, Dr. Alfred Rosenberg, as emissary to the Geneva disarmament conference. Rosenberg had once asserted, "On every telegraph pole from Munich to Berlin, the head of a prominent Jew must be stuck": not an especially auspicious choice of ambassadors to talk about arms control.[5]

But there was more to worry about than Nazi Germany on the foreign policy scene. In the Far East, the Japanese were now controlled by an increasingly aggressive military government that seemed intent on conquering all of Asia. Already in possession of Korea, the Japanese army overran the massive nation of Manchuria in 1931 to obtain its natural resources, as well as the island nation of what is currently Taiwan. Now, it was sweeping across mainland China toward Peking. Condemned by the League of Nations, Japan simply withdrew from it. The Japanese had already flouted the Washington Naval Treaty of 1922 by building aircraft carriers and battleships far in excess of what they had agreed upon. Called to account for this, the Japanese representative walked out of that convention as well.

Roosevelt had never trusted the Japanese; partly because his family had been in the China trade, he tended to side with the Chinese. In his first cabinet meeting, he had said that a war with Japan was not unlikely, and he later shocked brain truster Rex Tugwell by musing whether it would be better to start a war with Japan now, rather than later. In 1934, naval intelligence had shown Roosevelt a Japanese comic book that began with an air attack on Pearl Harbor and ended with peace being dictated in the White House. Army Air Corps general Billy Mitchell had for years been publicly forecasting a Japanese attack on Hawaii.[6]

With the Great Depression still weighing heavily over the land, Roosevelt limited his response to Japanese aggression. He obtained House approval of an embargo on war materials to Japan, but isolationists in the Senate forced him to drop even that mild sanction.

ROOSEVELT DECLARED IN HIS second inaugural address that the New Deal was "far from over." But privately he was beginning to feel put upon by Supreme Court decisions that thwarted so many of his programs. He was determined to do something about it, and on February 5, 1937, he sent a message to Congress requesting that the Court be enlarged by six additional members for a total of fifteen judges on the panel. This effort blew up in his face.

As justification, he had cited the "heavy load" of cases before the Court and the number of judges over seventy (most of whom were Republicans). But the proposal drew immediate and ferocious criticism—not only from Republicans but from a number of Democrats as well. The Court itself weighed in on the matter by making public a letter showing a large number of cases heard and decided, reporting no backlog. Republicans charged that Roosevelt was attempting to "pack" the Court, and the term stuck. In the end it went nowhere.

Roosevelt continued his efforts to promote the latest New Deal programs, getting Congress to pass an act to create public housing for the urban poor. By mid-1937 the economy seemed to pick up smartly, with rising production and even signs of inflation. Roosevelt decided to take what amounted to a campaign trip across the country.

In whistle stops from Washington, D.C., through the Midwest and into the Far West, the president stood on the rear platform of his presidential train and told the people that the New Deal was working. He complained about the Supreme Court, and notably did not invite any member of

Congress—especially those of his own party, who had opposed his programs—to stand with him on the platform. It was a victory lap of sorts, with reservations over congressional inaction and judicial defeats. Roosevelt visited many of the huge construction sites of the New Deal—dams, roads, bridges, courthouse buildings—and the press gave him ample coverage. In Chicago hundreds of thousands lined the rail tracks along his route. The day before, he had told the press he had deliberately chosen Chicago to speak on a subject of "definite national Importance."

Nevertheless, the growing world crisis had been on his mind and his nerves for some time. In the Far East, the empire of Japan seemed intent on creating an enormous Japanese-led economic and cultural sphere of the entire region. In Europe, forces loyal to the Second Spanish Republic were in full-scale warfare with the fascist military army of General Francisco Franco, who was backed by Hitler's Nazis and the Fascist government of Italy. Nazi planes, Italian soldiers, and German "advisers" were wreaking havoc on loyalist guerrillas in a conflict that destabilized all of Europe.

These were only the rank beginnings of what would, not three years later, blow up into World War II. Roosevelt was perceptive enough to smell trouble in the air and understand full well that the United States did not exist in a vacuum.

Therefore, he told the Chicagoans that "the very foundations of civilization were threatened by the current reign of terror and international lawlessness." He said that if conditions got worse, America "could not expect mercy and the Western Hemisphere could not avoid attack."[7]

"The peace, the freedom, and the security of ninety percent of the world is being jeopardized by the other ten percent," he told the Chicagoans. "We are adopting such measures as will minimize our risk of involvement," he said, "but we cannot have complete protection in a world of disorder in which confidence and security have broken down."[8] When he had finished, Roosevelt went back inside his Pullman car and said to his secretary Grace Tully, "Well, it's done now. It was something that needed saying."

The uproar that followed was intense. Pacifists claimed that Roosevelt was leading the nation to war. The country remained deeply averse to conflict, and isolationist congressmen threatened the president with impeachment. Labor unions chimed in with resolutions of their own. Letters and telegrams poured into the White House, condemning the president's assertions. For his part, Roosevelt remarked to his speechwriter, "It is a terrible thing to look over your shoulder when you are trying to lead—and to find no one there."[9]

The next day, in answer to a barrage of question from reporters, Roosevelt seemed to take it all back. Or at least he didn't reassert his position as much as try to clarify that he wasn't about to get the United States involved in any war.

By the end of the year the steam had gone out of the false recovery and prices and production slumped once more. The stock market hit rock bottom again. Unemployment rose dramatically. No one seemed to know what to do, including Roosevelt. The New Dealers pushed for more spending, the Republicans pushed for more fiscal responsibility.

The anti–New Deal Democrats—and there were more than a few—seemed to be talking to the Republicans, with the result that by the end of the year Congress had passed only a small fraction of the legislation Roosevelt had proposed. Roosevelt and his aides Harry Hopkins, Ickes, and others set up a "hit list" of these errant conservative Democrats—mostly Southerners or Midwesterners—and sought ways to have them defeated in the coming elections. There was much grumbling among the president's opponents that Roosevelt was setting himself up to be a dictator—so much so that Roosevelt felt compelled to issue to the press a denial, stating that he didn't "have the qualifications."

John Maynard Keynes stuck his nose into it again, warning Roosevelt in a letter that "You are treading a very dangerous middle path. Your present policies seem to presume more power than you actually have." FDR gave him the brush-off.

By 1938 much of the New Deal was dead. The programs that were not killed by the Supreme Court had been killed by Congress, which had seen the election of a significant number of conservatives. Historian and biographer Alonzo Hamby sums up the situation succinctly: "Roosevelt, like most charismatic leaders, had generated intense emotions. Millions of Americans worshiped him; millions of others quite literally could not bear to speak his name." What had gone so wrong to bring his presidency "to a seeming dead end"? It was Roosevelt's "persistent quest to increase presidential power and probe its limits." It was as simple as that, and many people had tired of it.[10]

Yet neither the country nor the world was finished in 1938 with Franklin Delano Roosevelt. Nobody wanted to believe it: neither Roosevelt's America, nor Hitler's Germany, nor Churchill's England, nor Mussolini's Italy, nor Stalin's Soviet Union. But these nations, and many others, were on the verge of the most destructive war in the history of mankind.

As PRESSURE ROSE TO TAKE SIDES in the emerging European conflict, strong attitudes had developed among Americans. Because of close Anglo-American bonds and the brutality of Hitler's Germany, a majority of citizens naturally sympathized with England and France and deplored the Nazis. At the same time, there was a powerful division over whether or not to become involved. Many recalled all too well that the previous war had resulted in fifty-three thousand American combat deaths and apparently settled nothing, since the Europeans were at it again. No less a personage than former president Herbert Hoover complained of President Wilson's crusade to "make the world safe for democracy"; he observed that the previous effort of 1914–18 to "enforce civilization on the world resulted in at least fifteen dictatorships replacing prewar constitutional governments." Those against war frequently cited President George Washington's farewell address, which warned against "foreign entanglements."

But many others saw the imminent dangers of Nazism, which, if unchecked, posed a hazard not just to Western civilization but to the world itself. They pointed out that the Atlantic Ocean could not protect America, as had been demonstrated in the War of 1812 when British troops burned Washington, D.C.—let alone in the new age of submarines and heavy bombers.

The division manifested itself in a political split between the isolationists, who wished to remain neutral, and the internationalists or interventionists, who wanted to intervene. In Congress, the split leaned toward the isolationists, as it did on the editorial pages of most newspapers. Interventionists seemed more prevalent on the East Coast and New England, while isolationists remained centered in the Midwest.

An organization called America First emerged from a group of smaller antiwar associations, whose leadership included many prominent Americans including Charles Lindbergh, still at the height of his fame for flying solo over the Atlantic Ocean. They argued that America should rearm but save its power for defense of the country rather than go to Europe to fight. From the time the war broke out in 1939 through the fall of France in 1940, America First gained strength. By the time of Hitler's invasion of the Soviet Union, it was a million strong and blowing with the fury of a hurricane on America's airwaves. Rallies drew tens of thousands and received front-page coverage. Roosevelt was so incensed by Lindbergh's involvement that he publicly suggested that the great flier was an appeaser and a traitor, provoking Lindbergh to resign his colonel's commission in the Army Air Corps.

Roosevelt had long since concluded that sooner or later America would have to go to war with Hitler, but was loath to say so publicly, especially as another presidential election loomed. Based on reports he received from the Army and Navy, Roosevelt was very much opposed to going to war sooner because he was told that the U.S. military was completely unprepared for a major war. Even as late as 1941 there were only six ready-for-combat divisions in the entire Army, while Hitler alone had more than a hundred.

In the distasteful Munich Agreement of September 1938 the old European Allies—principally Britain and France—had agreed to let Hitler move on Czechoslovakia. Roosevelt held a conference at the White House with his military leaders. William C. Bullitt, now the U.S. ambassador to France, paid a dramatic visit to the president with alarming stories of Germany's overwhelming aviation might and the unpreparedness of the French. Roosevelt startled everyone in the room with a proposal to build ten thousand warplanes, an unheard-of number. It revealed a remarkable prescience that airpower would likely be the deciding factor in any future conflict.

Franklin Roosevelt was both an internationalist and an interventionist who had been carrying on a secret correspondence with Winston Churchill well before the war broke out. He then "lent" the British fifty older destroyers in exchange for ninety-nine-year leases on bases in the Caribbean and elsewhere, declaring that America was "the arsenal of democracy" (a phrase Harry Hopkins had picked up one day reading a newspaper).

Churchill desperately needed the destroyers to fight the growing U-boat menace around the British Isles. Knowing that the Republican Congress would "raise hell" over such a militarist venture, Roosevelt prepared the American people with a particularly Rooseveltian obfuscation: an offhand remark at a press conference that his administration was "holding conversations" with the British government about the acquisition of "land and air bases for the defense of the Western Hemisphere." Churchill, for his part, told Parliament that the United States resembled the Mississippi River. "It just keeps rolling along," he rejoiced. "Let it roll. Let it roll on—full flood, inexorable, irresistible, to broader lands and better days."[11]

Still later, Roosevelt persuaded Congress to go along with a program termed Lend-Lease, which was in practice an American giveaway of war matériel, food, and oil to the Allies fighting Germany (and later Japan). By the time it was done, U.S. factories and refineries had produced half a trillion dollars for the war effort, including seven thousand tanks and more than eighteen thousand warplanes for the Soviet Union alone. Stalin publicly admitted that he would have lost the war without American help.

During this period there was one thing that Roosevelt *could* do, which he *did* do, that became one of the most important acts of his political career. He set science into motion in defense of the country. He created a science and technology agency devoted to military development and selected the noted MIT scientist Vannevar Bush to run it. Employing a near majority of American physicists, chemists, engineers, and other scientists, this agency leaped ahead in the implementation of such new developments as radar, sonar, radio, high-altitude flying, ballistics, and so on, soon outstripping the Germans and the Japanese in these critical areas.

In October 1939 the president received a letter from the distinguished physicist and mathematician Albert Einstein, who had escaped Nazi Germany and was teaching at Princeton. Einstein told Roosevelt he and other noted scientists believed that "splitting the atom" was theoretically possible—and, more ominously, that the Germans were well along in the process. "This new phenomenon," Einstein informed the president, "would also lead to the construction of bombs, and it is conceivable—though much less certain— that extremely powerful bombs of a new type may thus be constructed."

Roosevelt, whose mind was doubtless on many things other than the theoretical exploration of the tiny atom, scrawled a note on Einstein's letter: "We ought to do something about this." He might just as easily have had his secretary dictate a thank-you note to the old math genius. Instead, the president's note led to the Manhattan Project and the first atomic bomb.[12]

BY NOW PEOPLE BEGAN TO NOTICE the dark circles under the president's eyes and craggy wrinkles along his nose to his chin. White House staff thought that he often looked weary. Yet for the most part, Roosevelt's cheerful personality shined refreshingly in his distinctive laughter that carried melodically down the long corridors from his office. His day began with breakfast in bed at about 8 a.m., amid half a dozen newspapers and conferences with his press secretary and other functionaries. Then he read cables from overseas and conferred with the Department of State. Harry Hopkins might drop in, or his appointments secretary Edwin "Pa" Watson. Near 10 a.m. Arthur Prettyman, Roosevelt's longtime valet with whom he'd grown close, would assist him into his small, armless wooden wheelchair and push him to the elevator to begin his workday in the Oval Office, which he'd had redesigned and rebuilt not long after his inauguration in 1933.

A look at his big desk in the sun-bright office with the sixteen-foot paned windows halfway round spoke volumes about the Rooseveltian character. It was cluttered with models of boats and cars, gifts of knives and pens, and every sort of doodad to delight the president's eye during a visit by a boring guest.

During a typical day he might see a dozen or more visitors, with about twice that many letters to be written in between. There would be papers to sign and often conferences with domestic or overseas implications. Evenings were not free either. "Eleanor is having a lot of do-gooders for dinner, and you know what that means," he would tell Grace Tully.[13]

The celebrated Harvard historian Samuel Eliot Morison observed that Roosevelt, during these fraught days, had a mind like a "political calculating machine." Morison, who wrote the official history of the U.S. Navy in

World War II, thought that the president's brain contained "an intricate instrument in which the Gallup Poll, the strength of the armed services and the probability of England's survival; the personalities of governors, senators and congressmen, Mussolini, Hitler, Churchill, Chiang Kai-shek and Tojo; the Irish, German, Italian and Jewish voters, the 'Help the Allies' people and the America Firsters" were combined with fine points on political maneuvering.[14]

WHILE ROOSEVELT SUPPLIED favorable belligerents, he cut off unfavorable ones, including the Japanese. He had long since banned the sale to Japan of scrap metals (which the Japanese were turning into warships) as well as tin and aluminum and the like. One critical item without which the Japanese Imperial Navy could not function was American oil. All through 1941, Japanese ambassadors in Washington protested and pleaded with the U.S. Department of State. But when Roosevelt cut off Japan's oil supply it produced the final crisis.

Desperate now for oil, the Japanese turned to the Dutch, who still governed the rich oil fields of Indonesia and Borneo. But the Dutch turned them away, prompting the Japanese government to take these places by force—even if it risked war with the United States. The U.S. Pacific Fleet, based at Pearl Harbor on Oahu, Hawaii, was the only thing standing in Japan's way.

The emperor's planners also decided that, while they were at it, they would seize the fertile rice fields of Southeast Asia—Vietnam, Laos, Cambodia—which were now in the hands of the French. From there they would embark on a "southward movement" to capture not only the oil-producing territories of the Netherlands but also the British prizes of Hong Kong, Singapore, and rubber-and-tin-rich Malaya and Burma. India could come later.

For years, the Japanese strategy for defeating the U.S. Navy was to create an "incident" that would somehow lure the American fleet across the Pacific. Cut off from its bases, the U.S. Navy could be harassed for thousands of miles by Japanese submarines and warplanes based on Japanese-mandated islands, until it would finally be destroyed by the Imperial Navy in Japanese home waters. Then a remarkable man with a novel and daring approach stepped into the picture.

Admiral Isoroku Yamamoto was commander of the Japanese Combined Fleet. Dead set against any war with the United States, the fifty-seven-year-old had been a naval attaché in Washington and attended Harvard University. He had seen the automobile factories of Detroit and the oil fields of Texas and correctly perceived that "Japan lacks the natural power for a naval race with America." He went on record to predict, "If I am told to fight regardless of consequence, I shall run wild for the first six months or a year—but I have utterly no confidence for the second or third years."[15]

Yamamoto was a realist, and he knew he stood little chance of preventing the army militarists from marching to the riches below the equator. If that came to pass he did not wish to leave his flank open to the powerful American fleet in Hawaii. Against decades of Japanese strategic thinking, he proposed instead to lure the American fleet out to sea via an enormous aerial assault on Pearl Harbor.

In its first iteration, Yamamoto's plan was conceived as a giant suicide attack, in which the valuable Japanese carriers would launch three hundred planes five hundred miles from Pearl Harbor and immediately head home—out of range of American response. These Japanese dive-bombers and torpedo planes would deploy their weapons on the U.S. ships and—their fate sealed because there would not be fuel enough to return to the carriers—the pilots would crash into the ocean in the ages-old Japanese tradition of seppuku, or honor suicide.[16]

Somehow, this solution didn't sit right with the naval authorities, who realized the impact of losing three hundred trained pilots, who took almost as long to train as it took to build an aircraft carrier. Nor did it sit well with Yamamoto himself, who became willing to gamble (he had been an inveterate poker player during his time in the United States) that his carriers could catch the Americans napping.

IN THE SUMMER OF 1940, Hitler's armies roared through Belgium and France. Roosevelt had convinced himself to run for an unprecedented third term. For several years, he had gone to great lengths preparing the nation for a vast conflict, eventually with the active support of Great Britain. Now a severe threat loomed from within—the isolationists—who could, if they gained power, reverse all of Roosevelt's enormous programs to build up the military. Worse, they might withdraw support for the British, who were now fighting the Nazis alone.

Instead of actively running for the nomination, Roosevelt conceived a strategy in which he would instead be drafted into candidacy by a convention that understood his overwhelming influence over the foreign policy crisis. It worked, and Roosevelt would run for president with agriculture secretary Henry Wallace as his vice president. Democratic Party bosses were relieved, as they felt Roosevelt was the only Democratic candidate who could beat a Republican. But those closest to Roosevelt were less enthusiastic. His personal secretary Missy LeHand had become so concerned about the president's health that she actually burst into tears when the results came in.

Unfortunately for the Republicans, their convention coincided with the fall of France to the Nazis. This possibly accounts for their selection of Wendell Willkie, an internationalist who four years earlier had been a Democrat, as the Republican presidential candidate in favor of the isolationist Robert Taft.

The election debates were exceedingly spirited, centered on whether the United States would go to war. Both Roosevelt and Willkie danced around the subject at first, although a week before the election Roosevelt famously told a national audience in a campaign speech broadcast from Boston that "while I am talking to you mothers and fathers, I give you one more assurance. I have said this before, and I shall say it again, and again, and again. Your boys are not going to be sent into any foreign wars."[17]

He went on to declare that the purpose of drafting and training millions of Americans was solely "to form a force so strong that, by its very existence, it will keep the threat of war far away from our shores."[18]

Much has been made of these statements in retrospect. Some insisted that they were out-and-out lies told by the president, a charge that is probably not far from the truth.

Roosevelt was savvy enough to understand the consequences of letting England fall to Hitler, who could then conceivably gobble up the rest of Europe, Scandinavia, the Balkans, the Middle East, Africa, and most likely India. Once that was achieved, it would be practically impossible to defeat him, because there would be no overseas bases from which to operate.

Roosevelt could talk a good game of pledging that the U.S. military buildup was strictly for home defense. But he also realized all too well that Hitler was going to have to be beaten in Europe, and that Great Britain couldn't do it alone. He knew that the American boys he spoke of, sooner or later, were going to have to carry the fight across the Atlantic, though he could not know or even guess at what shape the thing would finally take. Wars, especially one this size, are always subject to seismic changes.

Meantime, in anticipation of congressional opposition, Roosevelt pulled off one of the slickest political coups of modern times by snatching two of the staunchest Republicans for his new cabinet. They were the venerable Henry L. Stimson, former secretary of state under Herbert Hoover whom Roosevelt made secretary of war, and Frank Knox, former Republican vice presidential candidate and publisher of the *Chicago Daily News,* who became Roosevelt's new secretary of the Navy. This gave at least the appearance of the administration becoming more bipartisan, a condition Roosevelt knew he would need in the coming months.

The Republicans were so infuriated at this presidential expropriation that in the summer of 1940 they expelled both men from the party at their convention. They might not have bothered, for all the good it did. Roosevelt won by a landslide in the November election.

His speech at his inauguration on January 20, 1941, was particularly acute. He spoke of the so-called death of democracy in the wake of the rise of the Axis powers and the Hitler-Stalin pact. "Democracy is not dying," he told the throng from the steps of the U.S. Capitol, "and it is up to all of us to keep it alive." Seated next to him were Eleanor and his eighty-six-year-old mother, Sara. Once again, watching from a discreet distance, escorted by two Secret Service agents, was Lucy Rutherfurd. Her seventy-eight-year-old husband was ill and wheelchair-bound; Lucy and the president had found the time to take secret rides together in the

Virginia countryside near her home. She was almost fifty now, and still quite striking. According to White House ushers, Roosevelt took his Scottish terrier Fala along with him on these intimate trips—possibly as a beard![19]

★★★★★

IN SEPTEMBER, SARA ROOSEVELT DIED. She had been ailing, and when word came that the end might be near Franklin rushed to her bedside at Hyde Park and sat with her for a day, holding her hand until she was gone. The president was heartbroken, and the country mourned with him for this remarkable woman who had devoted her life to her son. In her daily newspaper column, Eleanor wrote that the expression "Grande Dame" was "truly applicable to her"—although later she told her daughter, Anna, that "I couldn't feel any emotion or any real grief or sense of loss, and that seem[s] terrible after thirty-six years of close association." Nevertheless, Eleanor dutifully made all of the funeral arrangements.[20]

Matters of state ground on, and the grieving Roosevelt now faced the task of winning congressional approval of his Lend-Lease program. The isolationist faction of the Republican Party fought him at every turn. They filibustered, made inflammatory statements to the newspapers, and stalled by tacking on a string of petty amendments. But in the end the act passed, much to Roosevelt's and Churchill's relief. In retrospect, this act might have won the war—for if Hitler had been able to beat the Russians in the summer and fall of 1941 there would in all likelihood have been no stopping him.

Next came another bombshell: the extension of the draft act. The legislation had been passed by a contentious Congress the previous year with a mind toward training young American men in the basics of military science—formations, drill, riflery, military protocol, and the like—so that if there was ever a need for their services they would have at least a head start. But with the evolving world situation, Roosevelt wanted to extend the one-year service provision to an unlimited time, as in a national emergency.

Republicans were vehement, accusing Roosevelt of mongering the country into war. One of his prime antagonists was the Republican congressman from his own district in Dutchess County: the strident, Roosevelt-hating Hamilton Fish. As the debate raged, congressional galleries were packed to the limits, watched over by nervous Capitol policemen. Pressure was applied without mercy, with prominent Democrats phoning prominent constituents to quell opposition: a deft Rooseveltian touch. At last a vote was cast on August 12. Tensions ran high as the clerk of the House polled all 432 members. When he was finished the House Speaker, Sam Rayburn, looked at the tally and declared that the draft extension had passed by a vote of 203 to 202—one vote! Confusion broke out as reporters rushed to telephones, the gallery erupted, congressmen cheered or swore, in some cases charging that their vote was not recorded. Hamilton Fish declared that Roosevelt had won a "Pyrrhic victory through the use of power, patronage, and political bosses." In the end all that didn't matter; the bill had passed. And it was a good thing too—for the summer of '41 was to be the last peaceful summer Americans would see for four long, blood-soaked years.

THE JAPANESE WARPLANES APPEARED over Pearl Harbor just before 8 a.m. on Sunday, December 7, 1941. They had been spotted an hour earlier on a rudimentary mobile radar set on the northernmost point of Oahu. The apparatus was manned by two army privates, who telephoned headquarters that a large flight of planes was appearing on their screen. All the radar operators had gone to breakfast, leaving a rookie lieutenant in charge. He told the privates "not to worry about it," as a flight of B-17s was due in that morning from the West Coast. This was only one of many breakdowns that day in the defense of Pearl Harbor.

A warning message from the War Department had been sent earlier that day after U.S. intelligence experts decoded a top secret message from Tokyo, ordering the Japanese Embassy in Washington to burn its code books and other secret documents. The message was delayed by solar interference to the radio waves and wound up being sent by regular Western Union delivery. It arrived at Pearl Harbor headquarters two hours too late.

An hour before the attack, just outside the harbor, the U.S. destroyer *Ward* had fired on and sunk a Japanese midget submarine. The *Ward* radioed a report of the incident, but it was received by people incompetent to decode it. When it was finally deciphered, the commanding officer could not decide whether to put everyone on alert. There had been too many similar reports in the past that turned out to be attacks on whales or giant blackfish or just plain old flotsam. So the commander turned to a time-honored Navy custom: he told the duty officer to tell the *Ward* to "await developments." These were not long in coming.

The Japanese attack was devastating. Of the eight battleships of the Pacific Fleet, four were sunk and the others badly damaged. All of the cruisers were badly damaged, and nearly four hundred U.S. planes were wrecked on the ground. More than two thousand servicemen lost their lives, and more than a hundred civilians were killed or wounded.

Japanese authorities had installed a nationwide system of loudspeakers on telephone poles on every corner. The night of the attack, the radio broadcast an address by the Japanese dictator General Hideki Tojo, who spoke of "annihilating" the West. Up and down the streets people cheered and clapped, then the radio played "Umi Yukaba," a kind of Japanese version of "God Bless America." It went this way:

> *Across the sea, corpses in the waters*
> *Across the mountains, corpses in the fields*
> *I shall die only for the Emperor*
> *I shall never look back.*[21]

In Washington, Roosevelt was having lunch at the White House with his troubleshooter Harry Hopkins when word came from Navy Secretary Frank Knox that a message was just received: "Air raid Pearl Harbor. This is not a drill."[22]

The president knew from the state of negotiations that the Japanese would probably start a war, but not where or when. This news, he told

Hopkins, proved that the Japanese had been planning the attack the entire time they said they were "negotiating in good faith." More information began to come in describing the damages; it was even worse than originally thought. Roosevelt didn't learn the whole story for several weeks. He was particularly irate about U.S. planes being caught on the ground.

Anger at the Japanese was palpable, but that toward the Army and Navy commanders at Pearl Harbor vied for a close second; they were immediately relieved of command and vilified throughout the land. But there was much more to the story than that. After vigorous investigations that lasted years, both commanders were shown to have been far less guilty of unpreparedness than was originally thought.

Roosevelt also soon came under suspicion, after the isolationist senator Gerald P. Nye told an audience on the evening of the attack, "The president has maneuvered us into this war." Generations of historians, critics, and cranks have amplified that statement—some going so far as to charge that Roosevelt actually knew the time and place of the attack but had withheld it in order to bring America into the war.

This last charge is ridiculous. Roosevelt was in fact looking for a reason to get the United States into the war but, as a former secretary of the Navy, the notion that he would allow all those sailors to be killed and ships to be sunk is too monstrous to contemplate. Besides, if he had known about the attack, why wouldn't he have warned Navy commanders so they could have ambushed the Japanese as they prepared to bomb Pearl Harbor and sunk *their* ships, and shot down *their* planes, and killed *their* sailors? That would certainly have been a far smarter choice for the president than seeing his Pacific Fleet at the bottom of the ocean.

"We are all in the same boat," Roosevelt told Winston Churchill, who could barely contain himself on the evening following the attack. Churchill had called the president from Chequers, the traditional country home of the British prime minister, at the close of a weekend in Kent. In a telegram next day, just to follow up, Roosevelt added, "And it is a ship which cannot and will not be sunk." Afterward Churchill wrote: "I knew then that the war was won."[23]

CHAPTER TEN

On the eve of World War II, Churchill and half a dozen conservative MPs had been at the Other Club in London to bemoan the appeasement of the Nazis by then prime minister Neville Chamberlain. On their way out, they passed "a large private-party room full of gay [in the old sense] diners and dancers." Churchill and several others stopped for a moment to look in. As they walked away, he muttered, "Those poor people! They little know what they will have to face."

Great Britain was officially at war in 1939, but there was precious little action except at sea. By October Hitler had absorbed Austria, Czechoslovakia, and Poland, aligned himself with Russia, and retained the military initiative. Now he was organizing his armies and biding his time. But there was plenty of work to do at the Admiralty. British intelligence knew the Nazis had been producing submarines far in excess of those sent to prey upon British shipping in the previous war, and these new models were far more sophisticated and dangerous.

To make matters worse, Irish prime minister Eamon de Valera, whose country had declared itself neutral in the conflict, had venally ensured that the British lost their rights to the so-called Treaty Ports on Ireland's Atlantic coast, making them unavailable to the Royal Navy's antisubmarine forces. This sudden, shocking unavailability, Churchill said, put England's very existence at peril, since she did not have the resources to defend the sea-lanes from England proper and the entire country was dependent on imported food. The agonizing remedy was for Britain to acquire enough destroyers to make up for this deficiency, but there was no way to build them in time for what was coming. He had hoped that the United States might spare some old destroyers left over from World War I but his entreaties thus far had been rebuffed.

Many people thought Churchill was too old for a job as demanding as first lord of the Admiralty during a war, but he proved them wrong. One of his staff secretaries reported: "When Winston was at the Admiralty, the place was buzzing with atmosphere, with electricity. When he was away on tour it was dead, dead, dead." At meetings of the war cabinet, Churchill was a perfect tornado of ideas, plans, and solutions, prompting one of his fellow cabinet members to complain: "Arguing with him is like arguing with a brass band."[1]

One day, Churchill was pleasantly startled to find a letter from Franklin Roosevelt in his box that began: "My dear Churchill, it is because you and I occupied similar positions in World War I [alluding to Roosevelt's time as assistant secretary of the Navy] that I want you to know how glad I am that you are back again in the Admiralty." It concluded with a personal note: "Winston . . . I shall at all times welcome it, if you will keep me in touch personally with anything you want me to know about," by sending sealed letters in each other's diplomatic pouches. He added, with typical Roosevelt charm, that "I am glad you did the Marlborough volumes before this thing started—and I much enjoyed reading them."

Churchill's mouth must have dropped open. He rushed with the letter to the war cabinet to point out its "enormous implications." To be able to open a regular correspondence with the president of the United States, who controlled the U.S. Navy! Churchill suggested that they might induce Roosevelt to use an executive order to create a naval protective belt around the United States that would extend down into the Caribbean, in which British merchant vessels might find safety from German U-boats. Churchill responded immediately in taking Roosevelt up on the offer for correspondence. He signed it "from Naval Person"—until, that is, he was made prime minister, after which he signed it from "Former Naval Person." It was the first of 1,688 letters between the two men.

All through the long winter the Allies had been scheming and jockeying for position against Hitler's Wehrmacht. Churchill pushed a plan to invade Norway, which was supplying Swedish iron ore for German steel mills. But on April 9, 1940, Hitler struck first with a large invasion force that took Denmark and Norway within a month. Churchill pushed to form a British and French operation to take Norway back.

The best thing to come out of it was the splendid action of Churchill's Royal Navy and the Royal Air Force (RAF), which sank two German heavy cruisers, two light cruisers, ten destroyers, and a dozen other war vessels and put a battleship out of commission. This great naval whipping helped to dissuade Hitler later that summer from trying to invade England across the Channel. Otherwise, the mission to Norway was a disaster, and the troops had to be evacuated (minus the six thousand who had been killed). Churchill was in for a roasting in the press for his sanctioning of the Norway operation, but the action of the Royal Navy got him off the hook.

The Norway fiasco and a ferocious assault by the Germans to invade and occupy the Low Countries had finally riled the House of Commons to change the government. Churchill made a fiery speech that did not mention his old friend Neville Chamberlain, but did make plain his dissatisfaction with the way things were playing out. Another member drew out for the prime minister's edification Cromwell's hoary old screed, "You have sat too long for all the good you have been doing. Depart I say, and let us have done with you. In the name of God, go."

Chamberlain got the picture and resigned. It emerged that a coalition government would be necessary. The king, George VI, liked Churchill personally but had been raised to regard him as a loose cannon. Nevertheless, Churchill's chief adversary for the job, Lord Halifax, declined to take the position, and on May 10, 1940, Winston Churchill at last became the prime minister of Great Britain, a position he had sought all of his life. He took it under the most dire conditions imaginable, for by then the Nazis were in the process of invading France. If France fell, Churchill knew that England would be next.

When he finally got into bed at 3 a.m. that morning Churchill said he "became conscious of a profound sense of the whole scene.

"I felt that I had been walking with destiny, and that all my past life had been preparation for this hour and for this trial. Ten years in the political wilderness had freed me from ordinary party antagonisms. My warnings over the last six years had been so numerous, so detailed, and were now so terribly vindicated, that no one could gainsay me. I could not be reproached either for making the war, or with want of preparation for it. I thought I knew a good deal about it all, and I was sure I would not fail. Therefore, although impatient for the morning, I slept soundly, and had no need for cheering dreams. Facts are better than dreams."[2]

Beginning in 1939, as the German menace loomed, Britain had sent an army of more than four hundred thousand men (including thousands of tanks, artillery pieces, transportation trucks, etc.) to help the French defend the uncompleted portion of their vaunted Maginot Line. Erected at great expense after the First World War, it had been built to ensure that the Germans could never again invade France.

Churchill visited France five times during the fighting, putting himself in danger of being captured and surely put to death by Hitler. In late May, the Germans crashed through the Ardennes forest southeast of the Maginot Line and the defensive fortifications erected by the French and British forces. They had expected the main enemy attack to come through Belgium, as it had in the First World War. Instead, they were outflanked by the Germans, whose armies were led by Panzer divisions of powerful tanks. It quickly became obvious to Churchill that the position of the British army was untenable, and that the only sensible thing was to try to evacuate it.

In military science, arguably the only movement more dangerous than an amphibious attack against a defended position is a withdrawal under fire—and that was exactly what the huge British Expeditionary Force (BEF) faced between May 26 and June 4. To evacuate that many men back to England, without much preparation, under air bombardment, and with only a few days' notice, was an act that came to be known as the Miracle of Dunkirk.

On May 28, Churchill convened a meeting of the government's twenty-five ministers in his room at the House of Commons. "I described the course of events and showed them where we were, and all that was in the balance," he wrote later in his history of the war. "Then I said quite casually . . . Of course, whatever happens at Dunkirk, we shall fight on." Instead of any signs of ambivalence, all of the ministers rushed to his chair and grasped his hand or patted him on the back.

"I was sure that every minister was sure to have been killed quite soon. And to have all his family and possessions destroyed, rather than give in . . . There was a white glow, overpowering, sublime, which ran through our island from end to end."[3] That was honest valor, pure and simple, from an old gentleman who had seen enough war to last a lifetime and was now confronting the greatest danger of it all: the destruction of his home and hearth.

Every available military craft in England, every ferry, every suitable ship and boat, including fishing vessels and private motor yachts, was assembled. During the evening and night hours of May 26, the rescue armada made its way across the English Channel to save the helpless soldiers stranded on the beaches of northern France. Of the 400,000 soldiers, 338,000 were evacuated—and in the days to follow, more than 150,000 French soldiers and civilians, as well as troops from Poland, Norway, and other nations overrun by the Nazis, were also brought to England to fight another day. They had snatched victory from the jaws of defeat, and the whole of England celebrated.

When the last of the soldiers had been returned to British soil, Churchill made one of his most famous speeches to Parliament in which he concluded: "Even though many large tracts of Europe and many old and famous states have fallen or may fall into the grip of the Gestapo and all the odious apparatus of Nazi rule, we shall not flag or fail. We shall go on to the end. We shall fight in France, we shall fight on the seas and oceans, we shall fight in the air, we shall defend our island no matter what the cost may be. We shall fight on the beaches, we shall fight on the landing grounds, we shall fight in the fields and in the streets; we shall fight in the hills; we shall never surrender."

To which he added ominously: "And if, which I do not for a moment believe, this island or a large part of it were subjugated and starving, then our Empire beyond the seas, armed and guarded by the British fleet, would carry on the struggle until, in God's good time, the New World, with all its power and might, steps forth to the rescue and the liberation of the old."[4]

These were strong words for perilous times. As they spread by radio and newspapers throughout the British Empire, people obtained pictures of Churchill and had them framed. Or they tacked them to the walls of their homes or offices with the most celebrated lines affixed.

Churchill's speech also found its way across the Atlantic. The part about the "New World stepping forth to the rescue of the old" was not lost on the isolationists, who used it to rally their supporters, nor the interventionists, of whom Franklin Roosevelt was becoming an ardent champion.

On the last day of the Dunkirk rescue, Churchill was already thinking of ways to beat the Germans. And he was not thinking defensively either. Instead, he proposed offensive amphibious hit-and-run actions against the Nazis using armored vehicles. This plan resulted in the construction of the great shipyards of the Clyde and numerous vessels designated Landing Craft Tank (LCT).

On June 22, 1940, France fell to the Germans and signed a disgraceful armistice. According to the terms of the French defeat, the Germans occupied the northern, industrial part of the country and set up a puppet system in the south and the French colonies, in which the French were allowed to govern themselves through bureaucrats who took their orders from the Nazis. This government's seat was in the town of Vichy, and thus became known as the Vichy government. Now that Hitler had conquered and consolidated most of Europe the British were, at last, alone.

As soon as France was occupied, Hitler began building airfields along the French coast across the Channel from England, as well as improving half a dozen ports to pen the German submarines. In harbors up and down the Pas de Calais the Germans began assembling an armada of barges and other transport craft in preparation for an invasion of England. From Dover to Folkestone, people using strong telescopes could actually see the enemy on the cliffs of France constructing fortifications and building gun emplacements. They could even spot knots of German officers, pointing and gesturing. They were coming.

On the day of the French capitulation, Churchill gave another of his memorable addresses to the British people. "The Battle for France," he said, "is over. I expect that the Battle for Britain is about to begin . . . The whole fury and might of the enemy must very soon be turned on us . . .

"Let us therefore brace ourselves to our duties, and so bear ourselves that if the British Empire lasts for a thousand years, men will still say, '*This* was their finest hour.'"

It was an immensely stirring speech, met everywhere with accolades and acclaim. But it was also beginning to seem that famous words were all that Britain had to defend herself. The retreated Dunkirk army, in disarray, had left its arms and equipment in France. Britain had a navy, but so did Germany. Britain also had the Royal Air Force, so far indefinite and untested. But there, in the hearts of those young men, lay the reckoning for the balance.

IMMEDIATELY AFTER THE FALL OF FRANCE, a significant crisis arose over the disposition of the great French navy. With France now for all intents under German control, what was to become of its fleet, second only to the Royal Navy in power? There were seven French battleships, a dozen cruisers, scores of destroyers, and a large complement of submarines, oilers, tenders, and so on. If they should fall into German hands it would tip the balance of sea power in the Atlantic to the Nazis. Worse, if this were combined with the Italian fleet as well, the balance would tip the entire world to the Nazis.

Churchill was determined not to allow this to happen. But the scenario presented a difficult diplomatic predicament, as Great Britain still had important relations with the Vichy government and with the French colonial possessions. Any attempt to strong-arm the French navy would be seen as a dramatic breach of faith.

On one of Churchill's visits to France during the German invasion, Admiral François Darlan, commander of the French fleet, assured him that he would never allow the fleet to fall into German hands. But now Darlan was minister of marine under Vichy, equivalent to first lord of the Admiralty, or secretary of the U.S. Navy. So long as France was controlled by the

Germans, and its fleet remained in contested waters, there was no telling what might happen. To Churchill, the mere possibility that the Germans could suddenly incorporate the French ships into their own fleet was in itself an unparalleled disaster.

At the time, the bulk of the French navy lay inactive at Mediterranean ports in French Algeria, watched by British warships lest the French suddenly try to break into the open sea. In June, right after France fell, Churchill approved a plan under which the British admiral commanding a larger fleet in the Mediterranean would present the French naval commander at the Algerian port of Oran with a series of choices that amounted to an ultimatum.

1. Sail away with the British and fight the Germans and Italians.
2. Sail to England, the United States, or French-owned Martinique—out of the war zone—and remain there, demilitarized and out of the action.
3. Sink your ships at their present moorings within six hours.
4. Or we will sink them for you.

The ultimatum was presented to the French commander Admiral Marcel-Bruno Gensoul, who refused to answer it. The British naval officers found their duty highly distasteful, for the French ships were sitting ducks and everyone knew how many French sailors were aboard. When they so informed the Admiralty, the following word came back: "The French ships must comply with our terms or sink themselves or be sunk by you before dark."

With that, the British commander ordered the bombardment to begin. Before dark, most of the French naval fleet was either sunk or put out of action, and some two thousand French sailors were dead.

This caused many hard feelings among Frenchmen (Vichy or otherwise), and also in the French colonies, which now considered the British to be enemies. But Churchill, according to his secretary, had an ulterior motive: he wanted to impress on the American people—in particular, Franklin Roosevelt—that Great Britain was so deadly serious about continuing the fight against Hitler that it would take this unprecedented action against an ally (or former ally). That message was fully conveyed through the American press, which took serious note of British tenacity.

The next day, Churchill had to tell the House of Commons what had transpired in Britain's name, and he was greatly concerned about the reaction. As historian Roy Jenkins writes: "One cannot imagine a Halifax-led government giving the order for Oran."

When he had finished his address, Churchill sat down while the members seemed for the moment stunned; then cheers broke out all around that lasted a long time. Churchill sat on his bench "with tears pouring down his cheeks."[5]

Years later when he wrote his series on the war, Churchill summed up his country's situation and the uncertainties of the times in a philosophic passage that bears repeating here.

> After Oran it became clear to all countries that the British government and nation were resolved to fight on to the last. But even if there were no moral weakness in Britain, how could the appalling physical facts be overcome? Our armies at home were known to be almost unarmed except for rifles. There were in fact hardly five hundred field-guns of any sort and hardly two hundred medium and heavy tanks in the whole country. Months must pass before our factories could make good even the munitions lost at Dunkirk. Can one wonder that the world at large was convinced that our hour of doom had struck? . . .
>
> The buoyant and imperturbable temper of Britain, which I had the honor to express, may well have turned the scale. Here was this people, who in the years before the war had gone to the extreme bounds of pacifism and improvidence, who had indulged in the sport of party politics, and who, though so weakly armed, had advanced light-heartedly into the centre of European affairs, now confronted with the reckoning alike of their virtuous impulses and neglectful arrangements. They were not even dismayed. They defied the conquerors of

Europe. They seemed willing to have their island reduced to a shambles rather than give in.

The threat of German invasion was foremost in everyone's mind—most especially Churchill's. Britain watched defiantly as Hitler's invasion barges piled up in French harbors and construction on large-caliber guns proceeded on the cliffs of France. But the more Hitler and his generals considered it, invading England—or, as they referred to it, Operation Sea Lion—was going to be far more difficult than previously imagined.

For one thing, Britain had more than a thousand warships in its navy, some of which ceaselessly patrolled the Channel; behind them were powerful squadrons of destroyers, cruisers, and battleships, ready to take action. Then there was the Royal Air Force with more than a thousand warplanes. Every prospective beachhead would be heavily fortified and the British army could reinforce easily by busing or trucking units to the scene of action. By one British estimate, even if Hitler could somehow avoid detection and land up to a hundred thousand men on British soil, Britain's destroyers and other large warships would cut his supply line within an hour and turn their guns on the enemy and his equipment ashore, while the fighters and bombers blew the hapless invaders into pieces.

The more the Germans considered it, the more they didn't like the looks of it. By mid-July Hitler had decided to make a backhanded "peace offer" of sorts in a speech aimed at the British—and at Churchill in particular—in which he basically offered to let bygones be bygones. Churchill was having none of it and had his foreign secretary dismiss the gesture by declaring, "We will not stop fighting until freedom is secure."

Hitler was not a man to be jilted in such a fashion, nor could he allow an armed and hostile England to remain in his rear for long. After conferring with his army commander General Gerd von Rundstedt and air force chief Hermann Göring, Hitler took their advice, concluding that there could be no invasion of England until the Germans had destroyed the British air force and had complete air superiority over the proposed landing beaches. There were six of these, stretching along a hundred miles from Ramsgate to Portsmouth.

This began what became known as the Battle of Britain, which was fought almost entirely in the air. First came German bombing raids on English cities, accompanied by German fighters. The plan was that the Messerschmitt aircraft and their hotshot pilots would quickly overwhelm and destroy the green British youngsters in their Hurricanes and Spitfires.

Although the Messerschmitt was an excellent specimen, especially at high altitudes, it had a fatal flaw. Even coming from fields right over in France, it burned up so much fuel that by the time it got over England there was precious time left for a dogfight; the British pilots simply had to go up to meet them. Moreover, the British quickly discovered the Messerschmitt's superiority at altitude and refused to rise to the bait.

And the British also had a further advantage. In the late 1930s, the famous American flier Jimmy Doolittle visited England as a representative of the Shell Oil Company and convinced the minister of defense that he could get almost a third more power out of the Rolls-Royce engines in both Hurricanes and Spitfire fighter planes by using very high octane fuel. Doolittle, who had a PhD in aeronautical engineering from MIT, knew what he was talking about. After the war, the British credited him with saving England from a German invasion.

Day after day, British citizens could stop in their fields, or go out into the yard, or get off their bicycles to watch the air show. Hundreds of men flew planes that hummed, mosquito-like, high up in the sky. They left long white contrails, twisting and diving and quite often falling in flames.

When it came to air battles, the Germans had yet another problem they did not put into the equation until too late: When a British pilot's plane was downed, he parachuted out in his own country, or was fished out of the Channel, to fight another day. When a German went down he was lost for good, one way or the other.

The campaign went on from the middle of July through the first week in September, when German intelligence falsely concluded that the RAF was on its last legs. This induced them to commit a huge number of bombers— and their fighter escorts—in daily attacks on London and other cities. It was the beginning of the London Blitz (short for *Blitzkrieg,* or lightning war) and was supposed to commence the final destruction of British airpower.

It did no such thing. Despite wildly outrageous claims on both sides, Germany and Great Britain had about the same number of aircraft starting out. British tenacity, and the above-mentioned advantages of the RAF, reduced the German strength considerably. Although the prevailing view at Göring's headquarters was that the Royal Air Force was finished, the British by this point had an advantage in planes and were turning out fighters at a rate of a thousand a month.

After two weeks of unsustainable losses, Hitler called the battle off on this front and moved to the night bombing of British cities, thus giving up on air superiority, or supremacy: the major precondition of the vaunted Nazi invasion of England. For his part, Churchill famously remarked in the House of Commons on the skill and bravery of the young pilots and air crews: "Never in the field of human conflict was so much owed by so many to so few."

The British did not yet know that the Battle of Britain was completely over, and many still feared a German invasion. But the statistics make clear that Germany had suffered a major defeat. The Luftwaffe had 2,585 pilots and crew killed (and 925 captured) compared with 1,262 in the Royal Air Force. The Germans lost 1,977 aircraft (out of 2,550 at the start of the campaign), compared with an RAF loss of 1,744 planes (out of 1,963 to start). Also, some forty thousand civilians were killed by German bombs in the eight months of the Blitz, about half of them in London.

If Hitler thought he could bomb the British into accepting his peace offer, he was by now sorely disabused, and the Germans would soon abandon the invasion plan entirely. Not only that, but at the end of his speech to Parliament Churchill announced his agreement with the United States to send to Great Britain fifty World War I–era destroyers in exchange for military bases on British territory.

The destroyers were a godsend to stem the grievous losses from German U-boats. Roosevelt had refused to send them earlier, citing the Neutrality Act. But after the sinking of the French fleet, and the encouraging results of the Battle of Britain, Roosevelt determined to get around the act (which forbade the "selling" of arms to belligerents) with the "lease" gambit. This would lead to the famous Lend-Lease Act the following year, in which the United States abandoned practically all pretense of being neutral in the war.

This was itself a direct result of Churchill's near constant correspondence with Franklin D. Roosevelt.

WHILE THE BATTLE OF BRITAIN RAGED in the air over England, Churchill saw to it that the British were not idle in fighting the Axis, which would include Italy, under its Fascist dictator Benito Mussolini.

On June 10, 1940, while a German invasion of England was still a very real possibility, Mussolini declared that Italy was at war with Great Britain. Two days later, the British Mediterranean fleet, with the aircraft carrier *Ark Royal*, attacked the seaport city Tobruk in Italian-occupied Libya and sank the Italian cruiser *San Georgio*.

Mussolini then ordered his North African Tenth Army, consisting of approximately 150,000 infantrymen under Field Marshal Rodolfo Graziani, to invade neighboring Egypt, a British possession. But Graziani moved at a snail's pace in preparation, stringing his army out along the only respectable road in the area, which runs along the Mediterranean seashore. There, he stopped and waited near the Egyptian border. Prodded constantly by Mussolini to advance and capture Egypt, with the riches of Alexandria and the priceless Suez Canal, Graziani at last began to move.

The British defense in Egypt at that point consisted of a few paltry infantry, motorized infantry, and armored infantry battalions—perhaps two thousand men—to face an Italian army well over a hundred thousand strong. But face them they did. Immediately, the British organized hit-and-run raiding parties to harass and disorient the enemy.

Churchill was delighted, for he loved going after the enemy. If he couldn't get him yet on the European continent, he would go after him in the African deserts, even when he knew his men were greatly outnumbered. His military adviser General Hastings "Pug" Ismay said of Churchill: "He is not a gambler, but never shrinks from taking a calculated risk. His whole heart and soul are in the battle, and he is an apostle of the offensive."[6]

These parties, consisting of motorized light artillery and machine guns, would come storming, mad dog–like, out of the desert and smack into an

Italian unit with all guns blazing. The shock was such that the British found, to their astonishment, that there was little resistance; they often shot up all their ammunition before roaring away again. A series of these raids cost the British forty killed and wounded—but the enemy's losses were "ten times as many, including a hundred and fifty vehicles destroyed," Churchill announced.[7]

The head of Graziani's long column came to rest in Egypt's Sidi Barrani, a coastal town about sixty miles into Egypt, and instead of continuing the advance there it remained. For reasons that are not clear, Graziani had decided to stop and fortify Sidi Barrani and several other towns along the coastal road, apparently to wait for developments. The developments were not long in coming.

Churchill, meanwhile, was desperately trying to bring adequate military forces into Egypt. But he was hampered by uncertainty over the possibility of a Nazi invasion of the home islands, as well as the enemy submarine menace in the Mediterranean that was presently causing convoys to steam all the way around the Cape of Good Hope in the far south end of Africa and back through the Indian Ocean to the western end of Suez. This tortuous route took three times as long, but the notion of having a wolf pack of German submarines suddenly descend on a convoy of troopships, or transports loaded with tanks, was too much to bear.

On the bright side, Churchill was delighted when elements of his Mediterranean fleet attacked the Italian fleet at its main base at Taranto. The British surprised the Italians with a moonlight aircraft carrier assault from a hundred and seventy miles away. The battle raged for an hour, with half of the planes carrying torpedoes and the other half bombs or flares. The Italians put up a ferocious antiaircraft fire, shooting down two British planes, but the result of the raid showed a clear Allied victory. Three Italian battleships were torpedoed as well as a cruiser and many other ships damaged. In addition, a substantial amount of damage was done to the main Italian dockyard. Churchill gleefully reported that the Italian battle fleet was put out of action "for at least six months. By this single stroke, the balance of naval power in the Mediterranean was decisively altered," he crowed.

"I am sure you have been pleased about Taranto," Churchill wrote to Roosevelt. "The three uninjured battleships have quitted Taranto today, which perhaps means they are withdrawing to Trieste."[8]

As the months passed by Field Marshal Graziani remained inert in his fortress towns along the Mediterranean coast, while Churchill strived furiously to reinforce the Egyptian garrison. The Italian delay was a godsend, although the British were able to muster only thirty-six thousand troops—including divisions from Australia and India—against Graziani's imposing host. This became the Desert Army. The men would call themselves "Desert Rats" but they fought magnificently.

Outnumbered four to one, the British force nevertheless had the advantage of being completely motorized: one division of tanks, brigades and battalions of motorized machine guns, and light artillery. Churchill was anxious for some kind of offensive action against the enemy, rather than simply waiting for him to make the first move. The Desert Army gave him all he wanted and more.

There was uncertainty over exactly what capabilities the Italians had for making war. To find out, the commanders of the Desert Army decided to stage a full-scale raid on their fortress cities. The first target would be Sidi Barrani, about sixty miles down the coast highway from the British positions. The British did not come down the highway, however; as with previous hit-and-run raids, they came out of the desert, where they lay motionless by day, camouflaged from the Italian air patrols.

At dawn on the ninth of December they charged into the environs of Sidi Barrani. The Italians had excavated a huge antitank ditch that stretched for miles, but British infantry crossed it and kept the enemy busy while British engineers filled in the ditch.

Taken by surprise, the Italians initially gave up ground and personnel. By that evening a battalion of the venerable Coldstream Guards reported capturing so many prisoners it was impossible to count them. Instead they radioed that they had "about five acres of officers and two hundred acres of other rank."[9]

Churchill was following the battle late into the night from the map room at 10 Downing Street. He was actually patched in to the radio transmissions from the various units engaged in the fight, which sometimes, but not always, made it more difficult to follow the action. At one point some tank commander interrupted to report that he had reached "the second B in Bug Bug." Churchill went to his map table and traced along with his finger until he found a village named Bug Bug and was much pleased.[10]

Great Britain's Mediterranean fleet provided enormously effective artillery fire to support the operation, as did the Royal Air Force, which bombed, flew reconnaissance missions, and strafed the hapless Italians. By December 12 Churchill could tell Parliament that the fortress of Sidi Barrani was in British hands and the Desert Army—which had expected to conduct only a raid-in-force—had destroyed five enemy divisions and captured thirty-eight thousand prisoners.

Next on the list was the fortified town of Bardia, which was struck by the Desert Army on January 3. It also had an antitank ditch that ran for seventeen miles, but in practice it was too shallow to stop any. The British and Australian soldiers swept across it singing "We're off to see the Wizard, the wonderful Wizard of Oz," the theme song from the MGM movie that had been released worldwide a year earlier.

For his part, General Graziani complained bitterly to Mussolini about the injustice of his being ordered to make the attack in the first place, comparing his army to "a flea" that had been attacked by "an elephant"—when in fact it was exactly the other way around. Of Field Marshal Graziani, Mussolini waxed philosophically, "Here is another man with whom I cannot get angry, because I despise him."[11]

When all was said and done, Fortress Bardia was in British control by January 12, 1941. As a result, the Desert Army now had on its hands 113,000 Italian prisoners, some seven hundred pieces of Italian artillery, and hundreds of Italian trucks, planes, tanks, and other vehicles, and it had driven the Italians out of Egypt in disgrace. All of this was captured by newsreel cameras and disseminated in British and American movie theaters, a first sign that the Allies were winning at least something.

After exulting in a telegram to Roosevelt over the results of the battle, Churchill thought it would be a good time to address the Italian people by radio.

"Italians, I will tell you the truth. It is all because of one man. One man, and one man alone has ranged the Italian people in a deadly struggle against the British Empire, and has deprived Italy of the sympathy and intimacy of the United States of America." Churchill reminded them that Mussolini was against the Italian royal family, the pope, the Vatican, and the Catholic Church, as well as the Italian people "who had no lust for this war, and arrayed the inheritors of ancient Rome upon the side of pagan barbarians."

Next, the British prime minister took stock. Great Britain had been at war for a little over a year, much of it spent in great danger. The vast Nazi army had gathered across the narrows of the English Channel to finish off the last of the defeated Allies. He rated 1940 as "the most splendid, the most deadly year in our long English and British history." Writing that while a million Britons died in the First World War, "nothing surpasses 1940. We had not flinched. We had not failed," he said. "We had defied the tyrant at the height of his triumph, and the soul of the British people proved invincible."[12]

THAT MAY HAVE SEEMED TRUE in Churchill's fertile mind at the beginning of 1941. But the fact remained that England was still in a precarious position, with Hitler and Stalin holding all of Europe.* The most imminent danger came from the hundreds of German U-boats that prowled the sea-lanes leading to Great Britain. England for years had not been able to produce enough food to feed its growing population and depended on imports from the Americas, India, Africa, and other regions for survival. France, the Netherlands, and many other European countries were now closed for business.

Britain had around two thousand transport ships that were either at sea or in ports unloading or loading around the clock. By early 1941 the

---

* The countries Spain, Ireland, Portugal, and Switzerland remained neutral. The rest were conquered.

Germans were sinking one in four of these, and British industry could not replace them fast enough. Sonar (or asdic, as the British called it) was in its early stages and not always reliable. At this time, the fifty destroyers for antisubmarine warfare promised by Roosevelt had still not arrived, owing to extensive refitting required after their long deactivation. Gasoline, as well as foodstuffs from bacon to sugar, were strictly rationed by government order.

One bright ray of hope to counter the U-boat menace hinged on developments in the London suburb of Bletchley Park, where a top secret operation to break the German military codes had been in progress since the beginning of the war. Code-named Ultra, the procedure was being carried out, like the Americans' Magic program in the Pacific, by a peculiar collection of cryptologists, card-counting poker players, Oxford dons, mathematicians, classical musicians, crossword puzzle whizzes, and others with an ear for the intricacies of encoding and decoding. So far, they had been able to produce for Churchill and others at the very top levels of government rudimentary signal intelligence on Germany's dispositions and plans. By the end of the war they would be reading all of the German signals, down to battalion level and individual U-boats, and have been credited by some with winning the war. That would be a stretch, perhaps, but certainly the Ultra information was invaluable and saved many lives.

Hitler had not forgotten Great Britain, even though his immediate invasion plans were thwarted. The nightly bombings continued into 1941, killing, maiming, destroying, and causing a full blackout of London and other cities. Through it all, Churchill's was a voice of strength and inspiration. Even he was not immune from the bombing, however, and often times was forced to operate from a "war room" deep beneath the Treasury Department in Whitehall.* Incidentally, ensconced at his weekend house Chequers,

---

* After the war, when news of the German code-breaking operation at Bletchley became public, a rumor started circulating that Churchill had known of a German air raid on the city of Coventry that killed more than five hundred people but didn't warn them because he was afraid the Germans might figure out that he was reading their wireless signals. There is nothing, however, to substantiate that hypothesis.

Churchill was sometimes forced on moonlit nights to seek shelter elsewhere, for fear that German bombardiers could identify the place by the moon's reflection on the many lakes and ponds he'd had dug on the property.

DESPITE THEIR DECISIVE VICTORY over the Italians, the British were far from triumphant in North Africa. Feeling obligated to prop up his hapless ally, Hitler sent General Erwin Rommel, a highly accomplished officer, and two Panzer divisions to Libya. There, they would operate with the remains of the Italian army, which still consisted of more than one hundred thousand troops. "Now a new figure sprang upon the world," Churchill said, with a pungency that betrayed his love of a good contest.

The German air raids were costing three thousand to five thousand English men, women, and children's lives each month: a "sustainable rate," the authorities said. Meantime, the Royal Air Force under Marshal Arthur "Bomber" Harris was conducting a bombing campaign of its own on German cities. Because of distance and a lack of fighter cover, the pilots were not yet able to reach eastern Germany and Berlin. But the British conducted regular raids on Cologne, Essen, Mannheim, Frankfurt, and other cities in western Germany with hundreds of their big, four-engine Lancaster bombers. In addition, the British invention of radar gave at least ample warning to its citizens of an impending German air raid on the home islands.

Churchill found himself in a quandary that was palpable. Despite what he'd told the British people about the continued danger of a German invasion of England, Churchill personally had concluded that any such action would prove to be disastrous for Hitler: British sea power would wreck any attempted Channel crossing, and he had now assembled enough land power to destroy an invasion force on or near its beachhead. He nevertheless maintained the fiction to keep everyone on their toes.

What Churchill could not grasp for now was how the British army could destroy the Germans, who so vastly outmanned them. His own experience in the Great War had taught him that once the two armies came to grips on the European continent, the warfare would probably stabilize as it had in 1914 and a great butchery would begin. But without the manpower of France and Italy, Great Britain would be outbutchered by the more numerous Germans and Italians. Thus, Churchill persisted in his almost pathetic entreaties to Roosevelt and the Americans, who, as in 1918, seemed the last, best hope to win the war.

DURING THE FIRST MONTHS OF 1941, British strength in Africa and the Middle East had grown to 370,000 but was spread out over vast areas in this immense territory.

With much of Mussolini's army either captured or in disarray, Churchill prompted General Archibald Wavell, commander in chief in the Middle East, to take the final Italian stronghold at Tobruk. After several days of siege and fierce fighting, the Italians surrendered twenty thousand troops, two hundred guns, and about one hundred tanks. Nearly a thousand Italian soldiers had been killed. The British occupied the fortress city but, because Mussolini had now invaded Greece, Churchill decided to send an expeditionary force there from North Africa. This stripped General Wavell of sizable elements of his battle-experienced army and it soon led to a calamity.

Tobruk became garrisoned by, as Churchill put it, "less well-trained troops." To make matters worse, much of their equipment and armored vehicles had been stripped from them to beef up the Greek expedition. At the end of February, London sent a warning to General Wavell—based on Ultra decodes and air reconnaissance—that German units might be gearing up to attack his army from neighboring Tripoli, another Italian possession to the west. Wavell dismissed this, saying the single road through the desert was too long, narrow, and severe for an enemy to employ down it.

By the end of March Wavell began to realize the predicament he was in. He had stripped his army of so many arms and men for Greece that he telegraphed, "I am weak at present and no reinforcements of armoured troops, which are a chief requirement, are at present available."[13] In fact, he was about to be struck by a tornado in the form of the veteran German officer Erwin Rommel, soon to be Hitler's favorite general.

On March 31, Rommel roared out of the deserts of Tripolitania into Libya in four columns: one along the feeble coast road and the other three along desert tracks. As a result, he was able to overrun British positions all along the Libyan coast, except for the critical citadel of Tobruk, which held out in the storm. Churchill was shocked and dismayed: "Thus at a single stroke, and almost in a day," he agonized, "the desert flank upon which all our decisions depended had crumpled, and the expedition to Greece, already slender, was heavily reduced."[14]

The shoe now was on the other foot, with Rommel at large with his vastly superior armored force. The British fortress at Tobruk had been reinforced by sea with an Australian division, but the Germans laid siege. Churchill wrote Roosevelt, "We are, of course, going to fight all out for the Nile Valley. All questions of cutting the loss are ruled out. Tobruk must be held, not as a defensive position, but as an invaluable bridgehead on the flank of any serious by-pass advance on Egypt."[15]

FROM THE OUTSET OF MUSSOLINI'S INVASION, the Greek army had held the Italians at bay along the Albanian border, producing evidence that the Germans might again have to come to their allies' rescue. Churchill had sent his British expeditionary force from North Africa consisting of an Australian division, a New Zealand division, and an armored brigade of British soldiers, for a total of sixty-two thousand men. This small army proved wholly inadequate on April 6, 1941, when the Germans attacked across Bulgaria (which had again thrown in its lot with the Germans) with an army of seven hundred thousand. There was fierce resistance but the Germans outmanned the Allies in every category—ten times as many tanks, twice as many warplanes—and Greece was rapidly overrun. It soon became apparent that the British force must be evacuated. This was more or less successfully done in a heroic effort culminating on April 30—but with the loss of seven thousand troops captured.

Churchill viewed the defeat as a tragedy and blamed himself. Roosevelt telegraphed to buck him up, calling the British entry into Greece "heroic." Churchill telegraphed back, reiterating their intention to "fight it out to the last inch and ounce," and closed for the first time with a plea for America to "immediately range herself with us as a belligerent power." This, he said, would most likely cause the Axis to think twice before further invasions in the Mediterranean and North Africa; the British would be able "to hold the situation until the weight of your munitions gained the day."[16]

Churchill expected no affirmative reply to this, and he received none. But the next night in his highly emotional Sunday radio address, after warning British citizens against "becoming discouraged or alarmed," he closed with some lines of verse from the English poet Arthur Hugh Clough. It was a direct allusion to his plea for Roosevelt to bring the United States into the war.

> For while the tired waves, vainly breaking,
> Seem here no painful inch to gain,
> Far back, through creeks and inlets making,
> Comes silent, flooding in, the main.
>
> And not by eastern windows only,
> When daylight comes, comes in the light,
> In front the sun climbs slow, how slowly,
> But westward, look, the land is bright.

The situation at Tobruk now remained precarious, where some twenty-seven thousand besieged British and Australian troops held out against Rommel's outnumbering onslaught. On the night of April 10 a German Panzer unit attacked Tobruk after receiving information from air reconnaissance that the British were evacuating the garrison by ships in the harbor. As it turned out, the British were *reinforcing* Tobruk with the battle-hardened troops who'd just escaped Greece, and the German assault was thrown back.

The good news from Tobruk was, however, followed immediately by a revolt in British-held Iraq. It seemed that one Rashid Ali, an Arab warlord, was in cahoots with the Nazis and had attacked a British flying school at the desert town of Habbaniya with troops and artillery. The flying school students, commanding a wide variety of aircraft, took off under Rashid Ali's artillery fire, bombing and strafing their assailants. Churchill told General Wavell, with whom he had become great friends, that he needed to send some troops from North Africa to put down the Arab rebellion. Wavell recoiled, saying he was stretched to the limits trying to defend Egypt, Palestine, and Abyssinia (Ethiopia); supply Tobruk; and fight Rommel all over the desert, all at the same time. "I have consistently warned you," he telegraphed Churchill, "that no assistance could be given to Iraq from Palestine, and have always advised that a commitment in Iraq should be avoided."[17] In a telegraph several days later, Wavell warned Churchill of the possibility of an Arab revolt throughout the Middle East, such as the one against the Turks led by Lawrence of Arabia in the previous war.

Churchill reacted frostily to these tidings, telling Pug Ismay, "I am deeply disturbed at General Wavell's attitude . . . He gives me the impression of being tired out."[18]

Meantime, the war was about to blow up on the large Greek island of Crete, which, other than Gibraltar, was the last holdout of the Allies in the northern Mediterranean.

After the German victory in Greece, a sizable number of British soldiers were evacuated to Crete, which was now in danger of attack, according to Ultra intercepts. The Germans were planning a large airborne operation as a prelude to invasion. Churchill telegraphed Wavell that "to lose Crete would be a crime."

On the early morning of May 20, five thousand German paratroopers began dropping from the skies above Crete. It was a sight never before encountered in battle: a division-size airdrop into hostile fire. The highly motivated Nazi paratroopers suffered heavy casualties from the British and New Zealand defenders, as well as from native Cretans. But by the end of the second day the Germans had taken the main airport, and more fresh enemy troops began arriving. It was the relentless bombing by the German air force that tipped the balance. The Allies did not have fire-interceptor aircraft that could reach so far as Crete, and the skies were dominated by the Luftwaffe. Its planes knocked out most of the Allied guns and antiaircraft weapons on the first day. Churchill stayed in daily contact with the commanders on the island.

Simultaneous with the land battle was the naval battle of Crete, a contest between the German air force and the Royal Navy, which was in the vicinity to keep enemy convoys of troops from landing in Crete. Several convoys were sunk, but the price was high: three British cruisers and six destroyers were sunk and two battleships suffered crippling damage during the eventual evacuation of the twenty-two thousand British troops on the island. Despite such heavy losses, the navy rescued nineteen thousand of these in daring and gallant sorties into the maelstrom of aerial assault.

By the fifth day, much of the Allied resistance had been broken, and in another week the island belonged to the Nazi empire, completing its conquest of the Balkans and the Peloponnesian Peninsula. Not only that, but in its weakened condition the British fleet now faced a rejuvenated Italian navy, which had come out from its hiding place in Trieste. "The period which we now had to face offered to the Italians their best chance of challenging our dubious control of the Eastern Mediterranean," Churchill wrote solemnly. "We could not tell they would not seize it."

ALL THE WHILE, THERE REMAINED a furious battle for control of the Atlantic Ocean. Three German battle cruisers, *Sharnhorst*, *Gneisenau*, and *Hipper*, remained poised at Brest under the protection of powerful antiaircraft batteries, awaiting their moment to prey on Allied convoys. Then, late in May, as the conflict on Crete reached its most pitiless intensity, the Admiralty got word that the newly constructed German battleship *Bismarck*— supposedly the most powerful and heavily armed and armored warship in the world—was loose somewhere in the North Atlantic. On May 21 this ship and her accompanying cruiser *Prinz Eugen* were spotted by British aerial reconnaissance in the fjord at Bergen, Norway.

Although he knew his war vessels were outgunned, Churchill ordered an all-out search-and-destroy mission against this new and formidable menace. Next day air reconnaissance revealed that the *Bismarck* and *Prinz Eugen* had steamed into the open Atlantic and were headed for the Denmark Strait, an icy, misty Arctic narrows to the north of Iceland where the precious convoys cruised.

Every available ship was sent to predetermined positions, hoping to ambush the monster. Soon after midnight on May 24, Britain's most powerful battleship, HMS *Hood,* and the new battleship *Prince of Wales,* along with six destroyers, set out for the Denmark Strait. As a former first lord of the Admiralty, Churchill nourished a keen interest in the proceedings as they developed.

At 5:37 as the cold day dawned, spotters on the *Hood* and *Prince of Wales* identified the *Bismarck* and *Prinz Eugen* about fifteen miles distant. Fifteen minutes later they opened fire. The Germans returned the fire within three minutes. The *Hood* was hit amidships, setting a large munitions fire spreading rapidly, and the *Prince of Wales* also caught a salvo. At six o'clock, barely eight minutes into the action, a shell from a *Bismarck* salvo tore into the *Hood* aft the conning tower; she blew up in a stupendous flash and roar, breaking the entire ship in two. Both parts sank within two minutes, taking all but three of her 1,418-man crew to the ocean bottom. The *Prince of Wales* boldly continued the fight, but a shell from the *Bismarck* wiped out everyone on the bridge. Because of mechanical troubles, the *Prince of Wales* retired under a smokescreen but remained shadowing the *Bismarck* just out of range.

The *Bismarck,* however, had not escaped the battle unscathed. Two heavy shells from the *Prince of Wales* had penetrated beneath her waterline and she turned course, heading for German-occupied France and leaking a trail of oil. For four days the *Bismarck* was dogged by several British cruisers and by the limping *Prince of Wales.*

Churchill was in an anxious frame of mind. The House of Commons was to meet that morning in an improvised Parliament building; they had been blown out of their chamber by German bombers two weeks earlier. How, he wondered, would they receive the news that Crete was lost and even now being evacuated, that the mighty *Hood* was sunk with nearly all hands, and that the *Bismarck* was at large on the high seas with precious British troop and commodities convoys helpless against her?

Every available battleship of the Royal Navy was returned from convoy duties to engage the *Bismarck,* but these were scattered from Gibraltar to Nova Scotia and time was very dear. In addition to the battleships, two aircraft carriers were sent out: the HMS *Victorious* and the *Ark Royal.*

Just before sunset on May 26, Fairey Swordfish biplanes from the *Ark Royal* spotted the *Bismarck* and launched a torpedo attack, several of which hit the German behemoth. One explosion jammed her rudder, causing the *Bismarck* to steam in circles, a pitiful, helpless target for the converging British battleships.

Churchill had been in the Admiralty war room all evening, watching the charts and listening to the constant stream of reports. When he arose the next day the *Bismarck* was still afloat and her commander, Admiral Günther Lutjens, had sent a defiant message to the Kriegsmarine: "We shall fight to the last shell. Long live the Führer!"

When he arrived at Parliament shortly after 10:30 that morning, Churchill was handed a note saying that after repeated hits the *Bismarck* at last had sunk with nearly two thousand hands. He arose with great pleasure, and so informed the House, to long and grateful cheering.

The next day, Churchill wrote Roosevelt of his intense relief that such a monster would no longer menace the sea-lanes. "Now it is a different story," he told the president, adding, "The effect upon the Japanese [who were already threatening war in the Pacific] will be highly beneficial. I expect they are doing all their sums again."

In June 1941, Hitler invaded the Soviet Union without warning, despite the German-Soviet peace pact. Stalin had plenty of warning from Winston Churchill himself, whose intelligence agents and Ultra contacts told him that the movement of three entire Panzer divisions to Poland could only mean that the Nazis intended to attack Russia. On April 3 Churchill sent a secret message concerning this matter, to be delivered personally to the Soviet dictator by his Soviet ambassador, Sir Stafford Cripps.[19]

Stalin didn't believe it, apparently thinking the message was a capitalist trick. All spring and into summer, the Germans massed their armies toward the Soviet border until they had assembled a hundred and fifty divisions— upwards of two and a half million men—along an 1,800-mile front. At 4 a.m. on June 22, the German ambassador to the Soviet Union delivered a declaration of war from Hitler, although by then the German air force was already bombing Russian cities. The German attack was furious. Much of the Soviet air force was destroyed on the ground, and those Russian army units that were poised at the border recoiled from the overwhelming might of the German host.[20]

Churchill had already made up his mind on what stance the British should take in this development. Bitter and disgusted as Churchill was at Stalin's failure to take warning, as well as the Soviets' partnering up with the Nazis, he felt the only logical recourse was to hold his nose and go to Stalin as an ally. The night after the invasion, Churchill delivered one of his highly emotional broadcasts on the BBC, which bears repeating in some length.

> The Nazi regime is indistinguishable from the worst features of Communism. It is devoid of all theme and principle except appetite and racial domination. It excels all forms of human wickedness in the efficiency of its cruelty and ferocious aggression. No one has been a more consistent opponent of Communism than I have for the last twenty-five years. I will unsay no word that I have spoken about it.
>
> But all that fades away before the spectacle which is now unfolding . . .
>
> We have but one aim, and one single irrevocable purpose. We are resolved to destroy Hitler and every vestige of the Nazi regime. We shall fight him by land, we shall fight him by sea, we shall

fight him in the air until, with God's help, we have rid the earth of his shadow and liberated its peoples from his yoke . . .

It follows, therefore, that we shall give whatever help we can to Russia and the Russian people . . .

When I spoke a few minutes ago about Hitler and his blood-lust . . . I said there was a deeper motive behind his outrage. He wishes to destroy the Russian power because he hopes that if he succeeds he will bring back the main strength of his army and his air force from the East and hurl it upon this island, which he knows he must conquer or suffer the penalty of his crimes. His invasion of Russia is no more than a prelude to an invasion of the British Isles . . .

The Russian danger is, therefore, our danger, and the danger of the United States. Let us redouble our exertions and strike with united strength while life and power remain.

At that point Churchill represented a lone voice standing against the mighty Nazi juggernaut; he was certain to be among the first on the gallows should Hitler ever find his way to London. The notion of Hitler returning victorious from the Soviet Union with his whole army to conquer England was enough to stir patriotism in many an Englishman's breast. By this stage, Churchill had even managed to drag the United States into it, much to the consternation of the American diplomatic corps—though probably not to Roosevelt, who was at the time vowing never to send anybody's children off to foreign wars.

For his part, Stalin was handicapped with the absence of five hundred Soviet army generals who had been liquidated in the purges. He soon found that promoting colonels unready for high command was a risky business. When the attack opened, Stalin was in his dacha. He remained there a full week in a state of utter shock, not once venturing to the Kremlin. Molotov tried to get him to return to his office but Stalin demurred. "Lenin left us a great legacy," he replied, "and we, his heirs, have fucked it all up."[21]

THE GERMANS HAD DIVIDED their army into three groups: north, south, and center. Within a month, they had driven an equal number of Russians back three hundred miles into their own territory. Headed for the oil fields of Baku and the wheat fields of Ukraine, the Germans hit the surprised Russian army in a blitzkrieg of 3,600 Panzer tanks, 2,700 fighters and bombers, and some 3 million German soldiers. They could, however, have driven the Russians back a thousand miles—or five thousand miles—and still would not have pushed the Russians' backs to the wall. Russia is a country with great depth and elasticity, as we shall see.

The invasion force consisted not of Germans alone, but of others who had thrown in their lot with the Nazis. Finland, for example, an age-old enemy of Russia, sent ten divisions. Romania and Bulgaria contributed heavily to the invasion troops; even the Spanish Communists, who had lost the civil war to Franco in '39, scraped up a regiment or two to aid their fellow communists in the fight.

For their part, the deceived and incensed Soviets began making demands on their new allies that were difficult, if not impossible, to fulfill. From the United States, they demanded at least the same—if not more—munitions and other war-making equipment as England had received. And from the British they demanded an immediate cross-Channel landing of troops to establish a second front to relieve the pressure on Moscow, Leningrad, Stalingrad, and other soon-to-be besieged cities. Churchill laughed at the impossibility of such a maneuver. England was barely holding on against invasion herself. But he deeply resented Britain's own Communists, mostly factory organizers, who until now had denounced the fight with Germany as a "capitalist and imperialist war"; suddenly, overnight in fact, they were doing a hypocritical about-face. Soon the slogan "Second Front Now" began to appear, scrawled on fence walls, sidewalks, and buildings throughout the land.

ON AUGUST 9, CHURCHILL and Roosevelt met in a secret nautical rendezvous by warship. Roosevelt had eluded the press by sailing off from

Washington on the presidential yacht for unknown parts north, then transferring to the heavy cruiser USS *Augusta* in the Atlantic off Nantucket. A Secret Service man in a deck chair wrapped in a blanket fooled reporters into thinking the president was aboard, headed for Campobello. In fact, he was headed to Placentia Bay, Newfoundland, where Churchill was waiting on board the *Prince of Wales,* which was still somewhat battered from her valiant fight with the *Bismarck.* Both old sea dogs enjoyed high times on their voyages; Churchill read C. S. Forester's Horatio Hornblower novels and watched Hollywood films in the wardroom.

Dressed in a dark blue Royal Navy coat with two rows of brass buttons and an officer's hat, Churchill the "former naval person" took a launch to the *Augusta* where Roosevelt awaited him, standing on the deck in a light summer business suit and clutching the arm of his son Elliott, who was wearing his Army captain's uniform. Churchill and Roosevelt had met briefly in England toward the end of World War I but neither had much recollection of it.

A movie camera caught Churchill eagerly clambering up the gangway, as well as a great shaking of hands and smiles between the two heads of government. "At long last," Churchill cried, and Roosevelt replied, "Good to have you aboard, Mr. Churchill," which should have told the prime minister of Great Britain where he stood in the order of things. After lunch, the two got down to business. Churchill had come with his vast wish list of American munitions and supplies, but Roosevelt made an additional suggestion: that the two create a joint statement of postwar aims. This famous and somewhat wishful document conceived by the president and written by Churchill came to be known as the Atlantic Charter. It called for a world free from war, from fear, from want, and was hailed in the press as the definitive guide for future world harmony.

The next day Churchill, Roosevelt, and several hundred sailors from the *Augusta* visited the *Prince of Wales* across the bay. They joined with the British sailors in singing "Oh God, Our Help in Ages Past." Churchill wrote in his memoirs that "it was a great hour to live," but he lamented ruefully that "nearly half who sang were soon to die."[22]

Once back on British soil, Churchill was more certain than ever that the United States would soon enter the war. At present, America was far from "neutral" under international accords, as she had been supplying war materials to both England and Russia and patrolling with warships and warplanes in the Atlantic far off U.S. shores. Roosevelt was fully aware of course of the powerful sentiment among many in the United States who abhorred the notion of sending American boys into another European bloodbath.

★★★★★

IN THE MEANTIME, CHURCHILL continued agitating for his generals to stay on the offensive where possible, particularly in Egypt's Western Desert, where the Nazi general Rommel was still marauding. In June 1941 Churchill had relieved the overtaxed and overwhelmed General Wavell, replacing him as Middle East supreme commander with General Claude Auchinleck, the former commander of the British Indian army (despite misgivings by some of the prime minister's close advisers). Auchinleck's first substantial change was to appoint Lieutenant General Alan Cunningham to command the Eighth Army. A career infantryman, Cunningham did not fully understand mechanized armored warfare and its ability to move quickly in a desert environment. With his appointment, Churchill had ordered Auchinleck to attack the Germans but was rebuffed by Cunningham's protest that he could not possibly have the army assembled for an offensive before autumn. Moreover, Auchinleck said that even though he had five hundred tanks he needed another two hundred and fifty to replace losses. This, Churchill responded, was "a comfort Generals only enjoy in heaven," adding that "those who demand them don't always get there."[23]

Following a series of telegrams between himself and Auchinleck, Churchill concluded that he and his general had "a serious divergence of views between us," causing him "a sharp disappointment." Still, he did not relieve and replace Auchinleck, possibly because he did not want to have to admit that he made a bad selection in the first place.

To further complicate matters, the Australian government was objecting to having its troops fight in the Middle East as the possibility of war with Japan loomed on the horizon; the three Australian divisions were all the Aussies had to defend themselves. Churchill smoothed the matter over but it left him with a bitter taste.

In the meanwhile, Rommel now sat sullenly in place, ordered by Hitler not to advance farther at that time, due to trouble supplying him with gasoline. His thousand-mile line of communication with his supply base in Tripoli was menaced by the British-held fortress at Tobruk in his rear, which remained supplied by the Royal Navy. This was how matters stood in the Middle East through the summer and early autumn of 1941.

IN THE SOVIET UNION, the German drive seemed to have stalled. Despite enormous losses, the Russians had regrouped and offered a spirited defense. Russian partisans, meanwhile, had risen behind the invading army and disrupted its communications. Roads were breaking under the constant strain of traffic. The Russian rail system, which the Germans had intended to utilize for transportation, was insufficient, and heavy rains had slowed things to a crawl.

The British were supplying the Russians with hundreds of fighter planes and munitions, which were shipped into the ice-free port of Murmansk. Stalin thanked Churchill for these, but he demanded still more and renewed his calls for a second front. The Soviet ambassador complained to Churchill that Russia was fighting the Germans "virtually alone." Churchill reminded him that four months earlier the British were not only fighting the Germans alone; they were highly concerned that the Russians would invoke their mutual defense pact with the Nazis and join them for an invasion of England. "We never thought our survival was dependent on your action—either way," he told the dumbfounded Soviet ambassador.[24]

Stalin, however, had a secret weapon he did not mention. It was the Russian winter, which had decisively defeated many a Russian invader, most notably Napoleon. It would soon become so cold that the oil in German tanks would freeze solid and the bolts on soldiers' rifles would become impossibly stuck.

Dissatisfied with the stalled condition of his blitzkrieg in the East, Hitler, the former World War I corporal, fired his top generals von Rundstedt and Walther von Brauchitsch and seized personal command of his armies, which were waiting grievously for the Russian spring. Here was where the Führer started to become visibly unhinged.

★★★★★

CHURCHILL ANXIOUSLY AWAITED General Auchinleck's big offensive in the Western Desert to drive Rommel back into Tunisia. Already Churchill was dreaming of invading Sicily, the key, he thought, to a "second front" of sorts against Italy—and the possibility of a drive northward up the Italian boot into Austria and Germany.

Churchill continued to parlay regularly with Franklin Roosevelt, whom he desired above all things to bring into the fight. But he could not as yet see how to do it.[25]

General Auchinleck's offensive, Crusader, at last got off in the dark and driving rain on November 18, 1941. The first three days produced hopeful results, and the surprised Germans recoiled from the British armor and mechanized infantry. Then, four days later, the British lost a terrific tank-on-tank battle at a place called Sidi Rezegh and withdrew to safety, having lost nearly a third of their tanks.

In an effort to confuse and panic the British, Rommel pulled a stunt that Auchinleck himself compared with Jeb Stuart's 1862 ride around McClellan during the American Civil War. He got his Afrika Korps in the British rear, taking many prisoners, cutting off British communications, destroying equipment, and generally disrupting everything.

The armored battle continued to seesaw until General Cunningham reported that "further continuation of our offensive might result in the annihilation of our tank force, and endanger the safety of Egypt." Auchinleck immediately flew to Cunningham's desert headquarters and relieved him, placing General Neil Ritchie in charge with orders to continue the offensive.

After more than a month, Rommel drew off to the west in retreat. The British relieved the siege of Tobruk and the four Allied divisions therein. Reported losses after a month's fighting were about three thousand British killed, seventy-five hundred wounded, and seven thousand missing, for a total of seventeen thousand and five hundred lost. The Germans suffered a combined thirty-three thousand dead, wounded, or captured.

Churchill and the army considered this a victory and exulted while Rommel somehow refitted, replaced, and replenished his vaunted Afrika Korps for another blow.

In the meantime, the appalling events on December 7, 1941, convulsed the United States of America. The Japanese sneak attack on the U.S. Pacific Fleet at Pearl Harbor prompted an immediate American declaration of war against Japan. Hitler, in one of the most ill-considered decisions of his reign, abided by his mutual defense pact with the Japanese and declared war on the United States.

CHAPTER ELEVEN

I n the opening months of 1942 Stalin was having a family crisis of sorts. He'd had one of his spacious dachas in the Moscow suburb of Zubalova repaired after bomb damage and moved in Svetlana, his sixteen-year-old daughter, along with the infant daughter of his son Yakov, who was presently trapped in a German POW camp, along with her nurse. Yakov's wife, Yulia, per Stalin's infamous Order 270, in which the families of soldiers taken prisoner were to be punished, was off to the gulag labor camps.

Stalin's other son Vasily—a "crafty little brat," according to his father—was a pilot in the Soviet air force, a raconteur, and a drunkard who brought a wide variety of acquaintances to the dacha, including "actors, athletes, and fellow pilots" to drink and dance. Stalin was furious when he learned that Vasily regularly used his status as the dictator's son to curry favor from senior officers, such as spiffy quarters, home-cooked meals, and use of a car. He was even less impressed when the ace pilot V. Tsukanov, Vasily's personal flying instructor who had been handpicked by Stalin, reported to the boss that Vasily "is an able flier but will always get into difficulties because of his drinking."[1]

In response to this feedback, Stalin grounded Vasily to a desk as an "aircraft inspector." But wary superiors saw to it that promotions came regularly, and almost before anyone knew it Vasily was a lieutenant general. On those frequent occasions when he was drunk, he would sometimes shoot his revolver at crystal chandeliers in restaurants; he also preyed on the wives of friends and fellow pilots. During this time, he introduced Russia's famous screenwriter and journalist Aleksei Kapler to his little sister Svetlana.[2]

A pretty, smart, shy red-haired teenager, Svetlana had been on the outs with her father for a year. Someone had showed her a British magazine story about her mother Nadya's suicide. Svetlana had been told that she'd died of peritonitis and was both horrified and resentful that the truth had been kept from her. Worse, she somehow suspected that her father may have had some hand in it.

Although Svetlana was the favorite of his children, on those occasions when he saw her Stalin was now very strict, especially about her clothing, which he thought was too revealing. Stalin installed an NKVD agent to shadow her everywhere, ostensibly for her protection but also to ensure she did not get into "trouble."

Trouble came in the form of brother Vasily's friend. The nearly forty-year-old Kapler was a spellbinding raconteur and ladies' man. For the first time in her life Svetlana fell in love.

MUCH AS ROOSEVELT AND CHURCHILL were discovering for themselves, world affairs did not slow down during periods of Stalin's family drama. At present, 3.5 million German soldiers were swarming over the western Soviet Union. Ferocious resistance and the Russian winter blunted the lightning speed of the Nazi blitzkrieg. But still the Germans came on, and 2 million Russian soldiers were dead. Hitler now controlled all the Soviet Republics in the western borderlands: Belorussia, Ukraine, Lithuania, Latvia, and Estonia. Fully half of Russia's industrial and agricultural output was now under German occupation, as was nearly half its population.

Hitler installed Nazi governments in every nation, state, city, town, and village. Then he began wiping out the population. The purpose of the invasion was ostensibly to obtain *Lebensraum,* or living space, for the German people. More to the point, Hitler wanted *Pflanzensraum,* or growing space, for crops to make Germany self-sufficient. So he needed to remove (i.e., liquidate) the collective farmers from their collective farms.

Stalin seemed hapless and helpless against the onslaught. Dmitry Pavlov, the commanding general of Stalin's Western Front defenses, and his entire staff were recalled to Moscow, where they were charged with treason for "cowardice, inaction, mismanagement, deliberate disorganization of the troops," and summarily sentenced to be executed. Per Politburo orders, all their wives and children were sent to labor camps. As ever, Stalin dealt ruthlessly with those he perceived as failures. The generals asked to be taken back to the front to fight as ordinary soldiers, as atonement for their sins and errors. Stalin had them shot anyway and distributed the execution order, signed by himself, throughout the army. This was the kind of grisly terror employed to keep underlings obedient. When Averell Harriman, a messenger from President Roosevelt, praised the bravery of the Russian soldiers in their fight against Hitler, Stalin replied with ironic understatement, "It takes a very brave man to be a coward in the Russian army."[3]

WHEN JOSEPH E. DAVIES, the former U.S. ambassador to the Soviet Union, received word of the Japanese attack on Pearl Harbor, he happened to be having lunch with Ivy Litvinov, the wife of the new Soviet ambassador to the United States, Maxim Litvinov. "Thank God!" Davies blurted out, startling the Russian, whose immediate reaction was that war between the Americans and the Japanese was a bad thing, since it might interfere with the shipment of war materials to the Soviet Union. This was the kind of shortsighted communist reasoning the Americans and British had to put up with.[4]

Roosevelt and virtually all of the U.S. diplomatic corps were besotted with the idea that the Soviets would now declare war on Japan, which would put the squeeze on the upstart island nation. But as it turned out that was wishful thinking. Stalin had always kept a wary eye on the Japanese, who had sunk two navies sent by the czar in the early part of the century, and who now glared at Russia across the Sea of Japan, bristling with guns and planes and ships and soldiers.

Litvinov met next day with the U.S. secretary of state Cordell Hull to give him the news. When the Russian informed Hull that Stalin did not "at this time" wish to enter into a war with Japan, Hull lied to him: "I now have information that Japan is under the strictest commitment to Germany to attack Russia." Litvinov absorbed the statement without comment.[5]

Hull then proceeded to threaten Litvinov by suggesting that if Russia did not declare war on Japan, "there will be a constant flow of criticism" about why the United States is aiding Russia. That didn't work either, so Roosevelt conceived the idea of arranging a special conference in the British-held fortress at Singapore to discuss the matter. But before anything could actually be decided, the Japanese invaded supposedly invincible Singapore and captured an entire British army of eighty-two thousand men. And there the matter rested until 1945.[6]

As a kind of consolation prize, however, and to show that he was not unaware of his country's image in the West, Stalin dropped the "Internationale" as the Soviet Union's national anthem on grounds that its threat of a worldwide communist uprising might unsettle his newfound allies.

By late fall most of the Moscow government and its war machine—including five hundred factories and companies and a quarter million skilled workers—had been evacuated to a remote area behind the Ural Mountains, eight hundred miles to the east. Dynamite was placed in all of the important buildings including the Kremlin, so that if the city fell nothing would be left for the Germans.

Roosevelt's emissary Averell Harriman reported that the Germans were so close he could see the flashes of their antiaircraft guns at night. A special train for high government officials and diplomats was waiting on a siding for the five-day trip, equipped with neither a dining car nor drinking water, let alone a lounge car or toilet. Then, at the last moment, Stalin refused to go.[7]

He and Harriman got down to business then and there. Stalin asked what exactly the United States was willing and able to provide in the way of assistance; at that point, the Soviet treasury was empty, he told Harriman.

The American envoy said that President Roosevelt was working to include the Soviet Union in its Lend-Lease program, and then returned to the United States with a grocery list of stupendous dimensions—everything from field telephones to undersea cable along with every imaginable type of weapon, ammunition, and transport vehicle. Two weeks later, Congress voted to give Lend-Lease status to Russia and the supplies began pouring out, thousands upon thousands of tanks, trucks, rail equipments, warplanes, and machinery of all description.

Getting these things from U.S. ports to Russia, however, was problematic. On average, the United States lost one-quarter of its convoy ships in a typical Atlantic crossing. Take, for example, a convoy of forty-five U.S. cargo ships that steamed eastward in the North Atlantic for the Russian port of Archangel. German U-boats sank twenty-two and damaged eleven, which were then abandoned and destroyed. Two had returned to port with engine trouble. Ten reached their destination. Granted, this is an extreme example, but most convoys did not get through without some kind of scrape.*

In the initial days of the invasion Stalin's confidence had faltered. He huddled in his dacha without hope. It was an apt time for him to engage in some self-reflection, for the enormous woes of the Russian army had mostly been caused by the Soviet premier himself, beginning with the mass executions of his top military officers during the show trials and purges of the late 1930s. But beyond that, Stalin had allowed the Soviet military to lapse into a state resembling malaise. According to one of his biographers Stalin, who had been bombarded for months with accurate intelligence on Hitler's preparations, "now ascribed early German successes to the factor of surprise!"

For years before the German invasion, Stalin consistently interfered and meddled with military matters to the detriment of Russian defense. For example, he intervened to impose the exclusive manufacture of a certain type of tank gun that he recalled from the World War I era. It was far too large a caliber to be of any use on present Soviet tanks, but the proper guns had been taken out of production, wasting precious time and resources. Stalin—who had never had military experience or training, let alone command of an army—put the people's commissar for armaments in prison

---

* The author's maternal grandfather, a recently retired ship's captain with the United Fruit Company, led ships from New York and other American ports to Archangel in Russia. It was a dangerous and nerve-wracking trip, both coming and going.

right before the German attack and caused the navy to build battleships that would prove ineffective. Everyone was afraid to contradict him, for fear of being shot or sent to Siberia. He stupidly dissolved his army's only tank corps in 1939; by the time it was resurrected a few days before the German attack, it was too late to be put effectively into action. He also kept the Soviet air force far too near the frontier; German bombing of the runways meant the planes were either destroyed on the ground or, because the runways had been ruined, captured by the fast-moving Germans.[8]

Meanwhile, the infantry was kept in static enclaves along the frontier, which were easily overrun by Hitler's tanks and mobilized forces. The most infamous example of this was at Kiev, the capital city of Ukraine, where a Russian army of seven hundred thousand lay in the city or its outskirts while a two-pronged German assault rolled steadily toward them. The commanding general wanted to withdraw but Stalin ordered him to stand fast.

It was about this time that Stalin issued his notorious Order 270, which made surrendering to the Germans a crime of "treason on the Motherland," punishable by all the grim weights the word "treason" embodied. Plus, he decreed, the families of those found guilty would also be punished. The order was read to every individual unit of the armies, down to platoon level. For years after the war ended, millions of returning Russian POWs were treated as pariahs.

As the Nazi juggernaut approached, the chief of staff in Kiev read the writing on the wall and sent a special message over the head of the commanding officer and his political commissar, pleading for a withdrawal to save the army. Stalin accused him of being a "panicmonger" and once more ordered them to hold on.

In the end, nearly the entire army was either captured or killed. It was considered the largest encirclement in the history of warfare. Some six hundred thousand Russian soldiers became prisoners of war. Both the commanding officer and the chief of staff died trying to break out.

Before the war, a member of the General Staff Academy had warned of all these potential errors in a book on new military strategies. But he was imprisoned until 1956 for the crime of being right. According to Stalin's biographer Ronald Hingley, "So catastrophic were the . . . calamities, [and] so directly did they stem from Stalin's directives and policies, that he [Stalin] could hardly have rendered Hitler better service if he had been an agent in German pay all the time."[9]

Now, however, after his initial psychotic fit and the consequent tactical and strategic errors, Stalin had gotten a grip on himself. His later-to-be-infamous spy in Tokyo, Richard Sorge, informed the Kremlin that the Japanese had no plans to attack Russia. That happy news freed Stalin to order his armies in the Far East to move to the Soviet front between Moscow and Leningrad. Marshal Zhukov had even begun to talk of an offensive.

There were five Russian armies fighting outside Moscow, holding the Germans at bay. They fought furiously until being ultimately surrounded but fought on to the death. When the exhausted but victorious Germans prepared to claim Moscow as their prize, Stalin unleashed five fresh Russian armies on them from the Far Eastern Front—"Lads with fat, red faces wearing newish white sheepskin coats," and armed with the powerful new T-34 tanks.[10]

Stalin had stumbled upon a surprisingly effective strategy. After their long, arduous battles with the initial Russian armies, the Germans had become temporarily worn out, and thus were unprepared for an entirely new onslaught. The result was defeat and ultimately stalemate outside the gates of Moscow and Leningrad. At around this time, Stalin received *Time* magazine's vaunted Man of the Year award—presumably, in part, for at least fighting back against the Nazis.

This was the new strategy then: to sacrifice one large fighting force to wear the enemy down, then hit him with a fresh bludgeon just when he thinks he's won. It works if you have the manpower and are willing to use it. Stalin did.

The Germans were in a state of disbelief. General Franz Halder, chief of staff of the German army, wrote in his diary: "When the war began we had 200 divisions against us. Now, after the bloody losses they have suffered, we estimate that the number of [Russian] divisions is 360. Even if we smash a dozen of them the Russians will organize another dozen."

Russian historian Edvard Radzinsky observed this dynamic firsthand.[11] "Stalin could afford to sacrifice millions. There were millions more where they came from. Halder believed that Stalin would be overthrown by his own people . . . But the Soviet people did not even dare ask [themselves] why their leader had been caught napping by the German invasion, why the army was unready to defend itself. Independent thought had evaporated completely in the white heat of terror. He had created a new society . . . based on fear, the great engine of despotism."[12]

NOW CAME THE CRUCIBLE of Stalingrad. Russia's great industrial city on the Volga, formerly Tsaritsyn until 1925 when it was renamed for the Man of Steel, stood astride the routes Hitler's army would take for the breadbasket of the eastern Ukraine. Stalin was determined they would not pass, even if it meant the destruction of the city and everything within it.

From the Germans' point of view, the capture of Stalingrad was not a great strategic military prize, but it would be an immense propaganda coup, demonstrating to the world that the Soviets were unable to keep even the city named for their leader. It proved to be a reckless adventure for Hitler, the amateur strategist.

In the meanwhile, a German mechanized army group marched south of Stalingrad to take the oil fields of Baku and the Caucasus (where Stalin's first wife, Kato, had taken ill in 1907 with the typhus that soon killed her). This was a crucial strategic area. Not only would Baku provide the vital oil for Hitler's armies; it would also deprive the Russians of their main source of oil, which would dry up their tank armies and their military aircraft.

The Battle of Stalingrad began in August 1942, when two German armies began to move on the Baku oil fields. The Fourth Panzer had a relatively easy march, though its soldiers had to cross the difficult Caucasus Mountains. But the Sixth German Army, which did not contain Panzer divisions, was ordered to take Stalingrad on its way to the Caucasus, a feat much easier said than done.

There was ferocious fighting north of the city, as Stalin had ordered "not one step backward." But German superiority in tactics slowly forced the Soviets back toward Stalingrad. Soviet propaganda (and some historians) have insisted that Stalin lured the Germans into a trap, but that is not the case.

Desertions were so common that Stalin ordered the NKVD secret police to form "blocking battalions" to stop soldiers from fleeing. Anyone caught was subject to being shot or imprisoned; others were returned to the front.

All through that summer, the Germans advanced on Stalingrad with Russian and German soldiers dying by the tens of thousands each week. Both sides sent in heavy reinforcements, so that by the beginning of September each opposing army contained approximately a million men, including more than half a million Italians, Romanians, and Hungarians fighting on the side of the Germans.

Stalin also had been building up a huge separate army made of "men beyond the Urals"—just as he had in the battle for Moscow. These troops were led by the man who was then Stalin's favorite general, Georgy Zhukov, who would make a counterattack when the moment was right.

By this point the German air force had bombed Stalingrad into piles of smoking rubble. Thousands of bodies were entombed inside and the smell hovered like a pall. The weekly casualty figures remained horrendous. On November 19, Zhukov launched his counterattack with the fresh army, which both surprised and overwhelmed the Germans. Zhukov's strategy was to envelope the Nazi army and surround it.

The Italians, Romanians, and Hungarians soon surrendered—but not the Germans, who were ordered by an idiotically outraged Hitler to fight to the last man. The German commander Friedrich Paulus now found himself vastly outnumbered. With another Russian winter coming on, he requested a withdrawal, but Hitler refused. Instead, the Führer promoted Paulus to field marshal on the novel theory that no German field marshal had ever surrendered.

The Russian winter was even harsher than the previous year, and the Germans troops had received no winter clothing. One soldier told in a letter home how he watched his fingers fall off his right hand "one by one." The last to go, he said, was his trigger finger. Conditions among the common German soldiers were appalling; they ate their horses and dray animals, lived in freezing basements of ruined buildings with squalid cesspools outside, and piled their frozen dead around the steps for barricades and to keep out the cold.

By December 1942 the city was a wasteland, but Stalin would not let the Germans have it. He ordered a counterattack that defied belief, with a huge number of troops and thousands of tanks and planes. The Russian army grasped the Germans who were slowly starving and freezing, while Field Marshal Paulus sat hapless at his headquarters in the basement of a department store. By February 2, 1943, the Germans had had enough.

They had been supplied intermittently by air, but by New Year's Day Zhukov's forces had captured the last remaining enemy airfield. With his army doomed, Paulus sought a surrender to Zhukov and was taken prisoner. He had lost a hundred and fifty thousand men, both killed and missing, and turned over ninety-one thousand as prisoners; only six thousand eventually returned from the Soviet POW camps. On their way there, "ragged, dejected, unshaven, in filthy greatcoats," Russian children pelted them with stones. In captivity, Paulus joined a Soviet anti-Nazi group and in 1953 was allowed to move to Soviet-dominated East Germany, where he died four years later.[13]

Hitler descended into a furious rage over the Stalingrad debacle, which was widely publicized through Allied propaganda. Germans generally became fearful, sullen, and depressed. So far the war had been easy and victories were the norm; now they had to stare into the abject face of defeat. Stalingrad is today considered to be a turning point of the war: the decisive strategic battle after which the Germans were never again successful in the field. But the Hitlerites, neither knowing nor accepting this, kept the war going for three more miserable years. It has been estimated that during that time the Nazi army, in an orgy of rapine and racial cleansing, murdered up to 10 million Russian civilians in the occupied territories.

Stalin was celebrated as the unquestioned hero of the victory and made himself a field marshal of the Soviet Union, whose uniform he wore from that time forth. Roosevelt sent a fulsome congratulatory telegram, in which he alluded to Soviet troops "covered with glory," "proudest chapter of the war," "forever honored your name," etc. Stalin wired back, predicting "ultimate victory over our common enemy."[14]

In Stalin's own paternal drama, his daughter Svetlana's romance with Aleksei Kapler proceeded apace. He was just as smitten as she, even though she was barely out of childhood, and the two quickly became a couple. This was in 1942, after the Germans had been driven from the immediate gates of Moscow. Aleksei waited for Svetlana after school; they went to art galleries and the ballet. They saw movies and plays and dined in what passed for fashionable restaurants according to the dialectical materialism of Moscow, all the while shadowed by the NKVD man, to whom Kapler sometimes gave cigarettes "to relieve his boredom."[15]

The NKVD evidently reported these goings on to Stalin, but the big boss was totally focused on the huge battle then developing at Stalingrad. Apparently he didn't think there was anything to worry about; after all, a forty-year-old Russian would have to be a total imbecile to try any hanky-panky with the sixteen-year-old daughter of a man such as himself.

And then one day Stalin picked up an issue of *Pravda,* of which he had once been an editor. It featured an article by Kapler, now on assignment as a war correspondent in the battle area. At the end of the piece, he described recent visits to art galleries and midnight walks around Moscow with an unidentified sweetheart. This coda was the kicker for Stalin, and if he'd had any doubts that a love affair was in progress it resolved then. "It must be snowing in Moscow," Kapler wrote to his unnamed sweetheart. "From your window you can see the crenellated wall of the Kremlin."[16]

It dawned on the Soviet dictator that Kapler had to be writing about Stalin's own dacha, where Stalin had installed Svetlana! Enraged, Stalin reached for the phone, and Aleksei Kapler was on his way to the Siberian labor camps before the day was out.

Stalin confronted Svetlana at the dacha two days later, angrily claiming that Kapler was of all things a British spy! When she declared her love for the journalist, Stalin slapped her—twice—for the first time in her life. He shouted, according to historian Radzinsky, "Why do you think he would want you? He's got women all over the place, you fool!"[17]

Thus, daughter and father were forever alienated, which resulted in Svetlana's escape years later from behind the Iron Curtain to the United States, where she wrote a best-selling autobiography.[18]

THE STRAIN OF THE WAR had begun to tell on Stalin, now well into his sixties. His eyes were often bloodshot and puffy from lack of sleep or heavy drinking at late night banquets. His hair had begun to turn gray. His nerves were jangled, and he was frequently annoyed though he didn't have the sort of querulous, shrieking temperament that was a personality trait of Adolf Hitler.[19]

Stalin also never went to the fighting front—neither to visit his troops, to see it for himself, or for any other reason (although various propaganda portraits show him there in heroic fashion, leading, daring the enemy, in front of his army). He once got within a hundred miles of the front for a photo op during the battle for Moscow. But that was as close as he came, although he continued to wear in public the uniform of a Russian field marshal: the rank he had bestowed upon himself.[20]

He persisted in his on-and-off routine of stag parties in the Kremlin or at his dacha with Molotov and other high-level Soviet officials. At these affairs, sumptuous food was served, awash in liters of wine, vodka, and brandy. They began late in the evening; Svetlana often served as a "hostess" but would usually leave before 10 p.m. The parties would frequently last until dawn and featured dirty jokes and practical jokes and ended with singing. Stalin was quite proud of his baritone voice, and sly, secretive Molotov, who came from a musical family, played piano and various stringed instruments. These long nights were apparently a way to let off steam and the strain of war. Stalin rarely arose from bed before noon.[21]

In December 1942 a U.S. team of scientists, led by the Italian Enrico Fermi, set off the first nuclear chain reaction in a top secret site in Chicago. Within a week this information was passed to Joseph Stalin by Lavrenty Beria, the head of the NKVD and one of communism's most unsavory associates. At the time, Stalin instructed Beria to look into the prospect of nuclear weapons. Beria snatched up a number of Russian physicists presently languishing in Soviet labor camps and set them to working on the problem. Then he sent his spies and agents to Britain and the United States to steal the secrets of the atomic bomb.

★★★★★

THE AGONY IN LENINGRAD, the once lovely St. Petersburg, was now palpable. There had been 2.2 million people in the city when the Nazis laid siege. Now, those who were left were cut off without power, sewage, facilities, and heat. Food was also scarce, except a scant amount brought in with great difficulty on the Ice Road, an eighty-mile-long thruway over the thick ice of Lake Ladoga.* Day after day, German artillery shelled Leningrad and Hitler's airplanes bombed it, bringing down buildings, raining down death. Hitler had declared in an order on September 29, 1941: "The Führer has vowed to wipe St. Petersburg [Leningrad] from the face of the earth. The objective is to approach the city as closely as possible and destroy it entirely by artillery fire and constant attacks from the air. Requests to be allowed to surrender will be rejected . . . We have no interest in preserving any part of the population of that large city."[22]

Soon Leningrad's citizens were dying of starvation, as well as from shells and bombs. Before it was over a million civilians would perish. "People would go to visit friends for half an hour, sit down, and die," recalled the scholar and writer Olga Freidenburg. "They would leave home on business and die on the way. Thousands of people sat down on the ground for a rest, couldn't get up from hunger weakness, and froze to death. The militia immediately stole their ration cards." But, she added, "No suffering inflicted on a living people . . . nothing whatsoever could have made the regime surrender that city. True to the usual law, omnipotence trampled human beings under foot, and spoke of patriotism and heroism of the besieged."[23]

But Stalin had neither forgotten nor forsaken Leningrad; in fact, he sent his favorite general, Zhukov, to lift the German siege. After the Battle of Stalingrad ended in a successful conclusion, Zhukov was ordered to Leningrad, where an operation called Iskra (or Spark) was in the late planning stages. It was focused on breaking through the German front to the west

---

* There were great difficulties in securing the Ice Road. In the first weeks, forty trucks plunged through the ice seven hundred feet to the bottom. During the day it was under constant air attack and at night from preset German artillery fire.

of the city and opening a corridor for supplies to get through. Already a quarter million Russian soldiers had died in various actions that seesawed along the German lines, none of which had produced the desired results.

Operation Spark got off January 12, 1943, following two substantial artillery barrages and the bombing of German positions and air bases by Russian planes. After nearly two weeks of fierce fighting, the Russians had opened a six-mile-wide corridor to the east of Leningrad, which they fortified and improved with a hastily built railroad that connected the city with the rest of the Soviet Union. Thereafter, even though the corridor was within range of German artillery, vastly more abundant foodstuffs and supplies began to reach the starving citizens.

Operation Spark had not lifted the siege but at least the German lines were permanently broken. Later that month Stalin ordered the first Order of Suvorov medal, first class (named for an eighteenth-century Russian commander), awarded to Marshal Zhukov for "exceptional leadership in combat operations."

The question has been raised by some historians over whether Stalin could at this point, or even earlier, have lifted the siege of Leningrad but purposely did not, in order to keep a German army occupied there that might otherwise have been used against Stalin's other forces. Radzinsky thinks so, writing that Stalin "for tactical reasons used the slavish patriotism of people who died without complaint for nine hundred days and nights. Perhaps no nation in the world could have tolerated this—only this people trained by him to be so meekly obedient."

It is lucky for Zhukov that he had gained such immense national confidence and popularity for his roles in beating the Germans at Moscow, Stalingrad, and Leningrad. Stalin deeply mistrusted any figure who might conceivably rival him. And in Georgy Zhukov, Stalin was beginning to think he had found his worst nightmare.

CHAPTER TWELVE

Franklin Roosevelt addressed Congress the day after the Pearl Harbor attack. The president made the speech standing, after being assisted to the podium before the dais of the Speaker of the House. He began, "Yesterday, December 7, 1941—a date which will live in infamy—the United States of America was suddenly and deliberately attacked by naval and air forces of the Empire of Japan."

He told the packed and furious joint House and Senate chambers that the attack was obviously planned far in advance and that the Japanese deliberately sought to deceive the United States, "by false statements and expressions of hope for continued peace," right up to the moment of the attack. Lamenting the high casualties at Pearl Harbor, Roosevelt listed the other Pacific entities presently under Japanese attack, including Hong Kong; the American possessions of Guam, Wake, and Midway Islands; and the U.S. Commonwealth of the Philippines. "No matter how long it will take us to overcome this premeditated invasion," the president said, "the American people in their righteous might will win through to victory."

It was a five-minute speech but the chamber erupted in a five-minute display of applause, shouting, foot stamping, and fist shaking. To show their solidarity, isolationist congressmen and senators marched through the Capitol corridors arm in arm with their interventionist cohorts. Everyone, from politicians to ordinary Americans, was in a kind of daze, with the enormous events around the world reeling in their minds. For two years they had known the thing was there, and groped to comprehend from headlines how it came to be and have so much power. Now it became clear for the first time: a true world war, and America was in it to the hilt.[1]

It was a rainy, blustery day in Washington when Roosevelt made his address to Congress, and the mood of the people matched the weather. All over America, starting at the crack of dawn, somber young men formed lines at military recruiting stations. From California to the state of Washington, military spotters dotted the coastline with binoculars, straining to pick up signs of a Japanese invasion. That same morning, Archibald MacLeish, the librarian of Congress, had original copies of the U.S. Constitution, the Declaration of Independence, the Bill of Rights, the Magna Carta, and the Gutenberg Bible packed up and sent by armed guards to underground safes at Fort Knox, Kentucky, where the U.S. gold reserve was stored.

It took Congress less than an hour to vote unanimously for war on Japan—except for one nay vote by the longtime Montana pacifist Jeannette Rankin, who had also voted against entering World War I. Several days later, Hitler's Nazi government declared war on the United States, which reciprocated by declaring war on Germany and Italy. As Winston Churchill doubtless rubbed his hands in glee, Stalin continued to press for more American munitions—and, of course, his vaunted second front.

For now, Roosevelt had his hands full in the Pacific. Immediately after the assault on Hawaii, the Japanese had attacked Guam and Wake Islands. Guam, which had been considered "indefensible" by the War Department, surrendered its garrison of three hundred marines and naval personnel after a brief battle with some five thousand Japanese invaders. But Wake was a buzz saw for the Japanese. Situated twenty-three hundred miles from Pearl Harbor, it was an important intelligence collecting center, warning outpost, and stopover atoll for the big China Clipper ships of Pan Am's flying boat operation. It was defended by a 450-man Marine Defense Battalion, equipped with half a dozen 5-inch guns from a World War I–era battleship and a small squadron of obsolete fighter planes.

After two days of intense bombing, the Japanese planned on landing a force that would easily overwhelm the few marines who survived. The marine commanding the island, Major James P. S. Devereux, had other ideas. After learning about Pearl Harbor, he had expected to be bombed and moved his guns, substituting "dummy" versions in their place. No guns were hit, and when the Japanese invasion fleet appeared the next dawn, Devereux held his fire until the enemy was within a mile of shore. Then he opened up, sinking three destroyers, a troop transport, and knocking out a cruiser. More than three hundred Japanese had been killed, and the enemy commander decided to steam away and fight another day.

When Devereux radioed the results of the action to Pearl Harbor, it was regarded as a grand victory, even though everyone expected it was temporary. It also was reported that when asked if he needed anything, Devereux had replied, "Send us more Japs." This received widespread coverage in the press and airwaves, electrifying the American people, who badly needed a lift.*

A relief task force was sent to the island, built around the carrier *Saratoga*, with a cruiser division and marine reinforcements, but it would take nearly a week to get there. Over the next several days the Japanese contented themselves with bombing Wake from their bases in the nearby Marshall Islands. Slowly, almost every sign of civilization on the island was obliterated. On December 21, two Japanese carriers on their way home from the Pearl Harbor operation peeled off to add to the carnage.

Shortly after midnight, December 23, the Japanese began landing troops on beaches all over Wake, outnumbering the marines three or four to one. Devereux's scouts were watching intensely for any signs of the relief force while his shore guns accounted for two other troop transports and eight hundred Japanese soldiers.

When Admiral William Pye (who was now in charge of the U.S. Pacific Fleet) received word that Japanese infantry were on the island, he decided it was too late to defend Wake or even to evacuate it and recalled the relief force back to Pearl Harbor. When word of this reached the marine pilots

---

* It wasn't true. "I would not have been damned fool enough to send such an idiotic message," Devereux said after the war. Nobody knows who inserted that sentence.

on *Saratoga* there was bitter consternation; in the cruiser division, there were even suggestions they should ignore the order and proceed with the mission. In the end, the task force came about and headed for Pearl, with the distressed marine pilots knowing full well what would become of their fellow marines on Wake Island if it were abandoned to the Japanese. Most cursed; some wept or bashed their fists against the bulkheads.

Devereux began organizing his remaining men for a last stand. They fought it out during the morning and most of the afternoon but were slowly overcome. Lest everyone, including civilian workers, be killed, Devereux surrendered and was taken to the Japanese commander, who immediately demanded, "Where are the women's quarters!" When Devereux replied there weren't any women on Wake, the Japanese refused to believe it and threw Devereux and other officers into a cramped and filthy prison building. From there, they were shipped to atrocious POW camps in China or Japan and, as with other prisoners of the Japanese, only about two-thirds of them returned after the war.[*2]

The president and many at the White House had been looking for a miracle at Wake. When word came that the Japanese had taken the island a disappointed Roosevelt declared, "It's worse than Pearl Harbor."

Since the day of the Pearl Harbor attack, intelligence officers had voiced concern over the large number of Japanese and Japanese Americans living on the U.S. West Coast, who immediately became the object of suspicion and contempt by their neighbors.

For the past several years the FBI and military counterintelligence services had been intercepting secret Japanese radio communiqués regarding the use of Japanese civilians in espionage work. West Coast ports were the jump-off points for the entire Pacific war, and it was disturbing to know

---

* More than one hundred U.S. civilians were forced by the Japanese to stay and work on Wake as slaves. By the end of 1943, their work done, they were marched to the beach and machine-gunned to death. After the war, the Japanese commander of Wake and eleven of his officers were sentenced to death by hanging by an Allied tribunal.

they could be (and probably were being) watched. Right after Pearl Harbor, the FBI rounded up several thousand persons of Japanese ancestry who were suspected of enemy activity and put them in internment camps for the remainder of the war. The agency at the same time also corralled several thousand persons of German and Italian ancestry and placed them in similar accommodations.

There remained what to do about the large number of Japanese against whom the FBI had no information of disloyalty, but who, it was generally assumed, remained loyal to their emperor and their homeland. The possibility of a Japanese invasion remained high in speculation and on February 23, 1942, a Japanese submarine surfaced off Santa Barbara and commenced shelling an oil field, killing a number of cattle. A clamor had begun to remove the Japanese, who were also becoming a target for mobs of angry Americans and Filipinos. Secretary of War Henry Stimson recorded that "anti-Japanese feeling had reached a level which endangered the lives of all such individuals; incidents of extra-legal violence were increasingly frequent."

In the face of mounting pressure Roosevelt signed an order of evacuation for the West Coast Japanese—two-thirds of them American citizens. The order called for a *voluntary* evacuation and relocation away from the coast; some ten thousand Japanese did this on their own, moving east into they knew not what. But for the remaining hundred thousand who chose not to avail themselves of this option, the Justice Department issued further instructions: that they were to be physically relocated to internment camps. The orders further stated that no military guards would be used, except for the protection of the evacuees, and that "all assistance" would be provided in helping the Japanese to move. Once assembled in the War Relocation Centers, the Japanese remained free to voluntarily relocate to points of their choosing in the interior of the country (a third, about thirty thousand, chose this option). The man Roosevelt placed in charge of this program was Milton Eisenhower, brother of General Dwight D. Eisenhower.

An impression has been formed, through the mists of time and temperament, that every person of Japanese ancestry on the West Coast was summarily rounded up by the U.S. government and thrown into "concentration camps," which subsequently developed a horrible reputation in the European war. In truth, the relocation camps of America were never places of torture or death, as were those in Europe. Additionally any Japanese (other than the ones already arrested by the FBI) could relocate voluntarily to any place inland.*

THE PLIGHT OF THE U.S. PHILIPPINES, which like Wake Island was also undergoing its ordeal, was particularly agonizing for Roosevelt. Five years earlier, U.S. Army Chief of Staff Douglas MacArthur, a hero of World War I, had retired to become chief military adviser to the Philippines, then a U.S. commonwealth. In prewar days, President Roosevelt had a cordial but wary relationship with the Army's chief of staff. Roosevelt actually once remarked to Rex Tugwell, one of his brain trusters, that MacArthur was "the most dangerous man in America."† MacArthur, for his part, regarded Roosevelt as a lightweight but in practice showed him great deference as president. In fact, they both showed each other respect, though neither fully trusted the other.

The American battle design for defense of the Philippines, War Plan Orange, was to assume that U.S. and Filipino forces would be able to hold out against a Japanese invasion for up to six months until a powerful U.S. naval force could fight its way across the Pacific with reinforcements. Asked by the Philippines commonwealth president Manuel Quezon how long it

---

* While the federally mandated Japanese internment camps were not places of torture or death, they were and are a tarnish on the history of America. Those who were sent to them lost everything after the war. For many, there was more to fear from their California neighbors and elected officials than from any overseas threat.
† Roosevelt said this early on, apparently in reference to MacArthur's suppression of the Bonus Marchers under the previous president. But there is no evidence that the president continued to feel that way during MacArthur's term as Army chief of staff—or later, when he was fighting in the Philippines. Others speculate that Roosevelt considered MacArthur dangerous as a political rival.

would take to build an army that could withstand a Japanese invasion for that long, MacArthur replied it would take ten years. That was in 1935. The Americans and the Filipinos had simply run out of time.

At this time, the United States Army had some thirty-one thousand men in the Philippines, along with a sizable air force of B-17 bombers and modern P-40 fighters. The Philippine army numbered seventy thousand, but most were reservists and not highly trained. MacArthur, representing both the United States and the Philippines, commanded them all.

When the Japanese attacked Pearl Harbor, an alert soldier listening to music on a San Francisco station through his shortwave radio heard the broadcast interrupted to announce the attack and ran hollering into the night to break the news. MacArthur, asleep in his luxurious penthouse in the Manila Hotel with his wife and four-year-old son, put on his uniform and asked his wife to bring him a Bible, which he read for about an hour before going to his headquarters.

The Army Air Corps commander wanted to immediately send thirty-one B-17s to bomb Japanese air bases on Formosa Island (now Taiwan). But MacArthur refused permission on grounds that Roosevelt had ordered him to let the Japanese strike first. It is unclear what the sixty-year-old Mac-Arthur thought the Japanese attack on Hawaii had represented. But the Philippine air corps was relegated to sending its bombers away at first light to keep from being destroyed on the ground in an enemy air raid they all assumed must be coming.

The fighters were sent out to patrol against enemy attack, which they did from first light till about noon, when they were brought down to be refueled at Clark Field, about forty miles northwest of Manila. By then MacArthur had changed his mind about bombing Formosa and the bombers, too, were recalled for fueling. So far, there were no signs of the enemy and the American pilots had gone into the mess hall for lunch when suddenly in the sky there appeared great formations of Japanese bombers. The pilots, rushing out to the airstrip to man their planes, could see high above them countless sticks of enemy bombs glinting in the noonday sun, headed their way.

Most of the American bombers and many fighters were destroyed or badly damaged by the explosions, and thirty men were killed. When this was reported back to Washington an irate Hap Arnold, chief of the Air Corps, telephoned the U.S. air commander in the Philippines and berated him: "How could you, an experienced airman, let this happen? This is what we sent you out there to prevent in the first place!" When Roosevelt got the news he could not seem to get over it, for several days repeating, over and over, "On the ground! On the ground! They were destroyed on the *ground!*"

Though MacArthur didn't know it, there *was* no U.S. naval fleet coming to relieve and reinforce the Philippines. Roosevelt was aware of this, and so was General George Marshall, the current Army chief of staff. The Japanese navy was running wild all over the Far East with a dozen aircraft carriers and division after division of battleships and cruisers, while the United States had but three carriers and *no* battleships or trained Army to send to the rescue. There were twenty-one thousand partly trained U.S. Army troops waiting on the West Coast to board ships for the Philippines, but they were diverted to Australia for fear of the Japanese navy. Like Wake's Major Devereux before him, General MacArthur was on his own.

ON THE TWENTY-FOURTH of December, Christmas Eve, the Japanese invasion fleet appeared and began landing an army at Lingayen Gulf, about 125 miles north of Manila. The enemy got their men ashore before MacArthur could react. War Plan Orange called for the Allied forces to move to the Bataan Peninsula across Manila Bay from the city. It was a dense, jungle-type terrain with mountains and unfordable rivers, ideal for defense. It was assumed that food stockpiled for six months would be sufficient for a forty-thousand-man army.

MacArthur, however, decided to meet the Japanese army head-on. After all, he had an army of more than a hundred thousand against an enemy nearly half that size.

It was not a wise decision. The Japanese were well-trained veterans; they had tanks and air support, as well as the cover of big naval guns. The fighting was bitter and bloody. It also featured the last large-scale cavalry charge in modern warfare, led by General Jonathan "Skinny" Wainwright, a hard-drinking former West Point first captain and cavalryman. "We lost more than a few of our first-class fighting men," Wainwright lamented later, "and a number of fine horses—including my Little Boy, who took a bullet through the head."

The Japanese pushed the Americans and Filipinos back until retreat into the Bataan Peninsula was the only option. On the evening of December 28, President Roosevelt delivered over the radio a "proclamation": "I give to the people of the Philippines my solemn pledge that their freedom will be redeemed and their independence established and protected," he said. "The entire resources, in men and material of the United States, stands behind that pledge."[3]

The Filipinos, already reeling from the bombings of their cities, received this promise as a godsend. So did MacArthur and his army, who believed that the Navy was coming to their rescue with reinforcements and supplies. Neither appreciated that this promise was just political palaver.

MacArthur was so confident that he cabled General George Marshall in Washington: "If the western Pacific is to be saved it has to be saved here and now." But by then Marshall had concluded that the western Pacific could *not* be saved—at least not here and not now. Yet he was averse to imparting that information to MacArthur, lest he lose confidence. A week earlier, a conference between Roosevelt and Churchill had secretly confirmed the "Europe First" policy for the United States and Great Britain, meaning that all major resources from both countries would go to the war against Germany. Japan could be dealt with later.

Yet the president and General Marshall had decided it was better for MacArthur to fight on rather than surrender. Who knew? Maybe he would somehow pull off a victory. The Philippines was getting big headlines back home, and MacArthur was portrayed as a great hero. It was good for morale because, at the time, it was the only place Americans were actively fighting any of the Axis powers. War Secretary Stimson was even more cynical about it. "Sometimes men have to die," he said.

Thus MacArthur charged hopefully backward, as it were—into the steaming mists of Bataan's mountainous jungles, believing salvation was at hand. He cabled Washington that he needed several dozen P-40 fighter planes, asking, rather pathetically, "Can I expect anything along that line?"[4]

MacArthur had set up his headquarters on the Rock, Corregidor, the thousand-acre granite island two miles off the tip of the Bataan Peninsula, across the bay from Manila. The American and Filipino resistance stiffened. MacArthur knew the terrain well ever since he had surveyed the entire peninsula as a young first lieutenant. He drew his defensive lines carefully across the hundred-mile-long, thirty-mile-wide finger of land. In all there were five defensive lines, each about ten miles distant from the other, most drawn up where rivers impeded the Japanese way and bridges could be blown.

For nearly three months, MacArthur's army put up a magnificent fight. The Japanese hurled entire regiments against the Americans in reckless, suicidal banzai charges and were shot down by the thousands. But still they came, and by late February MacArthur's defensive lines began to give way. It turned out there had been only a month's supply of food; although MacArthur had put the men on half rations, hunger began to be rampant. As the days passed, the men killed off all the carabao (a kind of water buffalo) on Bataan; when the cavalry horses had eaten up all the grain and were themselves starving, they were killed and consumed. Men shot monkeys from the trees and made soup. Most of the soldiers had lost twenty or thirty pounds and their uniforms, now in tatters, hung on them as if on scarecrows. Experimentation with consuming local flora and fauna sometimes came with a high price: a lot of it was poisonous, from snakes, toads, and nettles to luscious-looking jungle plants.

Finally, MacArthur learned the truth about his situation, that there would be no powerful relief fleet from the Navy. He was informed by an intelligence officer from Washington, who had arrived by submarine to take the Philippines' gold reserves out of the country.

In disgust, MacArthur wired General Marshall in Washington: "I intend to fight it out to complete destruction." Marshall tried to soothe him by pointing out that as long as MacArthur was fighting the Japanese army in the Philippines, he was at least keeping them from fighting elsewhere. This offered MacArthur some new sense of purpose but it had a hollow ring.

For Roosevelt and Marshall, the possibility of MacArthur as a prisoner of the Japanese was awful to contemplate. Tokyo Rose, the Japanese radio propagandist, had gleefully told of marching him in chains through the streets of Tokyo to the Imperial Plaza, his eventual hanging place across from the emperor's palace. To preserve his safety, Marshall and Roosevelt decided to send MacArthur to Australia to command U.S. and Allied forces there. At that point the Japanese were occupying the northern half of New Guinea, from where they intended to launch an invasion of the Australian mainland.

MacArthur furiously declined to leave his troops at the hour of their great peril. After a series of terse back-and-forths between him and Marshall, MacArthur refused to go unless ordered by President Roosevelt personally. Roosevelt gave the order and promised MacArthur he would be in command of a great army with which to fight the Japanese.

Getting the general, his family, and their faithful Cantonese *amah* (nurse) "Ah Chew," plus his immediate staff, out of the Philippines was no sure thing, however. The enemy had thrown up a tight naval blockade, and no large plane could land safely anywhere near Corregidor. Escape by submarine might take too long to arrange, and MacArthur didn't like the idea anyway. Finally it was decided that they go by PT boat to the island of Mindanao, five hundred miles south, where they would be picked up at the Del Monte pineapple plantation by a B-17 bomber from Australia.

On March 12, 1942, MacArthur's entourage boarded one of four PT boats and roared off into who knew what. Extremely rough seas caused everyone to become seasick; MacArthur later compared the trip with "spending two days in a cement mixer."[5]

On March 26 MacArthur and his party arrived at Darwin, Australia—just in time for a Japanese air raid on the city. Luckily, they had left the airfield only ten minutes before Japanese dive-bombers obliterated it, including the plane they rode in on. MacArthur, known for his steely bravery under fire in World War I, remarked to his chief of staff Dick Sutherland: "It was close. But that's the way it is in war. You win or lose, live or die—and the difference is just an eyelash."[6]

MacArthur continued to insist that he would not abandon the Philippines. "I came through," he famously told reporters, "*and I shall return.*" MacArthur faced accusations of having abandoned his troops, but amid the tragedy of the Philippines and the infamous "Death March" atrocity that followed, his defiant promise resonated with the American people and many Filipinos as well. Roosevelt awarded MacArthur the Medal of Honor to head off suspicion, and thanks to MacArthur's gift for self-promotion his catchphrase was soon stamped on matchbooks, provided by the general's headquarters, and given to all troops in the Pacific theater. His words were heralded in newspaper headlines and radio broadcasts. They were engraved on cigarette lighters, glazed into pottery ashtrays, painted on walls, and, in many fraught cases, scrawled above public toilets. The phrase slipped easily into the American lexicon. MacArthur's propaganda campaign worked: he became a legend in his own time and, to Franklin Roosevelt, a possible rival candidate for the U.S. presidency.

But there was no great army in Australia for MacArthur to command, as Roosevelt had promised. What existed there were recently arrived parts of an American infantry division, an incomplete air force with old planes, and not much navy, most of it having been sunk at the Battle of the Java Sea.

THE CONFERENCE BETWEEN Roosevelt and Churchill that decided MacArthur's fate was code-named Arcadia. The two leaders met in Washington, D.C., in late December 1941 through the early weeks of January to discuss a wide range of war issues. The meeting was secret for good reason. It turns out that a few weeks after Pearl Harbor, a large seven-ship convoy *had* in fact been assembling on the West Coast designed for the relief of MacArthur in the Philippines. It contained munitions, warplanes, tanks, guns, food, and a force of twenty-one thousand U.S. Army troops. But Roosevelt suggested to Churchill at a Christmas Eve dinner at the White House that he might reroute the convoy to Singapore, where the British were trying to stave off the Japanese. When confronted about this by members of the War Department, both Roosevelt and Churchill denied that the conversation had taken place, until a memo taken by a British officer who had attended the dinner surfaced. Secretary of War Stimson was so irate that he threatened to resign if such a breach of protocol reoccurred.[7]

As these conversations continued through Christmas and into the new year, the intensity of war-related matters was beginning to tell on Roosevelt. His sunny disposition had all but disappeared; he had what *Time* magazine called "war nerves." It was horridly frustrating to sit by, unable to strike back, with the fleet destroyed at Pearl Harbor, Wake Island, and Guam lost, and the Philippines in its death agony. German submarines were obliterating dozens of convoy ships a month, while other Nazi U-boats were torpedoing scores of oil tankers coming north from the fields of Texas and Oklahoma. Russia was on the verge of defeat and possibly considering a deal with Hitler.

It was maddening and strength-sapping, but the war must go on, and Roosevelt somehow summoned the inner courage to face whatever each day brought—if not with a sunny smile, then at least with a determined eye.

One of the bright moments in the Arcadia conference had been a spontaneous idea of Roosevelt's to create a document, similar to the Atlantic Charter, that would set out not only war aims but postwar goals. It would be a sort of new world order for all the countries opposed to Nazism, fascism, and Japanese imperialism. He and Churchill began counting the probables and possibles until they had about two dozen countries listed. When the question arose of what to call the new organization, the two men decided to sleep on it and retired.

The next morning, Roosevelt's engaging smile had returned, and he asked to be wheeled to Churchill's quarters in the White House. While waiting in the living room, the story goes, Roosevelt was startled to behold Sir

Winston emerge from his bath stark naked, joking that he "had nothing to hide from the President of the United States."*[8]

A delighted Roosevelt responded that he had during the night come up with the name for their new organization: the United Nations. Churchill not only liked the name but thought it was a stroke of genius and went around all day trying it out on people. Thus came a glimpse of sunshine amid the gloomy clouds of war. And so it went, day in and day out, in the place where wars and battles were conceived, and the big decisions were made.

As the months passed, there were large, terrible, and complicated international questions that begged settling, including how to deal with Japanese designs on China, Burma, and India. Since before the war, when he was an American military attaché in China, General Joseph Stilwell had served as a U.S. commander in that theater; at the moment, he was heavily engaged by a large force of Japanese who were seeking to overtake Burma, possibly as a takeoff point to conquer India. Stilwell was suspicious of British intentions in the area, suggesting that they were more motivated by their efforts to keep their empire intact than in fighting the enemy.

Roosevelt sympathized with Stilwell. The president had long ago developed an antipathy toward imperialism, and he unsuccessfully nudged Churchill to give India its independence, as was being pressed by Mahatma Gandhi and other Indian activists. Churchill resisted Roosevelt's meddling, and privately he told friends he did not intend to be the prime minister who gave away the empire. Churchill had made representations to Gandhi about offering independence to India once the war was won. But the ascetic Indian leader didn't believe him, comparing Churchill's offer to "a postdated check." The issue remained a point of friction between Roosevelt and Churchill throughout the war but neither man allowed it to come before the main object, which was defeating the Axis powers.

---

* Some versions have Churchill with a bottle of champagne in his hand. Churchill later denied that he was naked, saying he was wrapped in a bath towel.

IN FEBRUARY 1942 the U.S. Navy suffered one of its worst sea disasters at the Battle of the Java Sea. The Navy's small Asiatic fleet, built around the heavy cruiser USS *Houston,* had escaped destruction by Japanese planes in the Philippines. While steaming to the South Pacific, it linked up with a Dutch and British force consisting of nine cruisers and eleven destroyers. On February 27, this task force was confronted by a superior Japanese fleet; most of the Allied ships were sunk with a terrific loss of life, including the *Houston,* which went down with 622 hands. Afterward, Roosevelt cabled Churchill, "The Pacific situation is very grave."

Following this debacle, Roosevelt felt a change was needed at Navy headquarters. The chief of naval operations, Admiral Harold R. "Betty" Stark, whom the president liked personally, appeared unequal to the task of running the entire naval operation. So Stark was put in charge of the Atlantic Fleet. In his place as CNO, Roosevelt installed Admiral Ernest J. King, a gruff sailor of the old school of whom it was said, "Not only did he not suffer fools gladly, he didn't suffer *anybody* gladly."*

Roosevelt hoped that King would bring to the Navy, which was still reeling from Pearl Harbor and other defeats, a sense of control, purpose, and adherence to duty. King would achieve this, though not without many sparks and contentious episodes. Given the future importance of naval carrier warfare in the Pacific, it was also notable that King was the first aviator to attain leadership of the Navy.

Another officer whose name began to surface around this time was the new brigadier general Dwight D. Eisenhower, who had appeared in General Marshall's fabled "black book," a list of men Marshall regarded as highly capable leaders that dated from the mid-1930s, when Marshall commanded the U.S. Army's Infantry School. Eisenhower had been moved from War Plans to the defense of the Philippines because he had served as an assistant to MacArthur there and knew the territory. After the Philippines fell Eisenhower would become the focus of much more important tasks.

---

* King's daughter said that her father was "very even-tempered. He had only one mood: furious."

★★★★★

IMMEDIATELY AFTER THE Pearl Harbor attack, Americans were both out-raged and humiliated that they were forced to stand by while the Japanese octopus scuttled across the Pacific, gobbling up nations and island chains.

No one was more outraged than Franklin Roosevelt, who had asked permission from his newfound ally Joseph Stalin to conduct an American heavy bomber raid on Japan from the Russian city Vladivostok. He was rebuffed with a stern *nyet*. Uncle Joe had his hands full fighting the Germans and didn't want to provoke Japan too.

Since then, Roosevelt had been pressing the chiefs of the armed services to find a quick way to retaliate against the Japanese homeland. So far everyone had drawn a blank. Regular carrier aircraft were too small to do any significant damage and didn't have the fuel range; bombers were thought to be too large to take off and land from a carrier. Then one cold January day, someone got the idea that the B-25 Mitchell, a relatively new twin-engine medium bomber, might just be able to take off from a flattop deck. It couldn't re-land, but after bombing Japan it had just enough range to make friendly fields in China.

Army Air Corps commander Hap Arnold sent for Lieutenant Colonel Jimmy Doolittle, already one of the most famous aviators in the world, whom he knew to be brilliant and "absolutely fearless." Doolittle found his raiders among the only major organization with pilots qualified to fly a B-25 in combat: the 17th Bombardment Group stationed at Fort Pendle-ton, Oregon. He had the word passed among the men of the 17th that volunteers would be needed "for a very hazardous mission." Anyone who wanted out could do so, "and nothing would ever be said about it." Nobody dropped out.[9]

Three months later a full Navy task force, including the aircraft carriers *Hornet* and *Enterprise,* would steam westward into harm's way, carrying the B-25s lashed to the flight deck. If the Japanese got wind of it, the expedition would be headed into a terrible trap, which would mean nearly the end of America's remaining naval power in the Pacific. The mission was so secret that at first even President Roosevelt wasn't told of it.

On April 2, 1942, the carriers slipped out of San Francisco. That afternoon, when it was safely at sea, the Navy task force commander sent a signal to all ships: "This force is bound for Tokyo."

The Army pilots and crews studied maps, gambled, watched movies, ate ice cream, and contemplated their fate. Two weeks later, as they approached enemy territory, the weather began to deteriorate and the seas grew tall as three-story buildings.

The original plan had called for planes to be launched about three hundred miles from Japan—but they had not realized that the Japanese had a second picket line seven hundred miles offshore. The extra four hundred miles would become a major factor because of fuel.

After a brief discussion with naval commanders, Doolittle got the okay to proceed anyway. The klaxon sounded immediately and the captain of the USS *Hornet* gave the order: "Army pilots, man your planes!" Doolittle himself had given the odds of the squadron returning alive as less than fifty-fifty.

The ship was rolling and pitching wildly as Doolittle became the first to take off. The flight officer was timing the rise and fall of the carrier's bow so that the pilots would have the benefit of a rising deck from which to fly off. "It was like riding a seesaw," Doolittle said.

Just as the carrier lifted up on a wave, Doolittle became airborne with only yards to spare. Five hours later, flying low, he and his squadron reached the coast of Japan. Fishermen and farmers looked up and waved to them. The weather had cleared.

Doolittle spotted a large munitions factory that was his target and pulled up to 1,200 feet, which was his bombing altitude. The bombardier dropped four incendiaries that set the factory afire. Another pilot headed across Tokyo for a large naval base in Yokohama. As the bomb bay doors opened, the plane was jolted by bursts from flak guns. But the bombardier pulled the lever and after a few seconds shouted jubilantly, "We got an aircraft carrier!"

Everyone half expected a cloud of Japanese Zeros to descend on them, but the unit was in and out so quickly that it didn't happen. It was the same in the other cities that were attacked: flak but only a few enemy fighters.

The squadron reassembled over the Sea of Japan and flew into the setting sun. None of the B-25s had been shot down, but one had engine trouble and was forced to land in Russia.* Now all they had to do was make the preprepared landing fields in friendly Chinese territory.

The *Enterprise* and *Hornet,* now speeding home, were picking up signals from Radio Tokyo telling of the raid. Great cheering broke out among the thousands of sailors aboard. They had done it, America had struck back!

The Doolittle raid set into motion a number of consequences in Japan far beyond its modest intention of dropping bombs on an enemy city. Like the Americans after Pearl Harbor, the Japanese were furious and humiliated. The Imperial government had always promised that the Home Islands were immune from enemy attacks.

So agitated and confused was the reaction during and immediately following the raid that large numbers of Japanese warships in the area broke radio silence and began communicating with one another. These signals were, in turn, snatched from the airwaves by U.S. radio listening posts from the Aleutian Islands to Australia and sent to Commander Joseph Rochefort's code-breaking operation in Hawaii. Where before, because of the paucity of samples, Rochefort's wizards were able to decode and read only a small portion of Japan's top secret naval code, they were soon reading most of it—and later still, they were reading almost all of it. This would have tremendous repercussions in the naval battles to come.[10]

The raid so embarrassed Admiral Yamamoto, the commander of the Imperial Navy, that he took steps to ensure such attacks would not be successful in the future. The first was to recall a significant number of Japanese fighter interceptors back to the Home Islands from the southern area, where they had been instrumental in Japanese victories. In this way, Doolittle's raid had at least slowed the pace of enemy conquests.

A far more critical reaction was Yamamoto's decision to expand the defensive perimeter around the Home Islands from 700 to 1,200 miles into the Pacific. This would necessitate the invasion and occupation of

---

* The pilots and crew were detained as prisoners in the Soviet Union until, two years later, they managed to escape into Iran.

Midway Island, an important U.S. observation and listening post. There, Yamamoto decided, he would bring about the destruction of the remainder of the U.S. Pacific Fleet. The plan was to lure the ships from Hawaii and deceive them into thinking the Midway operation was a run-of-the-mill Japanese advance on the scale of Wake Island or Guam. Instead, Yamamoto would be waiting with the most powerful force the Imperial Navy had ever assembled, including six aircraft carriers and the giant battleship *Yamato.* It was a trap that had been the dream of Japanese naval planners since the 1920s.*

In late April 1942, a task force set out from the Japanese Home Islands, bound for Port Moresby on the southern coast of New Guinea. Consisting of two heavy aircraft carriers, one light one, and other warships escorting fourteen troopships, it was a formidable lineup. The strategy was that the light carrier would cover the invasion's landing, while the two heavy carriers would ambush and sink the relief force that was sure to come.

What the Japanese didn't know was that the Americans were reading their mail and, also, that an American aircraft carrier, the *Yorktown,* was already operating in the Coral Sea to support the Australians. By late April 1942 U.S. Pacific Fleet headquarters at Pearl Harbor was able to piece together a picture of a major southward movement by the Japanese.

Two American carriers, the *Enterprise* and the *Hornet,* were returning from the Doolittle mission in the northwest Pacific; the *Saratoga* was laid up in a West Coast shipyard after being torpedoed the previous month. That left the *Lexington,* back at Pearl, to race south to join the *Yorktown* and intercept the Japanese force.

---

* Since the raid, the Doolittle fliers met annually for a reunion. A tradition developed that they would drink from silver cups engraved with their names. When a raider died, his cup was placed in a glass case. When it came down to the last two survivors, they would open a bottle of fine brandy, vintage 1896, the year of their leader's birth, and that would end the tradition. The brandy bottle was opened in 2016.

The loss of the *Lexington* and ensuing defeat sustained by the Americans at the Battle of the Coral Sea had repercussions far beyond the sinking of ships. First, it caused the Japanese to withdraw their task force with all its troopships bound for Port Moresby, which, if they had not been opposed, would undoubtedly have successfully established a base in southern New Guinea from which to invade Australia. Subsequent events caused the Japanese to give up the idea entirely. Second, the two Japanese carriers that returned to the Home Islands were so badly damaged they would be unable to join the Midway battle force. Admiral Yamamoto's fleet, now with four carriers instead of six, steamed from the Inland Sea toward its mid-ocean rendezvous with destiny.

When the *Yorktown* returned to Pearl Harbor, engineers and marine surveyors forecast it would take up to three months for repairs. Admiral Chester Nimitz, in one of his most critical decisions of the war, ordered that every available workman be immediately sent to the *Yorktown's* berth. He decreed that the repairs must be done in three days; with three thousand men working around the clock it was accomplished.

In retrospect, these events would have an immense bearing on the course of the Pacific war.

★★★★★

NIMITZ'S FIXATION ON HAVING *Yorktown* made seaworthy so quickly was inextricably connected with a discovery made by Commander Rochefort and his code breakers: the Japanese were planning a big operation in the central Pacific. Cryptologists working night and day had even figured out roughly when, but not where—only that the Japanese identified their target as "AF."

Rochefort suspected the target might be Midway Island, which was the only U.S.-held possession remaining in the central Pacific. Soon, he hit on a subterfuge stunning in its simplicity. He sent a top secret message to the commander of Midway, telling him to report, falsely, over the open airwaves, to Pearl Harbor that the freshwater distillation plant at Midway was broken. A day or so after the false report the Japanese took the bait. U.S. radio intercepts picked up a Japanese message to Tokyo that "AF was running low on water." Everybody knew there was a chance now for the United States to ambush the ambushers.[11]

Now that they knew *where,* naval intelligence desperately needed to know exactly *when.* One of the cryptologists, Lieutenant Commander Wesley Wright, who had just finished his regular twelve-hour shift, took a crack at it. He attacked an infinitesimally complex cipher until, at last, at 5:30 a.m. he was able to report a solution: the Japanese attack on Midway would begin at daybreak June 3.

This priceless information was clouded only by the staggering inferiority of the U.S. force against the Japanese fleet, which contained, so far as the U.S. Navy knew, up to eight large aircraft carriers, eleven battleships, sixteen cruisers, and fifty destroyers. Against this, the Navy could muster only three carriers, zero battleships, eight cruisers, and fourteen destroyers. If surprise ever counted for anything it had better be now.[12]

As anticipated, on the morning of June 3 a Navy PBY "flying boat" long-range reconnaissance plane spotted the Japanese ships right after dawn, about 375 miles from Midway. But what the pilot actually saw was not the main attack force with the carriers but the troop transports with the invasion force. The Japanese attack bombers had taken off for Midway Island at 4:30 a.m., before dawn.

Based on this report, seventeen B-17s took off from Midway to bomb the ship—but not a bomb struck home. The lone saving grace was that at least the B-17s were not on the Midway runways when the Japanese attackers came roaring in.

The Japanese strike wreaked havoc on Midway, not only causing major damage to buildings, hangars, shops, and fuel dumps but also destroying dozens of the "older, heavier, and slower" American planes that had been shot down by Zero fighters.

In the meantime, Admirals Raymond Spruance and Frank Jack Fletcher had launched planes of their own at dawn. The first Americans to find the enemy carriers were forty-one Douglas Devastator torpedo planes. It was a slaughter by the Japanese, whose faster Zeros and ship-to-air defenses knocked practically all of them from the sky without a single American torpedo hit being scored. Only six made it back to the U.S. carriers.

Again, the rule of unintended consequences tilted in favor of the Americans. The U.S. torpedo attack, which lasted about forty minutes, had discombobulated the Japanese. Their big carriers had to take jolting actions to evade U.S. torpedoes and were thus unable to bring their own torpedo planes and bombers above decks to launch them, or to switch armaments to planes on deck.

At this crucial moment, the American dive-bombers, notably in the new Douglas SBD Dauntless, arrived on the scene and caught the Japanese, their decks filled with planes, just returned from Midway. Moreover, their air cap—the defensive squadrons of Zeros that hovered above the carriers—was caught down "on the deck" chasing the American torpedo planes. As a result they were unable to gain altitude before the dive-bombers screamed in and unleashed their loads.

When it was over, about 10:30 a.m., three of the enemy carriers, *Kaga, Akagi,* and *Soryu,* were aflame from stem to stern; they later sank three miles down to the ocean floor. The fourth carrier, *Hiryu,* was also located and attacked late that afternoon and joined its friends beneath the waves— but not before it had launched planes that found the unfortunate *Yorktown* and bombed her so severely that her speed was reduced just enough for a Japanese submarine to put in a fatal torpedo.*

Thus the Battle of Midway concluded, a decisive American victory that permanently disarranged Japanese designs for control of the Pacific. The Midway invasion was thwarted, and Yamamoto withdrew his fleet to fight another day. But from the date of this key battle the Japanese did not conquer and keep another square foot of Pacific soil for the rest of World War II. The Midway battle was crucial. In exchange for 307 lives, the *Yorktown* and a destroyer, and 147 airplanes, the American fleet had destroyed four Japanese carriers, more than three hundred planes, a cruiser and a destroyer, and nearly five thousand Japanese sailors

---

* The planes that had bombed the *Yorktown,* however, were in for a wrenching surprise when they returned to find the *Hiryu* capsized and sinking. All they could do was circle pathetically above their mother ship with nowhere else to go until their fuel ran out.

and airmen. It has been called, with justification, "the turning point" in the Pacific war.

NOT LONG AFTER THE AMERICAN VICTORY at Midway, Churchill returned to the United States and stayed with Roosevelt at Hyde Park, lobbying valiantly for him to support a U.S. invasion of French North Africa. He persisted in his argument that although the Allies were not strong enough yet for a cross-Channel invasion of France, they could in fact oppose the Germans in North Africa. This would serve to deny them the rich spoils of the Arabian oil fields and the Suez Canal—if not of the entire Mediterranean, which would be lost if the Germans successfully persuaded the Spanish dictator Franco to allow them access to attack the British stronghold of Gibraltar, which sat at the Atlantic entrance to the Mediterranean Sea.

Marshall and the entire military establishment were against this strategy, via what might be termed the Marshall Dictum: diversions beget other diversions. If they had known what was in Churchill's devious mind, they would have been doubly opposed. After clearing North Africa of the Axis, Churchill reasoned, the next step would be an Allied invasion of Sicily, followed by an invasion of Italy to knock her out of the war. From there loomed the infinite possibility of a slash at Germany from Europe's "soft underbelly," up into Austria's thin border with Italy, and into southern Germany itself, thereby avoiding a dangerous amphibious landing in France altogether. Churchill saw the big picture clearly in his mind, just as he had seen it in the tragic Gallipoli invasion that had gone awry during the previous war.

At length Roosevelt relented and Churchill got his American invasion of North Africa, but not necessarily into the soft underbelly of the Balkans. It seemed to American citizens a long way from conquering Germany, and they knew nothing about it until the radio, newspapers, and newsreels announced on November 8, 1942, that a U.S. naval fleet and invasion transports had appeared at dawn off the coast of French Morocco.

★★★★★

Roosevelt faced a fraught dilemma of how to proceed with the Vichy French prior to the U.S. invasion of North Africa. Because Vichy controlled the French North African colony of Morocco, with its large garrison of soldiers, no one knew how the invasion would be received. Churchill and Roosevelt guessed—hoped, actually—that when American and British forces landed on the Moroccan coast they would be greeted as liberators. On the other hand, if the invasion was resisted, it could result in a great loss of life and possibly in failure.

Three characters emerged as possibilities to disarm the French troops: Charles de Gaulle, the leader of the Free French, consisting of about ten thousand French soldiers rescued during the British evacuation of Dunkirk and others scattered around Central Africa; General Henri Giraud, a popular figure who had recently escaped from the Nazis and was hiding in southern France; and Admiral François Darlan, an odious collaborator with the Germans who was then in charge of the Vichy affairs in the Mediterranean.

The stakes were high. There were some 120,000 Vichy soldiers in France's North African colonies, armed by the Germans to put down just such an invasion as the Allies were now contemplating. They'd had several years to fortify, and there was still enough French navy remaining to put up a fight, as well as a Vichy air force of 170 fighters and bombers.

Roosevelt plunged personally into the political intrigue, sending as his special representative Robert Murphy, a young career diplomat who had been the chargé d'affaires at Vichy. Murphy schmoozed with all the unctuous Vichyites, and soon he was able to identify those who might be amenable to coming to terms with an American invasion. He was a foreign dignitary, so Murphy also had access to French North Africa, where he proved himself a valuable spy, noting Vichy French fortifications, aerodromes, warships, tides, roads, and radio stations. Roosevelt also sent his close aide Admiral William D. Leahy as ambassador to Vichy, for which the president paid a steep political price. His enemies in the press and elsewhere assailed him mercilessly for cooperating with such a malodorous regime.

For a while, Roosevelt felt that the sixty-three-year-old General Giraud was the best choice of a go-between who could command Vichy troops to lay down their arms. He was a legendary soldier in the French army, as well as a master of disguises. Captured by the Germans in World War I, Giraud escaped and faked his way across half of Europe posing as "a butcher, a stable boy, a coal merchant, and a magician." Until recently he had been held prisoner in the Konigstein dungeon, where he "shaved his mustache, darkened his hair with brick dust, and, with a homemade rope he had plaited by hand, lowered himself 150 feet to the Elbe." Passing himself off as an engineer, he made it back to France with a 100,000 mark price on his head.[13]

After indicating that he was receptive to helping the Allies, Giraud was loaded into a British submarine and taken to Gibraltar where, on the eve of the invasion, he made himself unbearable. Through an interpreter, Giraud told Eisenhower, who was in overall command of the invasion, that he expected to be in supreme command of all Allied troops during the operation. Furthermore, he produced a detailed set of plans for liberating France and defeating Nazi Germany. Taken aback, Eisenhower offered Giraud command of all the French troops he could recruit, but he was not about to offer him his own job. Giraud persisted, however, sulking, grandstanding, and in the end he threatened not to help the Allies at all.

After this unhappy encounter, it was learned that Admiral Darlan, the Vichy commander of North Africa, had gone to Algiers to visit his son, who was sick with polio. He was promptly captured by a pro-Allied group and brought to the American high command. At first Darlan agreed to tell the Vichy troops to join the Allies; then he waffled and said he would have to speak with Marshal Philippe Pétain at Vichy. When Pétain told him instead to resist the invasion, Darlan again promised Eisenhower that he would order the French troops to cease fire, then lied and said he had no authority outside the city of Algiers.

Roosevelt had indeed gotten in bed with skunks, but it was the kind of political intrigue he enjoyed. When the press and politicians excoriated him for dealing with Vichy, Roosevelt followed the advice Winston Churchill had given him: "Just tell them it's a temporary expedient of war."[14]

★★★★★

IN THE MEANTIME, something dreadful was being hatched in the South Pacific. In May 1942 the Japanese had established a small seaplane base on the island of Tulagi in the Solomon Islands to the northeast of Australia. By July aerial photos showed they also had begun constructing a major air base on the much larger nearby island of Guadalcanal. Evidently, even though their surprise attack on New Guinea's Port Moresby had been thwarted at the Coral Sea battle, the Japanese had not given up on their designs for taking Australia—or at least in establishing a base to bomb the American shipping lanes and their supply and support facilities in the New Hebrides and New Caledonia chains of islands.

The development was alarming and clearly would need to be countered, since what the Japanese were building amounted to an unsinkable aircraft carrier that could do immeasurable damage. The U.S. Army as yet could not provide trained troops to attack the enemy. So the Navy decided to send in the Marines. Roosevelt was briefed and gave his approval, not knowing that he had just sanctioned one of the most storied battles of the Pacific war. The issue seesawed back and forth so often it gave the president and his cabinet cause to question its wisdom in the first place.

The First Marine Division, seventeen thousand strong, was escorted by a task force commanded by Admiral Fletcher that included the carriers *Saratoga, Enterprise,* and the new carrier *Wasp.* Because of the danger of enemy air attacks, Fletcher agreed to stick around for only two days. This horrified the Marine commander, Major General Alexander A. Vandegrift, because the troop transports would be unprotected for one to three days while unloading—as would the Marines, from who-knew-what might be encountered on the island.

At dawn on August 7, 1942, the American task force began landing Marines on Guadalcanal and Tulagi.

The Solomon Islands are one of the darkest, most forbidding territories on earth. No tropical paradise like Tahiti or the beaches of Waikiki, it was a mountainous, slug-shaped tropical hell about ninety miles long and twenty-five miles wide. When the transports arrived at night (in what would be known as Ironbottom Sound for the number of warships soon to be sunk there), the aroma of fresh ocean breezes soon changed into a fetid, sinister stink of rotting tropic vegetation and scummy, stagnant "rivers" filled with ferocious crocodiles. The widely traveled writer Jack London remarked in his *South Seas Tales* that "the worst punishment I could inflict on my enemies would be to banish them to the Solomons."[15]

Shortly before dawn the cruisers and destroyers opened up with their batteries on the beaches of Guadalcanal. The Japanese radio on Tulagi, twenty miles away, sounded the alarm to the big Japanese base at Rabaul, six hundred miles north, which immediately dispatched a flight of twenty-seven twin-engine bombers to forestall the Allied invasion. From their hiding places far up the island chain, coast watchers—former Australian coconut planters—sighted the Japanese aircraft and broadcast a warning to the fleet, causing the ships to stop unloading and scatter.

Planes from the U.S. carriers shot down fourteen of the bombers, and no hits were scored on American ships. Landing forces were pleasantly surprised to find that on Guadalcanal there were mostly only Japanese laborers and Korean slaves building the aerodrome. The Japanese on Tulagi were likewise dispatched, but not without a sharp fight. All in all it had been a good day. As the Americans would soon discover, however, nights were a different matter.

The Japanese had immediately dispatched a power naval fleet of seven cruisers and escorting destroyers to deal with the U.S. warships. Six Allied cruisers and nineteen destroyers were cruising Ironbottom Sound the night of August 8, protecting the eighteen troop transports that continued to unload. The night was squally, and lightning flashes eerily lit up the cone of an extinct volcano named Savo Island that lay at the north of the sound.

Upon their approach, the Japanese cruisers launched a number of floatplanes with flares, which suddenly lit up the sky above the Allied ships. A U.S. destroyer came to life: "Warning! Warning! Strange ships entering the harbor!" The Australian cruiser *Canberra* was the first to go, torpedoed and sunk by a salvo of twenty 8-inch shells. The cruiser

Chicago was nearly blown in half. The *Astoria* was set aflame, as was the *Quincy,* which, in a gallant action, got off a salvo before starting to go down; this probably saved the American troopships still unloading at the beaches. The *Quincy's* final shots hit the chartroom of the Japanese command cruiser; without navigation tools, and in the narrow confines of the sound on a rainy night, the Japanese broke off the action. But not before another U.S. cruiser, the *Vincennes,* was sent to the bottom in flames.

Thus ended the Battle of Savo Island, the new worst disaster the U.S. Navy had suffered in a sea battle. From beginning to end, it took just thirty-five minutes. A thousand and twenty sailors were dead, and the U.S. cruiser force was decimated. Japanese skill at night fighting was stunning. Their use of superior night glasses, as well as optics, searchlights, flares, night gunnery, and torpedo training, had completely overwhelmed the Americans. The defeat was so horrendous that Admiral King actually kept it from Roosevelt for a time.

This was the first of six naval battles for Guadalcanal, with the Americans getting the worst of it for the first half, before getting the hang of it and sinking most Japanese ships in the end.

The U.S. Marines on Guadalcanal were on their own. Standing on the beaches, they gaped as dozens of small boats began to arrive with hundreds of oil-blackened, burned, dismembered, or dead bodies of sailors fished from the bloody, oil-slicked waters of Ironbottom Sound.

Every night on Guadalcanal the Japanese dispatched a bomber known as "Washing Machine Charlie," for the queer sound of his engines. He would drop a load of bombs on the marines' camp at the airfield and then fly back to Rabaul. Five days after they had landed, a patrol had gone out to investigate reports that the Japanese were flying the white flag of surrender. It was led by the colonel in charge of the intelligence section (who should have known better) and contained intelligence analysts, medical officers, and others unaccustomed to combat. They were ambushed on the beach and slaughtered. Of twenty-six men in the patrol only three escaped.

The next week, the Japanese—under the impression that the marine landing was merely a raid—sent a thousand-man detachment composed of soldiers who were supposed to have captured Port Moresby on New Guinea but for the Battle of the Coral Sea. Their commander decided to attempt one of the Japanese army's infamous banzai charges, in which large bodies of troops screaming *Banzai!* ("May the emperor live a thousand years!") rush and overwhelm an enemy position with shock and speed.

This time it did not work.

The marines, acting on information from a native constable who had been savagely beaten by the Japanese, set up an ambush by the Tenaru River and partially avenged the killing of the intelligence patrol. Forty-three marines lost their lives in the melee that followed, and more than eight hundred Japanese bodies were counted; scores of Japanese soldiers were killed crossing the river and were later eaten by crocodiles. The Japanese commander committed hara-kiri, and General Vandegrift, appalled at the slaughter, wrote in his report, "I have never heard or read of this kind of fighting. These people refuse to surrender."[16]

An air force arrived at Guadalcanal after the marines finished the runways that the Japanese had started. This relieved the overall military situation, as the planes limited the Japanese ability to reinforce their ground troops and send their navy down from Rabaul to shell the marines.

Between defending against regular Japanese infantry attacks, their air attacks, naval shelling of the airfield, and troubling losses from malaria and other tropical diseases, the question arose of whether the marines could hold on. Roosevelt himself commented to a cabinet meeting that even if the marines were forced out of the Solomon Islands, the press could be told that "the delaying action had been of great value."[17]

The Japanese continued reinforcing their positions nightly on Guadalcanal by means of destroyer convoys from Rabaul known as the "Tokyo Express," until, at the height of the battle, they had nearly thirty thousand men there.

On the night of September 13, Washing Machine Charlie clattered over the airfield and dropped a pale green illumination flare; simultaneously twenty-four hundred Japanese soldiers screaming *Banzai!* attacked a six-hundred-man marine position on what would be named Bloody Ridge, and were repulsed with heavy losses. All night, the Japanese regrouped after these suicide charges and came again over ground littered with their dead. By morning, only eight hundred Japanese remained; they staggered off into the jungle. A *New York Times* correspondent, Hanson Baldwin, arrived to ask Vandegrift, "Are you going to hold this beachhead? Can you stay here?"

Vandegrift didn't hesitate. "Well, hell yes. Why not?"

The air above the Solomons was consumed with daily dogfights and other run-ins between Marine F4F Wildcats and Japanese bombers, with their escorting Zeros. The Wildcat was heavier and not as maneuverable as the Japanese planes, but it was better armored and soon the Americans began to take a heavy toll of the enemy planes. In late October, a naval engagement known as the Battle of the Santa Cruz Islands resulted in the sinking of the carrier *Hornet*. In a delicious irony, all of her planes had taken off and landed at the Marine airstrip at Guadalcanal full of fight.

Roosevelt was highly apprehensive about the marines' perilous circumstances, which he feared might end in disaster as it had in the Philippines. "My anxiety about the Southwest Pacific," he told his aide Harry Hopkins privately, "is to make sure that every possible weapon gets into that area to hold Guadalcanal. And that having held it in this crisis, that munitions and planes and crews are on the way to take advantage of our success."[18]

Publicly, however, Roosevelt was less confident, and he seemed to prepare the American people for a disappointment, speaking in diminishing terms of the "importance of the Solomon Islands." The public did not yet know of the terrible naval losses, and Roosevelt, according to his biographer Robert Sherwood, was "seeking to prepare the people" for the loss of Guadalcanal.

The marines, however, were preparing themselves for what they knew would be the most powerful enemy assault yet. Fortunately, they too had been reinforced with an additional Marine regiment plus two Army regiments, bringing Vandegrift's strength to twenty-two thousand. Fighting and dying continued on a daily basis, but the Americans still awaited the big attack they felt was coming.

All the same, the American naval successes and Japan's own inability to reinforce their ground troops without terrific loss of life were enough to convince Japanese naval authorities at Rabaul that continuing the offensive was futile. Still, somebody was going to have to tell the emperor—and nobody wanted to. So it was not until the end of December that the order was given to evacuate the Japanese army from the island. By that time they were starving, disease-ridden, and steadily being driven away from the airfield by the marines and the Army soldiers.

The Battle of Guadalcanal was a humiliating defeat for the Japanese, whose army until then had gone undefeated throughout the Pacific. Their losses were estimated at between twenty thousand and thirty-six thousand total, including the naval dead and soldiers drowned on the transports. Worse, many Japanese troops died from disease or starvation due to their superiors' inability to support them. If ever there was hubris in a battle, Guadalcanal stands as a shining example in military science. The Japanese consistently underestimated their enemy, put their troops in piecemeal, and continued to make the same mistakes in infantry tactics. Eventually, they would do the same in their sea battles.

The Allies lost some seven thousand soldiers and thirty-six ships, including an aircraft carrier. But now they had a strong base from which to operate as they slogged their way up the Solomon chain, pushing the Japanese before them. Upon learning of these happy results, President Roosevelt remarked, "It would seem that the turning point in this war has at last been reached."[19]

FRANKLIN ROOSEVELT WAS HAVING a casual dinner party at Shangri-La, the presidential getaway in the Maryland mountains. But to some of his guests he seemed nervous and preoccupied. It was November 7, 1942, the eve of the American invasion of North Africa, and the president was waiting for an important call. The phone rang late, and some noticed that his hand shook as he picked up the receiver. He listened, and then said, "Thank God, thank God. That sounds grand." He put the phone down and turned to his guests. "We've landed in North Africa. Casualties are below expectations. We are striking back."[20]

It was, as the British are fond of saying, a near run thing. American troops had come under shore fire from the Vichy French as the landing craft hit the beaches, but they withstood the storm with minimal casualties. The French navy came out to fight but the U.S. Navy sunk it.

Meanwhile, the Allied high command had tried out General Giraud over the radio to silence the French batteries, but no one paid him any attention. De Gaulle was not on the scene, but Admiral Darlan proved to be the ace in the hole. Despite Darlan's earlier dithering, Robert Murphy persuaded him to issue an order for a French cease-fire and proclaimed him the civil governor of French Morocco. That did the trick—though it put Roosevelt in a sticky spot with much of his liberal base, who did not fancy working with a collaborator and turncoat. Roosevelt tried out Churchill's explanation that Darlan was merely a military expedient, but this did not sit well with the press and many in Congress.

On Darlan's orders, which stemmed from Nazi puppet strings pulled back in Vichy, all Jews in Morocco had been rounded up for eventual transportation to concentration camps. An order to set them free had come from the Americans, but Darlan protested that it might lead to a civil war with the Arabs. Roosevelt was on the verge of firing Darlan and clapping him in jail when fate saved him the trouble. On Christmas Eve, a twenty-year-old lunatic who wanted to restore the French monarchy assassinated Darlan in his office, thus putting the Allies firmly in control.

Meanwhile, the British general Sir Bernard Law Montgomery, who had replaced Claude Auchinleck, had scored a great victory at El Alamein. This at last began to push Rommel's Afrika Korps out of Egypt, through the vast Libyan desert and into Tunisia, where the Americans, it was hoped, would overwhelm them.

It was a good strategic plan on paper but, as is often the case, difficult upon execution. First, this was the rainy season and the roads quickly turned into a muck that was impassible for large vehicles. Second, the weather became freezing cold; the men had not been issued winter gear, the idea apparently being that it did not get cold in Africa.

The American advance labored mightily through Morocco and crossed into Algeria but, once in Tunisia, became utterly bogged down by the weather and very stiff resistance by the Germans, who were being reinforced there. Orders came down to attack, but were impossible to execute, due to weather conditions. One GI quipped (after Churchill) that "Never in the field of human conflict have so few been commanded by so many, from so far away."

At length, Eisenhower came down from Gibraltar for a personal inspection. Once he reached the fighting front, he called off the entire advance until the spring, when the roads dried out.

In the meantime, Roosevelt and Churchill decided that now would be a good time to hold a grand Allied conference to discuss war aims, near to the battleground itself. They chose Casablanca as the meeting place and tried to persuade "Uncle Joe" Stalin to come. But the Soviet dictator demurred on grounds that he was needed in Moscow because of the fighting around Stalingrad. It was well known that Stalin didn't like to fly, which was the only secure way he could have gotten to Morocco.*[21]

A date for Casablanca was set for mid-January 1943. To celebrate, on New Year's Eve Roosevelt invited guests to the White House, no doubt with a taste of relish, to screen Hollywood's latest hit movie *Casablanca*, starring Humphrey Bogart and Ingrid Bergman.

In the meantime Stalin had sent Molotov as a special ambassador to the United States to agitate for continued Soviet Lend-Lease largesse. Like Churchill before him, Roosevelt welcomed Molotov to stay in the White House, where the staff was both startled and bewildered the next morning when they made Molotov's bed. Beneath his pillow, they found a loaded pistol and a slab of salami.

---

* Some attributed this to his fear that a bomb might be placed on his plane by a disgruntled fellow citizen. Other sources claim he did not trust airborne travel of any kind.

LEFT: Journalist Walter Duranty in 1935. His coverage of the Soviet Union for the *New York Times* was so biased toward communism that the paper later declared it was "some of the worst reporting to appear in this newspaper." RIGHT: Stalin with his henchman (and foreign minister) Vyacheslav Molotov in 1939. During the war Stalin confided to Winston Churchill, "That Molotov can drink!"

TOP: Roosevelt cheerfully holds two of his grandchildren—
Franklin D. Roosevelt III and John Boettiger—on Christmas Day 1939.
BOTTOM: Roosevelt with Ruthie Bie and dog Fala at the "Little White House"
in Georgia. Roosevelt was so seldom photographed in his wheelchair that most
Americans were unaware that he was completely crippled by polio.

St. Paul's Cathedral, dating to 1697 and designed by Christopher Wren,
looms over the terrific damage to London by German bombing.
The church was one of the few structures in that area to survive intact
and in time to host the funeral of Winston Churchill.

Churchill in his ubiquitous flying suit talks with American general Dwight D. Eisenhower, commander of Operation Overlord—the Allied invasion of France.

The "Big Three," Stalin, Roosevelt, and Churchill, at the Tehran Conference in 1943

Roosevelt and King Ibn Saud of Saudi Arabia aboard the cruiser *Quincy* in the Suez Canal in 1945. Roosevelt attempted to get the king's permission to relocate ten thousand Jewish refugees to Palestine but was rebuffed by an answer the president described as "perfectly awful."

TOP: To celebrate V-E day on May 8, 1945, Churchill (center) stands on the balcony of Buckingham Palace to greet revelers with the royal family (from left) Princess Elizabeth, Queen Elizabeth, King George VI, and Princess Margaret. BOTTOM LEFT: At age seventy-five Churchill sits outside painting the Château de Lourmarin. BOTTOM RIGHT: In April 1961 Churchill joins Aristotle Onassis (left) aboard his yacht, *Christina*. He points to the shore from his chair as they arrive in the Hudson River, New York.

As Churchill's funeral barge proceeds up the Thames River past the London shipyards, dozens of stevedoring cranes dip their giant appendages in a final reverential bow.

CHAPTER THIRTEEN

Winston Churchill's elation at the news of Japan's starting a war with the Americans was dampened considerably three days later when he was awakened in the early hours of the morning of December 10, 1941, and informed that two of the Royal Navy's battleships had been sunk by Japanese airplanes in the Gulf of Siam: the HMS *Prince of Wales,* the fast, modern boat that had carried Churchill to the Atlantic Charter conference in Newfoundland four months earlier, and the HMS *Repulse,* a powerful battle cruiser. They had been sent to Singapore by Churchill himself as a symbolic deterrent to Japanese aggression in Indochina. At the time of their demise, they had been in the gulf looking for a Japanese landing force that had invaded the British-held Malaya on the same day as the Pearl Harbor attack.

This "special" British fleet was supposed to have been joined by a flattop to provide it with air cover. But the carrier ran aground in Jamaica and was laid up for repairs—a fatal coincidence. A studied arrogance by the fleet admiral and the navy high command had led to the belief that British battleships were invulnerable to air attacks from countries such as Japan; as a result, the ships went to sea in harm's way.

When word came to Churchill shortly after 3 a.m., "I writhed and twisted in the bed as the full horror of the news sank in," he wrote later. "In all the war I never received such a direct shock."[1]

One thousand two hundred and fifty sailors went down on the two ships, and an equal number were saved by destroyer escorts. But the loss of such valuable assets boded ill for the future of capital ships against airpower as practiced by the empire of Japan. As Churchill later apologized, "The efficiency of the Japanese at air warfare was at the time greatly underestimated by ourselves and by the Americans."[2]

After word of the *Repulse* and *Prince of Wales* arrived, Churchill went into a depression for several days. He had sent these great battleships as a warning to the Japanese of Great Britain's naval superiority; instead they became nothing more than targets. According to Churchill's bodyguard, Inspector Walter Thompson of Scotland Yard, the prime minister moped, wept, and sat staring out to nowhere, sometimes mumbling, "I don't understand what happened. I don't understand it." He did this for a couple of days; the Christmas holidays, his favorite time of year, were looming up. Then he shook it off and went back to war.[3]

The sinkings were but a harbinger of things to come for the British, French, Dutch, and other colonial powers in the Far East. Unpleasant surprises would now overtake the Allies as the Japanese swarmed across the Pacific like a biblical plague, devouring islands and nations from Indochina to Borneo.

In British-held Hong Kong on December 7, 1941, a thirty-thousand-man Japanese attack was met by eleven thousand Scottish, Canadian, and Indian troops, as well as a seventeen-hundred-man militia of local British subjects known as the Gin Drinkers. Fierce fighting went on for two weeks, until the British force was split in two and nearly out of food, ammunition, and water. The only thing they were not low on was courage, with some of the most heroic work done by the Gin Drinkers. The Japanese had captured the electric power depot and the water works, so the island's 2 million residents had neither.

Early on Christmas Day, Japanese soldiers entered a hospital where some sixty wounded defenders lay on cots. They immediately began bayoneting them under their blankets. A doctor who tried to stop them was shot. Eleven nurses were carried off to an adjoining room and gang-raped; seven of them were murdered. By that afternoon it was apparent that further resistance was futile and the British commander surrendered.

There was little that Churchill could do except grind his teeth and dispatch two infantry divisions destined for North Africa to the Far East. But before they could arrive everything fell apart.

The story was the same all over the Pacific. Singapore, the capital of British-held Malaya, was a gigantic fortress with 16-inch guns bristling to repel any invasion fleet. Except that the Japanese did not come by sea; they came by land after invading northern Malaya and making their way down its long peninsula, using a combination of tanks and bicycles.

Unable to stop the enemy onslaught, British commander Sir Arthur Percival ordered a retreat across the Strait of Malacca into the fortress, which was awash in terrified civilians drinking themselves stupid on gin at the famous Raffles hotel bar and other posh watering spots. Overhead, Japanese air raids bombed nearly every foot of the twenty-five-mile-wide island.

In January 1942 the Japanese invaded Singapore using inflatable rubber boats, often disguised as Singaporean citizens. The British seemed powerless to stop them. One reason might have been that most of the British troops consisted of Indian divisions, who might not have fought as hard for the occupiers of their own country. According to official records, some five thousand Chinese living in Singapore were decapitated in this brutal attack, their heads stuck on pikes around the city as a warning against working for Westerners. When time came for the surrender, Percival turned over an army of 130,000 soldiers, including recent reinforcements, the most humiliating surrender in British history. Many of these were sent to work building a Japanese railroad in the pestilent jungles of Thailand and Burma, where they died by the tens of thousands of disease, starvation, and murderous Japanese cruelty. (Their story was widely told in the Academy Award–winning David Lean film *The Bridge on the River Kwai*.)

The problem, in short, was this: the British simply didn't have the sea power, or the manpower, to defend their far-flung empire *and* fight the Germans and Italians simultaneously. In a cruel irony, they had been depending on America's eight Pearl Harbor battleships, which now were destroyed or crippled, to join them in the defense of Singapore.

On the plus side, after a ferocious tank battle in North Africa, the British had managed to break up Rommel's Afrika Korps siege of the Libyan fortress Tobruk, in which two British colonial divisions had held out for most of the year. This was a major feat of arms—but the British still needed to drive the Germans and Italians out of North Africa. This seemed increasingly difficult, as the Nazis were intent on reinforcing and resupplying the Desert Fox from bases across the Mediterranean in Italy and Crete.

THE WEEK AFTER PEARL HARBOR, Churchill headed back across the Atlantic in the battleship *Duke of York* (as it happened, the sister ship to his previous transportation, HMS *Prince of Wales*, which now rested at the bottom of the Gulf of Siam) to attend the Arcadia conference with Franklin Roosevelt. Accompanying him was First Lord of the Admiralty Sir Dudley Pound, Air Marshal Sir Charles Portal, Field Marshal Sir John Dill, eighty staff members, and twenty cryptographers. Once in the North Atlantic they encountered the worst winter storm of a decade. It kept the big warship battened down for the entire trip while towering waves threw it violently about—rolling, wallowing, heaving, and causing almost everyone to become seasick. Several of the party suffered broken legs or arms. Churchill wrote, "Being in a ship in such weather as this is like being in a prison, with the extra chance of being drowned."

Churchill stayed in his cabin in his nightshirt making notes but came out in the evenings to watch movies such as *The Sea Hawk,* starring Errol Flynn, or read the seafaring stories of C. S. Forester. The plan, once they had reached American shores, had been to steam up the Potomac River to Washington, D.C. But the storm had made them late by several days, and Churchill chose to take a plane at Norfolk.

When he arrived in Washington at the Anacostia air base, Roosevelt was waiting for him on the runway in a car. Churchill was exceedingly appreciative of the gesture. He stayed at the White House in well-appointed rooms next to Roosevelt's "fixer," Harry Hopkins, with whom he would become well acquainted in the years to come.

At their first conference meeting, Churchill was relieved that Roosevelt and his advisers had agreed Germany was the most immediate and dangerous threat, and that military efforts should be weighted toward the war in Europe instead of in the Pacific. He was horrified, however, that Roosevelt's military men—most prominently, the Army's powerful chief of staff General George C. Marshall—were already planning to stage a cross-Channel invasion of France in 1942. As much as anyone, Churchill understood the dangers of an amphibious assault, arguably the most complicated and perilous of military maneuvers. The enemy, if prepared and alert, always has the edge and, with sufficient force, could well turn such an operation into a slaughter of the Allies.

The Germans, meanwhile, had been preparing to repel an invasion of France for a year and a half, building row upon row of artillery positions and machine-gun pillboxes, beach obstructions, tank barriers, and other fortifications. They also maintained a formidable air force that could wreak havoc on the landing beaches. If an invasion was attempted hastily and without proper planning and support, the English Channel, Churchill again warned, "would run red" with Allied blood.

On Christmas Eve 1941, Churchill was present for the annual Christmas tree lighting at the White House—the last of these until 1945—in which the president flipped on the red, white, and blue lights that festooned a forty-five-foot spruce growing on the South Lawn. On Christmas Day the two attended services at the Foundry Methodist Church, a Washington institution, where the Briton was deeply moved by a children's choir's rendering of "O Little Town of Bethlehem," a song he'd never heard before.[4]

The next day, at the stroke of noon, Churchill strode into the U.S. Capitol to address the second joint session of Congress since America had entered the war. The congressmen were charmed by his opening remarks. "I cannot help reflecting that if my father had been American," he said, "and my mother British, instead of the other way around, I might have got here on my own."[5] But later, his I-told-you-so observation that "If we had kept together after the last war, if we had taken common measures for our safety, this renewal of the curse need never have fallen upon us," was met in the chamber with an uncomfortable stony silence.[6]

Still, as Churchill warmed to his subject, the mood lifted once more. "What kind of people do they think we are!" he spat of the Japanese. His eyes were flashing and glistening. The Washington politicians jumped to their feet—including the isolationists—with furious clapping, pounding, and fist shaking; some were cursing and others gave hurrahs. "Is it possible," Churchill shouted, "they do not realize that we will never cease to persevere against them until they have been taught a lesson which they and the world will never forget?"[7]

The congressmen remained on their feet amid the roaring and applauding, some with tears running down their cheeks, as the British prime minister strode from the platform flashing his signature gesture, the famous V for victory sign. This was Winston Churchill at his grandest.

BACK IN ENGLAND AGAIN, Churchill encountered a foul mood that matched the foul gray winter weather outside. Rommel had sprung up once more and was on the move in North Africa; the British armies seemed to be losing everywhere in the Far East. The Japanese had begun an invasion of Burma at the same time they had attacked Hong Kong and Malaya; indications were that they planned to use Burma as a staging area to invade India, the British Empire's crown jewel. To make matters worse, the code breaking at Bletchley had suddenly dried up. The Germans had added a new rotor to their enigma machine and, once again, there were precipitous merchant shipping losses in the North Atlantic.

The threat of a German invasion still hung in the air—and, though nothing like the Blitz, the Germans still carried out nighttime bombing attacks on major British cities, purposely targeting civilian buildings for the terror factor. When the people (and the press) are uneasy and unsatisfied they look for someone to blame—and Churchill was conspicuously at the top of that heap. He was uneasy and disconcerted himself by all the bad news. But deep down he was not unsatisfied, for when the Americans joined the fight against the Axis he was certain they would win.

As spring approached, Churchill called a special session of the House of Commons to cast a vote of confidence (or no confidence) in himself. He was even beginning to have second thoughts in his own mind as to whether he was the right person to lead the nation for the rest of the war. He handily won the vote of confidence, but rumors (usually with some foundation) circulated that thus-and-so person was going to challenge him. The threat never materialized.

During the spring and summer of 1942 Churchill was utterly consumed by the war and, as its chief architect in Great Britain, immersed himself in matters great and small. Unlike Roosevelt, who served as more or less the chairman of a kind of joint war management committee, Churchill featured himself as the arbiter of almost everything—and in many ways he was equipped for it. As first lord of the Admiralty he had absorbed an enormous working knowledge of naval affairs: how ships worked, what they were capable of, and what they were not capable of. He also understood everything from troop and cargo transports to aircraft carriers to battleships and submarines. Churchill was also a pilot, going back to the days of World War I, and he had kept well abreast in the ensuing years of important matters in the Royal Air Force. And so far as the army went, he had cut his teeth on the dangerous mountains of the Punjab, the deserts of North Africa, and the plains of the Transvaal as well as in the trenches of Flanders fields.

Yet one dilemma that bedeviled Churchill almost to the end of the war was how to deal with the abominable losses in the Arctic convoys that the British navy was escorting past German outposts in the icy north. These ships would leave American ports with guns, planes, tanks, and other assorted supplies bound for the Russian port Archangel and the Russian front. The Russians had no navy to speak of, and so it fell to the British to protect them. The Germans had established numerous airfields in the north of Norway, which the convoys had to pass, as well as submarines and a sinister fleet of capital ships (including the battleship *Tirpitz* and a number of battle cruisers that were kept at Trondheim, Norway). On top of all this was the issue that for nearly half the year the sun shined almost twenty-four hours a day, removing at least cover of night as protection from the enemy.

One of these convoys, named PQ17, sailed from its rendezvous at Iceland on June 27, 1942. Consisting of thirty-four merchant ships and escorted by two cruisers, nine destroyers, and various support vessels, it was soon located by enemy air patrols. Word came down that the *Tirpitz* and her escorts had steamed out of Trondheim and were presumed to be on their way toward the convoy.

The cruisers' orders were not to go east of Bear Island unless the convoy "was threatened by a force [the cruisers] could fight." "Clearly," Churchill wrote, "this meant that [the cruiser force commander] was not intended to fight the *Tirpitz*," which could have blown him out of the water from sixteen miles away. The cruiser force commander chose to stay with the convoy anyway. But on the fourth of July word was received that the appearance of the *Tirpitz* was imminent, and orders came down for the convoy to "scatter." That meant that the cruiser force with its destroyers would turn back out of harm's way and the convoy ships would be at the tender mercies of the Germans. Of the thirty-four convoy ships, twenty-three were sunk; their crews perished in the icy wastes of the Barents Sea.

It was heartbreaking, depressing, and infuriating—to no one more than to Winston Churchill, who concluded that until some better way was found, he could not sanction any further convoys along that route while daylight hours prevailed most of the time.

In the aftermath of this disappointment Churchill received a "surly" letter from Stalin, all but accusing the British navy of cowardice in the face of the enemy. He further issued a veiled threat that the Soviet Union might drop out of the war, conveniently ignoring the fact that in their original Lend-Lease agreement the Russians had contracted to escort their own goods from U.S. ports. (The British, after all, had taken on the responsibility only as a matter of necessity after the Russians proved incapable of doing so.)

Infuriated, Churchill sent Stalin's letter to Roosevelt who, as was his custom, urged conciliation. "We have got always to bear in mind the personality of our Ally and the difficult and dangerous situation that confronts him," Roosevelt cautioned. Roosevelt suggested that they lead Stalin on about the possibility of a second front in 1942, when neither of them believed it could be accomplished.

So Churchill let the matter drop, with no rejoinder to the Soviet premier. "After all," he said, "the Russian armies were suffering fearfully and the campaign was at its crisis."[8]

The war in the air remained an issue of constant fascination and frustration to Churchill, who was still exultant over the results of the Battle of Britain two years earlier, but wary of Hitler's ability to damage his homeland. Technological developments came so fast—especially in the field of radar—that as soon as the British installed such devices in their airplanes, the Germans would shoot one down, find it, and copy it.

One very simple idea was suggested by the technicians eager to confuse German radar in their night fighters and ground antiaircraft batteries. Bundles of tinfoil—"the kind they wrap candies in"—would be tossed out of a plane to flutter down like a cloud and appearing on radar screens exactly like the image of planes. This would confuse the German radar operators completely. The bomber crews got wind of this development—they called it "Window"—and wanted to use it immediately to help make their flights more secure. But Churchill worried that if British bombers began using this strategy to protect themselves, the Germans would soon catch on and start using it when they bombed England, which would of course confuse the British radar operators. As Churchill put it, "A tense controversy ensued."[9] But after several months Churchill relented: British bombers could use Window to protect themselves and the British fighters. Should German bombers appear with a Window of their own the British technicians would just have to figure something out.

DURING THE SPRING AND SUMMER of 1942, Churchill was primarily occupied with the deteriorating situation in the North African desert of the British Eighth Army vis-à-vis Rommel's Afrika Korps.

Even though the British had relieved the siege of Tobruk and chased the German and Italian army westward in late 1941, by the spring of 1942 Rommel was back, resupplied and reinforced, and ready for another try. Tobruk was the only deepwater port in Libya, and Rommel needed it as a supply depot to achieve his ultimate goal of taking the Egyptian city Alexandria and the Port of Suez. This would mean control of the Suez Canal by the Germans: a major defeat for the British.

In January 1942, even though the British army outnumbered Rommel's forces in men, tanks, artillery, and airplanes, the wily German sent out a large reconnaissance that caught the British napping. Rommel decided to expand this raid into a battle, but the British rallied and stopped the Germans just short of Tobruk.

Churchill was concerned that the area commander, General Claude Auchinleck, was frittering away valuable time reorganizing the Eighth Army when he should have been attacking Rommel. On February 20, Churchill wrote to him: "According to our figures you have substantial superiority in the air, in armour, and in other forces over the enemy. There seems to be a danger that he may gain reinforcements as fast or even faster than you. Pray let me hear from you. All best wishes."

Auchinleck replied that he understood the situation but felt he was in a strong defensive position and would attack the enemy when he was able to pull together a set piece battle. This disturbed Churchill, but he didn't order an attack at that time, nor did he relieve Auchinleck. After all, the Scottish general was an officer of proven field merit, who had successfully driven Rommel from his siege of Tobruk the previous year.

As the weeks and months wore on, however, Churchill became increasingly anxious about the Eighth Army's inaction—in particular, because of the drastic situation on the island of Malta, located roughly in the center of the Mediterranean Sea. Malta was the Allies' only outpost from which British airpower could intercept and sink enemy convoys bringing troops and supplies to the Afrika Korps.

The Germans knew this, of course, and exerted every effort from their own air bases in Sicily and on Crete to ensure that no supplies got into Malta's ports. So severe were their exertions that the Malta base was at near starvation much of the time and without such essentials as antiaircraft ammunition with which to defend itself. The island, which had been a British possession since the era of the Crusades, was battered almost daily with air raids by German and Italian high-altitude fighters and dive-bombers, which left tens of thousands of British troops, as well as the civilian population, living like troglodytes in caves or beneath the ground. Its towns and cities were bombed to rubble, earning it the dubious distinction of being the Verdun of the maritime war.

On March 20 a convoy of four merchant ships left Alexandria with supplies for Malta but was attacked by a combination of Axis planes and warships. The escorting British convoy held off all of these, including an Italian battleship—only to see two of the convoy's ships sunk just eight miles from the island, and the other two sunk as they were unloading in the harbor. Of 26,000 tons of supplies, Malta received only 5,000. There were no more for another five months.[10]

Churchill continued prodding Auchinleck, asking for exact details of his plans, recounting the difficulties inherent in his inaction. But the Scotsman, though acknowledging each of Churchill's concerns with diplomatic aplomb, remained inert.

The situation on Malta was critical. When the British finally began trying to convoy to the island again, only two of the first seventeen ships got through.

At last, on May 10, Churchill sent this message to Auchinleck, backed by the army chief of staff and the entire defense committee: "We are determined not to let Malta fall without a battle being fought by your whole army for its retention. The starving out of this fortress would involve the surrender of over 30,000 men, Army and Air Force, with several hundred guns. Its possession would give the enemy a clear and sure bridge to Africa. Its surrender would sever the air route upon which both you and India depend for your aircraft reinforcements. It would compromise any offensive against Italy . . . Compared with the certainty of these disasters, we consider the risks you have set out and we accept them."

This was the first and only time that Churchill, as prime minister, ever told one of his generals to attack, or else.[11]

It took Auchinleck several days to make up his mind. But by the time he finally acquiesced, he'd already become victim of the full brunt of a surprise attack by Rommel, while still in the midst of preparing the attack of his own.

The battle raged for twenty-five days across the terrible desert, through the dreadful heat of day and bitter cold of night. It was mostly a battle between tanks and artillery, of machine guns mounted on trucks and jeep-like cars. Troops scrambled out of vehicles to scrape out holes in the sand to fire a 3-inch mortar—and knew how to do it. It was a war of constant motion, unlike any seen before the Nazi blitzkrieg. A tank would rumble warily along and suddenly be obliterated by an enemy land mine, or an artillery shot from a camouflaged position, or a bomb from an aircraft that came up behind.

Auchinleck continued to reassure Churchill that he had the matter in hand. Rommel, he said, was expending himself—his troops, and tanks, and planes—and would soon have to admit failure and retreat. The Scottish general was the epitome of the calm, cool, cheery, resolute British officer, and Churchill began to sleep easier, knowing that Auchinleck was at the helm. So much easier, in fact, that he planned another trip to Washington to see Roosevelt, for there were still things to achieve between them that were so much clearer in person than in telegrams and letters.

THIS TIME, INSTEAD OF ARRIVING on a British battleship, Churchill came to Washington in a flying boat. This giant creation of the Boeing aircraft company was very comfortable compared with other airplanes of the time. It featured freshly cooked meals and sleeping accommodations, and whereas a sea voyage could take up to ten days, the plane was able to fly from London to Washington in twenty-seven hours. It was not, however, a particularly safe aircraft, especially when German warplanes were roaming the skies.

Churchill had two main missions to accomplish in Washington. The first was to settle the idea, once and for all, that the Americans were still up to the invasion of North Africa, now code-named Torch. The second reason was the time had come to deal with the curious subject code-named Tube Alloys, which was what the British were calling their experiments in atomic fission. They had been working on nuclear energy since the 1930s—and so, Churchill knew, had the Germans. He wanted to share the considerable information gained by British scientists and let the Americans build the bomb.

The flying boat landed in the Potomac on June 18, 1942. Churchill was flown to Hyde Park next morning, where Roosevelt was vacationing. The president awaited him at the airfield with his personal automobile, a Plymouth Phaeton convertible with special hand controls for brakes and gas. In this vehicle, Roosevelt gave Churchill a tour of his estate, as well as the fright of his life, when Roosevelt cruised along the edge of the large bluff overlooking the Hudson with nary a foot on the brake.

On the matter of Tube Alloys, Churchill agreed to send his nuclear scientists to the United States to work with the team the Roosevelt administration already had in place. It was a portentous decision, for the British information cut months, if not years, off the time it took to build the bomb. They also agreed to keep this top secret project from their ally Joseph Stalin, lest he want to build a bomb of his own.

Two days later, the two men took the presidential train to Washington, where they were to meet with Roosevelt's military advisers on the matter of Torch. Churchill had just had his breakfast when he stopped by Roosevelt's study. He found the president studying a telegram he'd just been handed. Without saying anything he gave it to Churchill.

"Tobruk has surrendered, with twenty-five thousand men taken prisoners."

Churchill was dumbfounded. At first he didn't believe it and asked a military adviser to call London. When his adviser returned, he told Churchill that not only was it true, they were expecting heavy air attacks on Alexandria at any moment and Auchinleck's Eighth Army was being pushed back by Rommel hundreds of miles into Egypt.

"This was one of the heaviest blows I can recall during the war," he wrote afterward. When he arrived he'd been reassured that the situation in the desert was stable—and now this! Instead of arguing Torch from a position of strength, he was forced to beg for American troops to land in North Africa to save his own men.

As Churchill felt frustrated nearly to the verge of tears, Roosevelt said calmly, "What can we do to help?"

When he had composed himself, Churchill asked for Sherman tanks that were just now coming off the U.S. assembly lines. General Marshall arrived and gave the order: three hundred Sherman tanks would be sent immediately to the Middle East by fast boat.[12]

"Nothing could exceed the sympathy and chivalry of my two friends," Churchill said. Not only that, but before Churchill left, he'd received word that the highly trained U.S. Second Armored Division would be sent to reinforce the British Eighth Army in six weeks' time. "There were no reproaches. A friend in need is a friend indeed," he said.[13]

When Churchill returned to London's summer sunshine, dark shadows hovered in the House of Commons. Forty or fifty members had instigated a motion of censure against him, stating, "[The House] has no confidence in the central direction of the war."

Churchill dutifully set the motion up for argument. Auchinleck had sent him a graceful apology for the setback, which Churchill accepted with a warning. "Every fit male should be made to fight and die for victory. You are in the same kind of situation as we should be if England were invaded, and the same intense, drastic spirit should reign."

Debate on the motion to censure Churchill occupied two full days, going on until three in the morning. It was mainly old enemies venting their spleen. When a vote was taken on the morning of July 2, the motion was defeated by a vote of 475 to 25. Churchill reminded Parliament of how history repeated itself when, in 1799, a vote to censure Prime Minister William Pitt failed to muster more than twenty-five votes. Now he could set about finding ways to redeem Africa from Field Marshal Rommel and the Germans.

To SET THINGS IN MOTION, Churchill flew to Cairo to see what had happened to the Eighth Army. As it turned out, Auchinleck had simply been outmaneuvered by the Desert Fox. The army now held very strong positions for the defense of Egypt, starting around El Alamein, but was essentially right back where it had been a year ago, nearly five hundred miles to the east.

Churchill arrived in Egypt on August 4 after an all-night flight and beheld the sunrise from the copilot's seat of a British Commando bomber. "There in the pale, glimmering dawn, the endless winding silver ribbon of the Nile stretched joyously before us," he wrote. "Often had I seen the day break on the Nile. In war or peace, I had traversed by land or water almost its whole length. Never had the glint of daylight on its waters been so welcome to me."[14]

Churchill had consulted with his top military advisers, and it was clear that changes needed to be made. It was decided that General Auchinleck would be replaced as commander of Egypt and the Near East by General Sir Harold Alexander. The Eighth Army would be taken over by William Gott, a popular and highly respected lieutenant general who held the full confidence of the troops. No sooner had this decision been made, however, than General Gott was killed when his plane was shot down by half a dozen German Messerschmitts. It was then decided that General Bernard Montgomery—who would make a bold name for himself in the annals of World War II, and who was supposed to lead the British contingent of Torch—would replace Gott as commander of the Eighth Army.

Auchinleck was let down easy, and bore neither Churchill nor anyone else any animus. Always the gentleman, "the Auk" "received this stroke with soldierly dignity." Later he became commander in chief of the British Indian army, a post he held until the end of the war.

On August 10, 1942, Churchill enplaned in Cairo for Moscow, where he would meet for the first time "the great Revolutionary Chief and profound Russian statesman and warrior" Joseph Stalin. As his bomber weaved perilously between the towering mountains of Iran, Churchill mused on the purpose of his mission "to this sullen, sinister, Bolshevik State I had once tried so hard to strangle at its birth—and which, until Hitler appeared, I regarded as the mortal foe of civilized freedom."

Whatever else he intended to say, the most important part was that there would be no second front in France in 1942. Churchill had decided that Stalin needed to be told this in person, and with Roosevelt's infirmities he was the man to do it. Furthermore, Churchill always had a policy to hear bad news early, and he would make no exception with Stalin and the Soviet leaders.

They landed late in the afternoon and were put up in a well-lit dacha, complete with servants and "prepared with totalitarian lavishness." Churchill and Averell Harriman, the American representative sent by Roosevelt, met with Stalin at the blacked-out Kremlin at seven in the evening.

There, Churchill at last met "the ogre in his den," as his wife Clementine had described it in a letter. Stalin, all five feet four of him, appeared with his hair slicked back like a New Orleans bartender, pockmarked face, and tobacco-stained teeth. He was dressed in a rough-cloth peasant's blouse and trousers tucked into polished high leather boots. Harriman thought he looked much older and careworn than when he had visited him a year before.[15]

The first two hours of the conference were "bleak and somber," according to Churchill, who told Stalin right off that both the British and American military advisers had counseled against a cross-Channel invasion of France as too risky that year. Stalin, his face screwed up in a frown, responded that "a man who was not prepared to take risks could not win a war," and wondered aloud why the British "were so afraid of the Germans."

Churchill rejoined that Hitler had sat on the opposite side of the Channel for all of 1940 trying to decide whether to invade England, and in the end he opted not to risk it. But Stalin remained gloomy and unpersuaded, suggesting that the British and the Americans were afraid to "bloody their armies."[16]

Stalin perked up a bit when Churchill got around to describing the air war on Germany. When the Americans arrived with their large air force, Churchill told the premier, it would be enough to inflict ruin on Germany's industrial might. Stalin recommended bombing German homes as well as factories, to which Churchill replied righteously that only stray or mistargeted bombs would fall "on working men's houses."

Refreshments were served and Churchill, who made an art of presenting crucial points in speeches as deftly as a prima ballerina leaps in dance, suddenly unfurled a map of the Mediterranean and North Africa. "Is it written in stone that a Second Front has to be across the English Channel into France?" he asked. Then he took a pen and drew a crocodile. Jabbing the pen at the creature's belly, he declared to the startled dictator that it was better to attack such an animal "in its soft underbelly" than at its dangerous snout.[17]

Pointing to the map laid out before Stalin and his advisers, including the dour Molotov, Churchill began explaining Torch, which he described as a kind of second front of its own. A British and American army, he said, would land in French Morocco and French Algeria and cross the Atlas Mountains; meanwhile, the British Eighth Army would hammer the Germans westward out of Egypt, across Libya, and shatter them on the American anvil in Tunisia. He told Stalin that the destruction of his North African army would force Hitler to divert more troops and airpower to the Mediterranean, either from the Russian front or from France, which the Allies intended to invade next year.

Stalin asked exhausting questions about Torch, and when he was finally satisfied with the answers he said: "May God prosper this undertaking." It was a strange declaration coming from the world's most famous atheist, but nonetheless gratifying to Churchill and company.[18]

Back at Churchill's extravagant dacha next evening, the British contingent was assessing the productivity, or lack thereof, in the conference so far. The prime minister at one point casually described Stalin as "a peasant" whom he could handle, which produced a fervent reaction from Air Marshal Sir Arthur Tedder, who was certain that the walls were bugged. The airman grabbed for a sheet of paper on which he scribbled *Méfiez-vous!* ("Beware!") and flicked it across the table to Churchill, whereupon the prime minister read the note, put on his famous scowl, and, to the mortification of the diplomats present, turned and addressed the walls: "The Russians, I have been told, are not human beings at all. They are lower in the scale of nature than the orang-outang. Now then, let them take that down and translate it into Russian."[19]

The next morning at eleven the meetings were resumed. Stalin arrived surly and arrogant, thrusting at Churchill a paper making many accusations and demands—in particular, for the British to reverse their decision and invade France by the fall. Sensing that things were going badly, Churchill replied that he would answer it in writing. There then ensued a highly "unpleasant" conversation in which Stalin accused the British of being "too much afraid" of fighting the Germans, accusing them of breaking their promise, and stealing the Lend-Lease supplies destined for the Soviet Union. Churchill, seething at these charges but under complete control, answered each one succinctly, thoroughly, and profoundly—with frequent pauses, because he was speaking fast, to ask the translator: "Did you tell him that?"

The Soviet dictator showed little reaction at being spoken to in such a forceful manner. Churchill closed by saying that he and his people had come all the way to Moscow in the spirit of comradeship to establish good relations; that for a year and a half they had been left to fight the Germans entirely alone (a veiled allusion to Russia's nonaggression pact with Hitler); and that they resented the accusatory attitude of the Soviet premier. At this, Stalin called a halt to the meeting, saying that words wouldn't win the war, only action. At that, they all went to bed.

The next evening was a parting dinner for forty at Catherine the Great's dining hall. It was described by one of the British legation as "a complete orgy," with scores of courses including suckling pig, fish, chickens, and roasts, washed down with no less than nineteen vodka toasts. Stalin's aide, one General Kliment Voroshilov, "nearly drank himself under the table"— but the mood was robust and genial and the banquet went off well.[20]

The next evening around seven, Churchill went to Stalin's office to say goodbye; he was leaving for Cairo at dawn. They had an hour's "useful and important" conversation, in which Churchill expressed his concerns about the German drive toward the Caucasus Mountains, which was presently stalled at Stalingrad. If the Germans somehow broke through, they would take possession of the immensely rich oil fields of Baku and Persia.

"We shall stop them," the dictator told Churchill, "They will not cross the mountains." He then confided that he had twenty-five Russian divisions guarding the mountain passes.

When it was time to leave, Stalin cordially said to him, "You are leaving at daybreak. Why should we not go to my house and have some drinks?" Churchill rejoined that he was "in principle always in favor of such a policy," and off they went to Stalin's rooms in the Kremlin. They were there joined by the enigmatic Molotov, of whom Stalin said, "There is one thing about Molotov: he can drink."

They sat at a table in the dining room; a "handsome red-haired girl came in, kissed her father dutifully, and started laying the table," while Stalin began uncorking bottles. There they sat for the next six hours, eating leftovers and drinking wine. As the wine and the conversation began to percolate, Churchill asked Stalin whether the stresses of war were worse on him than his collective farm ordeal, in which tens of millions of peasants perished. "It was all very bad and difficult," the premier replied, "but necessary," going on to explain that unless agriculture were centrally controlled Russia would be subject to famines.

According to Churchill biographer Roy Jenkins, Stalin's technique was to play dual roles as "hard cop, friendly cop," to both "intimidate and bewilder. But at the same time to seduce his adversary—even if, to complete the paradox, the adversary was a necessary ally. Churchill stood up to this bombardment with remarkable tenacity, patience, and strength of character." In the end, the British leader left with a feeling of goodwill that had been absent until then. Each man had taken the measure of the other and found common ground.[21]

BACK IN CAIRO, Churchill was confronted with news of trouble in India. The independence party had suddenly fomented riots and other disorders throughout the enormous country. Railways were sabotaged and mob violence broke out in the cities and countryside alike. The viceroy reported that the deep unrest "threatened to jeopardize the whole war effort of India in the face of the Japanese invasion menace." His council recommended arresting the charismatic Mohandas Gandhi, his deputy Jawaharlal Nehru, and other members of the influential political party. It was a risk, but Churchill backed the viceroy; instead of a catastrophic revolution, the turmoil fizzled out and the population settled down for the duration. It was a small crisis amid the larger, more terrible crises, but Churchill excelled at dealing with each in its rightful place. In times of peace, rebellion in India would have been viewed in England as a calamity.

On August 19, Churchill drove out past the pyramids to the front lines, about 130 miles through the desert from Cairo, and down to Montgomery's headquarters by the sea. He arrived in the late afternoon at bathing time, where thousands of British soldiers were "disporting themselves" on the beach. Churchill wondered aloud why the War Department went to the expense of issuing the men white bathing trunks when they could just as easily go naked. Then he reflected on his own experience in this same desert forty years earlier, when military medical opinion was that the African sun was very dangerous to the skin and "must be kept away at all costs." "Spine pads" were attached to all tunics, which had to be tightly buttoned at all times cuff to neck; it was a military offense to appear outside without a pith helmet. Now, as he watched the soldiers in only swim trunks, he judged that the sun "apparently did them no harm."

Montgomery said an attack from Rommel was imminent, and that it would fall on his communications flank to take Cairo. They drove into the desert to the prospective battlefield, where the German Afrika Korps lay only a few miles away. Every crevice, every swale, every dune and hummock was packed with camouflaged tanks or artillery pieces: a grand and terrible spectacle. Montgomery was planning a nasty surprise for Rommel when he attacked under the impression that the Eighth Army was reeling. They returned to Montgomery's headquarters under the hard desert stars. That night, Churchill went to sleep peaceful as a baby, drenched in the solace of "the reviving ardor of the Army." Everyone said what a great change had come since Montgomery took command. "I could feel the truth of this with joy and comfort."[22]

Before departing—reluctantly—on the eve of the battle with Rommel, Churchill once more violated his policy against directly interfering with a military operation. He told General Alexander, the theater commander, to arm every staff officer and each of the thousands of clerks, lorry drivers, cooks, and bottle washers with rifles and drill them into defensive positions alongside the Nile in case Rommel broke through. It was the duty of every man in the army, Churchill had said, "to die for his country." Then he flew back to England.

Once back at the War Office, Churchill turned his attention to Operation Torch, the British-American landings in North Africa. The British had understood that the invasion would include landings in French-held Algeria as well as French Morocco. But at the last moment the American chiefs of staff balked on grounds that because of the sinking of the French fleet the British would likely be no more welcome in Algiers than they would be in French Morocco, which could be trouble. Churchill vehemently disagreed; it took two weeks of haggling to resolve the issue in Churchill's favor, with the invasion set for eight weeks' time.

★★★★★

IN THE MEANTIME, the British Eighth Army languished in the North African desert, waiting for an attack from Erwin Rommel. It came, as predicted by Ultra, on August 31, 1942. Churchill telegraphed to both Roosevelt and Stalin: "Rommel has begun the attack for which we have been preparing. An important battle may now be fought." For his part, Montgomery declared, "What I now needed was a battle that could be fought in accordance with my ideas."[23]

As expected, Rommel tried to turn the British southern flank. When that proved too difficult, he attempted to punch a hole in the middle of the British line. The German plan was to let the anticipated British counterattack succeed to an extent, then blow past it with a powerful force, get into the rear of the Eighth Army, then destroy its communications, its stores, and ultimately the Eighth Army itself. But as it happened things didn't work out that way.

First off, Montgomery refused to take the bait. Instead of counterattacking, he drew up a hundred tanks on a ridge facing the Germans and dared Rommel to come on. "The swine will not attack," the German commander telegraphed his boss, Mediterranean commander Field Marshal Albert Kesselring, in a rage. Wherever the German tanks and troops plunged forward, they were met with a wall of steel. Montgomery had given the order that under no circumstance were troops or units to withdraw. "We would fight on the ground we held," Montgomery said later, "and if we couldn't stay there alive, we would stay there dead." After a week of attacking, Rommel backed off. Not only was his attack not getting anyplace fast, but out on the Mediterranean the Royal Air Force had sunk three large fuel tankers destined for the Afrika Korps. The German commander was all too aware that you can't fight a battle between armor with an empty tank.[24]

Next it was Montgomery's turn. It took some time after Rommel's attack to reorganize and resupply the Eighth Army. But on the full moon of October 23, Montgomery gave the order for a thousand heavy artillery pieces to open up a three-hour barrage, announcing that General Bernard Montgomery and Co. were advancing into the German lines.

Thereafter, an entire part of the Western Desert—or so it seemed—began to rise up from its camouflaged haunts and surge forward with a roar, like a wave of prehistoric beasts. Tanks, self-propelled guns, tractors towing artillery, armored cars, trucks filled with infantry, and infantry afoot arose from their desert concealments and headed for a break in the vast German minefield that British engineers were trying to create.

Breaking the minefield was easier said than done, and for a time the attack stalled. The Afrika Korps violently counterattacked—but without the services of Erwin Rommel, who had gone back to Germany on medical leave. The battle seesawed up and down for several days, with commensurate loss of life. On October 26, the day after Rommel hastily resumed his command, an Australian and New Zealand infantry division, supported by several British divisions, broke the enemy line while the RAF shot down what few German planes were sent to assist Rommel. When these had been disposed of, the Germans were unable to re-form their units for attack, because British airpower would obliterate them.

Hitler issued another of his famous "fight and die to the last man" orders, but nobody in the Afrika Korps paid attention. By November 4 British armor was pursuing the German tanks and infantry trucks over open desert. What became known as the Battle of El Alamein had been won by Montgomery, and Rommel's army was in full retreat toward Italian-held Tunisia, more than a thousand miles to the west. If things went according to Churchill's and Montgomery's plan, the Germans and Italians would be met there by an American army commanded by General George S. Patton, which was supposed to go ashore in Morocco and Algeria in five days' time.

The Eighth Army had lost nearly five thousand men, but Rommel's army lost more: nine thousand killed, thirty-five thousand taken prisoner, five hundred tanks lost. Eleven Afrika Korps divisions ceased to exist.

In Churchill's mind, Alamein was a crucial turning point of the war. "It might almost be said," he wrote, "that before Alamein, we never had a victory. After Alamein we never had a defeat."[25]

CHAPTER FOURTEEN

Almost immediately after the German defeat at Stalingrad in February 1943, Field Marshal Erich von Manstein, now in charge of all German troops in Russia, decided to reorganize his forces and stage a massive surprise attack on the Red Army. His reasoning was that the war-weary Soviets would be in vulnerable disarray after the ordeal of the onerous siege. The new battle was to be fought in the vicinity of the city of Kursk, about 330 miles south of Moscow near Russia's border with Ukraine, where the Red Army line bulged out into a salient. About a million Germans faced more than 2 million Russians. By comparison, when Napoleon invaded Russia in 1812 he brought half a million men to fight nearly a million Russians.

At the same time Stalin, who had consistently pushed the Soviet armies to attack, now called for an all-out assault on the Germans. He was talked out of this by his own great general Zhukov, who in Stalin's mind had become a rival. Zhukov insisted that a well-prepared defense in depth was the better way: let the Germans come on until they were "bled white." (The Germans had in fact used a similar tactic in the First World War at Verdun—except that it was the Germans who were "bled white" instead.) That lesson was not lost on Zhukov, whose plan was to defend ground fiercely, then fall back to the next position; when the exhausted Germans thought they had won the battle, he would then unleash an overwhelming counterattack upon them.

Stalin was not pleased with this stratagem but gave way after Zhukov was backed by all of his generals and the State Committee of Defense. Soon,

Manstein's attack on the Russian salient near Kursk became apparent, just as Zhukov had predicted. Fifty German divisions—850,000 men—were drawn up in front of the spot by early April. But weeks went by, and no attack was forthcoming. Hitler had gotten cold feet.

It was by then a well-established principle in both armies that massive attacks were likely to be successful only after careful preparation. This was on Hitler's mind when he postponed Manstein's operation. His mistake was that it also gave the Russians time to prepare their defenses.

Unlike those of the previous century, modern armies were highly complex in their mechanization and aeronautical features. In Russia, an army could attack along a front as long as four hundred miles—but only with a stupendous amount of preparation. Stalin had at long last grasped this after immersing himself in military planning with his generals. Zhukov himself wrote that Stalin had become "master of the basic principles of the organization of frontline operations and the deployment of frontline forces. He controlled them completely and had a good understanding of major strategic problems. He was a worthy Supreme Commander."[1]

In the meanwhile, Stalin had set out, at home and abroad, to reconfigure his image as a godless, bloodthirsty tyrant into something more palatable to a wartime public. He perceived correctly that if he let up on stringent control over the Soviet population and strict adherence to Marxist doctrine, the Russian people would endure their hardships and more happily fight harder for the Motherland.

In his quest to become popular, Stalin was aided by Hitler himself, whose monstrous policies were even worse than Stalin's now. While they were in the Soviet Union, it is estimated that including the SS and other murderous groups, the Nazi armies killed between 15 and 30 million citizens, almost as many as Stalin during his twenty years as dictator. Those who survived were prone to gravitate to the least monstrous of the monsters.

Stalin relaxed his harsh Communist policies regarding the Russian Orthodox religion, which was (or had been) the national church for centuries; during the past twenty years, the Communists had murdered tens of thousands of priests. He also liberalized the suppression of nationalism in the conquered Soviet states such as Georgia, Ukraine, and the western "-stans," allowing the people to celebrate their nationalities and customs, a practice that had been strictly forbidden under communism.

Stalin also relaxed the tight restraints he had placed on intellectuals and intellectual activity. Ever since the revolution poets, authors, and even composers of classical music, such as Dmitri Shostakovich, had been threatened, imprisoned, and sometimes faced the firing squad for anything perceived by the authorities as counterrevolutionary. Now, with specific reservations, some of their patriotic poetry and other writing was read over the radio. Shostakovich was permitted to write patriotic musical compositions, some of which remain well regarded for their beauty and stirring emotion.

Stalin even relaxed his approach to certain forms of private enterprise. Peasants arriving in cities with a sack of vegetables or a pig slung over their backs were no longer subject to arrest and imprisonment; they were now allowed to trade or even accept cash for their produce. There was an ulterior government motive for this, of course. The Germans occupied so much Russian territory that the loss of the great harvests of wheat, grain, sugar beets, and stock from Ukraine, Belarus, and other massive Soviet territories was putting severe pressure on the government to ensure a regular food supply. So for Stalin these peasant entrepreneurs filled an important gap.

As a sop to his allies, Stalin very publicly dismantled the Comintern—the international organization responsible for infiltrating, agitating, and sowing communism throughout the world—which was viewed as a subversive threat by Western nations. Stalin's efforts to remake his public image worked. By 1943 most everyone was feeling somewhat kindly toward Uncle Joe, whose heroic people, under his steady leadership, were defeating the Nazi scourge.

None of this would last long after the war. Although the Comintern had been publicly dismantled by Stalin, its apparatus was kept firmly but quietly in place, and put back in use to subvert and enslave eastern European nations after peace was declared. Likewise, the Communist boot was returned squarely onto the neck of the Russian Orthodox Church as soon as the war was over. There was a new clampdown on intellectuals, and would-be capitalists faced stiff punishment for peddling fruit and vegetables without authority. Any signs or sentiments of nationalism in the provinces once more became grounds for sentencing to the gulags. Stalin was certain that nationalism was a mortal threat to Marxism—a view that was unequivocally vindicated forty-five years later when East Germans began tearing down the Berlin Wall that had kept them penned in for more than a generation. After his 1942 Man of the Year cover, Stalin would grace several more *Time* magazines during his lifetime, but the photo editors returned to portraying his expression as menacing.

As the years passed, Stalin also used the war as a pretext to organize mass deportations of citizens who clung to national identities. Thus, in 1942 and 1943 millions of Chechens, Kalmyks, Ingushes, Karachays, Meskhetians, Tatars, and other groups were either "liquidated" to extinction—some by units of the Soviet army—or deported beyond the Urals to Siberia or remote places in Central Asia (often in U.S. Lend-Lease trucks or packed inhumanely into railroad cattle cars). For Stalin, according to Ronald Hingley, the redistribution of entire populations was no more than a "minor administrative adjustment"—and the fact that the "freight was, as ever, liable to perish in transit" merely an incidental inconvenience of a necessary action by the state.[2]

The man principally responsible for carrying out the disposition of the so-called freight was Lavrenty Beria, described in the London *Daily Telegraph* as "Stalin's depraved executioner." Beria in 1938 had taken over the NKVD, the Soviet secret police, from his boss Nikolai Yezhov, a drunkard and homosexual predator, whom it was Beria's pleasure to shoot in the basement of the Lubyanka, the Soviet prison and torture chamber used by the NKVD.

The history of the secret police in Soviet Russia does not have many commendable chapters. The original iteration, the Cheka, had killed off so many people it actually put a dent in the Russian population. Many felt a shudder of relief when Stalin and the Politburo replaced it with the OGPU, which began its own binge of torturing and executing Russian citizens. Then came the NKVD, which, when Stalin decided to purge the country of anyone with an uncommunistic thought in his head, restarted the slaughter on an unprecedented scale.

Ironically, Stalin selected Beria to rein in the Great Terror that he had unleashed a year earlier. Beria, a tight-lipped, beady-eyed, smallish man, got the job after he faked and "broke up" a phony assassination plot against Stalin and executed the unfortunate "perpetrators." At the time he was chief deputy of the NKVD. What Stalin did not know then was that Beria was a serial rapist and a practicing sadist who enjoyed personally beating and killing people suspected of being enemies of the state.

Stalin seemed to enjoy this bloody chaos, defending it as "necessary." He befriended Beria, who once posed for a photograph at Stalin's dacha with twelve-year-old Svetlana bouncing on his knee. At the Yalta Conference Stalin jokingly introduced Beria to a startled President Roosevelt as "My Himmler," a reference to the war criminal Heinrich Himmler, head of the Nazi Gestapo.

Stalin may not have personally gone to the dreaded Lubyanka to see how the sausage was made—but he knew what was going on and had his hand in a lot of it. It wasn't necessarily information from Beria, either; Stalin had back channels and, to quote his biographer Robert Service, "daily collaboration with Beria was like being tied in a sack with a wild beast."[3] On occasion, Beria would have drinks at Stalin's dacha. There, the two would make veiled, knowing references to departed associates, producing a tremendous, warped sense of power in both of them.

OVER TIME, IT BECAME NOTICEABLE to anyone dealing with Joseph Stalin that just the tiniest thing that annoyed him was grounds for that person to disappear. This yielded a strong current of fear—of terror—in those who might have reason to come into contact with him.

That fear apparently did not extend to his children, each of whom disappointed him in different ways. Yakov had let himself be captured and then shot by the Germans. Vasily remained an overpromoted drunkard and ne'er-do-well who was a Soviet air force general at the age of twenty-three. He was divorced several times with much acrimony, but Stalin somehow was able to remain cordial with him.

After her lover was sent to the gulags by her father, Svetlana chased after Lavrenty Beria's son for a while. But when he remained married she settled on a university student in her class. He was Jewish; Stalin did not like Jews and would not approve the marriage. "Do what the hell you like," was the best she could get out of him. She wasn't allowed to bring her husband home. She had a child, also named Joseph, but the marriage didn't last and she remained more or less estranged from her father.

In time, Svetlana married again—this time, to the son of Andrey Zhdanov, a powerful figure in the communist hierarchy. But that didn't last either. There were long periods when father and daughter never saw each other; then, Stalin would contact her and a reunion of sorts would ensue. It was not until after Stalin's death that Svetlana finally realized the extent of his crimes. She defected to the West in 1967.

AT LAST, IN JUNE 1943, Hitler took the bait and attacked the Soviet positions at Kursk. He had no choice. Retreat from Russia was unthinkable and would inevitably lead to an attack while withdrawing, or degenerate into a World War I–style static battlefield, inviting an Allied air campaign that would reduce Germany to brick dust and rubble.

On July 5, 1943, nearly eight hundred thousand German soldiers attacked the ninety-by-one-hundred-thirty-mile Kursk salient with tanks, artillery, planes, and infantry. For two days they slowly pressed the Soviet army backward along both sides—but then Red Army resistance stiffened. A week and a half later it appeared the Germans had run out of momentum. That's when the Soviets counterattacked.

The scale of the battle was stupendous, dwarfing anything seen in World War I. Because the Germans had attacked both sides of the salient, they had created a fighting front well over three hundred miles in length. In this roaring, flaming cauldron, roughly fifteen thousand tanks were fighting each other, forty thousand artillery pieces were shelling one another, eight thousand planes were bombing and strafing, and nearly 3 million men were at one another's throats. The fighting lasted for nearly two months.

Zhukov had numerical superiority everywhere. In addition to having nearly 2.5 million men, he had more tanks, guns, and warplanes than Marshal Manstein—and he wasted them commensurately. Stalin, still smarting from being "overruled" by Zhukov and the army generals, took no part in directing the battle, instead sulking in the high command head-quarters and phoning Zhukov for information.

By the end of the month it was clear that the Germans were stalled, exhausted, and being bled white. The German strategic reserve, which might have made a difference in the battle's outcome, had been diverted to North Africa to support Rommel, who was being pressed hard by the British and American armies.

By August 23, Manstein had given up and he withdrew. In addition to thousands of wrecked tanks, planes, and artillery pieces, the Germans had lost a quarter of a million men and the Red Army lost some four hundred thousand. It was one of the bloodiest battles in history, and one of the most historic. Kursk is generally viewed as the turning point in the Second World War in Europe, for the Germans never again launched a successful offensive.

Once the Russian battle was declared won, Stalin called for a tremendous military parade in Moscow complete with tanks, motorized artillery, and endless divisions of infantry marching for so long that Stalin and his guests in the reviewing stand took time out to sit down for a luncheon before returning to the spectacle continuously unfolding before them.

AFTER WINNING THE BATTLE OF KURSK, Stalin now had the tiger by the tail. Germany had been beaten badly at Kursk, but if the Germans withdrew, the Russians would be on their backs as soon as possible.

Hitler reasoned that if he could keep Poland and the Balkan countries as battlegrounds, he could regroup and hope the Allies would slip up. Perhaps they would be defeated in a cross-Channel invasion, or stuck in Italy or elsewhere, and a deal might be made: an armistice or truce that would ensure the leavening out of issues and territory. At this point, it must have been clear to Hitler that he'd made a grievous mistake at Kursk. But in the fog of war commanders often do not always appreciate the errors they've made, and hope that Providence or the errors of the enemy will help them prevail. At this point, that was about all the German generals could hope for.

CHAPTER FIFTEEN

I n January 1943, while furious tank battles rumbled across Tunisia, Roosevelt and Churchill convened in Casablanca as planned. The conference was Churchill's idea; he thought the Allies ought to define and restate their war aims at this point in the conflict. Roosevelt agreed. He also felt that Allied interests would be advanced by having such highly publicized meetings between leaders, which would show a common resolve. Stalin absented himself, admitting that he didn't like to fly.

The trip wasn't very difficult for Churchill, who arrived from London in an RAF bomber after refueling at Gibraltar. But Roosevelt's journey was more arduous. He was spirited out of the White House by the Secret Service guard, who took him across the Mall to the Bureau of Printing and Engraving, where the money was made; his special train waited on tracks that ran inside the redbrick building in the shadow of the Washington Monument.

For security reasons, the regular dining car waiters had been replaced with Filipino mess stewards from the presidential Shangri-La retreat in Maryland. The train then took off for Miami with General Marshall, Admiral King, and their staffs, as well as Harry Hopkins, aboard.

At the Miami Naval Station, Roosevelt boarded a big Boeing flying boat that refueled at Trinidad and Belém, on Brazil's south coast, before an exhausting flight across the South Atlantic. Roosevelt didn't like to fly, but for reasons different than Stalin's. Polio had destroyed his leg muscles, so that in turbulent weather he couldn't brace himself and it was very uncomfortable. (He wrote Eleanor that the plane trip was "bumpy.") Finally, after eighteen hours, they landed at Gambia, the old slave port in French West Africa. Roosevelt was appalled at the living and working conditions of the natives, who received less than twenty-five cents a day and a half bowl of rice. It reinvigorated his opposition of empires—French, British, Japanese, whatever—and made him more determined that the postwar world would not be an imperial one. An army transport plane then carried the party north across the Atlas Mountains to Casablanca.[1]

Eisenhower had been anxious ever since he'd received word that the president and prime minister were coming to Casablanca—as if he didn't already have enough on his plate. He assigned George Patton to make the arrangements for their comfort and safekeeping, and though Ike had his doubts he also knew that pomp and circumstance were Patton's specialty. Patton, however, was more concerned with safety and secrecy than with pomp, and when the dignitaries arrived they were smuggled into Army Cadillacs with mud-smeared windows to conceal their identities.[2]

Outside Casablanca, Patton found a comfortable, secure resort compound located in the suburb of Anfa. To Roosevelt's delight the Third Division Artillery Band was playing "Hail to the Chief" when they arrived, as well as "Missouri Waltz," "Deep in the Heart of Texas," "Alexander's Ragtime Band," and, for Churchill, "The Naughty Marietta Waltz."

Patton felt it had gone off quite nicely (except for Roosevelt's entourage of Secret Service agents who had tagged along behind the mud-plastered limousines in an open jeep, brandishing pistols). In Patton's view his fifty-thousand-man Western Army Corps provided more than adequate security. He dismissed the Secret Service men as "a bunch of cheap detectives always smelling of drink."[3]

For Roosevelt it was a happy occasion; his sons Elliott and FDR Jr. were both there in their Army and Navy uniforms, respectively. (His son James was off in the Pacific with the Marines.) Churchill's son Randolph was also there, serving with the British commandos at the front. And Sergeant Robert Hopkins, Harry's son, whom Eisenhower had dug up out of his foxhole in Tunisia, completed the party.

When the conference convened next day, the first order of business was what to do next, if the Allies were successful in whipping the Germans and

Italians in North Africa. (There seemed to be no plans for what would happen if the reverse occurred.) Roosevelt and Marshall still favored an attack across the English Channel by the summer, a strategy Churchill vehemently continued to oppose. By clearing the Axis out of the Mediterranean, he argued, Italy could be taken and knocked out of the war. That would relieve much pressure on Stalin, Churchill said, and give the Allies air bases from which to bomb Germany from the south, as well as a possible entrée from northern Italy into Austria and then Germany.

It was the same old argument going round like a carnival ride—not only the premiers but their staffs had it out. The British gave a presentation pointing out their disastrous raid on the French port of Dieppe the previous summer. It had been planned partially as a response to Stalin's insistent calls for a second front, and partially to test the enemy defenses.

At Dieppe the Germans were waiting for them. Artillery and machine guns lashed out at the invaders even before they could get out of their barges. British tanks foundered on German obstacles along the beachhead. Of six thousand soldiers who landed there—most of them Canadians—a thousand were killed and two thousand were made prisoners. The rest managed to escape to the barges that ferried them back to England. It proved that a landing in France was going to be an extremely tough proposition. The hundreds of thousands of American soldiers who were to be a part of it were just beginning to arrive in England, Churchill pointed out, and had not yet been trained.

The British argument at long last proved persuasive, and it was finally agreed that Sicily would become the next invasion point, once the Allies had cleared North Africa. This was easier said than done, as the Americans fighting the Germans in Tunisia and the British fighting Rommel in the Libyan desert were finding out.

One of the matters partially settled at the conference had both diplomatic and political reverberations for Roosevelt. He had been enduring considerable vitriol from his enemies in the Democratic Party over the administration's continued dealings with the discredited Vichy regime in France. It remained Roosevelt's view that all avenues of approach should be kept alive, but this left him open to criticism on both military and moral grounds.

Roosevelt and Churchill had invited to the conference both the vain General Giraud and the even more vain General Charles de Gaulle, who hated Vichy and proclaimed himself the only true leader of the French army. The goal was to get these two bitter antagonists to cooperate in order to ease the political strain on Roosevelt.

De Gaulle, for his part, refused to leave London when he heard Giraud also would be at Casablanca; Churchill prodded him by threatening to cut off his funding. At the conference, de Gaulle and Giraud avoided each other entirely, but Churchill shooed them out onto the lawn and made them shake hands while a photographer snapped their picture. The photograph was flashed around the world as proof that Roosevelt had patched up French dissension, when in fact he had produced only a reluctant photo op.

Members of these Frenchmen's staffs somehow cracked the ice. It was suggested that one should become the civilian authority of all French North African territories, while the other would be the military authority. Giraud said he would be the civilian leader and de Gaulle could be the military man, but then de Gaulle, probably out of spite or pique, suggested he wanted it the other way around. Upon hearing this, Roosevelt remarked of de Gaulle sarcastically, "Yesterday he wanted to be Joan of Arc," to which Churchill riposted, "Well, fine. We just need to find some bishops to burn him at the stake." And there the matter rested.[4]

Churchill, who had loved North Africa ever since he had fought the Mahdi in the Sahara, took Roosevelt on an exotic sightseeing tour of Morocco, with the pistol-packing Secret Service men dogging them from behind. They drove through Casablanca's bazaar, with its markets of fake antiquities, snake charmers, and veiled dancing girls, and into the countryside, where they passed Arabs riding camels and women hauling water. Finally, they arrived at a six-story observation tower near Marrakech.

As Churchill led the way, the Secret Service agents lugged Roosevelt's wheelchair up the stairs. In the quiet of the tower, the two world leaders were treated to a spectacular vista of the distant Atlas Mountains painted purple by the setting sun, a sight that made the war seem far away.[5]

To end the conference, Roosevelt and Churchill seated themselves in small white chairs on the lawn of the compound amid the African palms and fruit trees. Together, they gave the gaggle of reporters a brief recitation of what had been decided—omitting, of course, the next invasion target. Then, Roosevelt made one of the most startling and controversial statements of the war.

He and Churchill, the president suddenly declared, had determined that the only way the war could end was by the unconditional surrender of Germany, Italy, and Japan. Among the many people who were shocked by this stark declaration was Churchill, who claimed this was the first he'd heard of it. British diplomacy, in its illustrious history, had always tried to leave a little wiggle room where military matters were concerned. Later, Roosevelt told newsmen that the idea just "popped into my mind," but this turned out to be not exactly true. Harry Hopkins revealed that he had found it in Roosevelt's notes the night before.

The announcement caused a considerable uproar that lasted for some time afterward. After the war, "there were many experts," explained Hopkins's biographer Robert Sherwood, "who believed that the utterance of these words would put the iron of desperate resistance into the Germans, Japanese, and Italians, . . . needlessly [prolonging] the war and [increasing] its cost; there are some who still believe that it did so . . . There were others who violently opposed the principle itself, and . . . still [attribute] the world's postwar troubles to the enforcement of unconditional surrender."

After the war Churchill was asked about the matter and said: "I would not have used those exact words but I stood by the president. Negotiation with Hitler was impossible. He was a maniac."[6]

AFTER EISENHOWER CALLED OFF the Tunisian advance during the previous winter, the Americans had used the time to get their tanks and trucks unstuck, improve roads, build airfields, land reinforcements, and regroup and reorganize for the coming dry season offensive.

Unfortunately, that is what the Germans used the time for as well. The original Allied plan had been to seize Tunisia and its valuable port in Tunis before the Germans could reinforce it. But now Hitler had rushed in an army of more than fifty-six thousand troops and heavy weapons. Moreover, after its defeat at the Battle of El Alamein, Rommel's army, rather than implementing a slow, methodical withdrawal, made it a race back to Tunisia; if they arrived in time, the Germans would give the Americans double trouble. By midwinter the vanguard of Rommel's eighty-thousand-man army had indeed reached Tunisia.

Tunisia is about the size and shape of the state of Florida. Its northern half is covered with mountains and valleys, with little infrastructure except for the coastal cities. When news of the American landings became known, the Germans thoughtfully covered all the mountain passes, roads, and bridges with powerful artillery and machine guns, backed by tanks and antitank guns and bristling with land mines. This spelled trouble for the green American soldiers who were anything but battle hardened.

Worse, much of their armor was out of date and no match for the German Panzer and Tiger (88mm cannon) tanks. Many U.S. armored units were equipped with the old General Lee (37mm cannon) and General Stuart tanks because most of the newer General Sherman and General Grant tanks had been sent to the British for their fight against Rommel. These obsolete vehicles ran on gasoline instead of diesel oil and came to be known as "flaming coffins." One old soldier, seeing a column of General Lees with their high profiles clanking down the road, described the tank as looking "like a damned moving cathedral."

The first major American action in North Africa was not impressive. It was a battle for the Medjerda River valley, and it seesawed back and forth for more than a month. The Americans would attack and then withdraw in the face of German counterattacks. American tank shells simply bounced off the thick-armored German tanks, and hideous scenes were offered up of U.S. crews roasted alive in their inferior vehicles or blown to atoms by German guns. British troops were there too, fighting alongside the Americans, and included among their numbers certain ethnic groups fighting alongside the Allies. A mercenary tribe known as the Goums, from the deserts of Algeria and Morocco, were infamous for coming into Allied camps carrying the severed heads of German soldiers; for these, they were paid a bounty. Likewise, a terror tactic practiced by the British Gurkhas, learned in their native Nepal, was to creep up on a sleeping patrol of Germans and slit every throat but one, leaving him, when he awoke, to spread the news.[7]

In February, the Americans tried to break out to the coast but received an awful setback at the Kasserine Pass. Rommel had finally arrived, but he was still stinging from his army's loss to Montgomery and the British and determined to secure a victory over the green American army. The Germans overwhelmed the U.S. forces in both firepower and tactics, causing them to retreat back across miles of ground they had already taken. It remains one of the greatest defeats in U.S. military history with ten thousand casualties and hundreds of tanks lost. The American forces, it seemed, were simply not performing. Amid reports of undaunted courage, there was evidence also of shirking, incompetence, and even cowardice.

In Eisenhower's view the army was poorly led—and, indeed, if anything good came out of the Kasserine tragedy it was Ike's appointment of George Patton to take charge of the entire operation in Tunisia. The American Army, from its generals to its lowliest private, now thoroughly understood this was no lark adventure they were embarked on but deadly serious business. From then on, the soldiers responded accordingly. They'd become battle hardened the hard way.

The fighting went on all through the spring, with Patton constantly pushing forward. Scripps-Howard correspondent Ernie Pyle described the incongruity of the battlefields with the Arabs "herding their camels, just as usual, some of them plowing their fields. Children walked alongside their sack-ladened burros, as tanks and guns clanked past them. The sky was filled with planes and smoke-bursts from screaming shells."[8]

ONE OF THE SUBJECTS DISCUSSED at the Casablanca Conference was the need to step up the bombing of German industrial and military facilities. By then, what would become the U.S. Eighth Air Force was organized and operating out of bases in England.

Both the British and the Germans had tried out daylight bombing on each other but soon dropped the idea because of heavy casualties. The brash Americans, however, left it to the British to restrict themselves to night bombing and took on the job of daylight sorties. The British said it couldn't be done without a fighter escort—and no fighter at that point could then carry the fuel to accompany a long-range bombing mission.

But the Americans had a weapon they felt could do the job. The four-engine B-17 Flying Fortress—so toughly constructed and so well armed, bristling with up to fourteen .50-cal. machine guns—presented a formidable challenge to any foe that ventured near it.

The famous *Memphis Belle* flew its first mission November 7, 1942. Over the next seven months, while performing her required twenty-five combat missions, the *Belle* shot down at least eight enemy fighters, remarkably without a single loss of her own crew.

While the B-17 of the Eighth Air Force was a tough customer, it was certainly not invulnerable to the enemy. More than five thousand B-17s were shot down by German flak or fighter planes, and twenty-six thousand men of the Eighth were killed during the course of the war. The chilling irony and shocking conclusion of Randall Jarrell's "The Death of the Ball Turret Gunner" tells the story in one of the best-known poems to come out of the war.

> *From my mother's sleep I fell into the State,*
> *And I hunched in its belly till my wet fur froze.*
> *Six miles from earth, loosed from its dream of life,*
> *I woke to black flak and nightmare fighters.*
> *When I died they washed me out of the turret with a hose.*

The last commander of the Eighth Air Force was none other than Jimmy Doolittle, leader of the famed raid on Japan. Before it was over, the Eighth had reduced to rubble not only most of Germany's industrial might but its cities as well. Aside from the flak and the fighters, the bombers fought a sterile, impersonal kind of war, flying in at thirty thousand feet and higher. But it wasn't impersonal for everyone. As Jarrell put it,

In bombers named for girls, we burned
The cities we had learned about in school.

If Roosevelt thought about any of this, it would mostly have been in the abstract. There was so much to do and so little time to do it, so more and more he left military matters to the military via General Marshall. He still worried about the American marines fighting on Guadalcanal, and the terrific price in lives and ships paid by the U.S. Navy. But about all he could do was inquire whether they were being properly supplied. Roosevelt was annoyed by statements MacArthur had given to newspaper reporters that this was not happening, but still he knew it was the truth. While every effort was being made to keep things flowing to the Southwest Pacific—airplanes, food, guns, ammunition—Roosevelt was also aware that the secret "Germany First" agreement was taking its toll on the entire Pacific theater.

BY THE LATE SPRING OF 1943 Patton's and Montgomery's armies began to wear down the Germans in Tunisia. Rommel had made a beeline in that direction, thinking that Hitler would evacuate his army to Sicily—just a few hundred miles distant—so that it could fight another day. But now Hitler was thoroughly disgusted; after all, he had sent Rommel's force to North Africa only to prop up his idiot ally Mussolini, who was now getting beaten by the British. He would not allow himself to admit defeat and again told Rommel to fight it out to the last man.

It nearly worked out that way. Rommel in fact had gone back to Germany for continuing medical issues. In May the Allies captured some 275,000 Axis troops, more than half of them German. It was the greatest Axis defeat thus far, and North Africa was for the most part free of Axis occupation.

The next step, at least for Churchill, was Sicily. General Marshall and the Joint Chiefs of Staff had no great objection to invading Sicily, but they did not want to commit to any further operations in the eastern Mediterranean. As Marshall had warned, "Distractions only lead to more distractions," and Sicily—like the North African invasion itself—was distraction enough.

Churchill, however, didn't agree, and he boarded the *Queen Mary* with a staff of one hundred to argue his case at the so-called Trident conference in Washington. For his part, Roosevelt was adamant that there would be a cross-Channel landing in France in 1944. Churchill agreed to this, and he further agreed to provide seven divisions—about 120,000 men—from the Mediterranean theater. But Churchill continued his ramblings about hitting Europe's "soft underbelly" to get at Austria and southern Germany.

There were also lengthy discussions about how to help defeat the Japanese in China. When the Japanese invaded Burma in 1941 they had cut the Burma Road, Chiang Kai-shek's supply lifeline of Allied goods and munitions, through India. It was important to keep Japanese armies occupied in China, so that they could not be sent as reinforcements to counter American efforts to oust them from the myriad Pacific islands on the way to the Home Islands of Japan.

A year earlier, the Allies had organized the India-China Ferry, consisting of mostly American transport planes that would "fly the hump" between India and China with supplies to supplant the Burma Road. This involved extremely difficult flying conditions because the route led over the Himalaya, the highest mountains in the world. General Stilwell, the U.S. commander in China, wanted a joint operation to reopen the Burma Road. But Roosevelt and Churchill turned it down, believing that this would be too difficult and dangerous in the Burma jungles. Instead, they opted to beef up "flying the hump" operations.

There were approximately 350,000 enemy soldiers protecting Sicily, including two mobile German Panzer divisions. This meant in practice that a far larger Allied force would be needed than for the North Africa invasion.

On the evening of July 9, 1943, at a state dinner in the White House, President Roosevelt announced to his guests that the Allied invasion of Sicily had begun. Montgomery's army of one hundred thousand was landing on the eastern beaches of Sicily's southern "horn," and Patton's army of sixty thousand was invading along a thirty-mile stretch of western beaches. This would be the largest-scale Allied amphibious landing to date, as well as a practical education for the run-up to Overlord the following spring.

All things considered, the Sicily invasion, dubbed Husky, went off with surprisingly few hitches. As the two Allied armies moved inland, other American and British divisions began arriving until the forces reached more than four hundred thousand. Axis strategy under an Italian commander was to slowly give way to the Allies at first, only to meet them with over-whelming force as they drove into the country's mountainous interior. However, led by overpowering tank units, the Americans and British were able to move more quickly than the enemy believed possible. As the Allies passed through towns and villages, the people greeted them as liberators, with girls giving kisses and women handing out fruit and flowers. The Germans, it seemed, had not been seen as good stewards in Italy, probably owing to their high-handed treatment of civilians.[9]

Patton's army raced northward and took the large city of Palermo along Sicily's coast, then struck out for Messina, which was to have been in Montgomery's area of operations. The Germans, sensing the inevitable, detached themselves from Italian control and scrambled for Messina them-selves, which was the closest port to the Italian mainland. They began embarking on escape craft.[10]

To Montgomery's mortification, Patton had arrived in Messina first. But the last Germans had departed with most of their equipment, which would prove to be a problem when the Allies invaded Italy shortly afterward. About a hundred thousand Italian soldiers had also escaped, but another hundred and fifty thousand were taken prisoner.

The Sicily operation had taken just over a month and, among other things, had caused Hitler to quickly move two German divisions from Russia and postpone his attack on Kursk, which, to a lesser extent, appeased Stalin's demands for a second front.

On July 25, 1943, a coup removed Mussolini from power. The Italian government fell into the hands of Marshal Pietro Badoglio who, seeing the handwriting on the wall, secretly indicated a willingness to switch sides. This put Roosevelt's "unconditional surrender" to the test. As badly as he and Churchill wanted Italy, with all her arms and soldiers, on the Allied side, Roosevelt knew that an unconditional surrender edict might likely keep the prideful Italians in the fight.

This notion must have been on his mind since May, after the Allied victory in Tunisia and the great surrender of Italian troops. In any case, Roosevelt had sought to mitigate his unconditional surrender position by assuring the Italian people in a Voice of America broadcast that once the Fascists and Nazis were removed they were free to choose their own form of government, and that Italy could take her place "as a respected member of the European family of nations."[11]

For nearly two months, the Allies remained in a kind of limbo over what exactly was going on in Italy. The Germans, suspicious of Badoglio's intentions, began rushing tank and infantry divisions into northern Italy. Meantime, peace talks with the Allies were secretly being held and on September 8 it was announced that Italy had formally and "unconditionally" surrendered. American troops began crossing from Sicily to Naples and moving up the Italian mainland toward Rome. The furious Germans had by then fortified the mountainous terrain north of the Italian capital. The terrible and deadly battle that commenced to eject them lasted until the end of the war.

By then the American marines had defeated the Japanese on Guadalcanal and were fighting their way up the Solomon Island chain toward the big Japanese base at Rabaul, while other marines escorted by the U.S. Navy were taking Japanese-held islands ever westward across the central Pacific. The fighting in New Guinea was drawing to a close and MacArthur now pointed his men northward toward the Philippines to fulfill his "I shall return" promise.

As they entered the fourth quarter of 1943, it was becoming apparent to the Allies that they would likely win the war—although in war nothing is certain and who knew what secret weapons or tactics the enemy might employ. Nevertheless, both Roosevelt and Churchill were becoming increasingly concerned about maintaining a lasting peace after the conflict officially ended. A major question among many in the State Department was how the Soviet Union would fit into this peace. The Americans and British continued supplying Stalin with arms and equipment, but both governments had begun to mistrust his intentions for postwar Europe.

Roosevelt was far more sanguine about Uncle Joe, and he wanted that kind of optimism to pervade not only his White House counselors but the nation at large. Stalin was deliberately presented by the Roosevelt administration as a benevolent dictator, a fatherlike figure, beloved by his people. When, for example, Chip Bohlen, State's new number two man on the Russia desk, attended a White House dinner, he was buttonholed by Roosevelt's top troubleshooter Harry Hopkins, who demanded to know if he was a member of "that anti-Soviet clique." Hopkins then lectured Bohlen on Russia's contributions to the war effort.[12]

To encourage this way of thinking, U.S.-made propaganda films were produced. They showcased the Soviet Union as a peaceful, idyllic place populated by happy citizens who worked joyfully together, engaged in folk dances in their time off, and fought Germans with the ferocity of lions. These films were shown repeatedly at neighborhood theaters throughout America. Nothing was mentioned about what happened to Russian soldiers who did not fight lionlike, or who surrendered when surrounded. As it happened, of the hundreds of thousands of captured Soviet troops repatriated to Russia after the war, practically all were immediately sent by Stalin to spend their lives in shame and hard labor in the Siberian gulags.

Gradually, however, the propaganda campaign worked, and many Americans began to reverse their previous notions of the Soviet Union as a violent dictatorship that aimed to spread communism throughout the world. Instead they began to see Stalin as a worthy ally in the fight against Nazism who would become a faithful peacekeeper once the war ended.

Roosevelt continued to believe that he could deal with Stalin better than Churchill could—even better than he and Churchill together—and wanted to arrange a one-on-one conference with the dictator in Alaska. To do so, Roosevelt sent his trusted counselor Joseph Davies to see Stalin personally in May 1943. Davies, who had been ambassador to the Soviet Union from late 1936 to 1938, was highly sympathetic to the Soviet regime and in 1941 had published a well-received book titled *Mission to Moscow* about his experiences. (It was later made into a Hollywood feature movie starring Walter Huston as Davies and Ann Harding as his wife, the former

Marjorie Merriweather Post.) Both the book and the movie painted a rosy picture of Stalin's Soviet Union, whitewashing the purges, the show trials, and the executions, and concluding that Americans had "nothing to fear from communism."

Roosevelt knew his man. Davies not only got the president's letter delivered, but secured an agreement from the Soviet dictator to meet the U.S. president in Fairbanks.[13] A photo of the meeting shows a grinning Stalin clasping hands with an equally sunny Joseph Davies.

Every time they tried to set a firm date for Roosevelt's proposed conference, however, Stalin balked—usually as a sulk against some perceived offense by either Roosevelt or Churchill. He was skeptical, for example, when Eisenhower announced the surrender of Italy, reasoning it was somehow a "separate peace" that the Allies had made with the enemy, after agreeing to avoid such arrangements. There was some truth to this observation, because the Americans didn't consult Stalin beforehand. But that diplomatic overlook seemed more of an afterthought as everyone but the Germans wanted Italy out of the war.

Then an incident came to light that gave even Roosevelt serious pause about the intentions and methods of Stalin's Soviet regime.

German troops entering the Katyn Forest in the western Soviet Union had discovered mass graves containing the bodies of tens of thousands of Polish military officers who had been executed Soviet style with a bullet to the back of the neck. These men, who were rounded up in 1939–1940, after the German-Russian invasion of Poland that had started the war, had been ostensibly bound for Russian concentration camps to prevent them from organizing any resistance to Soviet rule. But the NKVD (with Stalin's blessing) decided they were too much trouble to keep in Russia and had had them murdered instead.

The Soviets, of course, blamed the massacre on the Germans, who vehemently denied it. The Polish government-in-exile—citing the fact that the men were last seen in Soviet custody—demanded an investigation by the Red Cross. This gave Stalin the excuse to cut off diplomatic relations with Polish authorities (headquartered in London) and organize his own Polish government-in-exile in Moscow, known as the Union of Polish Patriots, which he obviously intended to install in the country after the war in order to absorb Poland into his empire.[14]

All of this had a terrible smell to it and caused Roosevelt to rethink his relationship with Uncle Joe. He still wanted to meet with him, and he remained of a mind to continue for the war's sake to portray him and his country in the brightest terms. But there was now an element of unsettling mistrust. The warnings that Roosevelt had brushed off, the dark reports coming from junior officers in the State Department, some of them directly from the U.S. Embassy in Moscow, now had a different and alarming ring.[15]

On a more favorable note, Eleanor Roosevelt had just conducted a two-month, twenty-five-thousand-mile tour of American fighting units in the South Pacific. This included Guadalcanal and other of the Solomon Islands, during which she is said to have told an audience of marines: "The marines that I have seen around the world have the cleanest bodies, the filthiest minds, the highest morale, and the lowest morals of any group of animals I have ever seen. Thank God for the United States Marines!"

Her report to the president was filled with useful observations, insights, and recommendations regarding treatment and care of troops in the rear areas and the occasional deficiencies of the military and the Red Cross. "I think perhaps I shouldn't have gone," she lamented to her husband later, "because of all the trouble I caused by simply being there."

In November 1943 Roosevelt set out for the Big Three conference in Tehran. Stalin had insisted on the location because, he said, there were telephone and telegraphic communications available there with Moscow. He could also ride down in his special train, which consisted of comfortable, if spartan, accommodations. Roosevelt and Churchill had also decided to use the occasion to meet with Chiang Kai-shek in Cairo, which Stalin declined to do because the Soviet Union was not at war with Japan—and also because it would have required him to fly over the Mediterranean.

There was a minor but telling to-do over Roosevelt's choice for a State Department officer to accompany him to the conference. The president wanted a young assistant secretary named Sumner Welles, not the elderly secretary of state Cordell Hull, to be his right-hand man in Tehran. But suddenly Welles was identified by the FBI with affidavits and other evidence as having "solicited homosexual services" from the porters on a train returning from the funeral of House Speaker William Bankhead in Alabama.

Roosevelt attempted to keep Welles through mighty opposition, but at last he was confronted by Hull with an "It's me or him" ultimatum. Welles was then forced to tender his resignation, on grounds that he was vulnerable to enemy blackmail.

ON NOVEMBER 11—Armistice Day—1943, Roosevelt was spirited out of the White House at 9:30 p.m. and driven to the presidential yacht *Potomac* at the Quantico, Virginia, U.S. Marine Corps base south of Washington. Before sunup the boat anchored off the mouth of the Potomac River. In the dark to the east could be seen the great shadowy hulk of the USS *Iowa,* one of the new, larger class of battleships, now commanded by the president's friend and former aide Captain John McCrea, who had at last got his sea command. Adding to the president's party of ten were Marshall, King, and Hap Arnold, commander of the Air Corps, who had come aboard the night before. They joined 107 staffers, planners, clerks, typists, translators, security people, and others involved in the mission. More than one person remarked that if a bomb had sunk the ship the entire top echelon of war directors would be wiped out.

The president had special bath facilities prepared for his condition, private phone lines, a private dining room, and a private elevator to take him between decks. Three destroyers would screen for enemy submarines. By the morning of November 13 the *Iowa* had cleared the Chesapeake Bay and stood out to sea under cloudy skies at a speed of 25 knots.

Next day, a Sunday, the weather turned sunny and warmer; the president was wheeled out to the deck by his valet Arthur Prettyman to observe antiaircraft exercises. He and a contingent of his party were duly impressed by the powerful curtains of fire laid down by the ship's antiaircraft weapons. They had been given cotton to put in their ears and seemed to be enjoying themselves immensely when, suddenly, an alarm began to clang and the shooting stopped. Someone shouted over the loudspeakers, "Torpedo defense! This is not a drill!" The ship put on full speed and was heeled in an evasive maneuver when the hull momentarily quivered from an underwater explosion. An officer shouted, "It's the real thing!"

Harry Hopkins shouted to the president to go inside, but instead Roosevelt told Prettyman, "Arthur, take me over to the starboard side. I want to watch the torpedo!" It was pure Roosevelt. Whether it was in France when he wanted to see some action as assistant secretary of the Navy or in the open convertible in Miami when the shots rang out, the president, like Churchill, was a picture of controlled, excited calm in moments of danger.[16]

It turned out that the torpedo had been fired by a careless accident from one of the screening destroyers during the antiaircraft drill. The tube had detonated astern of the *Iowa* from the roiling prop wake of the ship. Admiral King was of course outraged and had summoned the skipper of the offending destroyer over to the *Iowa* to personally relieve him of command; Roosevelt intervened and no action was taken. Hopkins, however, probably made an understatement when he observed that "the Navy will never hear the end of it."[17]

THE REMAINDER OF THE VOYAGE was uneventful and on November 20 the *Iowa* arrived in Mers el-Kabir, the great harbor of Oran in Algeria. General Eisenhower was there to greet the president when he landed on the quay, as were two of the president's sons, Navy Lieutenant Franklin D. Roosevelt Jr. and Colonel Elliott Roosevelt. That day, they flew to Eisenhower's theater headquarters in Tunis, where the president stayed in a villa once used by Germans. Ike took FDR, Marshall, and King on a tour of what used to be Carthage, two thousand years previous, which they had studied in their military academy textbooks. The intimacy of the occasion was palpable owing to the fact that either Eisenhower or Marshall was going to get the nod from Roosevelt as the commander of Overlord, the Allied invasion of France. Before dinner, Admiral King embarrassed everybody by weighing in on the subject of who should head the upcoming invasion. He suggested that the president preferred Marshall, but that the Joint Chiefs thought Marshall was more needed in Washington and that Ike should have the job.

Roosevelt was to fly on to Cairo next morning, but Eisenhower intervened on grounds that in the daylight the German fighters might make the presidential plane their target. That gave Eisenhower a day with Roosevelt by himself. The general used the opportunity to take the president on a tour of old Roman-Carthaginian battlefields, during which he gave him a lengthy and compelling discourse on how the Allies had whipped the German-Italian army in the area. During a roadside picnic, Roosevelt got to banter with Ike's red-haired Irish driver, Kay Summersby, whose romance with the commanding general was becoming an open secret. If word of this indiscretion got back to the president he never mentioned it—and likely, given his own situation with Lucy Rutherfurd, he put it out of mind.

The presidential party arrived in Egypt after a night flight and, with the pyramids as a backdrop, began the Cairo Conference featuring not only Chinese generalissimo Chiang Kai-shek, but his wife, Madame Chiang, who arrived in a slinky black satin dress slit up the sides that caused at least one British officer to offer up "a suppressed neigh."*[18]

Churchill was furious that Roosevelt had put the Chiangs at center stage, when he wished the conference to concern itself with plans for next year's fighting in Europe. But Roosevelt had already stated his hopes that, after the war, the 400 million–strong Chinese nation would become, along with the United States, Great Britain, and Russia, the "peacekeepers of the world" under the aegis of the new United Nations. In fact, Roosevelt was so con-

---

* The lush-figured Madame Chiang, who spoke English and was ubiquitously at the side of her husband, was said to be the model for the evil Dragon Lady in the popular comic strip "Terry and the Pirates," which lasted until 1973.

vinced that the Chinese would acquit themselves on the world stage that he reportedly offered them the job of occupying Japan after that country was defeated. Chiang politely turned him down, saying he didn't think China was the right country to occupy Japan—remembering, no doubt, the horrific atrocities committed on his countrymen by the Japanese, as well as the war with Mao Tse-tung's Communists that he knew would commence as soon as the Japanese threat was quelled.

Roosevelt also told Chiang that he would launch an amphibious attack on the Japanese in Burma to reopen the Burma Road for supplies, a promise that caused Churchill to become almost apoplectic. The prime minister wanted the United States to concentrate resources on the Germans in the Mediterranean, not on the Japanese in the jungles of Asia.

On Thanksgiving Day Roosevelt entertained the entire conference with a turkey dinner. The birds were provided by Undersecretary of State Edward Stettinius Jr., from his Virginia farm, and from Joe McCarter, a black farmer from Burnt Corn, Alabama, who had personally sent the president a turkey because he thought he was a good man.

Roosevelt, who was helped in by his son Elliott, sat down in a dinner jacket while Churchill appeared in coveralls. A U.S. Army band played tunes during dinner, including "Carry Me Back to Old Virginny" and "Old Man River," requested by Churchill; Roosevelt gave the nod to "The White Cliffs of Dover" for the British contingent. At the playing of the "Marines' Hymn" to celebrate the recent capture of Tarawa Island in the Pacific, Churchill rose to his feet flashing the V sign. After that, the party seemed to degenerate slightly when Churchill insisted that Roosevelt's military adviser Major General "Pa" Watson dance with him while the orchestra played a waltz. Roosevelt's laughter at this bizarre scene was "enough to wake the pharaohs," according to one of his aides.[19]

LESS THAN A WEEK LATER Roosevelt and party found themselves in Tehran, staying in (of all places) the Soviet Embassy. Stalin had insisted that Roosevelt stay at the Soviet Embassy for the course of the meeting, owing to a reported assassination plot ginned up by the Russian foreign minister Molotov, who spoke vaguely of German "saboteurs and parachutists." While American diplomats and security personnel concluded the thing was a hoax to maneuver Roosevelt and others into a place where they could be secretly surveilled, the president welcomed the opportunity to "make a positive gesture toward the suspicious Stalin," according to the historian Thomas Parrish. "What better way to start than by accepting Russian hospitality?" he wrote.

In any event, Roosevelt was reading cables in his suite at the Soviet Embassy on a Sunday afternoon when a short, stocky, pockmarked man entered without knocking. He was wearing a Soviet army tunic with a gold star signifying the rank of a marshal of the Soviet Union. It was Stalin, at last come to meet the president of the United States.

The big question that had loomed all through the preconference days for the Americans was what the Soviets' policies would be after Germany was defeated. It was obvious that if they continued their successes on the battlefield, the Russian army would break through eastern Europe, the Balkans, all the way into Germany itself. Would the Communists remain there to claim spoils or return to their own boundaries? The answer came more quickly than anyone thought possible. Stalin surprised Roosevelt before their meeting even formally began by volunteering that he "had no desire to own Europe," and that his countrymen had "plenty to do at home, without undertaking great new territorial responsibilities." This was what Roosevelt had wanted to hear, and it certainly got things off to a good start, although there were those among the president's diplomats and military brass who remained suspicious of the Soviets' intentions.[20]

For Roosevelt, there were more pleasant surprises in store. In early 1943 the War Department had produced a top secret strategic assessment, concluding that "the most important factor the United States has to consider in relation to Russia is the prosecution of the war in the Pacific." At the rate things were going, the paper said, "if the United States alone had to fight a ground war on the Japanese mainland, the costs and casualties would be immeasurably increased," and the action might even fail. It was thus imperative because of their strategic location and powerful military that the Russians join in the defeat of Japan.

When Stalin agreed to join the fight against Japan as soon as Germany was defeated, it was music to the U.S. military contingent's ears. Again, however, some of the more cynical diplomats wondered what reward the Communists would want for their services against Japan. Would it be concessions elsewhere? Japanese territory? Japan itself?

Throughout the conference, Roosevelt's firm commitment to Operation Overlord put him at odds with his friend Churchill. But Roosevelt was pleased with himself to be ganging up on the British prime minister in order to curry favor with Stalin. Almost invariably in a trio, at some point two will turn against the third, and Churchill had been asking for it, Roosevelt thought. "Winston just lost his head when everybody refused to take the subject seriously," Roosevelt told his son later. "He was going to take offense at what anybody said, specially if what was said pleased Uncle Joe."

Yet Roosevelt didn't forget the importance of his relationship with Churchill. The next morning the president had himself wheeled through the embassy's post exchange and "from among the Persian knives, daggers, rugs, he selected a Persian 'bowl of some antiquity'" as a gift he would present to Churchill that evening. Roosevelt knew how to play it. And he played it to the hilt.[21]

On the final day of the conference Roosevelt participated in meetings "that could have been done by the foreign ministers." Then, without consulting or even inviting Churchill, he got down to business with Stalin, divvying up the countries of Europe after the war.

Roosevelt conceded the fate of Poland to Stalin's Communist state, as well as that of the Baltic countries Latvia, Estonia, and Lithuania. He blithely explained to Stalin that if the war was still going on in 1944, he intended to run once more for the presidency, and that he would "need the votes of the six hundred million Americans of Polish descent" (there were in fact only 3 million of these). Therefore, he begged Stalin not to formally occupy the country until after the American elections.

As for the Baltic states, Roosevelt observed that they had once been a part of the old Russian Empire, and that he had no objection to the Soviets reabsorbing them after the war, provided there would be "some expression of the will of the people . . . perhaps not immediately after their re-occupation by the Soviet forces, but some day."[22]

He also seemed willing to concede Finland, with whom the Soviets had been at war. But Stalin didn't want it. He asked for only one of its ports on the Gulf of Bothnia, and that was okay by Roosevelt.

Despite the apparent treachery of condemning these European nations to the tender mercies of Soviet communism, there was a method of sorts to Roosevelt's seeming madness. First, he told people both within and without the U.S. Department of State that these were countries the Soviets could take at will anyway. They were all states in the far north bordering the Soviet Union, whose provenance was vaguely Russian anyway. The idea was, Roosevelt noted, that if he conceded their occupation to Stalin, the Soviets would not cast an envious eye on the larger, more European states such as Austria, Hungary, Czechoslovakia, the Balkans—even Germany itself. As for Poland, Roosevelt explained that he had no confidence in its government-in-exile anyway, which, he said, consisted of "landed aristo-crats" who intended to rule over a feudalistic system to the detriment of the masses.

Much of the talk centered on the critical second front issue. Stalin had long called for an invasion of France from the West in order to draw some of Hitler's power away from the Russian front. At Tehran, he was finally going to get what he wanted. Against Churchill's counsel, Roosevelt con-cluded that western Europe would remain the chief military focus, and that the longed-for cross-Channel invasion—now dubbed Overlord—would definitely take place in the spring of 1944. When this was translated to Stalin, he stunned conference participants by reiterating that "after the defeat of Germany, the Soviet Union would join the Allies in war against Japan."[23]

Churchill fumed at Roosevelt's concession, yet even the prickly British statesman was able at times to play the diplomat. At an elaborate dinner Churchill presented Stalin with the so-called Stalingrad Sword, a gift from the English king. Churchill told the Soviet dictator that he could "take his place among the major figures of Russian history," and deserved to be known as "Stalin the Great."[24] The Soviet premier replied that it "was easy to be a hero when you were dealing with people like the Russians," which was a fairly easy thing to say considering he had given orders that anyone who *wasn't* heroic would be shot.

When the discussion turned to what should be done with Germany after the war, Stalin suggested that the country should be dismantled and broken up into parts, so as to never again become an aggressive force. "You will not change Germany in a short period of time," Stalin declared, citing that country's aggression in 1870, 1914, and yet again in 1939. "There will be another war with them." Two years later, he told a delegations of Czechs, "I hate the Germans. We can't get rid of them. We Slavs must be prepared for the Germans to rise again against us."[25]

Roosevelt seemed outwardly sympathetic to Stalin's position but said his military planners and diplomats favored turning the country into zones administered for a specified period of time by Britain, France, the United States, and, of course, the Soviet Union, to ensure that a peaceful Germany reappeared.

Churchill, once again, was uneasy. In fact, he secretly wanted a strong Germany after the war as a bulwark against Soviet communism, which he believed to be the greater threat once the Nazis had been defeated. During the discussions he kept muddying the waters, insisting that the Allies should consider his Balkans strategy, as well as Overlord. But according to Elliott Roosevelt, who was present, "It was quite obvious to everyone in the room what [Churchill] really meant. He was above all else anxious to knife up into Central Europe, in order to keep the Red Army out of Austria and Romania, even Hungary. Stalin knew it, I knew it, everybody knew it."[26]

Dinner that evening was less convivial, owing to Churchill's brush with a brandy bottle and an apparent black-dog mood. The Big Three, along with their aides, translators, and diplomats, were dining in the embassy's Great Hall at the behest of Stalin. After a multicourse dinner the toasts began, led by Stalin, who was drinking vodka. Churchill had been drinking brandy all afternoon and was conscious of being needled good-naturedly during dinner by Stalin, who seemed to enjoy the activity. (After all, for years Churchill had quite publicly denounced Soviet communism as the archenemy of the West.) The Soviet premier was also apparently peeved over Churchill's Balkans scheme, which he saw for what it was. As Charles "Chip" Bohlen wrote afterward, Stalin "lost no opportunity to get in a dig at Mr. Churchill. Almost every remark he addressed to the prime minister contained some sharp edge."[27]

At length Stalin rose for what Elliott Roosevelt deemed his "umpteenth toast," which was a proposal for "the swiftest justice for all Germany's war criminals." At least fifty thousand [German officers] must be immediately shot upon capture, Stalin continued, in what the younger Roosevelt thought was a "jocular fashion."[28] At this Churchill could contain himself no longer and growled, "The British people would never stand for such mass murder." It was "wholly contrary to our British sense of justice. I feel most strongly that no one, Nazi or no, shall be summarily dealt with, before a firing squad, without proper legal trial."[29]

Stalin then asked for FDR's opinion. The president, evidently sensing Stalin's mood, replied, "As usual, it seems to be my function to mediate this dispute. Perhaps we could say that instead of executing fifty thousand war criminals, shall we say forty-nine thousand five hundred?"

At this Churchill, who had a reputation for holding his liquor, seemed to become unhinged. He arose in a flush, in the process knocking over his brandy glass, and declared again with that famous scowl that war criminals "must be allowed to stand trial." He then staggered out of the room, slamming the door behind him. In fact, he had not gone into the hallway but blundered into a darkened cloakroom, where he languished for several long moments before he felt arms "clapped above my shoulders from behind." It was Stalin, "grinning broadly, declaring he was only playing."[30]

"I consented to return," Churchill later wrote, embarrassed to have caused a scene, "and the rest of the evening passed pleasantly."[31]

By the end of the conference Stalin extracted from Roosevelt the promise of a date for Operation Overlord in spite of Churchill's vehement objections, just as the Soviet dictator had hoped. But Stalin's gratitude toward the American extended only so far. When Molotov asked Stalin later which of the other two Big Three he liked the most, the premier replied, "They're both imperialists."

At one point in the conference, Churchill could not resist bringing up Stalin's view of territorial claims in the postwar world. But the cagey old dictator pushed the question off. "There's no need to talk about that at the present: when the time comes we will have our say." It may have been the understatement of the century.[32]

PRESIDENT ROOSEVELT LEFT TEHRAN for Cairo, where he at last let be known his choice of the commander for Overlord. It was Eisenhower. Roosevelt had wanted to appoint George Marshall but, wrote Marshall in his memoirs, in the end the president had told him, "I feel I could not sleep at night with you out of the country." It was a major disappointment but Marshall, fine soldier that he was, accepted his fate and plunged back into his chief of staff work.

The *Iowa* was waiting when the president returned from Tehran; he ended his seventeen-thousand-mile odyssey in the Chesapeake Bay on December 16, when Roosevelt transferred from the battleship to his presidential yacht for a trip up the Potomac to Washington. In his diplomatic pouch, a piece of information awaited him that was so stunningly valuable Roosevelt could scarcely believe his eyes. The signals intelligence people, who had cracked the Japanese diplomatic and naval codes, had intercepted a document sent to Tokyo by Hiroshi Oshima, the Japanese ambassador in Berlin. A graduate of the Japanese military academy and student of military tactics, Oshima had just been given a tour of all the fortifications, gun positions, and defenses along the French coast that the Germans had erected to thwart a cross-Channel invasion from Great Britain. At night Oshima had sketched out in high detail everything he had seen during the day and sent this information to his superiors in Japan. It was now in the hands of the president of the United States, and soon would be in the hands of General Eisenhower.

When Roosevelt was wheeled into the White House he was greeted with cheers and applause—not only by the entire staff but by diplomats from the State Department, high-ranking military officers, and a delegation from Congress. Word had come out that he had had great success at Tehran, which he intended to announce in a fireside chat to the American people on Christmas Eve. He obviously could not talk much about Overlord, but he dwelled on the "spirit of cooperation" between the Big Three leaders. Of Stalin, he remarked that he "got along fine" with him.

"He is a man who combines a tremendous, relentless determination with a stalwart good humor," Roosevelt said in a radio broadcast from his home in Hyde Park a little more than a week later. "I believe that he is truly representative of the heart and soul of Russia, and I believe that we are going to get along very well with him and the Russian people—very well indeed."

Of the Germans the president said, "We intend to rid them once and for all of Nazism and Prussian militarism and the fantastic and disastrous notion that they constitute a 'master race.'"[33]

But Roosevelt was most proud of getting Stalin's agreement on his United Nations scheme for keeping the peace after the war ended, as well as his assent for the Soviet Union, along with Great Britain and China, to become one of the four peacekeepers of the world. This, in the president's mind, was to become his shining achievement: an organization for world peace that was actually backed up by military power.

At the beginning of the Tehran Conference, Roosevelt had worried that Stalin did not trust him at all, and had lumped him with Churchill, whom he vastly mistrusted. By the end of the conference Roosevelt believed he had mostly won over Stalin's trust. The president's close aide and speechwriter Robert Sherwood assessed the Tehran Conference to be the "supreme peak of Roosevelt's career," on grounds of the cooperation it elicited from the Big Three, especially Stalin.

Stalin saw more than the president suspected, however. For his part Stalin analyzed the character of his two fellow leaders as follows: Churchill was as he appeared—there was no guile, an open book. Roosevelt was not. A few months after the conference ended Stalin informed a delegation of Yugoslavians that Churchill was the kind of man "who would steal a kopek [worth less than a penny] out of your pocket." Roosevelt, though, "only dips his hands for bigger coins."[34]

CHAPTER SIXTEEN

C hurchill had left the Tehran Conference a very ill man. He had ailed with a sore throat and cold since leaving London, which he self-medicated with whisky. But since arriving in Tunis to pay a courtesy call on Eisenhower, Churchill seemed to have succumbed to a state of physical and mental exhaustion on the verge of collapse. His temperature rose to 102; it was feared he was infected with a particularly virulent strain of influenza that was killing thousands across Europe.

His doctor, Charles Wilson (Lord Moran), was beside himself with worry. They were in a primitive country with no respectable hospitals and no place for a proper diagnosis. Under the circumstances, Moran summoned from Cairo a heart specialist, a pathologist, and an X-ray machine with technician. On December 13 the X-ray revealed that Churchill was suffering from pneumonia. Moran prescribed sulfa drugs, but the next day Churchill's heart went into cardiac fibrillation. "My heart is doing something funny," he told the doctor, "can't you do anything to stop this?" Moran sat by his bedside and held his wrist, taking his pulse and trying to calm him for the four hours it took the digitalis drug to return the heartbeat to normal. The pneumonia, however, was not improving; Winston Churchill, after all, was entering his seventieth year. On December 15, Moran sent a special military transport for Clementine, who flew the twenty-six hours to Tunisia to be at her husband's bedside in a villa at Carthage. She arrived expecting to see a gray, dying man but instead was greeted by a cheerful pink-faced cherub "with a large cigar and a whisky and soda in his hand." The worst had passed. Churchill later remarked that if he had in fact died it would have been all right. "The plans for victory have been laid," he said, "it is only a matter of time."[1]

The Germans were having none of that, however, and were putting up a ferocious fight about eighty miles south of Rome at a Gethsemane called Monte Cassino. Once the Allies landed in Italy and Mussolini, deposed, fled to Germany, he did not stay there. The Germans cannily reinstalled him as head of a puppet government in the part of Italy that the Germans still controlled, known as the Italian Socialist Republic, which had scraped up a small military arm to fight alongside the Nazi armies.

The German army was ensconced at Cassino in a large, sixth-century Benedictine monastery atop the mountain. Neither shelling nor bombing would drive them out. From their artillery positions on the heights, the Germans made the land below impossible to cross; Rome, which the Allies had hoped to take by Christmas, was now a distant goal. Churchill had hoped that by now the Allies would have been in the far north, if not across the Alpine passes and into Austria. Italy is a long, narrow, north-and-south country flanked on both sides by seas; east and west, it's ribbed, washboard-like, with multiple mountains and valleys. This makes it ideal ground for the kind of defensive warfare the Germans were waging under possibly the greatest German general of them all: Field Marshal "Smiling Albert" Kesselring.

Two months earlier, the Allies had conceived a plan, code-named Shingle, that involved an amphibious end run through the Tyrrhenian Sea along the coast to a town called Anzio, which would bypass Monte Cassino and link up with the British Eighth Army. Ike reconsidered the plan because the stalemate was costly, in terms of both Allied lives and the timetable for ridding Italy of Germans. But in the end he decided the scheme was too dangerous and could lead to a catastrophe if the troops—two reinforced infantry divisions totaling about twenty-five thousand men—landed on the Anzio beaches facing a strong German army where they could be cut off and annihilated.

Churchill, naturally, loved the idea. It was just his sort of plan—daring, surprising, and forceful. If it were a success, both the U.S. Fifth Army and the British Eighth Army that was operating on the Adriatic Sea side of the Apennines could link up for the final march into Rome, with the Germans scattered and in disarray.

Ill as he was, Churchill said all of this to Eisenhower during a visit on Christmas Day, 1943. But Ike remained skeptical and spoke of the "hazard of annihilation." Churchill lacked a sufficient number of landing craft, which had been sent back to England for the invasion of France. Nevertheless, in the end Eisenhower approved the operation.

The plan stalled when Eisenhower left for a long-deserved two-week leave in the United States, after which he was to go to England to take charge of Overlord, never to return to the Italian theater. So Churchill tried an end run of his own. He cabled Roosevelt that an Allied amphibious landing beyond Monte Cassino "should decide the battle of Rome"—but, for the want of fifty-six landing ships, couldn't go forward. Could Roosevelt order the fifty-six ships to remain in the Mediterranean theater long enough for Shingle to proceed? It made no sense, Churchill argued, not to supply them with the tools they needed in the one place they were actually fighting Germans. Failure to do so, he told the president, would result in a deadlock, or worse, in Italy. Overlord was six months distant: plenty of time to get the landing ships to England after the touchdown at Anzio, Churchill pleaded.

Roosevelt considered the matter, and two days later he approved delaying the return of the landing craft. Shingle was a go.

Churchill remained weakened by his bout with pneumonia and was recuperating in his favorite villa in Marrakech, attended by Clementine, Moran, and his daughter Sarah, among others. Sarah remained his favorite daughter, but she had married the stage comedian Vic Oliver, whom Churchill described as "common as dirt" and refused to shake his hand.

News from the sea was good. During the year, between the reconstituted Ultra intercepts that once more located the position of German submarines and the increased presence of U.S. and British destroyer escorts, the German undersea blockade of Great Britain and the terrible losses on the ocean crossings were significantly abated. The Battle of the Atlantic appeared to be won. A majority of German U-boats had been sunk.

More good news arrived on the day after Christmas, Boxing Day in England, when the German battleship *Scharnhorst* was sunk off Norway by the HMS *Duke of York,* taking all but thirty-six of her two-thousand-man crew to the bottom with her. The *Scharnhorst* and her sister ship *Gneisenau,* now damaged beyond repair, had been the scourge of the North Atlantic. With the *Bismarck* and *Scharnhorst* gone, and the *Gneisenau* and *Tirpitz* badly wounded, Hitler's once vaunted surface fleet was all but wiped out.

The air war was likewise showing terrific success, with the RAF and U.S. Eighth Air Force turning much of western Germany, including the industrial Ruhr valley, into piles of crumbled, bloody brickbats. To accomplish this, these air forces braved Germany's formidable air defenses day and night, aided by the development of longer-ranged fighter escorts. Hamburg, for example, a city of a million, had twelve square miles completely leveled one night by ten thousand tons of high-explosive bombs that caused a firestorm with 150 mph winds and temperatures exceeding three thousand degrees, killing forty thousand residents, and leaving eight hundred thousand homeless. A German official described it as "beyond all human recognition."[2]

Churchill once pondered aloud whether this sort of total destruction, with its horrendous civilian casualties, wasn't being "beastly." But he apparently answered his own query by telling a reporter, "Opinion is divided whether . . . air power could by itself bring about collapse in Germany. There is no harm in finding out."[3]

There was a heavy price to pay for this, however. The Germans had gradually adapted to British and American aerial tactics, including ruses to throw off radar. To combat the British, German night fighters used new, more powerful radar to track the bomber streams and new radar-controlled anti-aircraft guns. By the middle of 1943 the RAF was losing an average of six hundred airmen every week, killed or captured. The Americans, who bombed in daylight, lost sixty of two hundred and forty B-17 bombers and their ten-man crews in a single raid on a ball-bearing factory in Germany.

ON JANUARY 22 THE SHINGLE landing force under Major General John P. Lucas achieved complete surprise when it landed on the Anzio beaches behind German lines. Unfortunately, Lucas was not the man for the job. He never liked the plan to begin with, referring in his diary to Churchill's involvement as "amateur" and making a snide reference to Gallipoli. Lucas's orders were somewhat vague about taking Rome, but he seems to have interpreted them as "get on the beach at Anzio and dig in," which was exactly the opposite of everyone's intentions. The Germans quickly brought powerful forces to the area and contained the Allied beachhead with artillery that they installed in low mountains that ringed the area. The Americans were in a terrain of reclaimed marshland kept dry by giant pumps. The Germans immediately turned the pumps off, flooding the land. Adding to the misery was terrible winter weather. As Churchill sourly put it, "I thought we were hurling a wildcat on the beaches at Anzio—but what we have instead is a stranded whale."[4]

Following his failure to break out after a month, Lucas was relieved of command and replaced by Major General Lucian Truscott. By that time more U.S. and British divisions were poured into the Anzio pocket, bringing the Allied total of men to a hundred and fifty thousand, which the Nazi radio propagandist Axis Sally described as "the largest self-supporting prisoner of war camp in the world." Even when a breakout was at last achieved in May, followed by the fall of Rome the next month, Anzio was roundly criticized in military circles for its forty-three thousand casualties and poor execution. Still, Churchill argued that the ultimate goal of capturing Rome was in fact achieved; it kept the Germans from moving five divisions to France. But for long, agonizing weeks, pinned to the beaches while Allied soldiers died, the Anzio operation indeed looked to be an eerie repetition of the Gallipoli debacle, which must have caused Churchill considerable discomfort.

When at last, after sixty-seven days in the Middle East and North Africa, Churchill felt up to coming home to resume his daily duties, he surprised Parliament, which was conducting routine business. Harold Nicholson described in his diary the prime minister's triumphant return: "We were dawdling through questions . . . when I saw (*saw* is the word) a gasp of astonishment pass over the faces of the Labour Party opposite. Suddenly they jumped to their feet and started shouting, waving their papers in the air. We also jumped up and the whole house broke into cheer after cheer while Winston, very pink, rather shy, . . . crept along the front bench and flung himself into his accustomed seat."

With Overlord now the preoccupying feature of the war for the Allies, there wasn't a lot for Churchill to do in the four-month period before it launched. And so he set himself to worrying. In the off-year elections, his Conservative Party took a beating in several important seats that had been considered "safe," a fact Churchill viewed with grave foreboding. In February his dictating secretary wrote, "Somehow today he looks ten years older"; his aide Jock Colville told of Churchill sitting in his study "look[ing] old, tired and depressed."[5]

He had reason for depression.

As Stalin's armies moved through Poland, the Communists installed stooge regimes. In England they refused to accept the Polish government-in-exile for which, in fact, England and France had gone to war against Germany in 1939.

Churchill was further depressed that Roosevelt had turned down an invitation to meet with him in Bermuda at Easter, fearing that the president might be drawing closer to the Soviet Union. He was beginning to wonder whether the Big Three was actually the Big Two and a Half, with him being the half.

Nevertheless, at times he was compelled to show the old Churchill pugnaciousness, especially in times of danger. The closer to the actual war he got, the more animated he became. He was especially indignant after German bombs exploded on the Horse Guards Parade and blew out the windows of 10 Downing Street. Each night, when the warning sirens wailed, Churchill would pace restlessly until the guns began to fire, then put on his tin hat and coat and go to the roof of the building, where he could see the action. Sometimes he would go to the Hyde Park battery, where his daughter Mary was a gun captain, and "hear the child ordering the guns to fire."[6]

More and more he lunched, dined, and even slept in his private train, which kept him closer to the war by visiting troops engaged in Overlord training. There was an ongoing argument over the implementation of Anvil, a plan to simultaneously land a large force of Allied soldiers in the South of France along the Mediterranean. These would consist mostly of the 250,000 Free French forces in North Africa, plus black troops from French and British colonies, and some American divisions. The Americans were all for it. Churchill preferred his strategy of landing somewhere in the Balkans. But for now he had to bend to Roosevelt, and Roosevelt wanted Anvil.

He continued to brood about the Normandy invasion, always returning to the possibility of failure and what that would mean. Aside from a great loss of life and treasure, it would be a great propaganda weapon for the Germans and a ghastly morale killer for the Allies. Blame would have to be assessed, which would lead to more low morale. There was a good likelihood that the Americans would pull out and devote their efforts to the Pacific. What would happen in Italy would be anybody's guess. Could the Russians alone beat Hitler? If so, what would the world look like then?[7]

Churchill also worried over his party's losses in recent elections. The war was wearing on everyone—the food, clothing, and gasoline rationing—and it had been going on five years now. Labor unions were threatening strikes. All the young men were in the military. The Germans still managed to send over the occasional bombing raid. People's nerves were jangled. Inside a lavatory, one of Churchill's friends saw a graffiti message scrawled above a mirror: "Winston Churchill Is a Bastard."[8]

These daunting issues wore on a man of Churchill's age. He was at present not only prime minister but minister of defense and foreign minister, at least temporarily, in place of an exhausted Anthony Eden. Everyone associated with Churchill seemed to keep a diary—and almost to a one they agreed that he looked "tired," "aged ten years," "memory was unclear," "perfectly exhausted." But he just kept running, like an aged racehorse, because he didn't know what else to do. A vacation was out of the question.

In March one of the ministers with knowledge of Tube Alloys—the British name for the atomic bomb project—told Churchill that the matter should be presented to the entire war cabinet, and to the Soviets as well. Churchill thought otherwise. Of the war cabinet he responded, "What can they do about it?" And as far as the Russians went: "Absolutely not."[9]

As D-day for Overlord approached, Churchill began to immerse himself in the invasion plans. General Montgomery had told him he needed far more men on the initial landings, and Churchill went to Eisenhower about it. There arose a controversy over the bombing of French railroad junctions prior to the landings that would thwart the Germans bringing reinforcements to the beachhead. The problem was that the rail junctions were invariably located in French towns and cities; the loss of life for civilians would be horrendous. Churchill felt such slaughter was hard to justify, but the Americans felt otherwise. Finally it was left to Roosevelt to break the impasse, and he did not stoop to scruples. If destroying the rail junctions would help the invasion, then it must be done.

Lastly, Churchill concocted a wild plan to get to the Normandy beaches for a "tour of inspection" on D-day. He succeeded in getting a navy admiral to write up an order with Churchill boarding the cruiser *Belfast,* which would take him to Normandy. There he would debark on a destroyer, which could get him in closer for a visual inspection of conditions on the beaches. This scheme set into motion a general kerfuffle that would lead straight to Buckingham Palace.

The admiral, Sir Bertram Ramsay, told Churchill that he had respected his wish to keep the matter from the first sea lord but had thought it necessary to inform General Eisenhower, who was in charge of the invasion. This created an uproar in both camps when Eisenhower, who was very much against the idea, immediately informed the British, whose higher ranks were also fiercely opposed to it. Churchill's military adviser General Ismay "rather cleverly made the point that the problem was not so much safety, but being cut off from communications during a short period when crucial decisions might be necessary." Churchill replied that if Ismay remained opposed to him making the trip he would take him along!

At length it was left to King George to deal with the issue. He solved it by threatening to come along as well, a risk that Churchill felt he could not allow. So instead of being aboard a cruiser the night before D-day, Churchill "spent the night like a gentleman in England now abed." He left Clementine with the morbid comment, "Do you realize that by the time you wake up in the morning twenty thousand men may have been killed?"

IN THE MISTY FALSE DAWN of June 6, 1944, German lookouts all along an eighty-mile stretch of coastline in Normandy, France, were staggered to behold an armada of thousands of ships looming in the English Channel, two hundred miles to the south of where the Germans had been expecting them. Soon, naval gunfire from destroyers, cruisers, and battleships began blasting German defenses and installations along what Hitler called his "Atlantic Wall," while hundreds of landing craft headed toward the beaches. The night before, the American 82nd and 101st Airborne Divisions and a British airborne division had dropped behind German lines to create confusion and panic. By afternoon more than a hundred and sixty thousand Allied soldiers of Omar Bradley's American First Army and Bernard Montgomery's British 21st Army Group would be on the Normandy beaches. Overlord had arrived.

There were a great many ruses used to fool the Germans as to when and where the invasion would take place. One, known as the Man Who Never Was (aka Operation Mincemeat), involved floating a corpse dressed in an officer's uniform, shackled to a secret messages briefcase, which washed up on a Mediterranean beach and was immediately examined by the Germans. The briefcase contained a top secret message indicating that the Allied landings would be in the Mediterranean. Another ruse involved an army that never was, commanded by General George S. Patton in the south of England. It consisted of thousands upon thousands of tanks and trucks, artillery pieces, sleeping tents, and lots of radio traffic. The tanks, trucks, guns, and sleeping tents were life-size balloons to trick German reconnaissance intelligence into thinking that this phony "army" was intended to land at the Pas de Calais, France's closest point with England. And fooled the Germans were.

An even more elaborate ruse involved the RAF and its use of Window—the little strips of tinfoil used to confuse enemy radar. For hours before the landings, British planes in continuous columns bombarded the German-held shores with tons of the stuff, which muddled their radar while seven thousand Allied ships approached the Normandy coast undetected.

Simultaneously, throughout France another Allied army rose up to torment the German foe. These were the underground fighters of the French Resistance, or Maquis, who on signal began derailing trains, attacking German convoys, puncturing tires, blowing bridges, throwing bombs, and otherwise disrupting the German occupying forces.

By late afternoon the Allies had taken most of their objectives and were holding a defensive line several miles inland from the Channel. About ten thousand casualties had been suffered, with about half of them killed in action. Also, some ten thousand French citizens died when the Allies bombed the rail junctions. Within two months nearly 2 million Allied troops—American, British, French, Polish, and others—would be ashore.

Thwarted in his desire to go in with the men on D-day, Churchill nevertheless arranged to visit the battle area less than a week later. He did this in conjunction with the American chiefs of staff, who had decided to fly to England the day after the landings to be on hand if anything went wrong (and, one suspects, to get a look at the greatest of all invasions: the one they had planned over, argued over, sweated over, and often anguished over, which would anticipate the liberation of Europe and the end of the war).

Churchill took George Marshall and the heads of the U.S. Army, Navy, and the Air Corps into his private train, feting them with an elaborate banquet and many toasts of fine champagne as the train slowly wound its way to Portsmouth and the embarkation point. They were greeted there by a glowing Eisenhower, and then split up for the voyage to the battle area: the Americans in the USS *Thompson* and the British in a Royal Navy destroyer that would take them to the coast of Normandy.

Once on French soil, the distinguished American visitors were greeted by the U.S. Army commander Omar Bradley. It was Marshall's first visit to France since he had fought there twenty-six years earlier during World War I. From the beaches the party moved inland past a sobering temporary cemetery where at least a portion of the several thousand American servicemen killed in action had been lain.

It was hot and dusty, and the roads were overflowing with American soldiers, German prisoners, trucks, tanks, jeeps, guns, and ambulances filled with the wounded and the dead. Bradley suddenly realized, as he put it later, "the catastrophe that a single German sniper could cause." He took everyone to his headquarters in an old apple orchard, where they lunched al fresco on C rations washed down with water in tin canteen cups.[10]

For his part, Churchill entered France in a pugnacious frame of mind. He seemed delighted at the frenzied invasion activity: German bombers coming and going, British antiaircraft guns blasting, men marching, tanks clanking, people hollering. He rode happily in the rear of Montgomery's open jeep, pink-faced and waving a cigar and his famous V for victory sign to passing troops. On the way back to the destroyer to return to Portsmouth, they passed a large monitor warship firing its big 14-inch guns at the Germans. Churchill insisted on climbing aboard, saying he'd "never been on one of his Majesty's ships engaging the enemy." But the rough weather would have made the transfer too risky and there the matter ended—almost.[11] Still, when boarding his destroyer Churchill persuaded the ship's batteries to begin blasting away at some target beyond the beachhead, "to take a plug ourselves," he said. "Winston wanted to take part in the war, and was longing for some kind of retaliation [from the Germans]," General Alan Brooke surmised in his diary, but they refused to engage in the exchange.[12]

Brooke was astonished at "how little [France] had been affected by the German occupation and five years of war." The crops were good, the farms neat, and there were plenty of fat livestock, he said, adding grimly that the French population "did not seem in any way pleased to see us arrive to liberate France. They had been quite content as they were, and we were bringing war and desolation to their country."[13]

THE NIGHT OF CHURCHILL'S RETURN to London coincided with the arrival in the city of Hitler's new top secret weapon with which he believed he would win the war: a pilotless rocket, or "flying bomb" (or, as the military called it, V-1). Londoners called them "buzz bombs" for the queer buzzing sound they made with their pulse-jet-propelled engine. They were equipped with a rudimentary gyroscope that was supposed to keep them straight and level across the Channel, where they were designed to fall indiscriminately on greater London. Most of this first batch went far off course. But several did in fact reach London and killed half a dozen people.

Hitler and his propagandists had been hinting about such secret weapons of "retaliation" for more than a year, and Churchill had requested that his staff prepare for them. After that first day's inconclusive raid, suddenly there were hundreds of the flying bombs in any given twenty-four-hour period. "The blind, impersonal nature of the missile made the individual on the ground feel helpless," Churchill wrote. There was little that he could do, no human enemy that he could see shot down.

The following Sunday, one of the things fell on the Guards Chapel, killing two hundred guardsmen and demolishing the building. The RAF souped up and stripped down some of its Spitfires, which could sometimes overtake the weapon and shoot it down—or, in some cases, get close enough to nudge it and throw it off course. It was possible to shoot down the device with antiaircraft guns as well, but this did little good because nearly all the antiaircraft guns were in and around London, and the thing exploded on contact with the ground anyway.

The British also made a point of bombing the launching sites, but the Germans made new ones and kept up the raids. Then intelligence reports came back that the Germans were storing the things in caves outside Paris. These were bombed mercilessly and several thousand missiles were destroyed. But the Germans had more where those came from, built by slave labor. One landed on a building housing twenty-two homeless children and their caretakers; none survived. It was simply another thing to be endured, and people more or less got used to it. Within a month nearly three thousand Londoners had been killed and ten thousand injured by the flying bombs.[14]

At length, the British decided to move all the antiaircraft guns in London to the coast in hopes of shooting down the missiles as they came ashore. This was an enormous undertaking, moving six hundred huge Bofors guns weighing up to 10,000 pounds each along with tens of thousands of gun crews—including Mary Churchill. But between this tactic and the air-to-air destruction by British Spitfires, Churchill declared in September that "the V-1 had been mastered."[15]

Then came the V-2.

The Germans had also been working on a rocket-propelled ballistic missile, tall as a five-story building, with a nearly 2,500-pound warhead. This was a far more serious threat. Its trajectory took it fifty miles into space, and with a speed of 3,500 mph it was impossible to shoot down with guns or planes. Its engine cut out right before it reached London, so it was also impossible to hear it coming and take cover. Its explosion could erase a city block. The rockets began falling on September 8, 1944, and continued until near the end of the war, when the Allies pushed the Germans beyond the V-2's two-hundred-plus-mile range. Londoners felt quite helpless and frustrated. Churchill admitted, "We could do little against the rocket once it was launched." On a snowbound New Year's Day, 1945, Jock Colville told his diary, "The rockets are falling like autumn leaves."

The RAF strenuously bombed launching sites and the manufacturing facilities at Peenemunde, deep into Germany, but at a terrible cost: some fourteen thousand airmen were killed or missing on anti-V-2 missions.[16] The rockets fell at a rate of fifteen to twenty a day, around the clock. Before it was over tens of thousands of Londoners were killed or injured and thousands of homes were destroyed.

Meantime, the British and American air forces had just about given up on limiting their bombing to military targets and were quickly reducing more German cities, Berlin included, to piles of brick dust and sad heaps of debris.

NEARLY TWO MONTHS AFTER the D-day landings, the Allies were still holding their slender beachhead in Normandy. There was daily fighting along the front lines, but the situation had reached a stalemate. That part of Normandy was *bocage* country: farmland divided by thick hedgerows designed to resist soil erosion. Each hedgerow contained a potential trap for enemy machine guns or antitank weapons. The Allies thought it was too dangerous to break out, and the Germans thought it was too dangerous to break in. Then the U.S. Third Army got cranked up, with General George Patton at its helm.

Finally Eisenhower and his generals settled on Operation Cobra to bust out of Normandy and get into the open country. Patton's army led the way, exclaiming, "Let's cut the guts out of these Krauts and get on to Berlin," adding with a flourish, "And when we get to Berlin, I am personally going to shoot that paper-hanging son of a bitch!"*

---

* Hitler at one time held a job as a wall paperer.

On July 25, 1944, the Allies began the big push with First Army in Normandy, breaking through the German lines by the second day. Patton immediately ordered two armored divisions through the break and began moving so fast he ran himself off the maps. Ike had to slow him down to keep continuity in the line.

Hitler continued to aid the Allies by insisting on directing the battle from his comfortable aerie high in the Bavarian Alps. He had fired Erwin Rommel for letting the Allies get ashore and replaced him with Field Marshal Günther von Kluge (who, unbeknownst to Hitler, had been involved in the July plot to kill him). Hitler kept ordering costly counterattacks that were quickly chewing up Kluge's command. When Kluge complained, Hitler ordered him back to Berlin; fearful that the Gestapo had learned of his involvement in the bomb plot against the Führer, Kluge committed suicide by swallowing a cyanide capsule. Rommel later did the same, given a choice by the Gestapo between suicide and a war hero's funeral or execution.

Hitler sent Field Marshal Walter Model to replace Kluge, but Model's report was devastating: withdraw the army immediately or lose it. Thus the Germans began a long, fighting retreat into Germany, with the Allies right behind. German troops left Paris fairly quickly, and quietly, chased by an uprising of French Resistance fighters. German commanders had refused Hitler's orders to destroy the city.

Churchill, meanwhile, had failed to persuade Eisenhower to scrap Operation Anvil in favor of an immediate Allied push up the Adriatic into the Balkans and Austria. On September 12, 1944, he went to a conference in Quebec, where he hoped to persuade Roosevelt to adopt the plan. Churchill warned him of what would happen if the Soviet army got to the Balkan states before the Allies: communism and more communism. Roosevelt was unmoved. Churchill reported that Roosevelt looked "frail."[17]

Churchill was certain now that Stalin intended to expand the Soviet empire wherever he could project power. The prime minister had expected as much from the start, though at first he'd been tempted to believe Stalin when the premier promised he had no designs on European lands. That had simply been a lie. With Stalin's armies there would come new commissars to organize new government employees, who would put in place the brutalized systems that would last for people's lifetimes—and, so far as Churchill knew, forever.

The Soviets, Churchill now believed, would take over Romania and Bulgaria and the Baltic countries, then Hungary, Czechoslovakia, Austria, and perhaps Germany itself. Having grabbed all that, and killed the system of capitalist trade, the rest of Europe was likewise in danger. And who knew, Churchill worried, if Turkey and the whole of the Middle East would be left for the Communists to pick off one state at a time?

When he returned from Quebec, Churchill cabled Roosevelt that he would go and visit Stalin to see what he could do.

On October 9, 1944, Churchill found himself sitting at a conference table in Moscow opposite Joseph Stalin. Present also were the ubiquitous Molotov, as well as the current U.S. ambassador to the Soviet Union, Averell Harriman. Earlier, Churchill and his party had been received in "an extraordinary atmosphere of goodwill." The Russians had presented them at the Bolshoi and the opera, and wined and dined them late into the night. There was none of the suspicion that had pervaded the Tehran Conference, nor the tension and apprehension, now that the Germans had been pushed back hundreds of miles. Churchill opened by magnanimously informing Stalin that the British "were right in interpreting your dissolution of the Comintern as a decision by the Soviet government not to interfere in the internal political affairs of other countries." In truth, the Soviets had done no such thing, and Churchill had actually raised the issue in the manner of a hopeful question.[18]

He was pragmatic enough to see that once the Soviet armies were in a country, there wasn't a lot Great Britain or the United States could do about it. His Mediterranean strategy had been designed to get there first, at least in the Balkans and eastern Europe. But that was history now. Then Churchill did an extraordinary thing. He had arrived at what he thought was a second-best solution. "How would it do for you," he told Stalin, "to have ninety percent predominance in Romania, for us to have ninety percent of the say in Greece, and go fifty-fifty about Yugoslavia?"

While this was being translated, Churchill tore a sheet of paper in half and scribbled down the ratios of proportional interests in what he had just proposed, as well as similar recommendations for Bulgaria and Hungary, and then carrying on the divvying up into Europe as well. He pushed the paper across the table to Stalin, who stared without picking it up, then took a blue pencil and made "a large tick" upon it before passing it back toward Churchill. "It was all settled," Churchill wrote afterward, "in no more time than it takes to set down."[19]

There was a long silence. "The pencilled paper lay at the centre of the table," Churchill recalled. At length Churchill said, "Might in not be thought rather cynical if it seemed we had disposed of these issues, so fateful to millions of people, in such an offhand manner? Let us burn the paper," he proposed.

"No, you keep it," the Soviet premier told him.[20]

By the time Churchill returned to London, the Allies were in Paris, which had been abandoned by the Germans. The city had been officially "liberated" by the French general Jacques Leclerc; de Gaulle arrived shortly afterward at the Ministry of Defense and took charge of everything, General Giraud having faded into the background. Churchill was appalled but nevertheless made a point of persuading Roosevelt that, under the circumstances, the insufferable Frenchman was the best person to lead a country so wounded and discouraged as France.

Ten days before Christmas 1944, American and British troops advanced to the Rhine, having fought their way across all the lurid battlefields of the First World War—Ypres, Belfort, and Verdun. They were poised to cross the river but were held up by floods caused by heavy rains. On December 16, the spearhead of a large German force attacked the center of the Allied line in the heavily forested Ardennes region.

The blow landed on four unprepared divisions of the American VIII Corps, who were in the area for a period of rest and recreation. Eisenhower and the U.S. intelligence services had suspected that "something was afoot" but "its scope and violence came as a surprise," Churchill wrote. The German plan was to cut the Allied line in two with armor and capture the port of Antwerp, the supply lifeline of the British and American forces. The enemy assault created a sixty-mile-deep bulge that lent itself to the name of the battle.

Bad weather kept the Allied air force out of action for the first critical week. Churchill immediately crossed the Channel and went to Eisenhower's headquarters. Unable to offer more infantry when all he had was fighting there already, Churchill promised eighty thousand Royal Marines from the British navy. The situation was so desperate that Churchill ordered a new draft in England for a quarter of a million men.

Eisenhower had been trying without success to relieve the pressure by having the Russians start a large offensive on one of their fronts. Churchill offered to use his personal contacts with Stalin to achieve this end. Without hesitation, Stalin came through, promising a major offensive in his central front as soon as weather permitted.

By Christmas the German offensive had spent much of itself except for a savage Panzer attack on the 101st Airborne that was holding the town of Bastogne. When the Germans came under a flag of truce to demand the 101st surrender, General Anthony McAuliffe replied, "Nuts."

George Patton, meantime, was speeding the U.S. Third Army from about a hundred miles in the south to join the fray; by December 26 his tanks had pitched into the German flank. By January 16 the Allied northern and southern wings closed upon the Germans and began forcing them back eastward. The bulge was soon erased, and the enemy's final offensive of the war was over.

Churchill sent a large force to Greece to intervene in the vacuum left by the Germans, who were now retreating. They had left an army of irregular "partisans," dominated by Communists fighting for control of the country. Churchill was determined that the cradle of democracy would not fall to a totalitarian regime. After heavy fighting in Athens and elsewhere, the Communists asked for a truce, and democracy, or something like it, was restored in Greece.

This did not come without a price to Churchill. The action had "caused a great stir" in both the press and the House of Commons, and nearly undid the fragile coalition government. Churchill defended it, writing in his history of the war, "I saw quite plainly that Communism would be the peril civilization would have to face after the defeat of Nazism and Fascism . . . When three million men were fighting on the Western Front and vast American forces were deployed against Japan in the Pacific the spasms of Greece may seem petty, but nevertheless they stood at the nerve center of power, law, and freedom in the Western World."[21]

By the beginning of 1945 both the Russians and the British-American armies were on the verge of crossing borders into Germany. To Churchill, however, the political situation that was shaping up was less than satisfactory. Romania, Bulgaria, Hungary, and Yugoslavia lay in the Soviet shadow, and Poland, though liberated from the Germans, "had merely exchanged one despotic conqueror for another."

Churchill had been pressing both Roosevelt and Stalin for another Big Three conference, and at length one was organized for February 4, 1945. It would be at Yalta, an old Russian resort in the Crimean Peninsula on the Black Sea, which Stalin could reach by train. This would pose a difficult journey for Churchill, who had developed a fever and was confined to bed aboard his plane—but more so for Roosevelt, who had become gaunt and haunt-eyed. Churchill confided to Harry Hopkins that, "from all the reports I have received about Yalta, we could not have found a worse place for a meeting if we had spent ten years in looking for it."[22]

Roosevelt never shared Churchill's overpowering distaste for communism, viewing it as a sort of rough but benign philosophy for the edification and improvement of lower classes; this was also the position taken by his Department of State. Before Soviet expansion in Europe and elsewhere, before subversion in the United States, before the Communist takeover of China, and before the Soviets' atomic bomb, Russia was an ally.

Not only that, but the president remained mildly suspicious of Churchill's motives vis-à-vis the far-flung British Empire, an enterprise of which Roosevelt disapproved. Though Churchill had signed the Atlantic Charter back in 1941 calling for people to be able to choose their own form of government, it did not square with colonialism and empires, and Roosevelt saw no signs that the British were ready to give up theirs.

Churchill had asked for a preliminary one-on-one meeting with Roosevelt before the Yalta Conference to reach agreement on how to deal with Stalin and his aggressive and expansive ideas. But the president declined on grounds that he didn't have time. In truth, he simply didn't want to get into intrigues with the prime minister. Europe was a long ways off across the Atlantic Ocean, and America at great cost had saved it from the scourge of Nazism. The scourges of communism were not on the president's radar screen.

However, the president did meet early with Churchill on the island of Malta, the prime minister having arrived in his special American C-54 Skymaster four-engine passenger plane, and Roosevelt on the U.S. cruiser *Quincy.* In Churchill's words they "reviewed the whole span of the war," from European operations, to the Pacific, to German U-boats, to the problems in Greece and the Soviet occupation of eastern European countries.

That evening the various parties took off for the Crimea, about twenty-five hundred miles distant. Churchill arrived first and watched Roosevelt being carried down the ramp of his own Skymaster, the *Sacred Cow.* He thought the president looked "frail and ill."

Yalta, on the subtropical shores of the Black Sea, was an old czarist resort filled with palaces and palatial villas that had until recently been occupied by Germans—and before that, for twenty-five years, by the Communist elite. Some of these buildings had been damaged by the fighting, and most were musty from disuse, though the Russians had done their best to bring them up to style and comfort. Churchill's daughter Sarah described their quarters, an 1857 vacation home to one of the Romanovs, as looking "like a Scottish baronial hall inside, and a cross between a Swiss chalet and a mosque on the outside." The grounds were littered with scores of stone lions in all manner of habitation. The British were warned not to stray off because of uncleared German land mines still in the area.[23]

Churchill opened with a hopeful toast. "The whole world will have its eyes on this conference," he said at a small dinner party hosted by Roosevelt. "If it is successful we will have peace for one hundred years." But that was not to be. Other than the lavish dozen-course feasts each night, washed down with "buckets of champagne" and endless vodka toasts, Yalta turned out to be a colossal waste of time. There was enough goodwill to fill a thousand Christmas stockings. But in the end all the major agenda matters were postponed. Roosevelt made the stunning declaration that he did not intend for American troops to remain in Europe more than two years after the war, and Stalin, apparently emboldened by that news, lied or prevaricated about his intentions in eastern Europe.

Roosevelt was anxious to move forward with his United Nations scheme, but a stalemate ensued over how the "Big Four"—the United States, Britain, Russia, and China—would handle voting and vetoing. After days of haggling with Stalin, it was agreed to postpone that question for a future time.

Churchill made valiant efforts to secure Poland for the Poles, going so far as to point out that England had gone to war over Poland in 1939. But Stalin, whose armies now occupied the entire country, obfuscated his designs and frustrated every question until everyone was ready to march off to the banquets and their relentless rounds of toasts. Roosevelt, who was obviously ill and according to Churchill had "only a slender contact with life," was of little help. He didn't want Stalin to feel the Western Allies were "ganging up on him." The president, Churchill told Lord Moran, "is behaving very badly. He won't take any interest in what we're trying to do."

For his part, Stalin had at last developed an effective negotiating style to use with the Allies, which is remarkable because he'd never had to negotiate before: what Stalin wanted he got, and vice versa. One ploy was to assert (falsely) that he had to get permission from the Politburo, or the "Supreme Soviet," or some other Communist council in Moscow, to which he was supposedly answerable. But in fact Stalin was answerable to no one. He reigned supreme.

Another maneuver was to give way on every small issue but stonewall like hell on the large ones until everyone's patience was so tried that the matter was postponed indefinitely. Also, he had developed his own peculiar debating definitions for such terms as "freedom" and "democracy," which he had freely promised for Poland and the other eastern European states as the Red Army cleared out the Germans. Whatever those terms meant to

Roosevelt and Churchill, to Stalin—at least when it came to Poland and the other countries that the Soviet army occupied—they meant "freedom and democracy as dictated in Moscow."[24]

CHURCHILL RETURNED TO LONDON in time for some of the most devastating RAF bombing raids of the war. Many of these were demanded by the Russian army, which was fighting tough battles against Nazi forces on Germany's eastern borders and was using interior rail lines to throw in troops at strategic points. The Russians wanted Allied planes to bomb the German rail hubs to prevent this. One rail center, Dresden, was firebombed by a thousand-plane RAF raid, incinerating nearly thirty thousand residents and even setting the Elbe River afire.

When Churchill inquired about the results of the raid, he was told that Dresden had ceased to exist. This set Churchill to wonder in a memo to the chief of staff whether wreaking such destruction on Germany at this point wasn't counterproductive. Though in the past he'd never expressed regret or moral qualms over such carnage, Churchill now concluded that with the war almost over it would be best to limit the damage to German cities and civil infrastructure to retain as much self-sufficiency as possible in the country after the war had ended. That way, the Allies would not have to spend their own precious resources coming to the aid of an utterly stricken Germany when they had their own rebuilding to do. Tens of thousands of British homes had been destroyed by enemy bombs and rockets; these continued to fall until April.

Soviet commissars marching westward and south with Stalin's armies continued setting up puppet Communist governments in the countries they invaded—Romania, Bulgaria, Yugoslavia, Austria, Hungary, Czechoslovakia—and now they were inside Germany. It was Churchill's worst nightmare, but there was little he could do. Even though Churchill had agreed on paper with Stalin several months earlier that in some of these countries Russia would have a majority of "influence," Churchill never envisioned the Soviets taking over their governments entirely. He continued to bombard Roosevelt with telegrams and messages begging for Eisenhower's armies to move into these countries before the Russians got there, but the president seemed unresponsive. At one point he told Churchill, "I do not get the point." Churchill responded that they were being "defrauded" by Stalin.[25]

When Montgomery's British army reached the Rhine, Churchill immediately departed London for the combat front: a most unwelcome visitor. Montgomery's terrified staff had great difficulty getting the prime minister clear of a hot firing area where enemy bullets kicked up sand and water all around him.

At one point Churchill meandered down to the Rhine and relieved himself in it, fulfilling a promise he had made since the early days of the war. It was undoubtedly a moment of immense satisfaction for the prime minister. Alan Brooke, chief of the Imperial General Staff, recorded that the "Old Man" wore a "boyish grin of contentment."[26]

With the big Soviet push across Germany aimed directly at Berlin, Eisenhower's focus was far to the south, where it had been reported—by Goebbels, of all people—that Hitler had separate armies in the Bavarian Alps that could fend off the Allies for months, if not years, in the rugged mountain passes. Ike's strategy from the outset had been to go after enemy armies—not territory, or places. He and his intelligence advisers apparently fell for this myth, spread via radio broadcasts by Hitler's propaganda minister. Eisenhower headed his forces there instead of Berlin.

The Russians, however, were under no such illusions and pointed their armies straight toward the German capital. Along the way, they carried out a policy of boiling vengeance—murder, looting, and rape almost unparalleled in the history of warfare. Thousands of women committed suicide, and fathers killed their wives and daughters rather than subject them to the depredations of Russian soldiers. The mayhem was horrifying and affected hundreds of thousands, if not millions, of German women.

On April 19, Eisenhower told Churchill that George Patton's Third Army had come across a scene of horrible degradation at a place called Buchenwald. There had been rumors of German slave-labor camps for Jews, Gypsies, and others "undesirable" to the Third Reich, but for the first time these were being discovered by Allied troops. Patton called it "the most horrible sight I have ever seen."

The place abounded in dead bodies, lying naked on the ground, stacked in sheds, buried in pits, and sprinkled with lime to decompose them faster. The Germans had tried to destroy the evidence. As the Allied armies neared, they forced some of the inmates to dig up pits filled with bodies and place them on what Patton described as "a mammoth griddle" composed of crisscrossed rail track set on a brick foundation. They then poured pitch on the bodies and roasted them on a fire of coal and pine.[27]

There was a "whipping table" upon which men were stretched and beaten with a stick the size of a pick handle. Inmates too weak to move were lying in tiers of bunks like "animated mummies." "When we went through they tried to cheer but were too feeble," Patton said. In a large building with tall smokestacks, prisoners were dropped down chutes to a basement where they were strangled with piano wire, then sent by elevator to the second floor where there were rows of furnaces resembling "baker's ovens."[28]

The American commander ordered that all citizens of the nearby town be "escorted into the camp and forced to see these scenes. After their tour, the mayor and his wife went home and hanged themselves."[29]

Churchill was deeply disgusted, not least because reports of such camps and activities had only been rumored and he and his whole staff had mostly dismissed them as exaggerations. He knew that the Nazis were brutal, even barbarous. But he had refused to believe that Germans could be so utterly sadistic.

By the end of April 1945 the Russian army was on the outskirts of Berlin and so began a terrific shelling of the city with several thousand heavy artillery pieces, reducing to rubble what the Allied bombs had missed. Little was spared, including beautiful parks and tree-lined boulevards, historic buildings, churches—even the Berlin zoo. Officially, 125,000 Berliners died or committed suicide during this bombardment. The rest either fled or survived in basements. The German soldiers fired back with artillery of their own and fought fiercely from the upper floors of buildings. Eighty thousand Russian soldiers were among the dead.

On April 20, during a lull in the shelling, Hitler emerged from his underground bunker into the chancellery garden to decorate a squad of boy soldiers, some as young as twelve, with iron crosses for fighting in defense of Berlin, before sending them back out to be killed by the Russians. It was the Führer's fifty-sixth birthday, and all the notorious Nazis were there to celebrate in the dining room deep underground: Göring, Goebbels, Bormann, Ribbentrop, Himmler—as well as the military headmen Admiral Karl Dönitz, Generals Jodl and Keitel, and Albert Speer, the Reich's architect.

Hitler gave Speer special instructions that day. The German people had failed their Führer, and deserved nothing in return. Speer was to order immediate destruction of all infrastructure throughout Germany—power plants, dams, factories, and so forth—the same things the British and Americans had been trying to destroy for four years. Speer ignored the order, which might easily have meant his head. But he was at least more honorable than that.

After dinner these worthies took their leave, some hoping to escape into other countries and others vainly hoping to supplant Hitler as the leader of Germany. What they didn't know was that Eisenhower had decided as a matter of principle that the Allies would not accept surrender from any of the notorious Nazis, Hitler included.

When the bombardment began, Hitler had convinced himself of the notion that the American and German armies would somehow link up and turn on the Soviets. After a solid week of shelling the deluded Führer gave up.

After watching the simpleminded Eva Braun, whom Hitler had married less than two days before, swallow a cyanide capsule, Hitler stuck a pistol into his mouth and pulled the trigger. The pair were later dragged up to the surface by aides and their bodies set afire with gasoline.

Meantime, Churchill received word that Mussolini and his mistress had been killed and hanged by a mob on a scaffold in the town square of a small village in northern Italy. Churchill—likely thinking of his daughter Sarah's Austrian stand-up comic husband—remarked, "Well, at least he had the pleasure of murdering his son-in-law." Il Duce had in fact accomplished this a year earlier by executing his own daughter Edda's husband, Count Galeazzo Ciano, for treason.

In the meanwhile, Yugoslavian Communists sensed blood at Germany's capitulation in Italy and agitated for their Italian Communist cohorts to rise up and seize power. But the Allied forces had split Italy in two and, to Churchill's eternal relief, the effort failed.[30]

Stalin's enormous army was conquering new ground day by day and turning it into Communist territory. "My mind," Churchill said later, "was oppressed with the new and even greater peril which was swiftly unfolding itself to my gaze." To Clementine he wrote, "The misery of the whole world appalls me, and I fear increasingly that new struggles may arise out of those we are successfully ending."

Churchill's gloomy frustration was palpable in remarks he made to the House of Commons in 1945, as Stalin annexed and absorbed European nations: "It is beyond the power of this country to prevent all sorts of things crashing at the present time. The responsibility lies with the United States, and my desire is to give them all the support within my power. If they feel they are not able to do anything, then we must let matters take their course."[31]

ON MAY 3 FOUR GERMAN OFFICERS appeared in General Montgomery's headquarters under a flag of truce. "Who are they? What do they want?" Montgomery asked an interpreter. They were, the Germans said, officers of Field Marshal Wilhelm Keitel. They knew they were surrounded now that the British had arrived, and they wanted to surrender the German army to Montgomery instead of to the Russians, whom they were presently fighting. In fact, they wondered if they might continue fighting the Russians without British interference. Montgomery refused, saying they should have thought about that before they started the war. The British general said that unless they surrendered unconditionally he would keep fighting them. He sent them to have lunch and think it over. They agreed to return next day with a reply. Late that night, Montgomery ordered his troops to stop firing.

The Germans returned next day, May 4, and signed an unconditional surrender document that Montgomery handed them.

Three days later, at Eisenhower's headquarters, General Alfred Jodl surrendered the remainder of German troops unconditionally. The European war was over. Forty million people were dead.[32]

The next day in London Churchill hosted a champagne lunch at Number 10 Downing Street for his closest staff and aides, whom he praised as the "architects of victory." The following afternoon Churchill addressed the nation in a BBC broadcast. A million Londoners, each seemingly waving a small Union Jack, thronged the streets toward Buckingham Palace. The royal couple, with the king wearing his Royal Navy uniform, obliged the crowd and appeared on their balcony to continuous cheering and waving of flags. When Churchill also appeared, the roar of the crowd became frenzied and almost overwhelming.

Church bells had been ringing since dawn all over England, and they continued ringing all day. At 3 p.m., when Churchill was scheduled to speak in the palace yard, a hush grew over a jam-packed crowd. Then the prime minister's voice came through over loudspeakers. His short speech ended with a rousing call: "The evil-doers now lie prostrate before us. Advance Britannia!" There was a gasp from the crowd; then a band struck up "God Save the King" and the throng chimed loudly in. That night, hundreds of huge searchlights were turned on for the first time in years, illuminating buildings instead of a night sky filled with enemy bombers. Throughout the British Isles bonfires burned from dusk long into the gentle night. After five and a half long years Europe was at peace.

CHAPTER SEVENTEEN

By late 1943 Roosevelt had decided to run for a wholly unprecedented fourth term as president of the United States. He was exhausted yet well aware of the pressures involved in being president. But as he considered the continuity of the job in the ongoing crisis, he concluded it would be dangerous to have a new man in his place when the major battles against the Germans and Japanese had yet to be fought. As he had in previous candidacies, Roosevelt shrewdly decided not to actively campaign but to merely shine a spotlight on his regular presidential activities. For vice president, he selected the Missouri senator Harry S. Truman.

In his January State of the Union message, Roosevelt startled everyone when he proposed what he called a second, or economic, Bill of Rights, "under which a new basis for security and prosperity can be established for all—regardless of station, race, or creed." These rights included for everyone:

- The right to a decent home.
- The right to a satisfactory job that would earn enough for adequate food, clothing, and recreation.
- The right to adequate medical care.
- The right to adequate protection from the fears of old age, sickness, accident, and unemployment.
- The right to a good education.[1]

This was as close as Roosevelt got to pure socialism. He laid it on Congress to pass the laws providing for these benefits, and he warned of political consequences if it did not. But legislators, already conscious of antagonisms toward the president's mushrooming social programs, let this pie-in-the-sky "Second Bill of Rights" die a slow but sure legislative death.

On June 14, 1944, Roosevelt left for a promotional visit to the West Coast by way of Hyde Park and, incidentally, a stop at the magnificent New Jersey estate of Lucy Mercer Rutherfurd, whose husband had died several months earlier at the age of eighty-two. There, while the Secret Service entertained Rutherfurd's younger children outside by letting them fire the agents' tommy guns into the lake, Roosevelt and Lucy enjoyed a long and private morning and afternoon together.[2]

Later that summer, Roosevelt felt well enough to sail to Hawaii on the heavy cruiser *Baltimore* to settle a prickly argument between General MacArthur and Admiral Nimitz over the course the war would take as the Allies closed in on Japan. MacArthur's Southwest Pacific command had cut loose from New Guinea and was now barreling northward, "bypassing" Japanese-held islands, toward the Philippines. Meanwhile, the Navy's marines under Nimitz were fighting their way westward across the central Pacific in a series of terrific head-on battles that MacArthur considered wasteful.

It was Nimitz's contention that MacArthur should not try to reconquer Luzon and Manila, but instead focus on invading Formosa (now Taiwan). Here, Japan had installed enormous aerodromes from which it was bombing the islands where the Marines were fighting. MacArthur argued the opposite, on grounds that it would appear to the world inhumane to deliberately bypass the Philippines (an American protectorate) and let the Filipinos continue to suffer under Japanese rule. Also, he continued, it strategically made better sense to reclaim the Philippines (and, not incidentally, fulfill MacArthur's famous pledge "I shall return").

On the first day of the conference in July, Roosevelt made MacArthur and Nimitz sit from morning to sundown in the rear of a large open car— the two of them with the president sitting in between—providing photo ops for newsreel cameras and the press while Roosevelt visited troops and made brief patriotic speeches. MacArthur claimed to be appalled. This was

Roosevelt's very effective notion of political campaigning, and MacArthur's feigned outrage seems almost comical, given his reputation as a camera hog whenever the press was around.

That evening, after dinner, they got down to business, with MacArthur and Nimitz each defending his position and the president acting as referee. In the end, MacArthur got his way in the debate, and the president got his in the upcoming election. He defeated New York governor Thomas E. Dewey, whom his cousin Alice Roosevelt Longworth later famously characterized as looking like the "little man on the wedding cake."

THE ELECTION OF 1944 was as close and contentious as any Roosevelt had endured. Considering his increasing ill health, the president managed to put up a front of high spirits and well-being that was truly remarkable. During October, the weather in the Northeast and Midwest turned miserably cold and rainy, but Roosevelt was up to the challenge. Stopping his train in Brooklyn, despite pleas from his doctor Admiral Ross McIntire to rest up and conserve his energy for a dinner speech that evening before the Foreign Policy Association, Roosevelt took to his open-topped Packard limousine in a freezing rain and made a four-hour waving tour of four of the five New York City boroughs, ending up in Manhattan with crowds along the sidewalks estimated by police as upwards of 3 million.

This reception so invigorated the old campaigner that he repeated it in Philadelphia and elsewhere, bolstered by the news that MacArthur had at last landed in the Philippines. A few days later, he learned that the U.S. Navy had won a spectacular victory over the Japanese fleet in Leyte Gulf, in what was claimed to be the largest naval battle in history.

Tom Dewey was a youthful and vigorous former prosecutor who had made a name for himself busting New York organized crime, an act that had carried him to the governor's chair. He had learned somehow of the existence of Magic, the top secret U.S. code-breaking operation that had been able to intercept Japanese naval communications. Here was proof, Dewey concluded, that Roosevelt knew in advance of the Japanese attack on Pearl Harbor but had kept it a secret so the United States would be led into the war.

Dewey was planning to use this bombshell information at an appropriate opportunity until George Marshall found out about it. He wrote him a letter, pleading against any unmasking of the code-reading capabilities of the armed services. As a patriot there wasn't much Dewey could do but comply with the Army's chief of staff. He was furious, though, because he considered Roosevelt a traitor and a liar in the Pearl Harbor affair. What he didn't know was that at the time of the Japanese attack on Pearl the American code breakers were reading only the Japanese diplomatic code, not the naval code that might have been useful to predict an attack on Hawaii.

In Chicago, a crowd of a quarter million cheered Roosevelt for ten minutes before he told them, "Well, they [the Republicans] say in effect just this: 'Those incompetent bunglers and blunderers in Washington have passed a lot of excellent laws about social security and labor, and farm relief, and soil conservation—and we promise that if we are elected we will not change any of them.'

"And they go on to say: 'Those same, quarrelsome tired old men—they have built the greatest military machine the world has ever known, which is fighting its way to victory.' And they say: 'If you elect us, we promise not to change any of that either.'[3]

"Therefore, say these Republican orators, 'it is time for a change.'"

About all Dewey had in the way of political argument was to point out that under Roosevelt's leadership the United States had been almost completely unprepared for the war. But that was four long years in the past, and the Allies were clearly winning now. His other argument centered on the president's cozy relationship with the possibly Communist-influenced CIO labor union, but neither did this seem a big concern to the voters, for the United States and the Communist Soviet Union were now allies in the war.

When the results were tallied, Roosevelt received more than 53 percent of the popular vote and 432 electoral votes to 99 for Dewey.

★★★★★

It was after this election that Roosevelt began to slip into a chronic spiral of ill health. Ever since polio had confined him to a wheelchair he had developed pulmonary disorders and other ailments consistent with living an inactive life, including a pack-a-day or more habit of unfiltered cigarettes. His daughter, Anna, who now lived in the White House, also was concerned over the palsied shaking of her father's hands and alerted his personal physician Dr. McIntire.

McIntire put Roosevelt in Bethesda Naval Hospital for a medical workup. Doctors diagnosed the president with dangerously high blood pressure, hypertensive heart disease, an enlarged heart with cardiac failure in the left ventricle, and troubling gastrointestinal problems. The president also had considerable bouts with breathlessness and a gray pallor in his face. He was sixty-two years old. McIntire gave orders that no one should reveal Roosevelt's diagnosis, including to Roosevelt himself.

In June, when the D-day landings took place on the coast of France, Roosevelt had wanted to be with Winston Churchill, among the first visitors to the fighting front. But his weakened condition foreclosed that possibility.

Roosevelt was put on a low-fat diet by his doctors to lower his weight. It worked, and he lost twenty pounds. But this served to make him look unusually sallow as he continued to wear the same shirts and suits, which didn't fit anymore. Rumors began to spread that he had cancer; *Time* magazine, then owned by Republican Henry Luce, declared that Roosevelt looked like "an old man."

Roosevelt paid these things little attention. He was more interested in promoting his design for a United Nations, which, led by the United States, Russia, Great Britain, and China, would "police" the world, making it free of wars and undemocratic uprisings.

Roosevelt was a Wilsonian idealist who always believed that the former president's League of Nations scheme, if it had been backed by America's might, could have prevented World War II. He never seemed to comprehend with Churchill's prophetic clarity that a titanic conflict over the future of the world between totalitarian communism and democratic capitalism was going to dominate the second half of the twentieth century. When he returned from the conference in Tehran, Roosevelt remarked to one of his aides that after the war he expected more trouble from the British than from the Russians. Every time he asked Churchill when the British were going to return Hong Kong to the Chinese, the president complained, "All I get is a grunt."[4]

Roosevelt continued to see Lucy Mercer regularly after her husband died. Daughter Anna Roosevelt would arrange small dinner parties at the White House, and sometimes at Warm Springs she would be the go-between. Eleanor by now had divested herself of Lorena Hickok and was said by some, including the FBI, to have become romantically involved with a radical young writer and drafted serviceman named Joseph Lash, who later won a Pulitzer Prize for writing the first lady's biography. According to Anna, a military officer one day brought her a packet of intercepted censored "love letters" to Eleanor from Lash, who was then posted (by personal order of Roosevelt) in the South Seas. The officer requested that she give them to her father. When she did, Roosevelt took them from her "without a word," she said, and put them away.*

WHEN ROOSEVELT ARRIVED AT YALTA in February 1945 many people commented on his sallow appearance, including Churchill's doctor Lord Moran, who diagnosed advanced hardening of the arteries of the brain and gave the American president only a few months to live. As leader of the discussions Roosevelt was said to have been lethargic but effective. He was certainly handicapped by the absence of Harry Hopkins, whose stomach cancer had confined him to bed during the entire conference.

On Roosevelt's return voyage, the battle cruiser USS *Quincy* anchored in the Suez Canal's Great Bitter Lake, known biblically as Lake Marah. (Ironically, this was the spot where Moses, leading the Exodus of Jews out of Egypt, had stopped over on his way to the promised land.) It was here that

---

* The FBI file asserts that Army counterintelligence officers who were surveilling Lash because of his radical associations made a recording of the two having intercourse in Lash's Chicago hotel room. Some historians and experts have questioned the veracity of the account.

the president met with Saudi Arabia's king Ibn Saud over the fate of Jewish refugees from Europe.

The king's arrival on the U.S. destroyer *Murphy* was an astonishing spectacle to the president and his entourage. Abdulaziz Ibn Saud appeared, like Cleopatra on her barge, perched on a gilded throne atop a pile of Turkish rugs on the destroyer's forward gun deck. The entire forecastle was bedecked by a ferocious-looking cadre of royal bodyguards, dark-skinned and barefoot, brandishing long-barreled rifles and unsheathed scimitars.

Behind the fo'c'sle, an enormous canvas sleeping tent had been erected for the king and his forty-eight-man retinue—including the king's personal food taster and an astrologer—all of whom slept on the rugs. On the stern of the destroyer was a flock of eighty sheep to provide the Arabs' meals. According to presidential biographer Frank Freidel, the *Murphy's* crew received "an unwanted thrill" when they discovered one of the king's servants cooking lamb on an open fire at the entrance to the ship's powder magazine. One American witness billed it as "a spectacle out of the past on the deck of a modern man-of-war."[5]

The sight became stranger still when the king, "a whale of a man" in abundant robes with gold bunting and a dagger at his waist, was hoisted in the *Murphy's* bosun's chair, transferred aerially across the waters of the Great Bitter Lake, and deposited on the *Quincy's* deck. Here, he was introduced to Roosevelt, who was wearing his long blue navy cape and battered fedora. At the behest of the Navy, among others, the president made every effort to flatter the king, whose small country was sitting atop the world's largest oil reserves that were presently under exclusive contract to California's Standard Oil Company.[6]

More important at the moment was the terrible issue of some ten thousand desperate Jewish refugees who had been driven from their homelands by the Nazis. They now wished to immigrate to Palestine, a British mandate from the old League of Nations largely influenced by the Arab League, of which Saudi Arabia was a founding member. The Saudi king's response to Roosevelt's entreaty that these Jews be allowed to settle in the highly disputed Palestinian lands was so emphatic that the president could not bring himself even to paraphrase it for the press, let alone repeat it verbatim. All he told reporters was that "it was perfectly awful."[7]

Never one to give up on an important issue, Roosevelt brought up the subject of Jewish immigration several times again during the next four hours of conversation. But each time, the king's response was more "emphatic" than the last. At length Roosevelt changed the subject to agriculture, an idea that ranged back to his flight over the Saudi desert en route to the Tehran Conference in 1943. The president raised the prospect of irrigating the desert by pumping a wealth of underground water that would make the arid land bloom with fruits and vegetables. The king replied that would be okay with him so long as such environmental prosperity "would not be inherited by the Jews."[8]

ON MARCH 1, SEVERAL DAYS AFTER his return from Yalta, Roosevelt addressed a joint session of Congress. This time he did not have to endure the agony of standing through his talk but was rolled out in his chair to a desk cluttered with a dozen microphones. He told the congressmen that he had seen what the Germans did in the Crimea, and that "there was no place existing on earth for German militarism and Christian decency."

During the speech, Roosevelt looked physically in good shape; his voice was strong and steady and the bags under his eyes had receded. He told his audience: "I come from the Crimea conference in the firm belief that we have made a good start on the road to a world of peace . . . a permanent structure of peace upon which we can build."

It was an early spring in Washington, the spring of 1945. The cherry blossoms dripped from the trees along the Tidal Basin and covered the ground like fruits from exotic cornucopias. In the White House, there was always the bustle of official business and correspondence, meetings, decisions, speeches, and letters to be answered. Roosevelt slept late more often now. When Eleanor wasn't around, Lucy Rutherfurd often came to dinners.

Roosevelt protested in writing the fact that Stalin was now closing off Poland and other areas under Soviet occupation; the notion of holding free elections seemed to have evaporated. Stalin did hold one free election—in Hungary—but the Communists were defeated, so he nullified the results.

"We can't do business with Stalin," Roosevelt declared privately. "He has broken every one of the promises he made at Yalta." In trying to square this disillusionment with what he'd told Congress earlier that month, Roosevelt confided to the *New York Times* that "Stalin is either not a man of his word or not in control in the Kremlin."

By the first of April Roosevelt was so run-down that he needed to go to Warm Springs for its restorative atmosphere. He always felt good at Warm Springs; the mere idea of the place revived him. Once in Georgia, he got from his train into his special car with the hand controls and drove himself to the Little White House. The troubles of the world of course followed him there: a bitter Communist uprising in Yugoslavia and Russian intransigence at the fledgling United Nations, which was then being organized in San Francisco. He began to tire again and easily became lethargic, especially in the afternoons.

But at night, Roosevelt became a different man. After a cocktail or two he perked up and was lively and smiling, the cares having vanished for that particular day. Accompanying him in Georgia were his two favorite cousins Polly Delano and Daisy Suckley. Lucy Rutherfurd was there as well, with her friend the artist Elizabeth Shoumatoff, who was painting a watercolor portrait of the president for Lucy.[9]

The morning of April 12 began on a high note. Roosevelt sat in his favorite leather chair at Mme. Shoumatoff's request, wearing his big navy cape draped over his shoulders. He joked and told stories as he worked on his papers at a card table set by the fireplace. Shoumatoff was at her easel with her watercolor paints.

At 1:15 p.m., right before lunch, Roosevelt suddenly put his hand up to his forehead. "I have a terrible headache," he said. His hand dropped and he slumped sideways. Mme. Shoumatoff gasped and let out a small scream. It happened very suddenly. Then everyone was moving around, fetching the doctor, calling the Secret Service men—doing something. Arthur Prettyman, the president's valet, rushed in. He and another man carried the unconscious Roosevelt to his bedroom, which was right off the living room, and laid him on the bed.[10]

The president was in a coma, perspiring heavily, his breathing slow and shallow. The doctor, a young Navy commander, administered drugs meant to revive him but with no effect. A long wait began; CPR was started. The doctor spoke with McIntire in Washington and told him the situation was serious. Eleanor was notified. Shoumatoff gathered up Lucy and summoned their chauffeur. Within a few minutes the two women were off the property, headed for Lucy's winter estate in Aiken, South Carolina.[11]

At 3:35 p.m. Franklin D. Roosevelt died.

ELEANOR ARRIVED EARLY the next morning, dressed in black, having flown to Warm Springs with Dr. McIntire and Roosevelt's press secretary Steve Early. She entered the Little White House cottage to find Roosevelt's cousins Polly Delano and Daisy Suckley, valet Arthur Prettyman, and his secretary Grace Tully. Also present were two local morticians.

Eleanor remarked to no one in particular that she was going in to see her husband. After about five minutes she returned, dry-eyed but slightly flustered. The morticians asked about caskets—mahogany, bronze? Eleanor wasn't sure. McIntire said bronze.

A funeral train was prepared by the Southern Railway Company, its engines and cars painted a gleaming forest green. Two thousand soldiers had been ordered up from nearby Fort Benning to line the road from the Little White House compound to the train station at Warm Springs; a military band was present with a drum corps to play the funeral dirge. Before the funeral party had departed, someone noticed there was no American flag draping the casket. One of the Army officers ordered that the one flying from the flagpole in the circle out front of the cottage be hauled down and used for the presidential shroud.

The train left at 10:13 for the twenty-four-hour trip to Washington. All along the route people lined the tracks in respect. The president's flag-draped casket could be seen through the big panoramic parlor windows in the last car. Men stood with their hats in hand, women and children looked on in awe. Some were daubing at their eyes with handkerchiefs or balled fists.

In the capital the next morning, the casket was removed from the train and strapped on a black artillery caisson pulled by six white horses from the elite honor guard unit at Fort Myer, Virginia. The procession was augmented by various units from the Army, Navy, Marines, and the Brigade of Midshipmen of the U.S. Naval Academy at Annapolis, as well as motorcycle police, bands, and guidon units with flags. Limousines bearing family and friends headed the procession, more than two miles long. An estimated 350,000 mourners lined Pennsylvania Avenue as the funeral cortege made its way to the White House.

The Blue Room was filled with prominent guests, including President and Mrs. Harry S. Truman and their daughter, Roosevelt's old opponent Thomas Dewey, Mrs. Woodrow Wilson, all the cabinet members and Supreme Court justices, a great many ambassadors, and office staff. The family sat in front of the casket, which was surrounded by heaps of flowers. At exactly 4 p.m. the Right Reverend Angus Dun, Episcopal bishop of the Washington diocese, stepped in front of the casket and told the mourners to sing the naval hymn "Eternal Father, Strong to Save," one of Roosevelt's favorites.

Among those *not* present was Winston Churchill, who had intended to come all along and actually had his Skymaster warming up on the runway. But minutes before takeoff he got into a snit with his foreign minister, Anthony Eden, who also wanted to go. In a decision that the prime minister regretted to the end of his days he decided to remain.

Churchill had, however, penned a note to Eleanor: "I feel so deeply for you all. As for me, I have lost a dear and cherished friendship which was forged in the fire of war. I trust you may find consolation in the glory of his name and the magnitude of his work."[12]

The Russians suspected Roosevelt had been poisoned, and Stalin himself recommended an autopsy. The Japanese, on the other hand, for reasons known only to themselves, sent planes out to the U.S. fleet fighting at Okinawa to drop leaflets expressing regret at Roosevelt's passing.[13]

Across America at that moment, most things came to a halt while a two-minute silence was observed for people to pause and meditate on the passing of their longtime leader. Radios went silent, as did Wall Street stock tickers. Hats were doffed; some people kneeled, some wept. The service was simple; more hymns were sung. It was over in twenty minutes.

After Eleanor had arrived at the Little White House and had her time with the deceased Franklin, she sat with the women in the small living room and asked each what had happened. When she got to Polly Delano she was told that Mme. Shoumatoff was there painting her husband's portrait for Lucy Mercer Rutherfurd, who was also in attendance. Not only that, she explained that Mrs. Rutherfurd was frequently present at White House dinners when Eleanor was away, and that her own daughter, Anna, was the facilitator of these rendezvous. Eleanor apparently absorbed this information without comment. But the news would have obviously come as a blow, for she had not only just lost her husband but suddenly come to the understanding that he had carried on a twenty-eight-year-long affair with the woman he'd promised never to see again back in 1919.

Following the funeral service in the White House, Eleanor had summoned Anna to her sitting room and confronted her furiously with Polly's revelations. Anna is said to have admitted to sponsoring the Lucy Rutherfurd dinners but said she did so only to assuage her father's "loneliness."

These scenes are recorded in detail in books by Jim Bishop and Joseph Persico. But only Bishop—whose book *FDR's Last Year* is unsourced—says, in his introduction, that Anna Roosevelt spoke with him at length about the relationship between Lucy Rutherfurd and her parents. I can find no reason not to take him at his word. However she mourned or remembered her husband, Eleanor continued to make her own important contributions to world affairs. After Franklin's death she would go on to serve as U.S. delegate to the United Nations.

LATE ON THE AFTERNOON of Roosevelt's funeral, the train departed for Hyde Park where the bells in the small St. James Episcopal church were tolling for its most illustrious senior warden. Family, friends, and dignitaries crowded into the small hemlock-hedged rose garden, where Roosevelt's parents were buried. A grave had been dug, surrounded by enormous sprays of flowers. A number of local residents had brought small handpicked bouquets that they laid beside the bier.

Cannons began to boom out the final twenty-one-gun salute as the artillery caisson with the casket was hauled up the hill by the six white horses. A seventh horse, in the lead, was caparisoned in black with boots reversed in the stirrups. The West Point band played the funeral march, while a drum corps beat out the muffled cadence. When the mourners were situated by the grave, the entire six-hundred-man body of West Point cadets in their dress grays filed into the enclosure, two by two, and took their places at attention in the rear along the hemlock hedge.

The rector of St. James, in full regalia, performed the brief burial service. At the end, a rifle salute was fired over the grave. Then, as the casket was lowered, the band played "Hail to the Chief" one final time.

Franklin Roosevelt's story thus was ended. Loved by many, hated by others, he had come into office as an optimist in the depths of the Great Depression. It took nearly a decade for the economy to rectify itself, and then only when the nation began gearing up for war. But Roosevelt's sunny disposition in his speeches and fireside chats reassured people that their government had not forgotten them. Then, as war clouds darkened, he was quick to see the dangers, and smart enough to navigate past the entangling fingers of the isolationists to help a struggling Britain when she had no other friend in the world.

After Pearl Harbor, Roosevelt became an ideal leader in the Allied arrangement. His judgments were cautious and well considered. Thankfully, he had listened to Winston Churchill's warnings about trying to invade France too early, even when his military advisers thought otherwise. There were great and terrible decisions to be made, and Roosevelt never shied from making them. If he had a fault, it was in placing too much trust in Stalin's Soviet Union. His role in the eradication of the evil Axis is undiminished. Roosevelt's hand, from the United Nations to the World Bank, is seen everywhere in the brave new world that emerged from the ashes of World War II.

IN 1944, WITH THE GERMANS now driven back across their own borders, Joseph Stalin turned his attention to domestic issues. He had become concerned that nationalism in his various provinces—especially the Caucasus—was holding sway over communism, a development that needed eradication at any cost.

Earlier on, the war had caused Stalin to relax some previous controls over nationalism on the theory that people would fight harder if they felt they were fighting for their national homeland. But now this must be reined in. He had already banished numerous ethnic groups to Siberia or Far East Asia—but there were yet more whom he feared were clinging to their national or ethnic identities. Stalin's version of communism had no use for "diversity" of any stripe; these people and all their instincts would have to be crushed. According to historian Edvard Radzinsky, "Terror had almost vanished from the land by 1944. But on the threshold of victory, Stalin began reviving it."

Lavrenty Beria, head of the secret police, was selected for the job. All through the spring and summer of 1944, NKVD agents uprooted hundreds of thousands of Chechens, Balkans, Ingushes, Kalmyks, Tatars, and other ethnic peoples and shipped them bag and baggage to the wilderness lands beyond the Ural Mountains, where many became indentured workers in the Soviet gulag system. Some of these ethnic groups had in fact defected or cozied up to the German occupiers—not because they were admirers of Nazism but because they abhorred Stalin's version of communism. Or any version of it, for that matter.*

Russia's Jews, whom Stalin referred to as "rootless cosmopolitans," came in for a special malediction. They had made the mistake of asking Stalin to give them a national homeland in the Crimea, which had recently been (forcibly) vacated by the Tatars. Instead, the Jews were denounced for stealing Russian inventions and giving them to foreigners, an accusation that soon "degenerated into lunacy." Public announcements were made

---

* There had been talk of deporting the population of Ukraine—all 50 million people—but it was dropped after calculations showed there were insufficient rail facilities.

that "the discoveries of Russian scientists had been pirated wholesale." The steam engine, for example, had not been invented by Watt but by a Siberian worker named Polzunov; Edison had not invented the electric lightbulb, a Russian named Yablochkov had. Popov, not Marconi, had invented the wireless radio; Petrov discovered the electric arc; and a man named Mozhaisky, not the Wright brothers, had built and flown the first successful airplane—and so on. These absurd claims generated gales of horse laughter worldwide and were soon put under wraps—except within the Soviet school system, where they continued to be taught as true. The Jews would not get the Crimea as a homeland, but Stalin needed them "temporarily." Later, their time would come.[14]

Religion also came under scrutiny. In early 1943, in the war's most critical stages, Stalin had relaxed the state's opposition to organized religion. He did so in order that people—soldiers and civilians alike—might find solace for their hardships through God. Twenty thousand Russian Orthodox churches reopened, and their priests were freed from the work camps. But pure, unadulterated communism had room for no god. Stalin understood that churches were by their very definition counterrevolutionary. Thus, he now installed as the official government overseer of the nation's churches one G. Karpov, a colonel in the NKVD. Observation and persecution of religion began anew, though not as blatantly as before. Stalin merely set into motion a higher authority to ensure that good Christians must be good Communists too.

As the German armies receded, the extent of the destruction they wrought was practically unimaginable. Nearly two thousand Russian towns and seventy thousand villages had been obliterated within the area of German occupation. Not a factory, mine, commercial enterprise, or home of any sort was left standing. Nor did schools, hospitals, libraries, or public or private buildings escape the Nazi torch. Millions of displaced people crowded the countryside begging for food. Gangs of orphaned children with neither public assistance nor private charity roamed about, stealing.

Repairing all this was a task of Herculean magnitude—which, at least, would be easier in a command economy such as the Soviet Union's, although terribly hard on the people. Every able-bodied man and woman must be put back to work, came the orders. Stalin gave the job of solving all this to Beria and the NKVD.

More than 26 million Soviet citizens had been killed during the war. Most were soldiers, but 8 million were civilians, most of these murdered by the Germans out of sheer meanness. The devastation was a breathtaking travesty.

★★★★★

WHEN NEWS CAME OF ROOSEVELT'S DEATH Stalin wrote a heartfelt letter in which he hardly mentioned wartime decisions or cooperation but spoke of the genuine friendship he felt for the American president. In private, however, he called him "weak and rapacious."[15]

As the Russians drove deeper into Germany, they recovered Soviet prisoner of war camps run by the Germans. An estimated 2 million Soviet POWs resided there—and, true to his declaration of 1942, these unfortunates were treated by Stalin as "malicious deserters."

As they were repatriated, the former POWs were sent immediately to prison labor camps in Siberia and elsewhere for long terms of incarceration. Some were singled out for execution. Not only that, but Stalin had demanded—and the British and Americans had shamefully acceded—that all Soviet prisoners of war in camps liberated by Eisenhower's armies also be returned to Russia. It was apparently quite a pitiful sight, as these miserable creatures who had been nearly starved for years in German POW camps lived to see victory in the war but resisted with all their might the possibility of being returned to their own homeland. Many cried and begged not to be sent back to Russia, but it did no good. The Americans and British turned them over anyway.

As well, the Soviet government had extracted from the Allies a promise to turn over all Soviet citizens living in areas under Allied control, many of whom had *escaped* from the Communist country years before; many of these had, in fact, fought for the White Russians against the Communists. There was little doubt of their fate when the NKVD finished investigating them. Count Nikolai Tolstoy-Miloslavsky (a relation of Leo) cataloged this eyewitness account of the proceedings in Graz, Austria, from a British sergeant as the former prisoners were handed over to Russian representatives: "As they reached the reception point, a woman rushed to the viaduct over the River Muir and threw her child into the water, then jumped in herself . . . Men and women were herded together into a huge concentration camp fenced with barbed wire . . . That nightmare will remain with me as long as I live."[16]

German prisoners did not fare well in Stalin's POW camps either. Of an estimated 3 million Germans captured by the Soviets, an estimated 1 million died in labor camps. Most were held long after the war had ended. The last German prisoner wasn't released until 1956.[17]

By 1945 STALIN'S AGE was beginning to catch up to him. He was slightly stooped, his hearing was weak, and he had begun to dodder. He had little in the way of family. His son Yakov, whom he had disavowed, had been killed by the Germans; Vasily was a hopeless alcoholic; and he was more or less estranged from his daughter Svetlana, although she occasionally still served as a hostess to his mostly stag dinner parties. These affairs over time had become more and more bizarre.

All manner of pranks and practical jokes were encouraged, such as unfastening the lid of the saltshaker so that it dumped its entire contents into the food of the unsuspecting butt of the joke—who, often as not, was Molotov, Stalin's longtime foreign minister. Large ripe tomatoes were slipped onto the seats of chairs. Vodka was poured into wine bottles. The banquets began late and ended in the early hours, with a great many vodka toasts that often devolved into levity, insults, and sometimes veiled threats. Charles de Gaulle was present at one of these; Stalin rose to toast his quartermaster general, who was charged with supplying the army on the fighting fronts. "And he'd better do his job," the Soviet dictator concluded of the quartermaster with a cringeworthy smile, "or he'll be hanged. That's the custom in our country." Later, Stalin jokingly threatened to banish his interpreter to Siberia because he "knew too much."

Stalin had tried of late to ingratiate himself with the large Alliluyev family of his wife Nadya; he'd made little headway, since he had imprisoned several Alliluyev women because they also "knew too much" about her suicide. The others were terrified of him.[18]

When the war finally ended, it was decided to throw the largest victory parade in the history of the world. Millions of Soviet soldiers, interspersed by an endless procession of tanks, artillery pieces, bands, and other military paraphernalia, marched before Marshal Stalin's reviewing stand. It was at first planned to have the nation's first marshal lead the parade on a white horse—but at the last moment Stalin demurred, citing his age and telling General Zhukov, "No, you ride it."

This was the last publicity stunt accorded Zhukov or any of the other Soviet marshals, whom Stalin feared might somehow eclipse him as the most worshiped figure in the Communist world. After this event Zhukov, who had been the head of the Soviet army, was reassigned to a lowly command in the Urals. Agents tapped the phones of generals and recorded their conversations. Some were confronted with the fact that they had made disparaging remarks about the Stalin regime; these men were shot, their families banished to Siberia. Posters of a heroic-looking Stalin, replete in his marshal's uniform, his pockmarks airbrushed and a little gray now added to his hair, flooded the land on billboards and the walls of schools, factories, and government buildings. The dictator's cult of personality was at its height.

The war had given Stalin total control of the government and its people, and he intended to keep it that way. Soviet Russia had become government by fear and firing squad (if it wasn't that before). No one felt completely safe, including Stalin. His most immediate threat would have been from Lavrenty Beria, with his huge secret police apparatus. So Stalin—gently, by his standards—stripped Beria of the part of his job having to do with internal affairs. Likewise, he removed Georgy Malenkov from the position of chairman of the Committee on the Rehabilitation of Liberated Areas, which had become, essentially, a criminal enterprise. Whole factories from

Germany were dismantled and "liberated" back to Russia under war reparations agreements. But many of the eastern European countries found that estate-size mansions, complete with their automobiles, livestock, shrubbery, and even their servants, were also "liberated" to the Soviet Union. This last was not the reason Malenkov was fired, however; the reason was that he was sloppy with the liberated factories, many of which stood for years with their machinery in rusting heaps beside railroad tracks.

In July 1945 the final conference of the Big Three was held at Potsdam, on the outskirts of ruined Berlin. The composition of the group, however, was much altered. Roosevelt had died in office earlier that year, and President Harry S. Truman now represented the United States among the Allies. In the British delegation, Churchill was joined by the socialist Clement Attlee; back home the British awaited the outcome of a general election, and Attlee stood to replace Churchill as prime minister if the Tories lost. When Churchill expressed anxiety about the election outcome, Stalin remarked that he was sure the British statesman had nothing to worry about. After all, one of Stalin's favorite aphorisms was: "It doesn't matter who votes, it only matters who counts the votes."

As he had at Tehran and Yalta, Stalin spent his time at Potsdam consolidating "his unavowed intention of dominating and, in effect, annexing eastern European states, which later became known as 'Soviet satellites.'"[19] Stalin's position on these matters was dictated by the fact that his armies occupied the territories in question. He once privately told a young Communist visitor from Yugoslavia that whoever rules a country militarily dictates the kind of government that it can have—"and that includes France, but we do not now have the ability to go into Paris," Stalin said.[20]

The war in Europe may have been over, but the war in the Pacific was very much alive. At one point, President Truman took Stalin aside and informed him that the United States had just successfully conducted its first test of an atomic bomb. The Soviet premier seemed unperturbed by this news—even disinterested.

Stalin, of course, had known about the British and American work on the bomb all along, from Soviet spies such as Klaus Fuchs, Julius and Ethel Rosenberg, and others. When he realized that the Americans actually had one of the weapons, Stalin immediately ordered Beria to redouble his efforts to produce a nuclear bomb in "a short period of time." This resulted in increased spying, and by 1949 the Soviets had assembled and successfully tested an atomic weapon along the American design. Two years later, they produced an even more powerful one of their own design.[21]

Stalin now commanded the world's largest modern military and, along with his satellite states, the largest bloc on the European continent. But the fact that peace was at hand was not what Stalin needed. In his Orwellian world, what he needed was enemies: something his millions of subjects could hate and strive *against,* something that would make them work harder and feel more loyalty to the Motherland. Ironically, it was Winston Churchill, the out-of-work former British PM, who fulfilled Stalin's need.

On March 5, 1946, Churchill took to the podium of small Westminster College in Fulton, Missouri, and gave his famous Iron Curtain speech. It received worldwide coverage, and its hostility toward the Soviet Union was the final straw. Stalin could now blame everything that was wrong on his former allies, who now had revealed themselves as enemies. The Comintern, which had never fully gone out of business, was back in operation at full speed—and all roads led to Moscow.

Churchill had lambasted the Russians openly at a time when the U.S. State Department was still trying to keep the Grand Alliance from falling apart. The United States did not officially break with the Soviet Union until June 25, 1950, when Kim Il Sung's Communist North Korea launched a full-scale attack on neighboring democratic South Korea, capturing its capital Seoul in three days. It appeared that nothing could stop the Communist onslaught, which was armed and supplied by Stalin's military via Russia's Trans-Siberian Railway. But Stalin had made a grave miscalculation.

Just as it appeared all of South Korea would fall, President Harry Truman sent his diplomats to Roosevelt's new United Nations, where they secured a favorable vote in the Security Council for armed intervention. The Soviet Union might have blocked the vote, but Stalin had been boycotting the UN over its policy of recognizing Chiang Kai-shek's government in Taiwan as the legitimate Chinese authority. As a result, Stalin found himself confronting an alliance of eighteen nations who agreed to join the United States in the fight against Communist aggression.[22]

Douglas MacArthur was selected to drive the North Koreans out of the South, which he did in 1950 with a brilliant seaborne invasion at the port of Inchon that split the Communist forces in two and soon pushed them back beyond their own border at the 38th Parallel. Then the Chinese Communists of Mao Tse-tung invaded South Korea, and the fighting began all over again until it bogged down into a bitter and protracted stalemate.

One thing the Korean War did was to cement Western nations, including Australia and New Zealand, against communism. It strengthened Stalin's case that capitalist countries were the implacable enemies of the Soviet Union. But the expense of the war was a strain on the Soviets, who were still trying to rebuild their shattered country after World War II. In the air, American jet fighters battled Russian MiGs flown by Soviet aviators, and the Americans were getting the better of it. Stalin had been promised a short, decisive war by Kim Il Sung. But instead the conflict dragged on for three years, with Kim continuously begging for more help until a Soviet-backed truce was finally declared, the North Koreans pushed back into their own territory.

IN 1950, THE MAYOR OF Leningrad and six fellow Communist Party officials were arrested, tried, and shot in one batch for treason. Stalin had begun another purge. Two thousand other officials from that city were exiled to Siberia. The Politburo, where the Soviet power lay, resembled as much as anything a den of thieves whose members were engaged in ongoing conspiracies against one another. The chief conspirator, Stalin, having disposed in one way or another of most of his old friends as well as enemies, now engineered Molotov's turn at the screws. First Stalin had Molotov's wife arrested. She was Jewish, and the rap was that she had become too friendly with Israeli envoy Golda Meir, whom she had known since school days. Next, Molotov was sacked as foreign minister. Stalin had his home telephone bugged, and Molotov was no longer invited to the dictator's dacha for banquets. His wife remained in jail, accused of being at the head of a Jewish conspiracy to turn the Crimea into "a California for Jews." In 1952, Stalin gave what would be his last speech to the Politburo, denouncing Molotov and others for being "cowards and defeatists." Later it was charged that Molotov was a British spy because he'd spent a few moments alone with British foreign minister Anthony Eden while on a Scottish train in 1943. He must have known what was coming next but fate intervened.[23]

ON THE NIGHT OF MARCH 1, 1953, Stalin suffered a cerebral hemorrhage. He was found by his bodyguards unconscious on the bedroom floor of his dacha outside Moscow, having spent the night before drinking heavily with his Kremlin cronies.

Stalin was placed on a couch and a blanket put over him. No one thought to summon a doctor; instead a call was placed to the minister of security in Moscow, who passed the buck to Beria and Malenkov. These two, plus Nikolai Bulganin and Nikita Khrushchev—the four top Communist lieutenants—drove out to the dacha to have a look. Once more, medical attention was not immediately sought, giving rise to suspicions that this was deliberately done to see if Stalin might die. All four, in some way or other, were on Stalin's hit list.

When doctors at last were summoned, they found that Stalin was paralyzed on his right side and his breathing was poor. Medical advice was sought at once from, ironically, Moscow's Lubyanka prison and secret police headquarters, where many of Russia's most distinguished physicians (most of them Jewish) had been recently incarcerated by Stalin, who insisted that they were traitors and spies. This consultation revealed that the prognosis was grave and death likely imminent. Svetlana, now twenty-eight and twice divorced, was called, as was Stalin's son Vasily, who arrived drunk and was asked to leave.

Stalin lingered for four days before expiring on March 5 after undergoing a massive stomach hemorrhage. He was seventy-four years old. Mr. and Mrs.

Molotov were off the hook. Meanwhile, like conspirators in a Shakespearean play, the four Soviet top brass began arguing over the order of succession. Intermittently, during the deathwatch, they had gone over to Stalin's unconscious form and touched him—Beria, according to one account, "slobbering on Stalin's hand in an unctuous display of fidelity."[24]

The world was informed of the death of the Soviet leader, while Stalin's body was embalmed at the special institute set up to keep Lenin's corpse in top shape. Word was put out that the four old Communists would each take charge of a ministry or ministries and run the Soviet Union as equal partners. Within six months, however, Khrushchev emerged as the first secretary of the Communist Party and first leader of the council of ministries. Malenkov was selected as leader of the Soviet Union but Khrushchev was effectively the new boss.

Within a few months Beria was arrested, tried, and shot, having been accused of initiating all the murders and other crimes that Stalin had ordered. Before his death, Beria had told the others that it was actually *he* who had killed Stalin by poisoning him. Nobody knows if that's true or not; the autopsy document has been lost.*

Stalin's funeral was a monumental affair. His body was laid out in a catafalque in the Hall of Columns on Red Square beneath a sign that read "Proletarians from All Countries, Unite!" In one of the great feats in the history of taxidermy, the corpse had been gutted, stuffed, and mounted to last a lifetime or longer on his funeral bier.

Tens of thousands, maybe hundreds of thousands, came by bus and by train from all parts of the Soviet Union in a tremendous outpouring for the man hailed for decades as "the greatest living human." More than two hundred people were trampled to death trying to pay their respects to the remains.

It had been decided to place Stalin's corpse next to Lenin's in a glassed-in coffin. Newspapers extolled his virtues, citing grand economic programs

---

* It has been said by various sources that Beria's successor at the secret police, now known as the KGB, stuffed rags into his mouth to keep him from screaming before he shot him between the eyes. Interestingly, all of the Soviet secret police heads, leading back to the 1917 revolution, had also been executed by their successors.

and the victory over the Nazis. It was written that Stalin had "been born into a Russia that used wooden rakes and left it with an atomic pile."

Khrushchev almost immediately began initiating reforms and innovations, most of which were kept secret from the people but that loosened the constant aura of terror always on everyone's mind. Cultural expression was permitted to some extent. The Korean War was ended. By 1956 Khrushchev was denouncing Stalin as a monster and a criminal, which set off angry strikes, protests, riots, and an anticommunist revolt in Hungary that was put down by Soviet tanks. By 1961 Stalin had been so discredited, and so many of his misdeeds uncovered, that by secret order his body was removed in the dead of night from the Lenin mausoleum and buried below the Kremlin Wall. As far as the Communists were concerned, Stalin's chapter in their great Marxist experiment was closed.

If Stalin had a legacy to be proud of, it was that he'd transformed Russia from an agrarian society to an industrial one—but at a terrible cost in lives and respect for the normal human condition. Mere peasantry had been replaced by a society in which mostly semi-impoverished state functionaries lived and worked with perhaps a slightly higher standard of living. But they lived in constant fear of their lives, and were instructed to worship the Communist state—and Joseph Stalin—instead of the god of their choice.

Life was cheap in Stalin's Soviet Union. The "state" was everything and, for Stalin personally, power was everything. Nowhere was this more evident than in the victory over Nazi Germany. Russia had three times the manpower of Germany; Stalin simply produced infantry division after infantry division to be slaughtered before finally overwhelming the foe. It wasn't pretty but it worked—that's about the best that can be said for the strategy. On the other hand, as one of Stalin's favorite Marxist-Communist doctrines held, revolutionary ends could justify even the most terrible means.

WINSTON CHURCHILL LIVED two decades longer than Franklin Roosevelt, and more than a decade longer than Stalin. But these weren't years of leisure and pasture as he had most deservedly earned; they were more the playing out of a great historical drama that had run for almost a century. His life was so rich, and so filled with energy and import, that it continued to enliven and inspire (and often exasperate) anyone who came within his radius.

When the European war ended, there remained the matter of Japan; Churchill plunged into that vicissitude with his usual vigor. The British did not take a great part in the battles that at last had cornered the Japanese on their island nation, but they had been victimized in 1942 by Japanese invasions of their colonies in Hong Kong, Malaya, Singapore, and Burma, featuring great loss of life, treasure, and massive incarceration of British prisoners in the brutal Japanese POW system.

As the war against Hitler ended, the British, like the Americans, began to mobilize their troops in Europe, Italy, and North Africa for the long journey to the western Pacific and the final battles against Japan. At the same time, Churchill was alarmed that this rapid demobilization in Europe would encourage the Soviets to invade and occupy even more nations.

In July 1945, the Big Three conference at Potsdam was meant to solve the questions of whether Stalin would accept reinstallation of the former Polish government and allow free elections in the European states Russia had occupied during the defeat of the German army. As well, there was the critical issue regarding which Allied country would occupy which part of the defeated Germany.

On the morning of July 24 Churchill met with President Truman at Number 2 Kaiserstrasse, Truman's residence at Potsdam, and there the final plans were made for the use of nuclear weapons against Japan. Churchill would later maintain that the decision to drop the atomic bomb on Japan had already been agreed upon by all parties. By this point the only questions that remained were when and where. Churchill assured the president that he favored using the weapon if it might help bring an end to the war. Truman informed Stalin later that day that the Allies had decided to use a new weapon of incredible force against Japan within the next few weeks, though he declined to specify technological details to the Soviet dictator. The Allies had been firebombing Tokyo and other major Japanese cities for some time, but a handful of targets had been deliberately spared from conventional attacks in order to demonstrate the true destructive power of the atomic bomb—including Hiroshima, which held an important military base.

AIR RAID WARNINGS SOUNDED in Hiroshima early on the morning of August 6, 1945. But by 8 a.m. the all-clear was given; only a single enemy plane had been sighted, and it was assumed to be on a reconnaissance mission. In fact there were three planes: the American B-29 bomber *Enola Gay*—piloted by Colonel Paul Tibbets—and two others carrying measuring instruments and photographic equipment. The bomber's cargo was a nuclear weapon code-named "Little Boy," but only Tibbets, his copilot, and the plane's bombardier knew what they were carrying. Tibbets and his crew had been training for the mission for months, and he was sanguine about it.

Just a short while later, at 8:15, a brilliant flash and earsplitting crack just above the city erased the lives of at least eighty thousand Japanese citizens and some military personnel. Twenty thousand more would later die of injuries or radiation poisoning.

When the atomic bomb detonated the *Enola Gay* was already ten miles away. But the shock wave shuddered through the plane as if it were being shaken by a giant hand. The crew had been given special dark glasses to protect their eyes from the flash that was bright as the sun itself. One of them later described the explosion and the giant mushroom cloud that followed as "awe inspiring."

The bombing came at a critical time in the war. The surrender of Germany on May 7 had ended the fighting in Europe, but Japan refused to concede the "unconditional surrender" that Roosevelt had called for at the Casablanca Conference in 1943. By the time of the Hiroshima bombing the Allies had conquered all of the outlying islands of Japan at a terrible cost in lives. Still, the Home Islands remained fiercely defended, with many Japanese ready to take up arms against any invaders, including various militias and reservists. General George Marshall estimated that it would cost up to 1 million American casualties to take the Home Islands by force. Marshall and President Truman had further predicted, based on a consensus of military and policy experts, that an invasion of Japan would cost more Japanese lives than atomic bombs, because a ground war would likely go on for at least two more years.

President Truman, aware of the condemnation the United States would receive in some quarters for using the atomic bomb, was unwilling to accept the enormous U.S. casualty figures that was the alternative and he ordered the air force to proceed with the mission. After the bombing Colonel Tibbets told reporters he believed the action had saved lives by shortening the war.

After Little Boy detonated over Hiroshima there was a wary silence from the Japanese. In fact, authorities in Tokyo didn't know what had happened. All communications with Hiroshima were suddenly silenced. The Japanese sent a small plane with a low-ranking officer to fly down for a look-see. He came upon an enormous fading mushroom cloud of smoke and debris and a scene below of unimaginable destruction.

Still the Japanese refused to surrender. Allied radio published accounts of the blast and threatened more to come, but the Japanese militarists were unmoved. They knew something of nuclear physics, and stupidly concluded that the United States possessed only one of the devices and would not be able to produce more for an extended period of time.

Meanwhile, Stalin decided at long last to declare war on Japan, hoping for last-minute territorial gains. The Allied vice was beginning to squeeze, but the Japanese held out for conditions: no Allied occupation of their country, the return of their outlying islands, no Allied trials for war crimes, and their emperor would retain his throne. For Truman, this was also unacceptable, and he ordered another nuclear attack to be unleashed on the port city Nagasaki.

The second bomb struck on August 9. Because Nagasaki's many hills absorbed a major portion of that blast, it was not quite as deadly as the first. Still, there was tremendous loss of life and destruction of property. The city, which existed mostly for military manufacturing, was almost obliterated.

Emperor Hirohito finally interceded with the military and called for a surrender on Allied terms. This caused several bloody insurrections among the hard-core militarists' ranks—but in the end the emperor delivered a surrender statement that contained two of the finest examples of understatement and overstatement ever fashioned in a single paragraph. The first was that "the war situation has developed not necessarily to Japan's advantage," and the other was that if the Americans kept dropping atomic bombs on Japan "it would lead to the total extinction of human civilization."

So the Japanese surrendered and lived to thrive another day. Peace once again descended upon the planet. But not for long. Stalin's spies—notably Klaus Fuchs, an English scientist and secret Communist agent—soon turned over critical information on building a nuclear weapon to the Soviet Union.

The Communists promptly began their own atomic bomb program, which in 1949 produced a successful blast in the desert of what is modern-day Kazakhstan. They immediately began to threaten the United States and other Allies with nuclear holocaust, and the world once more shivered at the ghastly prospect of a war not too far off the mark from Emperor Hirohito's dire prediction.

THE DAY AFTER THE FATEFUL MEETING in Kaiserstrasse, on July 25, Churchill returned home to discover the election results. Then came the breathtaking news: the Conservatives had lost. Churchill was out of a job. People worldwide were astonished when the British voters suddenly rejected the man who so prominently led them through the war. Clementine said to him immediately after they received the news, "It may well be a blessing in disguise"—to which Churchill replied, "If it's a blessing, at the moment it seems quite effectively disguised."[25]

After lunch he went into his study and composed a statement that he sent to the BBC: "The decision of the British people has been recorded in the votes counted today. I have therefore laid down the charge that was placed on me in darker times. I regret that I have not been permitted to finish the work against Japan . . . It only remains for me to express to the British people, for whom I have acted in these perilous years, my profound gratitude for the unflinching, unswerving support which they have given me during my task, and for the many expressions of kindness which they have shown toward their servant."[26]

The Churchill historian Brian Gardner called it "perhaps the most gracious acceptance of democratic defeat in the English language."

What had caused this amazing "act of ingratitude" (as one observer put it)? The immense sense of relief when the war finally ended had led people to reflect on all of their remaining privations. Food rationing, clothing rationing, coal rationing, durable goods rationing: there was almost universal scarcity, so tremendous was the effort put into the war. The opposing party spoke of the socialist utopia and railed that greedy owners of railroads, coal mines, oil and gas utilities, and other major industries were living in luxury while workingmen toiled for pittances in the mines and factories. Labour promised to socialize, or nationalize, these "central businesses" so that they would become owned and run by the state; everyone's paycheck would go up, people were told. For the masses, it was a message too tempting to resist.*

Churchill spent the weekend at Chequers after the election results were announced. There, he attempted to make merry with family and friends and ward off the black cloud caused by the extraordinary political blow. They watched *The Wizard of Oz* and played records, croquet, and cards, but the gloom continued to hover. Finally, at Sunday dinner, Churchill (after a robust serving of good champagne) announced, "It is fatal to give in to self-pity." He might be out of power, he said, but he was still a member of the House of Commons—and as such he would enthusiastically lead the opposition. Somebody had to lead the opposition. The notions of the Labour Party were fundamentally wrong to him, and dangerous.[27]

WHEN CHURCHILL WALKED INTO the House of Commons and took his place on the opposition bench for the first time in more than a decade, the

---

* Many companies were nationalized under the Labour government during the late 1940s. Many of these were "privatized" once more under the government of Margaret Thatcher, 1979–1990.

Conservative Party members arose and serenaded him with "For He's a Jolly Good Fellow." Labour members tried to drown them out with "The Red Flag," a socialist anthem. But for a change the Tory vocalists had their way.

As a member of the opposition Churchill had few, if any, peers in speechmaking abilities. And he did not stand idly by as the Labour government nationalized the coal, petroleum, and steel industries, the Bank of England, railroads, national trucking, and British Airways and installed a socialized medical system—all of which required nearly half a million new bureaucrats to oversee. These civil servants, Churchill told the House, constituted "a mighty army . . . that has been taken from production and added, at a prodigious cost and waste, to the oppressive machinery of government and control. Instead of helping national recovery, this is a positive hindrance.

"The queues are longer, the shelves are barer, the shops are emptier," he went on. "The interference of government departments with daily life is more severe and more galling. More forms have to be filled up, more government officials have to be consulted. Whole spheres of potential activity are frozen, rigid and numb."[28]

Churchill was preaching to the choir, of course, and he knew it. His tirades might have been comforting to Conservatives but Labour had a mandate, which it full well knew. No matter what Churchill said, the socialization of Great Britain rolled inexorably forward. This would not be forever, and Churchill understood this. Someday Labour would be out of power and the vast engine of government ownership they had assembled could be repealed—as in fact it was. But that was more than a decade into the future.

To suggestions within his own party that it might be time for him to retire, Churchill had this to say to his personal physician Lord Moran: "A short time ago I was ready to retire and die gracefully. Now I'm going to stay and have [the socialists] out. I'll tear their bleeding entrails out of them. I'm in pretty good fettle," he thundered, explaining that it was the "Jerome side" of him—his mother's people—that propelled him into this belligerent attitude.[29]

In the meantime, Churchill concluded that he needed to reinvent himself, which he did as an international statesman, traveling to world capitals to give political speeches and urge the formation of, of all things, "a United States of Europe," he told an audience in Zurich in September 1946. This, he explained, would unify the continent in a way "never known since the Roman Empire."[30]

This notion had become a recurring theme in Churchill's thinking after it became apparent that the Soviet Union was going to remain in control of Eastern Europe. It was the biggest modern land grab since the German rampage, and Churchill was fearful that Stalin wouldn't stop there.

Churchill's European union—including Germany—would presumably provide for a common defense, an idea that did not immediately go over well in France, given that nation's firsthand experience of what a rearmed Germany could do. (It almost certainly, however, did not envision the present European economic union with its capital in Brussels, from which Great Britain is presently in the process of seceding.)

In light of his decade-long rhetorical screeds against Germany it seems incongruous that Churchill was willing to invite the Germans back into the community of nations. But it was completely in character. He was "remarkably free from any grudges, let alone malice," wrote Paul Johnson, one of his biographers. For example, as bitter as his invective was against the Labour Party's socialism, Churchill was never hateful toward individual members of the opposing party; in fact, when the Labour members resigned in 1945 against his pleas to keep the coalition government together, he threw them a champagne going-away party when their departure became inevitable. For all of his long life, Churchill had lived by a simple dictum: "In war, resolution. In defeat, defiance. In victory, magnanimity. In peace, goodwill"—and he sincerely meant it. His friend the newspaper tycoon Lord Beaverbrook said of him, "Winston is never vindictive."[31]

On March 5, 1946, when Churchill gave a speech in the small college town of Fulton, Missouri, forty thousand people gathered hoping to get a glimpse of the famous British statesman. President Harry S. Truman, a Missourian who had succeeded to the presidency upon Roosevelt's death, accompanied him on the podium at Westminster College. Truman had read a draft of Churchill's speech on the train ride from Washington and predicted that it was going to "create quite a stir"—which turned out to be a vast understatement.

"A shadow has fallen on the scenes so lately lighted by the Allied victory," Churchill began, referring to the Soviet Union. "Nobody knows what Soviet Russia and its Communist international organization intends to do in the immediate future, or what are the limits, if any, to their expansive and proselytizing tendencies . . . It is my duty, however, for I am sure you would wish me to state the facts as I see them, to place before you certain facts about the present position in Europe.

"From Stettin in the Baltic to Trieste in the Adriatic," Churchill scowled, "an iron curtain has descended on the Continent"—a phrase that would resonate for the rest of the century. "Behind that line lie all the capitals of the ancient states of Central and Eastern Europe. Warsaw, Berlin, Prague, Budapest, Belgrade, Bucharest, and Sofia—all these famous cities and the populations around them lie in what I must call the Soviet sphere, and all are subject in one form or another—not only to Soviet influence, but to a very high and, in many cases, increasing measure of control from Moscow."

Churchill then called for an alliance of "the English-speaking common-wealths that would adhere faithfully to the Charter of the United Nations" to confront and contain further Communist expansion. Churchill knew that Britain couldn't go it alone, and he was determined to make his best case for the United States to remain a player on the international scene. America was at the "pinnacle of power," he told the audience, with an "awe-inspiring accountability to the future."

The speech might have been given to college students, but Churchill was quite aware that the presence of a Paramount Pictures movie camera would ensure that his remarks would soon reach a majority of Americans who still depended on local theaters for their weekly newsreels. He had hoped it would awaken American interest about conditions in Europe vis-à-vis Soviet aggression. Most U.S. citizens didn't know much about these things, nor did they much care; they were merely glad the ordeal of war had ended. Moreover, much of America wasn't ready for such a commitment—far from it. The country had lost four hundred thousand men in the war, and had made immeasurable material sacrifices at home. Like the British, American citizens had suffered from food and gas rationing, as well as shortages of just about everything for four long years, since all possible exertions had gone into the war effort.

One of Churchill's statements was particularly irksome to many: "From what I have seen of our Russian friends during the war, I am convinced that there is nothing that they admire more than strength, and there is nothing for which they have less respect than weakness—especially military weakness." The implication seemed to be that the United States needed to maintain a large military presence in Europe, staying armed and ready to fight a major war with the Soviet Union if challenged.

Reaction was overwhelmingly negative and provoked a storm of controversy. The *Chicago Sun-Times* declared that Churchill was trying to lead the United States into war and said it would be "disastrous" to follow this "great but blinded aristocrat." The *Nation* complained that Churchill sounded as if "the British and Americans were ganging up on Russia." Three liberal Democratic U.S. senators attacked Churchill in a joint statement, claiming that "his interpretation of international events would destroy what remained of Big Three unity and undermine the UN." Eleanor Roosevelt was deeply troubled by Churchill's position, fearing that it might push Truman into an anti-Soviet stance. Others heaped similar abuse, accusing him of being a "reactionary" and a "warmonger." Reporters demanded whether President Truman had read the speech beforehand when he was caught on the movie camera heavily applauding it. Truman lied and denied it.[32]

The speech might have been a controversial bombshell but it served to awaken a considerable number of Americans to the plight of the Soviet-dominated countries. Churchill's dramatic use of the Iron Curtain metaphor immediately entered the English lexicon and remained prominent as such for fifty years.

A year almost to the day from Churchill's speech, President Truman announced what would come to be known as the Truman Doctrine, a tectonic shift in U.S. foreign policy in which the president pledged that the United States would endeavor to give all possible assistance to the people of countries confronting a takeover by the Communists. It became the first iteration of what was to be the policy of "containment" of the

Soviet Union. This led directly to the formation of NATO, the North Atlantic Treaty Organization.

Stalin, for his part, declared that "Russia would rearm, at the expense of producing consumer goods," because "capitalist-imperialist monopolies guaranteed that no peaceful international order was possible." To make his point, within the year Russian MiGs shot down a British aircraft that had strayed into the Soviet sector of occupied Berlin.

Not long afterward, George Kennan, the chargé d'affaires in Moscow, sent a lengthy assessment of the Soviet situation to the U.S. State Department, in which he forecast that Stalin's "neurotic view of world affairs" would bring about a Russian foreign policy inclined to "use every means possible to infiltrate, weaken, and divide the West." Stalin, he said, was paranoid over "capitalist encirclement" from which, the dictator said, "in the long run there could never be a peaceful co-existence." Kennan wrote that for the West to make gestures of goodwill to the Soviets was a waste of time, because Moscow was convinced that the West would never "stand firm" against Soviet aggression. A new era was at hand.[33]

Noting these developments, George Marshall, former chairman of the Joint Chiefs of Staff and now secretary of state, had undertaken a fact-finding tour of Europe—and he didn't like the facts he'd found. He told President Truman that if something wasn't done to put the prostrated nations of Europe back on their feet, international trade would be crippled and some, if not most, of these countries would fall to Communist proselytizing and intrigue. What became known as the Marshall Plan was a multibillion-dollar American self-help handout in which war-torn nations could apply for direct aid from the United States after submitting a recovery plan. (The package was worth more than a trillion in today's dollars and up to 15 percent of the U.S. federal budget.)

Stalin stupidly forbade the Soviet Union or any of the countries it occupied in central and eastern Europe from participation, dooming them to backward shabbiness well into the 1990s, even after the collapse of the Soviet Union. The Marshall Plan is generally credited with speeding the recovery in western Europe by a decade or more, and Marshall was awarded the Nobel Peace Prize.

★★★★★

CHURCHILL REOPENED CHARTWELL in 1946 and began the lengthy process of restoring its gardens, orchards, and fish ponds after five years of disuse.* In between the landscaping projects and working on his long-awaited *History of the English-Speaking Peoples,*† he tended to his easel and paints.

In 1946, a wealthy Englishman removed a sharp financial burden from Churchill's shoulders when he convened a group of donors who purchased Chartwell and all of Churchill's papers for a considerable sum; the understanding was that the property would belong to Churchill for the rest of his life, after which it would be turned into a national monument. And at last, Churchill managed to permanently secure his financial future by signing an agreement to write his war memoirs. He created a six-volume first-person history of the Second World War, one of the most successful endeavors in publishing history, which would earn Churchill more than $50 million and secure his being awarded the Nobel Prize in literature in 1953.

Aside from the money, the mere writing of *The Second World War* served as a substantial buffer against the old "black dog" of depression that had nagged at Churchill from time to time—especially now, when he was out of power as momentous events clouded the world scene. He watched the horrific Hindu-Islamic violence accompanying the breakup of India (which he had warned of), resulting in the slaughter of up to 2 million people; the Korean War; the Berlin crisis; the British disarmament-rearmament argument; the rise of Communist China; and Russian development of nuclear weapons. To these things Churchill could only speak, not act, as the role of Great Britain in international affairs diminished year by year.

The British Empire did not dissolve peacefully. After India broke away, Burma followed suit and was soon taken over by Communists. A Communist insurrection broke out in Malaya that resulted in her departure from the empire, followed by Ceylon (Sri Lanka), which descended into a thirty-year civil war that ended with a republican government in 2009. The same

---

* German prisoners had been used to look after the place during the war.
† It would not be published for another decade.

was true for England's African colonies, where widespread fighting broke out as British rule ended, followed by dictatorial rule that remains destabilizing even today.

The breakup of the British Empire put an appalling strain on the British economy, as the country could no longer depend on the smooth conduct of trade between its former colonies and Great Britain. Roosevelt, who was strongly anti-imperialist, would no doubt have been pleased at this development (minus the slaughter). But he didn't live to see it.

His war memoir was Churchill's tonic against this sour state of affairs. Most of the writing was done at Chartwell, where he kept a staff of research assistants to help him sort the historical record and a gaggle of stenographers to whom he dictated passages, often well into the evening.

When the House of Commons was in session he also spent time in London—sometimes at the Other Club, where the future prime minister Harold Macmillan captured him vividly in his diary. "He has used these days to give a demonstration of energy and vitality," Macmillan wrote. "He has voted in every decision, made a series of brilliant little speeches, shows all his qualities of humor and sarcasm, and crowned all by a remarkable breakfast (at 7:30 a.m.) of eggs, bacon, sausages, and coffee, followed by a large whisky and soda and a huge cigar," after which he was prepared to face the day and the Labour Party in the House of Commons.[34]

In 1951, Churchill was back in power. By a minor miracle, Labour had been squabbling with itself and Prime Minister Clement Attlee felt compelled to call an election. In a narrow vote, Churchill's Tory Party prevailed, and he once more had his old job back. He didn't have the majority necessary to overturn the vast socialist legislation of the past five years. But now he could at least put a halt to its expansion.

Churchill himself had run a very moderate campaign in view of his previous political stridency, offering to work across party lines with Labour and what was left of the Liberal Party. The old king was dying of cancer, and there was something atavistically solid in Churchill that the British public felt would see them through.

By the time Churchill regained office the Russians had developed first the atomic bomb and then the much larger hydrogen weapon. In the words of his biographer Roy Jenkins, "The saving of the world from destruction in a reciprocal holocaust of H-bombs . . . became more important [to Churchill] than any policy issue."[35]

To that end Churchill frequently traveled to the United States, working with Truman and later President Dwight D. Eisenhower to convene a summit with the Soviets on preventing nuclear war. But the Russians, usually at the last minute, always seemed to throw a monkey wrench into the proceedings, and Churchill was never able to broker a rapprochement.

Otherwise, Churchill seemed preoccupied with simply staying in power, long after many in his own party thought he ought to retire. He had told his doctor, "If I leave office, I'll die."

That wasn't the case, at least not right away. After at last turning over his party leadership to Anthony Eden in 1955, Churchill, at the age of eighty, returned to his bench in the House of Commons as an ordinary, if singular, member. He had served four kings and two queens, including Victoria, fought in four wars, and received numerous honors including the Order of the Garter, considered England's most prestigious decoration for chivalry. He had sired five children, who gave him nine grandchildren. And he stayed married and faithful to the same woman for fifty-seven years.

Churchill had many defining moments in his long career. But his leadership during the Second World War stands at the pinnacle—especially as reflected in his brilliant speeches: "Their finest hour," "Never in the field of human conflict was so much owed by so many to so few," "We will fight them on the beaches . . . ," "What kind of people do they think we are!"

If there is a single shining moment among the others, it would certainly have been in May 1940, the "Darkest Hour" of the war. When France was falling and the British army had its back to the sea at Dunkirk, Churchill resisted the strong admonitions of his foreign secretary Lord Halifax that a truce, or "acceptable peace terms"—*surrender*—should be arranged with the Nazis. Halifax, moreover, was not alone in such thinking in the cabinet or in the House itself. But Churchill would have none of it. He told them, "If this long island story of ours is to end at last, let it end when each of us is choking on his own blood upon the ground." Forthwith, he ordered every ship and boat afloat to evacuate the Dunkirk army. Thus England was saved.

OUT OF POWER AT LAST he had a decade more to live. This period has been compared by a few historians to his "wilderness years," but that analogy doesn't hold. Churchill sought no government office but was often consulted by ministers on a variety of subjects. He also continued making speeches, though fewer than when he was actively in office. His life was far from dull and mundane.

In one infamous episode he had sat for a portrait by Britain's highly regarded artist Graham Sutherland, which was meant to be an eightieth birthday gift to him from the House of Commons. At the first few sittings, Churchill was allowed to see the basic drawing and was much impressed. But as time wore on Sutherland refused to let Churchill look at the canvas and follow the portrait's progress. When the finished product was unveiled Churchill not only didn't like it, he despised it, saying it made him look "old and spent" and his face "cruel and coarse."[36]

At the presentation ceremony he showed admirable restraint by declaring, "The portrait is a remarkable example of modern art. It certainly combines force and candor." In private he told his doctor, "I think it is malignant." The House divided along party lines as to whether the painting looked "remarkably accurate" or "disgusting."

Clementine stuck it down in the cellar and later had it cut up and burned.

During the 1950s and '60s, Churchill spent time at Chartwell reveling in his marvelous view of the Weald of Kent, or watching his racehorses run at the various meets nearby. He enjoyed gambling, at which he was not very good, in the casinos at Monte Carlo and other posh spots on the French Riviera. With the publication of his memoirs he had money to lose.

He became friends with Aristotle Onassis, the Greek shipping magnate who owned a spectacularly appointed yacht, aboard which Churchill traveled in the style to which he had become accustomed. His sailing companions at times included the English ballet doyenne Margot Fonteyn, the celebrated diva Maria Callas, and Jackie Kennedy's sister Lee Radziwill. He once refused, however, to sail with the Duke of Windsor, whom he considered an "empty man," and his wife, the Duchess, whom he considered not at all. He stayed for months at a time with friends at their luxurious villas in the South of France. And always, there were the ever present paints and easel.

Churchill toyed with the idea of buying a villa of his own but nothing came of it; in the words of biographer Jenkins he "wisely settled down to be a perpetual guest," even though there were at times spats over whom Churchill would stay with, or on whose yacht he would sail. Sometimes Clementine went along on these excursions, and sometimes not; in their twilight years she seemed more likely to go her own way. But they exchanged letters almost daily when apart.

In 1962, Churchill took a fall and broke his hip. That seemed to be the downward turning point in his health. He suffered heart and artery issues during the next several years, plus three minor strokes, which left him weak. He continued traveling but not nearly as much. His time was running out.

In 1963 Churchill was made an "honorary citizen" of the United States—the first time this honor had been bestowed since the Marquis de Lafayette—but he was too frail to attend his installation. On November 30, 1964, he turned ninety. Seven weeks later, on January 24, 1965, he passed away from a severe stroke that he had suffered two weeks earlier.

CHURCHILL'S BODY LAY in state at Westminster Hall for three days: the only other nonroyal besides Gladstone and the Duke of Wellington to be accorded such an honor. More than 320,000 people visited the catafalque.

At 9:30 on January 30, a bitter cold and damp gray London morning, eight Grenadier Guards placed Churchill's Union Jack–draped coffin on a gun carriage, drawn by one hundred sailors of the Royal Navy. Churchill's son Randolph and the older male grandchildren filed in behind the casket, while Clementine and the other women and girls of the family rode inside horse-drawn funeral coaches. Dozens of companies of the famous old regiments, some on horseback, some afoot, marched behind, as did dozens of heads of state, presidents, prime ministers, and other dignitaries from across the world come to pay their respects.

Hundreds of thousands of reverent spectators lined the route of the procession that moved slowly and deliberately to the jarringly muted beat of drums, while distant cannons every minute fired a final, haunting salute.

The funeral ceremony was conducted at St. Paul's Cathedral, designed in 1697 by Christopher Wren, which had miraculously survived the German bombing during the war. Afterward, the coffin was placed on the varnished stern of a Royal Navy admiral's barge in the Thames to be transported to Waterloo Station. There, a *Battle of Britain*–class locomotive named the *Winston Churchill* waited to carry it to the church cemetery near Blenheim Palace, sixty miles distant, where many of his distinguished relatives lay.

As the funeral barge moved past on the river, operators of the scores of huge stevedoring cranes that lined the banks of the Thames for miles dipped their vast mechanical limbs in graceful, final bows to the great man. A lone piper on the bow of a following barge played "Flowers of the Forest."

"At Bladon," wrote Lord Moran, "in a country churchyard, in the stillness of a winter evening, in the presence of his family and a few friends, Winston Churchill was committed to the English earth, which in his finest hour, he had held inviolate."[37]

EPILOGUE

Today Churchill, Roosevelt, and Stalin appear almost like dinosaurs: giants who ruled the earth in their time. Although the passing years fade their memories, they can never diminish the impact these three leaders had on the world. Two of them were good, honest men who suppressed pangs of regret for sending millions of men into battles where death was a constant companion. The third—Stalin—seems to have had no pangs of regret to suppress. But he was nevertheless steadfast in holding the line against the likes of Adolf Hitler and his Nazi hordes.

Although Roosevelt's and Churchill's lives were forged in the crucible of the shared British and American experience of the First World War—Roosevelt as assistant secretary of the U.S. Navy and Churchill as first lord of the British Admiralty—their countries were far from natural allies. The Americans had fought the British in a war of rebellion and revolution, and again thirty years later over some of the same issues. Forty-five years after that, during the American Civil War, Great Britain entertained strong notions of siding with the Confederacy against the United States, and declined to do so only as the tide of battle turned against the South. One might have thought from this past record that Americans would have recoiled from association with anything British. But fifty-two years after the Civil War the two nations were fighting side by side against the Germans in the squalid trenches of the Western Front. War, like Shakespeare's "misery," makes strange bedfellows.

Stalin sat out the Great War in a Siberian camp to which he'd been banished by forces of the czar. When danger arose twenty years later as Hitler's cult gripped an aggressive Germany, Stalin became an eager ally of the vicious Nazi regime until Hitler stabbed him in the back by attacking the Communist empire. During this time the United States sat by as a "neutral" nation until it, too, was drawn into the struggle when the Japanese attacked Hawaii.

Given this tangled web of diplomatic relations it would be surprising if any of these three men fully trusted the others. And indeed they did not. Roosevelt distrusted the British because of their colonial empire, of which America had once been a part. Churchill distrusted the Americans' commitment to the European war and he detested Stalin's Soviet Communist state. Stalin, who had risen to the top by killing off his opposition, distrusted everyone.

They nevertheless found themselves inextricably bound as the war progressed. Churchill was a hands-on style of leader who didn't order his commanders to attack or withdraw by certain dates or times. But he let his feelings and wishes be known, and he visited the battle areas as much as possible. He was able to influence Roosevelt to invade North Africa and join the Sicilian and Italian campaigns (these last two were for better or worse as the Allies were still fighting the Germans in northern Italy when the war ended). But Churchill was a terrific wartime leader; his stirring radio speeches resound clearly today with a resolve and bellicosity that saw the British people through the worst of the aerial Blitz and other indignities.

Roosevelt, on the other hand, acted more like a referee, deferring most decisions to George Marshall, his military chief of staff, but reserving the final say for himself. It was Roosevelt, for example, who decided in 1942 to join the British and invade North Africa, when his generals sought instead to concentrate everything on a cross-Channel invasion of France. And it was Roosevelt who decided—against the wishes of his U.S. Navy commanders—to let Douglas MacArthur invade the Philippines in 1944.

Stalin was a strange but tenacious wartime leader. He deferred to but distrusted Zhukov, by far his best general. He made few wartime speeches, even while the entire Communist system arrayed itself along a flood of propaganda. One thing about a dictator is that he gets to make the rules, and Stalin made rules that would cause even Nazis to cringe—including summary execution of retreating soldiers and banishment of prisoners of war and their families. He even denied having a son when his son was captured by German soldiers. In the end, Stalin had the luxury—if that is the word for it—of such excessive manpower that he could sacrifice whole armies to the Germans just because he had more whole armies waiting in the wings to finish the job.

Perhaps the most remarkable thing about Stalin was his ability to hang on as dictator of Soviet Russia amid the conniving gang of ambitious cut-throats who made up the Soviet government. In fact, he was able to develop such a cult of leader worship that his death brought genuine tears to the masses. It was only after his crimes were exposed and he was publicly denounced that the Russian people realized the truth.

Whatever the underlying makeup, these three men presided over three of the most powerful countries on the planet. Together, they saw and lived through the deadliest conflict in history from its beginning until its end. Even Roosevelt, who died a month before Germany surrendered, had the satisfaction of knowing that the end was coming. Each in his own way had high hopes for the brave new world that would arise from the ashes.

NOTES

Chapter One

1. William Manchester, *The Last Lion,* vol. 1, *Visions of Glory* (Boston: Little, Brown, 1983).
2. Winston Spencer Churchill, *My Early Life* (New York: Simon & Schuster, 1996 [1930]).
3. Ibid.
4. Ibid.
5. Randolph S. Churchill, companion, part 1 (documents) to vol. 1, *Winston Churchill* (London: Heinemann, 1967).
6. Ibid.
7. Randolph Churchill, companion, vol. 1, part 1, *Winston Churchill.*
8. Ibid.
9. Ibid.
10. Ibid.
11. Churchill, *My Early Life.*
12. Ibid.
13. Randolph Churchill, companion, part 1, *Winston Churchill.*
14. Ibid.
15. Ibid.
16. Ibid.
17. Manchester, *Last Lion,* vol. 1.
18. Randolph Churchill, companion, part 2 to vol. 1, *Winston Churchill.*
19. Ibid.
20. Ibid.
21. Ibid.
22. Churchill, *My Early Life.*
23. Quoted in Manchester, *Last Lion,* vol. 1.
24. Churchill, *My Early Life.*
25. Randolph Churchill, companion, part 2, *Winston Churchill;* Manchester, *Last Lion,* vol. 1.
26. Dennis Kincaid, *British Social Life in India* (London: Routledge, 1973).
27. Churchill, *My Early Life.*
28. Ibid.
29. Ibid.; Randolph Churchill, companion, part 1, *Winston Churchill.*
30. Winston Churchill, *The Story of the Malakand Field Force* (London: Longman, 1898); Con Coughlin, *Churchill's First War* (New York: Thomas Dunne, 2014).
31. Churchill, *My Early Life.*
32. Ibid.; Churchill, *Malakand Field Force.*
33. Churchill, *Malakand Field Force.*
34. Ibid.
35. Ibid.
36. Churchill, *My Early Life.*
37. Ibid.; Churchill, *Malakand Field Force.*

Chapter Two

1. Churchill, *My Early Life;* Churchill, *Malakand Field Force.*
2. Randolph Churchill, companion, part 2, *Winston Churchill.*
3. Ralph G. Martin, *Jennie: The Life of Lady Randolph Churchill* (Englewood Cliffs, NJ: Prentice Hall, 1969); Churchill, *My Early Life.*
4. Martin, *Jennie;* Churchill, *My Early Life.*
5. Randolph Churchill, companion, part 2, *Winston Churchill;* Churchill, *My Early Life.*
6. Churchill, *My Early Life.*
7. Ibid.
8. Ibid.
9. Winston Churchill, *The River War: An Historical Account of the Reconquest of the Soudan* (London: Longman, 1899); Churchill, *My Early Life.*
10. Churchill, *River War;* Churchill, *My Early Life.*

11. Frederick Woods, ed., *Young Winston's Wars: The Original Despatches of Winston S. Churchill War Correspondent, 1897–1900* (New York: Viking, 1973).
12. Woods, *Young Winston's Wars*.
13. Churchill, *My Early Life*.
14. Ibid.
15. Ibid.
16. Ibid.
17. Randolph Churchill, companion, parts 1 and 2, *Winston Churchill*; Churchill, *My Early Life*.
18. Randolph Churchill, companion, part 2, *Winston Churchill*; Churchill, *My Early Life*; Simon Read, *Winston Churchill Reporting* (Boston: Da Capo, 2015).
19. Read, *Churchill Reporting*.
20. Churchill, *My Early Life*.
21. Ibid.
22. Ibid.
23. Ibid. (The account of Churchill's escape is taken from his autobiography and from his contemporary dispatches to the *Morning Post*, which are substantially similar except where noted. Supporting documents, including a reward poster, are contained in his son's biography, part 2. These are by far the most reliable primary evidences of what occurred.)
24. Manchester, *Last Lion*, vol. 1.

Chapter Three

1. Simon Sebag Montefiore, *Young Stalin* (New York: Knopf, 2007). Montefiore has done by far the most exhaustive academic research into the Tiflis robbery of 1907 and I have relied on his account above various news stories of the day.
2. Edvard Radzinsky, *Stalin* (New York: Doubleday, 1996); Montefiore, *Young Stalin*.
3. Radzinsky, *Stalin*.
4. Montefiore, *Young Stalin*.
5. Ibid.
6. Ronald Hingley, *Joseph Stalin: Man and Legend* (New York: McGraw Hill, 1974); Emil Ludwig, *Stalin* (New York: Putnam, 1942).
7. Hingley, *Joseph Stalin*.
8. Ibid.
9. Oleg Khlevniuk, *Stalin: New Biography of a Dictator* (New Haven, CT: Yale University Press, 2015).
10. Montefiore, *Young Stalin*.
11. Ibid.
12. Radzinsky, *Stalin*.
13. Montefiore, *Young Stalin*.
14. Radzinsky, *Stalin*.
15. Ibid.
16. Ibid.
17. Montefiore, *Young Stalin*.
18. Ibid.
19. Frederic Morton, *Thunder at Twilight: Vienna 1913–1914* (New York: Scribner, 1989).
20. Ibid.
21. Ibid.
22. Khlevniuk, *Stalin*.
23. Ibid.
24. Robert Service, *Stalin: A Biography* (Cambridge, MA: Belknap Press, 2005).
25. Radzinsky, *Stalin*.
26. Khlevniuk, *Stalin*.
27. Radzinsky, *Stalin*.
28. Ibid.
29. Khlevniuk, *Stalin*.

Chapter Four

1. Geoffrey Ward, *A First-Class Temperament: The Emergence of FDR* (New York: Harper & Row, 1989).
2. Ibid.
3. Alonzo Hamby, *Man of Destiny: FDR and the Making of the American Century* (New York: Basic Books, 2015).
4. Geoffrey Ward, *Before the Trumpet: Young Franklin Roosevelt* (New York: Harper & Row, 1985).
5. Ibid.
6. Ibid.
7. Frank Freidel, *Franklin D. Roosevelt: A Rendezvous with Destiny* (Boston: Little, Brown, 1990).
8. Frank Ashburn, *Peabody of Groton: A Portrait* (New York: Coward McCann, 1944).

9.   Ibid.
10.   Ward, *Before the Trumpet.*
11.   Ibid.
12.   Hamby, *Man of Destiny.*
13.   Ibid.
14.   Ibid.
15.   Ibid.
16.   Joseph Lash, *Eleanor and Franklin* (New York: Norton, 1971).
17.   Hamby, *Man of Destiny.*
18.   Ibid.
19.   Alfred B. Rollins Jr., *Roosevelt and Howe* (New York: Knopf, 1962).
20.   *Troy* (New York) *Record,* March 4, 1912.
21.   *Wall Street Journal,* December 23, 2017–January 10, 2018.

Chapter Five

1.   Randolph Churchill, *Winston Churchill,* vol. 2.
2.   Ibid.
3.   Ibid.
4.   Ibid.
5.   Manchester, *Last Lion,* vol. 1.
6.   Ibid.
7.   Winston Churchill, *The World Crisis,* vol. 1 (London: Butterworth, 1923).
8.   Ibid.
9.   Ibid.
10.   Violet Bonham Carter, *Winston Churchill As I Knew Him* (London: Eyre & Spottiswoode, 1965); Churchill, *World Crisis.*
11.   Bonham Carter, *As I Knew Him.* Italian reporter quote in Manchester, *Last Lion,* vol. 3, *Defender of the Realm* (Boston: Little, Brown, 1995).
12.   Bonham Carter, *As I Knew Him.*
13.   Winston Groom, *A Storm in Flanders* (New York: Atlantic Monthly Press, 2002).
14.   Ibid.
15.   Churchill, *World Crisis.*
16.   Bonham Carter, *As I Knew Him.*
17.   Paul Johnson, *Churchill* (New York: Viking, 2009).

Chapter Six

1.   Johnson, *Churchill.*
2.   Winston Churchill, *Thoughts and Adventures* (London: Butterworth, 1932).
3.   Ibid.
4.   Ibid.
5.   Ibid.
6.   Ibid.
7.   Manchester, *Last Lion,* vol. 1.
8.   Ibid.
9.   Johnson, *Churchill.*
10.   David Lough, *No More Champagne: Churchill and His Money* (New York: Picador, 2015); Manchester, *Last Lion,* vol. 1; Mary Soames, *Clementine Churchill* (Boston: Mariner Books, 2003).
11.   Lough, *No More Champagne,* vol. 1.
12.   Ibid.
13.   Manchester, *Last Lion,* vol. 1.
14.   Martin Gilbert, *Winston S. Churchill,* vol. 5 (Boston: Houghton Mifflin, 1979).
15.   Manchester, *Last Lion,* vol. 1.
16.   Johnson, *Churchill.*
17.   *Daily Mail,* December 28, 1931.
18.   Manchester, *Last Lion,* vol. 1.
19.   Winston Churchill, *The Second World War,* vol. 1 (London: Cassell, 1948); Roy Jenkins, *Churchill* (New York: Penguin, 2001).
20.   Hansard.millbanksystems.com, March 16, 1936.
21.   Jenkins, *Churchill.*
22.   Edward Rothstein, *New York Times,* March 29, 2003.

Chapter Seven

1.   Rothstein, *New York Times,* March 29, 2003.

2.   Ibid.
3.   Ibid.
4.   Ibid.
5.   Lev Lurie, *New York Times,* May 7, 2012.
6.   Radzinsky, *Stalin.*
7.   Ibid.
8.   Ibid.
9.   Hingley, *Joseph Stalin.*
10. Julianna Pilon, *Wall Street Journal,* April 29–30, 2017.
11. Hingley, *Joseph Stalin.*
12. Ibid.
13. Manchester, *Last Lion,* vol. 1.
14. Stalin, speech to the Politburo, November 1931.
15. Service, *Stalin.*
16. Ibid.
17. Hingley, *Joseph Stalin.*
18. Ibid.
19. Ibid.
20. S. J. Taylor, *Stalin's Apologist* (New York: Oxford University Press, 1990).
21. Radzinsky, *Stalin.*
22. Kevin Kosar, *Moonshine: A Global History* (London: Reaktion, 2017).
23. Ibid.
24. Service, *Stalin.*
25. Susan Butler, *My Dear Mr. Stalin: The Complete Correspondence of Franklin D. Roosevelt and Joseph V. Stalin* (New Haven, CT: Yale University Press, 2003).
26. Ibid.
27. Ibid.

Chapter Eight
1.   Joseph E. Persico, *Franklin and Lucy* (New York: Random House, 2008).
2.   Ibid.
3.   Jonathan Daniels, *Washington Quadrille: The Dance Beside the Documents* (New York: Doubleday, 1968).
4.   Persico, *Franklin and Lucy.*
5.   Ibid.
6.   Joseph Lash, *Love, Eleanor* (New York: Doubleday, 1982); Ward, *A First-Class Temperament.*
7.   Lash, *Love, Eleanor.*
8.   Daniels, *Washington Quadrille.*
9.   Ibid.; Persico, *Franklin and Lucy.*
10. Ward, *A First-Class Temperament.*
11. Freidel, *A Rendezvous with Destiny.*
12. Persico, *Franklin and Lucy.*
13. Ibid.
14. Elliott Roosevelt and James Brough, *An Untold Story* (New York: Putnam, 1973).
15. Freidel, *A Rendezvous with Destiny.*
16. Ward, *A First-Class Temperament.*
17. Ibid.
18. *New York Times,* June 28, 1928.
19. Freidel, *A Rendezvous with Destiny.*
20. Ibid.
21. James MacGregor Burns, *Roosevelt: The Lion and the Fox* (New York: Harcourt, Brace, 1956); Ward, *A First-Class Temperament;* Freidel, *A Rendezvous with Destiny.*
22. Arthur Schlesinger Jr., *The Crisis of the Old Order* (Boston: Houghton Mifflin, 1957); Burns, *Lion and the Fox.*
23. Schlesinger, *Crisis of the Old Order.*
24. Ibid.
25. Ibid.
26. Ibid.
27. Ibid.
28. Freidel *A Rendezvous with Destiny;* Schlesinger, *Crisis of the Old Order.*
29. Persico, *Franklin and Lucy.*
30. Hamby, *Man of Destiny.*
31. Roy Jenkins, *Franklin Delano Roosevelt* (New York: Times Books, 2003).

Chapter Nine

1. U.S. Department of State bulletin. Office of the Historian, Milestones 1921–1936, *Recognition of the Soviet Union 1933*.
2. Lash, *Love, Eleanor;* Persico, *Franklin and Lucy.*
3. Persico, *Franklin and Lucy.*
4. Freidel, *A Rendezvous with Destiny.*
5. Ibid.
6. Ibid.
7. Burns, *Lion and the Fox.*
8. Ibid.
9. Ibid.
10. Hamby, *Man of Destiny.*
11. Winston Churchill, *The Second World War,* vol. 2 (London: Cassell, 1949).
12. Thomas Parrish, *Roosevelt and Marshall* (New York: Morrow, 1989).
13. Ibid.
14. Samuel Eliot Morison, *The Two Ocean War* (Boston: Little, Brown, 1963).
15. Samuel Eliot Morison, *The Rising Sun in the Pacific,* vol. 3 (Boston: Little, Brown, 1948).
16. Gordon Prange, *At Dawn We Slept: The Untold Story of Pearl Harbor* (New York: McGraw Hill, 1981).
17. The American Presidency Project, University of California, Santa Barbara. Franklin D. Roosevelt, Campaign Address at Boston, October 30, 1940.
18. Ibid.
19. Persico, *Franklin and Lucy.*
20. Ibid.
21. John Toland, *The Rising Sun: The Decline and Fall of the Japanese Empire* (New York: Random House, 1970).
22. Freidel, *A Rendezvous with Destiny.*
23. Churchill, *Second World War,* vol. 2.

Chapter Ten

1. Jenkins, *Churchill;* Johnson, *Churchill.*
2. Churchill, *Second World War,* vol. 2.
3. Ibid.
4. Ibid.
5. Ibid.; Jenkins, *Churchill.*
6. Johnson, *Churchill.*
7. Churchill, *Second World War,* vol. 2.
8. Warren Kimball, ed. *Churchill and Roosevelt: The Complete Correspondence,* vol 11 (Princeton, NJ: Princeton University Press, 1987).
9. Ibid.
10. Ibid.
11. Count Galeazzo Ciano, *Diaries* (New York: Simon, 1946).
12. Winston Churchill, *The Second World War,* vol. 3 (London: Cassell, 1950).
13. Ibid.
14. Ibid.
15. Ibid.
16. Ibid.
17. Ibid.
18. Manchester, *Last Lion,* vol. 3.
19. Churchill, *Second World War,* vol. 3.
20. Ibid.
21. Manchester, *Last Lion,* vol. 3.
22. Churchill, *Second World War,* vol. 3.
23. Ibid.
24. Ibid.
25. Ibid.

Chapter Eleven

1. Radzinsky, *Stalin.*
2. Svetlana Stalin, *Svetlana: The Story of Stalin's Daughter* (New York: New American Library, 1967); Radzinsky, Stalin.
3. Radzinsky, *Stalin.*
4. Susan Butler, *Roosevelt and Stalin: Portrait of a Partnership* (New York: Knopf, 2015).
5. Ibid.
6. Ibid.

7. Butler, *My Dear Mr. Stalin.*
8. Hingley, *Joseph Stalin.*
9. Ibid.
10. Radzinsky, *Stalin.*
11. Franz Halder, *The Private War Journals of General Franz Halder* (Boulder, CO: Westview, 1976).
12. Radzinsky, *Stalin.*
13. Ibid.
14. Butler, *My Dear Mr. Stalin.*
15. Radzinsky, *Stalin.*
16. Service, *Stalin*; Svetlana Stalin, *Svetlana;* Radzinsky, *Stalin.*
17. Service, *Stalin*; Radzinsky, *Stalin.*
18. Svetlana Stalin, *Svetlana.*
19. Radzinsky, *Stalin;* Service, *Stalin.*
20. Radzinsky, *Stalin.*
21. Service, *Stalin.*
22. Radzinsky, *Stalin.*
23. Ibid.

Chapter Twelve

1. Winston Groom, *1942: The Year That Tried Men's Souls* (New York: Atlantic Monthly Press, 2005).
2. Morison, *Rising Sun.*
3. The American Presidency Project. Franklin D. Roosevelt, Message of Support to the Philippines. December 28, 1941.
4. William Manchester, *American Caesar* (New York: Little, Brown, 1978).
5. Douglas MacArthur, *Reminiscences* (New York: McGraw Hill, 1964).
6. Groom, *1942.*
7. Freidel, *A Rendezvous with Destiny;* Parrish, *Roosevelt and Marshall.*
8. Freidel, *A Rendezvous with Destiny.*
9. James Doolittle, *I Could Never Be So Lucky Again* (Atglen, PA: Schiffer, 1991).
10. David Kahn, *The Code-Breakers: The Story of Secret Writing* (New York: Scribner, 1967).
11. Groom, *1942.*
12. Ibid.
13. Rick Atkinson, *An Army at Dawn: The War in North Africa* (New York: Holt, 2002).
14. Freidel, *A Rendezvous with Destiny.*
15. Toland, *Rising Sun.*
16. A. A. Vandegrift, *Once a Marine* (New York: Ballantine, 1964).
17. Freidel, *A Rendezvous with Destiny.*
18. Robert Sherwood, *Roosevelt and Hopkins: An Intimate History* (New York: Harper, 1948).
19. Samuel Eliot Morison, *The Struggle for Guadalcanal* (Boston: Little, Brown, 1949).
20. Grace Tully, *F.D.R., My Boss* (New York: Scribner, 1949).
21. Sherwood, *Roosevelt and Hopkins.*

Chapter Thirteen

1. Churchill, *Second World War,* vol. 3.
2. Ibid.
3. Manchester, *Last Lion,* vol. 3.
4. Groom, *1942.*
5. Winston Churchill, *Winston Churchill: His Complete Speeches* (New York: Chelsea House, 1974).
6. Ibid.
7. Ibid.
8. Churchill, *Second World War,* vol. 3.
9. Ibid.
10. Ibid.
11. Ibid.
12. Ibid.
13. Ibid.
14. Ibid.
15. Manchester, *Last Lion,* vol. 3.
16. Churchill, *Second World War,* vol. 3.
17. Manchester, *Last Lion,* vol. 3.
18. Churchill, *Second World War,* vol. 3.
19. Sir Alexander Cadogan, *Diaries* (New York: Putnam's Sons, 1972).

20. Manchester, *Last Lion,* vol. 3.
21. Jenkins, *Churchill.*
22. Churchill, *Second World War,* vol. 3.
23. Manchester, *Last Lion,* vol. 3; Churchill, *Second World War,* vol. 3.
24. Churchill, *Second World War,* vol. 3.
25. Ibid.

Chapter Fourteen

1. Georgy Zhukov, *The Memoirs of Marshal Zhukov* (New York: Delacorte, 1971).
2. Hingley, *Joseph Stalin.*
3. Service, *Stalin.*

Chapter Fifteen

1. Frank Freidel, *A Rendezvous with Destiny.*
2. Atkinson, *An Army at Dawn.*
3. Sherwood, *Roosevelt and Hopkins;* Atkinson, *An Army at Dawn.*
4. Freidel, *A Rendezvous with Destiny.*
5. Jenkins, *Churchill;* Atkinson, *An Army at Dawn.*
6. Sherwood, *Roosevelt and Hopkins.*
7. Gerald F. Linderman, *The World Within War* (New York: Free Press 1997).
8. Ernie Pyle, *Here Is Your War* (New York: Holt, 1943).
9. Winston Groom, *The Generals: Patton, MacArthur, Marshall, and the Winning of World War II* (Washington, D.C.: National Geographic, 2015).
10. Ibid.
11. Freidel, *A Rendezvous with Destiny.*
12. Bohlen, *Witness to History.*
13. Joseph E. Davies, *Mission to Moscow* (New York: Simon & Schuster, 1941).
14. Freidel, *A Rendezvous with Destiny.*
15. Ibid.
16. Sherwood, *Roosevelt and Hopkins.*
17. Ibid.; Parrish, *Roosevelt and Marshall.*
18. Sir Arthur Bryant quoted in Parrish, *Roosevelt and Marshall.*
19. Parrish, *Roosevelt and Marshall.*
20. Kenneth Davis, *Saturday Evening Post,* May 13–20, 1944; quoted ibid.
21. Elliott Roosevelt, *As He Saw It.*
22. Butler, *My Dear Mr. Stalin.*
23. Hingley, *Joseph Stalin.*
24. Radzinsky, *Stalin.*
25. Ibid.
26. Elliott Roosevelt, *As He Saw It* (New York: Duell, Sloan and Pearce, 1946).
27. Charles Bohlen, *Witness to History* (New York: Norton, 1973).
28. Elliott Roosevelt, *As He Saw It.*
29. Ibid.
30. Winston Churchill, *The Second World War,* vol. 5 (London: Cassell, 1951).
31. Ibid.
32. Butler, *My Dear Mr. Stalin.*
33. Ibid.
34. Manchester, *Last Lion,* vol. 3.

Chapter Sixteen

1. Charles Wilson (Lord Moran), *Churchill: Taken from the Diaries of Lord Moran* (Boston: Houghton Mifflin, 1966).
2. Manchester, *Last Lion*, vol. 3.
3. Churchill, *Second World War,* vol. 5; Manchester, *Last Lion,* vol. 3.
4. John "Jock" Colville, *The Fringes of Power: Diaries 1935–1955* (New York: Norton, 1985).
5. Jenkins, *Churchill;* Colville, *Fringes of Power.*
6. Jenkins, *Churchill.*
7. Manchester, *Last Lion,* vol. 3.
8. Ibid.
9. Jenkins, *Churchill.*
10. Groom, *The Generals.*
11. Alan Brooke, *War Diaries* (London: Weidenfeld & Nicolson 2001).

12. Ibid.
13. Ibid.; Churchill, *The Second World War*, vol. 6 (London: Cassell 1953).
14. Churchill, *Second World War*, vol. 6.
15. Ibid.
16. Ibid.; Colville, *Fringes of Power;* Manchester, *Last Lion*, vol. 3.
17. Manchester, *Last Lion*, vol. 3.
18. Churchill, *Second World War*, vol. 6.
19. Ibid.
20. Ibid.
21. Ibid.
22. Ibid.
23. Manchester, *Last Lion*, vol. 3.
24. Hingley, *Joseph Stalin.*
25. Ibid.; Churchill, *Second World War*, vol. 6.
26. Brooke, *War Diaries.*
27. Martin Blumenson, *The Patton Papers 1940–1945* (Boston: Houghton Mifflin, 1974).
28. Ibid.
29. Ibid.
30. Johnson, *Churchill.*
31. Churchill, *Second World War*, vol. 6; Soames, *Clementine Churchill;* Johnson, *Churchill.*
32. Manchester, *Last Lion*, vol. 3.

Chapter Seventeen
1. USHistory.org. Franklin Roosevelt, "Economic Bill of Rights," speech, January 11, 1944.
2. Rutherfurd family member Jane Walker Rutherfurd to author.
3. Samuel I. Rosenman, ed., *Public Papers and Addresses of Franklin D. Roosevelt* (New York: Harper, 1944).
4. Freidel, *A Rendezvous with History.*
5. Thomas W. Lippman, "The Day FDR Met Saudi Arabia's Ibn Saud," *The Link* 38, no. 2 (April/May 2005).
6. Ibid.
7. Ibid., Freidel, *A Rendezvous with History.*
8. Lippman, "The Day FDR Met Saudi Arabia's Ibn Saud."
9. Jim Bishop, *FDR's Last Year* (New York: Morrow, 1974).
10. Ibid.
11. Ibid.; Freidel, *A Rendezvous with Destiny.*
12. Freidel, *A Rendezvous with Destiny.*
13. Bishop, *FDR's Last Year.*
14. Radzinsky, *Stalin.*
15. Ibid.
16. Ibid.
17. Yuri Teplyakov, "Stalin's War Against His Own Troops," *Journal of Historical Review* 14, no. 4 (July/August 1994).
18. Hingley, *Joseph Stalin.*
19. Ibid.
20. Milovan Djilas, *Conversations with Stalin* (New York: Harcourt, 1962).
21. Radzinsky, *Stalin.*
22. Service, *Stalin.*
23. Ibid.
24. Ibid.
25. Churchill, *Second World War,* vol. 6.
26. Brian Gardner, *Churchill in Power: As Seen by His Contemporaries* (Boston: Houghton Mifflin, 1970).
27. Manchester, *Last Lion*, vol. 3.
28. Ibid.
29. Charles Wilson (Lord Moran), *Churchill: The Struggle for Survival* (New York: Basic Books, 2006).
30. Manchester, *Last Lion*, vol. 3.
31. Johnson, *Churchill.*
32. Manchester, *Last Lion*, vol. 3.
33. George Keenan, "Long Telegram," February 22, 1946 (accessed online at National Security Archive).
34. Harold Macmillan, *Tides of Fortune* (New York: HarperCollins, 1969).
35. Jenkins, *Churchill.*
36. Ibid.
37. Wilson, *Struggle for Survival;* Manchester, *Last Lion*, vol. 3.

NOTES ON SOURCES AND ACKNOWLEDGMENTS

A s I have written in my past three-person histories such as *The Aviators: Eddie Rickenbacker, Jimmy Doolittle, Charles Lindbergh, and the Epic Age of Flight* and *The Generals: Patton, MacArthur, Marshall, and the Winning of World War II,* I am allowed, in a way, to cherry-pick my subjects. One critic held this as a flaw, but in fact it's delightfully true. If I approached each of these august men in a full-blown biography the books would run three thousand pages or more.

So there. I cherry-pick, which is not to say that I skim; I just don't have to investigate every orifice, interesting or not, of the characters I write about. I do, however, try studiously to understand their natures, the forces that formed them, and what made them so distinct among men.

In particular, if one wants to fully understand Winston Churchill there are two principal sources to consider. One is the official biography (as it is referred to) of Winston Churchill, consisting of eight volumes with accompanying volumes of the definitive source materials. The first two of these volumes were written by Churchill's son, Randolph, who died at the age of fifty-seven before the biography was complete. The work was continued by the distinguished historian Martin Gilbert. It is massive, comprehensive, and, if one may say so, decisive.

The second most valuable source is Churchill himself, who wrote dozens of books during his lifetime, many of them autobiographical about his army service in India, the Sudan, and South Africa or memorials, such as his magisterial six-volume history of the Second World War, with himself at the center. It is occasionally, and quite naturally, self-serving but never deceptive or dishonest. It is also highly entertaining.

William Manchester began his authoritative three-volume biography *The Last Lion* in the 1980s, and there are also fine single-volume biographies by the British historians Roy Jenkins and Paul Johnson, as well as dozens of lesser works, many enumerated in the bibliography.

Roosevelt likewise had a worthy chronicler in the late American historian Arthur M. Schlesinger Jr., whom the author counted as a friend. His work consists of a three-volume biography of Roosevelt's life up to the days before World War II. There are also intimate Roosevelt biographies by James MacGregor Burns and Alonzo Hamby and the very informative *Roosevelt and Hopkins* by the playwright Robert Sherwood, who served in the Roosevelt administration as a speechwriter during the war. As with Churchill there are scores of more recent and less comprehensive studies of Roosevelt, including books on Roosevelt and Stalin, Roosevelt and Churchill, and many books on Roosevelt's wife, Eleanor.

Regarding Stalin, there is less information. In fact, during his thirty-year reign over the former Soviet Union, whatever information existed about Stalin's life was scrupulously edited by Stalin himself so that there was only one official history—and woe betide anyone who thought otherwise. In 1968, the British historian Robert Conquest published *The Great Terror* about Stalin's murder of tens of millions of his fellow citizens—as well as some dozen other books about the Russian communist empire.

Subsequent to the dissolution of the Soviet Union and the opening of official files, much has been discovered and brought to light. Biographies of Stalin by Simon Sebag Montefiore on the dictator's early life and by Ronald Hingley on his political machinations paint a much more nuanced picture of Stalin's character, as do biographies from Russian writers Edvard Radzinsky, Vadim Z. Rogovin, and Oleg V. Khlevniuk, who is chief researcher for the State Archive of the Russian Federation. Interesting, but suspect, is a book by Valentin M. Berezhkov, who was Stalin's longtime interpreter.

As I have in other books, my first acknowledgment is always to remind myself and others how earnestly and deeply I'm indebted to those dogged journalists and historians who have gone before. That said, the brilliant and comforting head and hand of Lisa Thomas, publisher and editorial director of National Geographic Books, has been an ever steady source of encouragement for nearly a decade, and especially for this present work. Likewise, her able deputy editor Hilary Black and senior editorial project manager Allyson Johnson have been invaluable in seeing the project through. And thank you to National Geographic's photography director Susan Blair, designer Nicole Miller, and cartographer Michael McNey who helped bring these pages to life, as well as to managing editor Jennifer Thornton and senior production editor Judith Klein, who worked tirelessly to get these pages in shape for print.

Andrew Carlson, my dazzling young editor, has once more made his indelible mark by unraveling so many clumsy chunks of my prose that it actually looks like I know what I'm doing. To him I owe a million thanks. And, as always, my enduring gratitude goes to my longtime copy editor Don Kennison who has saved me from myself more times than I care to remember. Finally, I wish to bestow profound gratitude and best wishes upon my very, very longtime research assistant and doer-of-all-other-things, Dr. Wren Murphy, whose retirement is well earned.

SELECTED BIBLIOGRAPHY

Ashburn, Frank D. *Peabody of Groton: A Portrait*. New York: Coward McCann, 1944.

Atkinson, Rick. *An Army at Dawn: The War in North Africa, 1942–1943*. New York: Henry Holt, 2002.

Bishop, Jim. *FDR's Last Year: April 1944–April 1945*. New York: Morrow, 1974.

Blumenson, Martin. *The Patton Papers 1940–1945*. Boston: Houghton Mifflin, 1974.

Bohlen, Charles Eustis. *Witness to History: 1929–1969*. New York: W. W. Norton, 1973.

Brooke, Alan. *War Diaries*. Alex Danchev and Daniel Todman, eds. London: Weidenfeld & Nicolson, 2001.

Burns, James MacGregor. *Roosevelt: The Lion and the Fox*. New York: Konecky & Konecky, 1984 (1956).

Butler, Susan, ed. *My Dear Mr. Stalin: The Complete Correspondence of Franklin D. Roosevelt and Joseph V. Stalin*. New Haven, CT: Yale University Press, 2003.

———. *Roosevelt and Stalin: Portrait of a Partnership*. New York: Knopf, 2015.

Cadogan, Alexander. *The Diaries of Sir Alexander Cadogan, O.M., 1938–1945*. David Dilks, ed. New York: G. P. Putnam's Sons, 1972.

Carter, Violet Bonham. *Winston Churchill As I Knew Him*. London: Eyre & Spottiswoode and Collins, 1965.

Churchill, Randolph S, ed. *The Churchill Documents*, vol. 1. Hillsdale, MI: Hillsdale College Press, 2006.

———. *Winston S. Churchill*, vol. 1, *Youth*. Boston: Houghton Mifflin, 1966.

———. *Winston S. Churchill*, vol. 2, *Young Statesman*. Boston: Houghton Mifflin, 1967.

Churchill, Winston. *My Early Life*. London: Butterworth, 1930.

———. *The River War: An Account of the Reconquest of the Sudan*. London: Longman, 1899.

———. *The Second World War*, vol. 1, *The Gathering Storm*. London: Cassell, 1948.

———. *The Second World War*, vol. 2, *Their Finest Hour*. London: Cassell, 1949.

———. *The Second World War*, vol. 3, *The Grand Alliance*. London: Cassell, 1950.

———. *The Second World War*, vol. 5, *Closing the Ring*. London: Cassell, 1951.

———. *The Second World War*, vol. 6, *Triumph and Tragedy*. London: Cassell, 1953.

———. *The Story of the Malakand Field Force*. London: Longman, 1898.

———. *Thoughts and Adventures*. London: Butterworth, 1932.

———. *Winston S. Churchill: His Complete Speeches*, Robert Rhodes James, ed. New York: Chelsea House, 1974.

———. *The World Crisis*, vol. 1. London: Butterworth, 1923.

Ciano, Galeazzo, and Hugh Gibson. *The Ciano Diaries: 1939–1943*. New York: Simon Publications, 1946.

Colville, John. *The Fringes of Power: 10 Downing Street Diaries, 1939–1955*. New York: Norton, 1985.

Coughlin, Con. *Churchill's First War: Young Winston at War with the Afghans*. New York: Thomas Dunne, 2014.

Daniels, Jonathan. *Washington Quadrille: The Dance Beside the Documents*. New York: Doubleday, 1968.

Davies, Joseph E. *Mission to Moscow*. New York: Simon & Schuster, 1941.

Djilas, Milovan. *Conversations with Stalin*. New York: Harcourt, 1962.

Doolittle, James H., and Carol V. Glines. *I Could Never Be So Lucky Again*. Atglen, PA: Schiffer, 1991.

Freidel, Frank. *Franklin D. Roosevelt: A Rendezvous with Destiny*. Boston: Little, Brown, 1990.

Gardner, Brian. *Churchill in Power: As Seen by His Contemporaries*. Boston: Houghton Mifflin, 1970.

Gilbert, Martin. *Winston S. Churchill*, vols. 3–8. Boston: Houghton Mifflin, 1971–88.

Groom, Winston. *1942: The Year That Tried Men's Souls*. New York: Atlantic Monthly Press, 2005.

———. *The Generals: Patton, MacArthur, Marshall, and the Winning of World War II*. Washington, D.C.: National Geographic, 2015.

———. *A Storm in Flanders*. New York: Atlantic Monthly Press, 2002.

Halder, Franz. *The Private War Journals of General Franz Halder*. Boulder, CO: Westview Press, 1976.

Hamby, Alonzo L. *Man of Destiny: FDR and the Making of the American Century*. New York: Basic Books, 2015.

Hingley, Ronald. *Joseph Stalin: Man and Legend*. New York: McGraw Hill, 1974.

Jenkins, Roy. *Churchill: A Biography*. New York: Penguin, 2001.

Jenkins, Roy, and Richard E. Neustadt. *Franklin Delano Roosevelt*. New York: Times Books, 2003.

Johnson, Paul. *Churchill*. New York: Viking, 2009.

Kahn, David. *The Code-Breakers: The Story of Secret Writing*. New York: Scribner, 1967.

Khlevniuk, O. V. *Stalin: New Biography of a Dictator*. Translated by Nora Seligman Favorov. New Haven, CT: Yale University Press, 2015.

Kimball, Warren F., ed. *Churchill and Roosevelt: The Complete Correspondence*, vol. 11. Princeton, NJ: Princeton University Press, 1987.

Kincaid, Dennis Charles Alexander. *British Social Life in India, 1608–1937*. London: Routledge & Kegan Paul, 1973.

Kosar, Kevin R. *Moonshine: A Global History*. London: Reaktion Books, 2017.

Lash, Joseph P. *Eleanor and Franklin*. New York: Norton, 1971.

———. *Love, Eleanor: Eleanor Roosevelt and Her Friends*. New York: Doubleday, 1982.

Linderman, Gerald F. *The World Within War: America's Combat Experience in World War II*. New York: Free Press, 1997.

Lippman, Thomas W. "The Day FDR Met Saudi Arabia's Ibn Saud." *The Link* 38, no. 2. April/May 2005.

Lough, David. *No More Champagne: Churchill and His Money*. New York: Picador, 2015.

Ludwig, Emil. *Stalin*. New York: G. P. Putnam's Sons, 1942.

MacArthur, Douglas. *Reminiscences*. New York: McGraw Hill, 1964.

Macmillan, Harold. *Tides of Fortune, 1945–1955*. New York: HarperCollins, 1969.

Manchester, William. *American Caesar*. New York: Little, Brown, 1978.

———. *The Last Lion: Winston Spencer Churchill*, vol. 1, *Visions of Glory, 1874–1932*. Boston: Little, Brown, 1983.

———. *The Last Lion: Winston Spencer Churchill*, vol. 3, *Defender of the Realm, 1940–1965*. Boston: Little, Brown, 2012.

Martin, Ralph G. *Jennie: The Life of Lady Randolph Churchill*. Englewood Cliffs, NJ: Prentice Hall, 1969.

Montefiore, Simon Sebag. *Young Stalin*. New York: Knopf, 2007.

Morison, Samuel Eliot. *The Rising Sun in the Pacific: 1931–April 1942*. Boston: Little, Brown, 1948.

———. *The Struggle for Guadalcanal: August 1942–February 1943*. Boston: Little, Brown, 1949.

———. *The Two-Ocean War: A Short History of the United States Navy in the Second World War*. Boston: Little, Brown, 1963.

Morton, Frederic. *Thunder at Twilight: Vienna, 1913–1914*. New York: Scribner, 1989.

Parrish, Thomas. *Roosevelt and Marshall: Partners in Politics and War*. New York: Morrow, 1989.

Patton, George S. *The Patton Papers: 1940–1945*. Martin Blumenson, ed. Boston: Houghton Mifflin, 1974.

Persico, Joseph E. *Franklin and Lucy: President Roosevelt, Mrs. Rutherfurd, and the Other Remarkable Women in His Life*. New York: Random House, 2008.

Prange, Gordon W. *At Dawn We Slept: The Untold Story of Pearl Harbor*. New York: McGraw Hill, 1981.

Pyle, Ernie. *Here Is Your War*. New York: Henry Holt, 1943.

Radzinsky, Edvard. *Stalin: The First In-Depth Biography Based on Explosive New Documents from Russia's Secret Archives*. New York: Doubleday, 1996.

Read, Simon. *Winston Churchill Reporting: Adventures of a Young War Correspondent*. Boston: Da Capo Press, 2015.

Rollins, Alfred B., Jr. *Roosevelt and Howe*. New York: Knopf, 1962.

Roosevelt, Elliott. *As He Saw It*. New York: Duell, Sloan and Pearce, 1946.

THE ALLIES

Roosevelt, Elliott, and James Brough. *An Untold Story: The Roosevelts of Hyde Park*. New York: G. P. Putnam's, 1973.

Rosenman, Samuel I., ed. *The Public Papers and Addresses of Franklin D. Roosevelt*. New York: Harper and Brothers, 1944.

Rothstein, Edward. "Churchill, Heroic Relic or Relevant Now?" *New York Times,* March 29, 2003.

Schlesinger, Arthur M. Jr. *The Crisis of Old Order,* vol. 1, *The Age of Roosevelt*. Boston: Houghton Mifflin, 1957.

Service, Robert. *Stalin: A Biography*. Cambridge, MA: Belknap Press of Harvard University, 2005.

Sherwood, Robert. *Roosevelt and Hopkins: An Intimate History*. New York: Harper, 1948.

Soames, Mary. *Clementine Churchill: The Biography of a Marriage*. Boston: Mariner Books, 2003.

Stalin, Svetlana. *Svetlana: The Story of Stalin's Daughter*. New York: New American Library, 1967.

Taylor, S. J. *Stalin's Apologist: Walter Duranty: The New York Times's Man in Moscow*. New York: Oxford University Press, 1990.

Teplyakov, Yuri. "Stalin's War Against His Own Troops: The Tragic Fate of Soviet Prisoners of War in German Captivity." *Journal of Historical Review* 14, no. 4 (July/August 1994).

Toland, John. *The Rising Sun: The Decline and Fall of the Japanese Empire, 1936–1945*. New York: Random House, 1970.

Tully, Grace. *F.D.R., My Boss*. New York: Scribner, 1949.

Vandegrift, A. A. *Once a Marine: The Memoirs of General A. A. Vandegrift Commandant of the U.S. Marines in WWII*. New York: Ballantine Books, 1964.

Ward, Geoffrey C. *Before the Trumpet: Young Franklin Roosevelt, 1882–1905*. New York: Harper & Row, 1985.

———. *A First-Class Temperament: The Emergence of Franklin Roosevelt, 1905–1928*. New York: Harper & Row, 1989.

Wilson, Charles (Lord Moran). *Churchill: The Struggle for Survival 1945–60*. New York: Basic Books, 2006.

———. *Churchill: Taken from the Diaries of Lord Moran*. Boston: Houghton Mifflin, 1966.

Woods, Frederick, ed. *Young Winston's Wars: The Original Despatches of Winston S. Churchill War Correspondent, 1897–1900*. New York: Viking, 1973.

Zhukov, Georgy K. *The Memoirs of Marshal Zhukov*. New York: Delacorte, 1971.

INDEX

ILLUSTRATIONS AND MAPS CREDITS

Front Cover: (Roosevelt), Oscar White/Corbis/VCG via Getty Images; (Churchill), Keystone-France/Gamma-Keystone via Getty Images; (Stalin), akg-images; (Flags), Art Media/Print Collector/Getty Images. Back Cover: (LE), Universal History Archive/UIG via Getty Images; (CT), Frank Scherschel/The LIFE Picture Collection/Getty Images; (RT), AP/REX/Shutterstock. Back Flap: Squire Fox.

Insert 1
1 (UP LE), Mary Evans/REX/Shutterstock; 1 (LO LE), The Print Collector/Getty Images; 1 (RT), Hulton Archive/Getty Images; 2 (LE), CORBIS/Corbis via Getty Images; 2 (RT), CORBIS/Corbis via Getty Images; 3, CORBIS/Corbis via Getty Images; 4 (UP LE), CCI/REX/Shutterstock; 4 (LO LE), Universal History Archive/UIG via Getty Images; 4 (RT), Bettmann/Getty Images; 5 (LE), SuperStock/Alamy Stock Photo; 5 (RT), PA Images via Getty Images; 6 (LE), CORBIS/Corbis via Getty Images; 6 (RT), CORBIS/Corbis via Getty Images; 7 (UP LE), Underwood Archives/Getty Images; 7 (LO LE), Hulton Archive/Getty Images; 7 (RT), Universal History Archive/UIG via Getty Images; 8 (UP), Keystone-France/Gamma-Keystone via Getty Images; 8 (LO), AP/REX/Shutterstock

Insert 2
1 (LE), ART Collection/Alamy Stock Photo; 1 (RT), Hulton Archive/Getty Images; 2 (UP), Everett Collection Historical/Alamy Stock Photo; 2 (LO), Universal History Archive/UIG via Getty Images; 3, ANL/REX/Shutterstock; 4, Capt. Horton/IWM via Getty Images; 5, U.S. Signal Corps photo/Library of Congress Prints and Photographs Division, LC-USZ62-32833; 6, Bettmann/Getty Images; 7 (UP), Historia/REX/Shutterstock; 7 (LO LE), Frank Scherschel/The LIFE Picture Collection/Getty Images; 7 (LO RT), AP Photo; 8, Popperfoto/Getty Images.

Map Sources
European Theater map: Esposito, Vincent J. *The West Point Atlas of War: World War II: European Theater.* New York: Tess Press, 1995.
Pacific Theater map: Esposito, Vincent J. *The West Point Atlas of War: World War II: The Pacific.* New York: Tess Press, 2007.